THE ENCYCLOPAEDIA OF MIDDLE EASTERN MYTHOLOGY AND RELIGION

Jan Knappert graduated from Leiden University, Holland, where he studied Oriental languages and cultures. He was Professor of Oriental Studies at Louvain University, Belgium, lectured at the School of Oriental and African Studies in London for many years, and has travelled widely in the Middle East, Africa and Asia. He is the author of numerous books and articles on mythology.

THE ENCYCLOPAEDIA OF

MIDDLE EASTERN MYTHOLOGY

AND

RELIGION

Jan Knappert

ELEMENT
Shaftesbury, Dorset ● Rockport, Massachusetts
Brisbane, Queensland

© Jan Knappert 1993

Published in Great Britain in 1993 by
Element Books Limited
Longmead, Shaftesbury, Dorset

Published in the USA in 1993 by
Element, Inc,
42 Broadway, Rockport, MA 01966

Published in Australia in 1993 by
Element Books Limited for
Jacaranda Wiley Limited
33 Park Road, Milton, Brisbane, 4064

Cover design by Max Fairbrother
Design by Roger Lightfoot
Maps by Countryside Illustrations
Typeset by Electronic Book Factory Ltd, Fife, Scotland
Printed and bound in Great Britain

British Library Cataloguing in Publication
data available

Library of Congress Cataloging in Publication
data available

ISBN 1–85230–427–8

PREFACE

The Middle East has been called the cradle of religions, although India might challenge that claim, being itself the mother of six religions (Hinduism, Jainism, Buddhism, Sikhism, Tantrism, and Ahmadiya).

The living religions which originated in the Middle East with their country and approximate date of origin are: Judaism (Israel, *c.* 1500 BC; Christianity (Israel, *c.* 30 AD); Islam (Mecca, 622 AD); Isma'ilism (Egypt, 969 AD); Druzism (Egypt, *c.* 1100 AD); Baha'ism (Iran, 1863 AD).

It has been argued that Sufism is not a form of Islam but a new religion, and so should be mentioned separately. Likewise the Shi'is call themselves good Muslims but are considered unorthodox by the Sunnis. The mythologist and the religiologist must not be a party to any of these conflicts. Nor is there an answer to questions like: In what way is a sect different from a religion? Is Theosophy a new religion?

The very fact that the debate about these questions is continuing demonstrates that these religions are alive and growing. Each religion grew out of an older one like a branch out of a tree. The three major branches of the tree of religion are Judaism, Christianity and Islam. Like Islam, Christianity has ramified into several branches, including Catholic, Maronite, Armenian, Syriac, Greek orthodoxy, Coptic orthodoxy and Ethiopic Christianity. Judaism too, has ramified; Hasidism and Cabbalism could be considered branches of Judaism. In the time of Jesus there were already several 'sects' in Judaism, such as the Zealots, the Sadducees and the Essenes.

It has been argued that all Jesus wanted was to make his followers into a new community of pious Jewish worshippers, not to create a new religion. Yet that was what happened. Christianity began as a 'branch' of Judaism but soon developed into a new religion, when his followers realized what Jesus had really meant, and what he had really been. Today, many Christians are convinced that Christianity never was a branch of Judaism, but that it was the true religion which the Jews did not accept. Likewise Muhammad told his followers that his Islam was not a new form of Judaism or Christianity but that it was the old and only correct form of the religion of Abraham. The very fact that all three religions accept Abraham and the Ten Commandments of Moses proves that they are three branches of the original religion of the Patriarchs. This congeniality is further demonstrated by the fact that numerous characters from the Bible are also mentioned in the Koran, beginning with Adam and ending with Jesus (see *Prophets*). Muslim writers after Muhammad have added to the already considerable number of Biblical tales and characters, making them part of the Islamic storytellers' repertoire, changing David and Solomon into Arab kings for instance.

The tree of the three religions does not only have branches, it also has roots. These roots have been discovered in the last 150 years when the great literatures of the Middle East in antiquity were deciphered: Old Persian, Babylonian, Sumerian, Ugaritic and other literatures have contributed incredibly rich material to our understanding of the Bible. That great tome, to which numerous writers contributed books for over a thousand years, from Genesis to Revelation, is therefore as it were the trunk of that great tree of religion. And yet, in spite of being sister religions, there is great division between them. Why? Because, as Sa'di, the great Persian poet wrote:

One follower of Moses has fought another follower of Moses,
ever since they tried to name the Unnameable.
Or, as this writer put it:
God, Allah, Dios, by so many names
they call Him like the fire by its flames.

The flames of a fire cannot be given individual names, they are only brief appearances of the one element Fire. The Divine Essence cannot be named either. Christians, Jews and Muslims are all followers of Moses' commandments, yet they are fighting murderously in many countries because each party believes it alone is right and all the others are wrong. In the face of that belief we should all repeat what Muslim scholars often write after reporting a disputation between theologians: *Allahu A'alam*! God knows better! You will find this exclamation several times in these pages. where contradictory tales are recorded. May this book serve to create better understanding between persons of different persuasions.

I should like to thank the publishers of Element Books for their help and expert advice.

INTRODUCTION

1. GEOGRAPHY OF THE MIDDLE EAST

Asia Minor, the Arabian Peninsula and the mountainous high plateau of Iran, Afghanistan and Baluchistan are three distinct tectonic plates with different characteristics. Arabia is historically a part of Africa from which is was separated in 'recent' geological times by the Red Sea and the Gulf of Aqaba. This deep rift continues in the Dead Sea (800 metres below the level of the Mediterranean) and the Jordan valley separating Israel from the Kingdom of Jordan. On the other side the Arabian-Syrian plateau is bordered by the valley of the Euphrates with its steep banks. This ancient river, called Furat by the Arabs and Firat by the Turks, rises near Erzurum in what used to be Armenia. In Roman and Byzantine times it was the frontier of Europe. Three Roman emperors have died in its defence, Gordian in 244, Valerian in 260 and Julian in 362. The Persian emperors Ardashir, Shapur and Hormizd were too strong.

Across the plain to the east, called in Arabic Al-Jazira 'the Island' and in Greek Mesopotamia 'Between the Rivers', flows the Tigris, the Asian River of the Tigers, called Diglat in the cuneiform tablets and Dijla in Arabic. East of its valley the land rises steeply towards the formidable Zagros mountains of Iran and Kurdistan. Beyond it lie the forbidding rock formations and salt deserts of Persia and Afghanistan, the ancient Bactria. Two thousand kilometres to the east the land finally drops down to form the green valley of the Indus river which gave its name to India. On the north side Iran is bordered by the vast steppes of Turkestan, which was

part of the Persian empire for centuries. West of the salty
Caspian Sea rises the Caucasus, a cradle of nations, steep
peaks forming the highest mountains of Europe. Several of
our most delicious fruits were first cultivated in this area:
plums, apricots and quinces.

Travelling west from Mesopotamia across the stony Syrian
and Jordanian desert the pilgrim, on his way to Jerusalem,
will suddenly descend from the endless dry plains and see the
green valley of the rolling river Jordan. A short distance – 50
miles – separates the Jordan from the Mediterranean coast at
Tel Aviv, 'Hill of Spring', in Israel. In that narrow strip along
the Levantine coast where Israel, Palestine and the Lebanon
are situated, many things have happened during the last 3000
years, filling many tomes (see *Palestine*).

West of Israel lies Egypt, a large country on the north-
east corner of Africa. Egypt has seldom looked towards
Africa, and then only for conquest. Since the earliest historical times, it has had very lively contacts with the Middle East. Even the art of writing must have come from
Sumer to Egypt.

These then, are the countries with which this book will be
concerned.

From the dawn of prehistory, tribes of all types have wandered through the Middle East and settled there. In early
times both Iran and Turkey were heavily forested. Cedar
trees stood majestically all over the Lebanon, while pine
forests covered most of northern Mesopotamia and Syria.
Animals of all species roamed the woods and the fertile
plains: wild boar, wild cattle, deer, gazelle, wild goats and
wild sheep in the hills; in the woods lived the elephant, wild
ass and wild buffalo, which were stalked by many predators,
including lion, leopard, bear, fox, wolf and hyena. Innumerable birds lived in the swamps of lower Mesopotamia:
ibis, stork, marabou, pelican, flamingo, heron, bittern and
many others. It is a sobering thought to realize that all those
deserts and rocks were once among the earth's finest natural
landscapes.

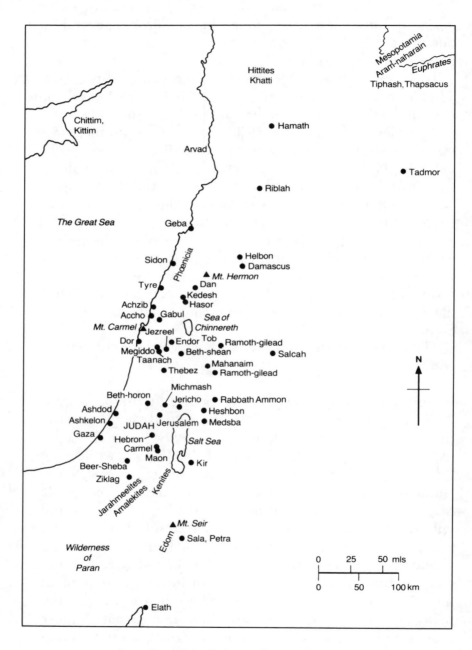

Israel and Judah 10th Century BC

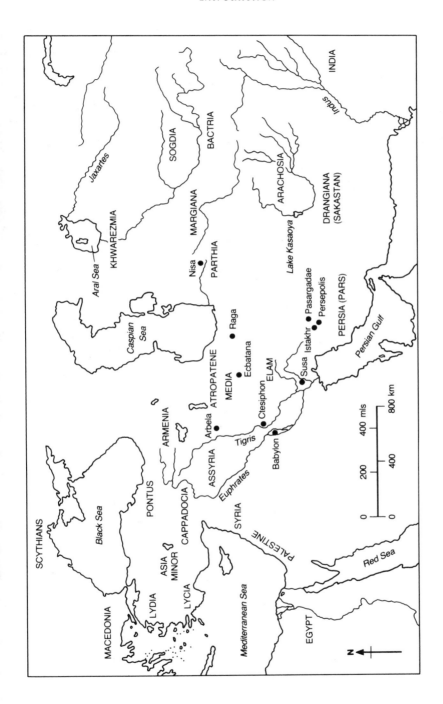

Imperial Persia

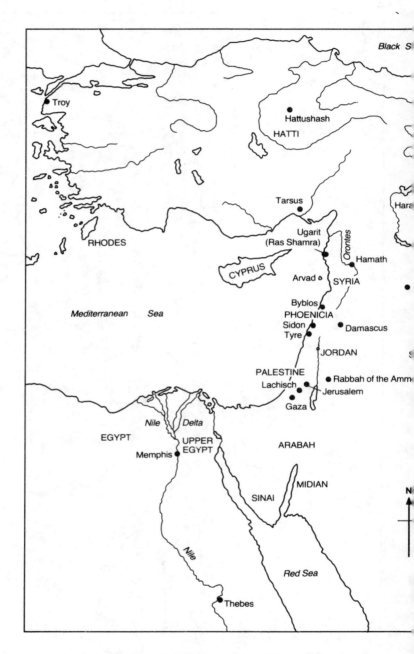

The Ancient Middle East

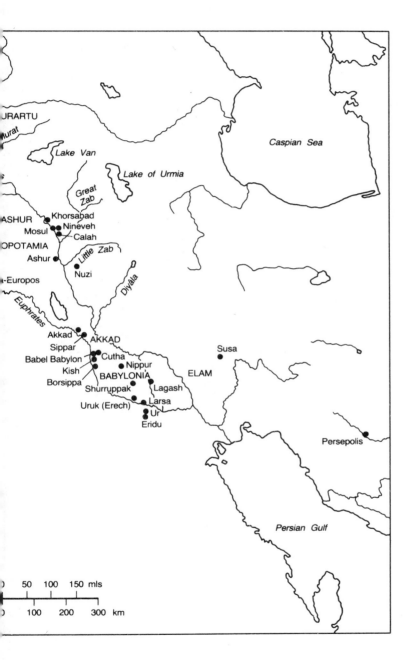

URARTU
Murat

Lake Van

Lake of Urmia

Caspian Sea

Great
Zab

ASHUR
Mosul
Khorsabad
Nineveh
Calah

OPOTAMIA
Ashur
Little Zab

Nuzi

Diyāla

-Europos

Euphrates

Akkad
Sippar
AKKAD

Babel Babylon
Cutha

Kish
Nippur

Borsippa
BABYLONIA

Shurruppak
Lagash

Uruk (Erech)
Larsa
Ur
Eridu

Susa

ELAM

Persepolis

Persian Gulf

50   100   150 mls

100   200   300 km

The Ancient Middle East

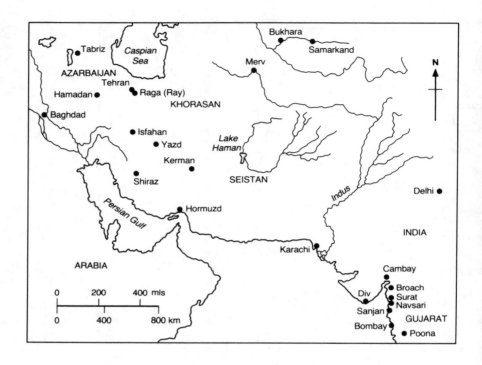

Islamic Iran

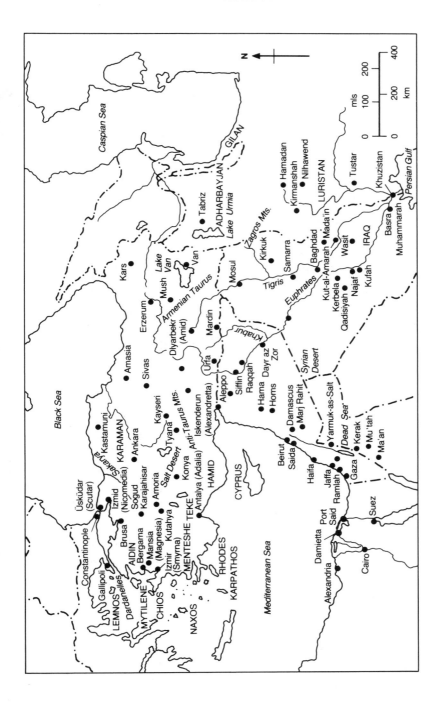

The Islamic Middle East

2. THE PEOPLES OF THE ANCIENT MIDDLE EAST

When the Children of Israel arrived in the Middle East, a great deal of damage had already been done to the environment by Gilgamesh and his successors — but we are running ahead of our story.

Archaeologists have unearthed the bones of early Neanderthal man and his successors in the area; they were the first toolmakers. The oldest ruins on earth are to be found in the Middle East, in the city of Jericho, some of whose walls are 9000 years old.

For millennia man was a hunter decorating himself with leopard skins and other trophies. Gradually he (or his wives) developed the art of leather work: carving, scraping, stretching, beating the skins and finally even sewing them. To this end various stone tools such as scrapers were manufactured, and also needles made of animal or fish bone. Nets were made for both hunting and fishing, and baskets to keep the fish in.

At some stage the goat was domesticated, the first animal to undergo that fate. Goats had to be kept in pens at night to protect them from predators, and to keep all their milk for their owners. Baskets were daubed with clay on the outside so that they could be used as containers for the milk. Later the clay was baked, and eventually the baskets were omitted (though the basket-like decorations continued). Thus was pottery invented, and it is still one of the world's leading industries.

However, by far the most important development in Mesopotamia was the selection of grasses with the aim of growing bigger grains. Obviously, the grasses had to be cultivated in very large numbers in enclosed fields. Weeds had to be cleared, goats and other animals had to be kept out, and the seed grains had to be chosen, dried and kept in a safe place until the new sowing season. This was the famous revolution that led to the invention of agriculture. It must have taken many centuries, since it was three revolutions in one: the introduction of deliberate reasoning in food-finding; the discovery of the concept of the selection of seeds; and the invention of cultivation.

The invention of agriculture led to the need for more pots and jars in which to store grain and other produce. Vegetables were kept in pots (sauerkraut is one of the few relics of that practice), and even meat was kept pickled in jars – remember the 'fleshpots of Egypt'. For pickling meat and fish, salt was needed, and it was first produced in the lagoons near the Persian Gulf. Most important of all was the system of irrigation canals, ever bigger and better, which criss-crossed southern Mesopotamia.

All this led to a need for a sedentary life. The herdsmen were ever in search of greener pastures, but the cultivators had to settle in one place to supervise sowing, harvesting, storing, irrigation and ploughing. They built themselves permanent homes and to that end they invented bricks; so another industry sprang up. This combined process took a very long time, some five millennia from about 8000 to 3000 BC.

The farmers settled together in villages and towns which they fortified against invasion by armed gangs of plunderers, who were irresistibly lured by those fleshpots, which helped the farmers survive the winter or the dry season. Such early centres of agriculture developed in the Nile Valley, in Mesopotamia and in the Indus Valley, as well as in the Huang Ho Valley of China.

Those four early centres of settled civilization had another fundamental asset in common: they each invented a system of writing, and with it they initiated the last period of human evolution, which we now call history. They were the first people to become more to us than skeletons in their tombs: they acquired a voice, for we know their languages. The scripts of ancient Egypt, Mesopotamia and China have been deciphered, but the Indus Valley script still awaits the genius who will unravel it for us. That civilization had close trade relations with the Gulf countries about 4000 years ago, but it falls outside our present survey.

The question of who lived in the Middle East in the days of Abraham is not easy to answer. The Bible gives a list of tribes or nations, which are all descendants of Noah. Only some of those names can be indentified with peoples of whom we have archaeological records. Often the Bible causes more problems than it solves. For example, were the Chaldeans (Genesis 11.28) the same as the Sumerians who, we know, founded the city of Ur? We know that the people who lived in central Anatolia in about 2000 BC, whom we call Hittites, were not the same as the Hittites of the Bible (Genesis 10.15; 26.34; Joshua 9.1; Judges 3.5). Canaan, the son of Ham, must have engendered a nation of Africans. However, the Canaanites whom the Children of Israel encountered as the inhabitants of Palestine, spoke a Semitic language quite close to Hebrew. The people of Sidon (son of Canaan) likewise spoke a Semitic language, but the Hittites, sons of his brother Heth, probably did not (Genesis 10:15).

Ever since the deciphering of the ancient inscriptions, the names of various Middle Eastern peoples have come to us, first as the writers of the rock inscriptions, clay tablets, etc., secondly as mere names of 'barbarians' vanquished by the kings of Egypt, Babylon, Persia, etc., and thirdly as the names of peoples in the more scholarly works of Greek authors such as Herodotus and later Babylonian scribes who compiled the first bilingual dictionaries. It is always essential to know what type of language people speak before we can identify them. Unfortunately the language of the inscriptions is not always the same as the language of the people. For example the Persian kings edited some of their inscriptions in Aramaic.

The number of ethnic groups living in the Middle East at any time in the past is very difficult to establish, even if we could clearly define each of them. The following is an attempt to list the main tribes or nations.

Chief nations of the Ancient Middle East

Akkadians on the Tigris from 2334 BC
Arabs in Arabia
Aramaeans in Syria
Aryans a large group of peoples *c.* 1500 BC in Iran and
  Afghanistan, speaking closely related Iranian Languages
Assyrians in northern Iraq before the Persians, from *c.* 2000
  BC
Babylonians in central Iraq before the Persians
Byzantines in Greece, Asia Minor, Egypt, Syria, Lebanon,
  Palestine and Jordan since *c.* 300 AD
Canaanites in Palestine before Solomon
Copts in Christian Egypt
Eblaites in northern Lebanon *c.* 2500 BC
Edomites in Jordan *c.* 1000 BC
Elamites in Western Iran around Abadan before the Persians
  c. 3000 BC
Greeks in all the cities of the Western Middle East after
  Alexander the Great
Hattians in central Asia Minor before the Hittites
Hebrews in Palestine since Abraham
Hellenes see Greeks
Hittites in central Asia Minor after 2000 BC
Hurrians or **Mitannians** in northern Syria *c.* 1500–1000 BC
Iranians see Aryans and Persians
Luwians or **Luvians** in Western Anatolia
Mandaeans in the delta of the Euphrates in Christian times
Moabites in Jordan *c.* 1000 BC
Nabataeans in southern Palestine before the Romans
Nazaraeans see Mandaeans
Nesites see Hittites
Persians in Iran since *c.* 2000 BC divided into Medians,
  Parthians, etc.
Romans in Asia Minor, Syria, Egypt, Palestine, Jordan,
  Lebanon, from *c.* 40 BC
Sabaic, Minaic or **South Arabian** peoples in Yemen before
  Muhammad

Sabians see Mandaeans
Sumerians the inventors of script, in the Euphrates delta
  c. 3000 BC
Syrians in Syria in Christian times, writing Syriac, i.e. 'Late'
  Aramaic
Ugarites in Lebanon preceding the Phoenicians, *c.* 2000 BC
Urartians in eastern Asia Minor (Lake Van)

3. THE PEOPLES OF THE MODERN MIDDLE EAST

The early civilizations accumulated riches and this wealth attracted numerous 'barbarian' peoples from the north who, in the course of centuries, settled down and became civilized. When the curtain of history is raised some 3000 years BC, the Sumerians and Elamites are in position.

In the third millennium the invasion of the Semites from the north was the first great movement of peoples. They were already divided into a large number of groups: first into south, east and north-west Semites, then again into Eblaites, Ugaritians, Canaanites, Phoenicians and Amorites. The south Semites moved on to fill the southern part of Arabia, driving out the Hamites and Cushites, who settled in Africa. Later several south Semitic groups also settled in Africa, forming the nucleus of the Ethiopian peoples. The east Semites divided into the Babylonians and Assyrians while the north-west Semites divided into the Arabs and Hebrews, fiercely independent nations.

The second great invasion before 2000 BC was that of the Indo-Europeans. To that group belonged the Indo-Iranians, the Hittites, the Luvians, the Lydians, the Greeks, the Armenians, the Scythians (of whom now only the Ossetians are left), the Hurrians, the Urartians and, much later, the Slavs. The Indo-Iranians were probably the first group to arrive. They settled in Iran and spilled over into India before 1500 BC. They divided into the Indian-Aryan peoples who spoke Vedic, and the Iranians who divided further into the Persians, the Medes, the Kurds, the Baluchis, the Pathans, the Tajiks, the Scythians and the Khotanese. The Armenians probably descend from the Urartians who have lived in the Ararat area at least since 2000 BC.

Thus the scene was set for the history of the Middle East to begin. First the Sumerians had all the power, thanks to their brilliant inventions. They were followed by the Babylonians, the Assyrians and the Hittites. Each nation had its time of greatness and its time of decline. In the sixth century BC the Persians rose to dominance, occupying not only Mesopotamia and Syria, but also Israel. Then, with great rapidity, within ten years (333–323 BC) Alexander the Great conquered all those lands and heralded the pre-eminence of Greek culture. In the first century BC the Romans became masters of the Middle East, including Asia Minor and Egypt but not Iran which had recreated itself under the Parthian kings. The Emperor Constantine created the Christian Eastern Roman Empire in 308 AD, with Greek as the dominant language. In 634, the Arabs abruptly exploded out of their desert and conquered all of the Middle East (but not Asia Minor), so that today Egypt, Palestine, Lebanon, Jordan, Syria and Mesopotamia are Arabic-speaking lands. In the late eleventh century the Turks broke through and finally organized themselves into the Ottoman Empire (1517–1918), making Turkish the dominant language. Meanwhile, the 'minor' peoples maintained themselves in their mountain redouts: the Armenians, the Kurds and the Georgians, of whom only the Kurds were Islamicized. Various other Christian groups, much persecuted, have managed to survive, some with their old Syriac language and liturgy, the Copts with their own liturgy. The Christians in southern Iraq have recently been massacred.

4. THE RELIGIONS

In antiquity every nation, every tribe, every village had its own religion. Still today in tropical Africa and other parts of the world where Christianity and Islam have not yet become dominant, every tribe has its own gods.

The Romans, when they organized an empire that encompassed many peoples with as many religions, referred to those peoples as *nationes* 'nations'. Every person was defined by his birth, *natio*, as belonging to a particular nation, so he must, by duty, worship the gods of that nation, since they were his own ancestor gods. One did not adopt another person's religion, nor was there ever a question of conversion before the revolution of Christianity. Jacob in the Bible worshipped the God of his father Isaac and his grandfather Abraham, but his uncle Laban had his own gods (Genesis 31.19, 31.53). Rachel took her father's gods with her because she was afraid she would feel homesick in her husband's home country. In Africa there are many tales of a young bride feeling desolate in her husband's house, especially when watching the (to her) strange rituals her in-laws perform for their gods. In many parts of Asia a wife is permitted to bring her own gods to her husband's home and arrange her own altar or shrine in a corner of the house.

It was only much later that wives were expected to embrace their husband's religion. In antiquity that was impossible. No one could change his or her gods.

Each tribe, every nation in history, has at some stage endeavoured to enlarge its territory at the expense of its neighbours, in order to gain more resources – more food. They could either eliminate the natives, as the Children of Israel did under Joshua and Samuel, or they could absorb them, as the Romans did. In either case the conquest was not only ethnic but also religious. The conquerors' gods had to be worshipped by all the subjected tribes. The Romans simply 'equated' the names of their gods with those of the Celts, Greeks, Germans and Egyptians. Tolerance was out of the question because the prestige of the state was dependent on its gods, who had shown by their favour that the Romans possessed the mandate of heaven, since all power is god-given.

'Live in my state, worship in my temple', the kings might

have said. The state was a universe, an ordered cosmos created by the gods as their own realm. No man could be permitted to live inside that state and not worship the gods that kept it alive and peaceful. This explains the fulminations of the prophets of Israel against heathen practices: the State was Jehovah's creation and would be broken by him as soon as its citizens broke the Covenant and worshipped other gods. The State was only the outside hulk, the skin inside which the nation lived safely with its divine spirit immanently presiding.

This unwritten law is still revered in the Middle East: there the people believe that the land belongs to whomever God gives victory. They believe that the earth belongs to its Creator who parcels it out to His stewards (*khalifa*). In China likewise, the emperor was the Son of Heaven. If the emperor was healthy and had many children, then the country would prosper. Without a good emperor the State would crumble and vanish. The king of Egypt too, was the sun-god in human shape. He rose every morning, sat on his throne and was rowed in his sun-boat (one such ceremonial royal vessel has recently come to light) on the Nile just as the sun-god Ra sailed along the blue sky.

There is an Islamic legend in which this idea survives. A young woman called Asiya, whose father had taught her to worship only Allah, refused to adore the Pharaoh as a god, so he had her cooked in a cauldron. Asiya is still venerated as one of the saints of Islam. There the concept of divine kings, still common in Africa, has ceased to exist, and with it the stability of the State. God's favour is then the mandate of heaven (Romans 13.1). Kings, especially new kings, love pomp and pageantry. They are convinced that worship is their due. The example of King Alexander the Great demonstrates that Persians and Mesopotamians were ready to worship their emperor as if he were divine.

Thus in the ever expanding states of antiquity, the religion of each empire was obligatory upon all citizens. The Akhaemenid emperors of Iran imposed their religion on all their citizens. Only the peasants in the countryside went

on tilling their soil and worshipping their ancient gods,
about whom they told the same age-old myths century
after century.

It is precisely these ancient myths that survive in the Bible
and in the Koran, as well as in the mouths of today's
shepherds and peasants in Egypt, Iraq and elsewhere. The
languages have changed, from Babylonian and Coptic to
Arabic; even the official religions have changed: after Paganism came Zoroastrianism, Christianity and finally Islam. But
the folklore has remained incredibly similar to what it must
have been in the second millennium BC.

Here are some examples of common religious elements:

1. In the Bible Adam is deceived and so loses his immortality.
   In the Sumerian (*c.* 3000 BC) myth Adapa is tricked by
   the god Ea, so he does *not* eat the food of immortality in
   heaven and becomes a mortal man.
2. Noah is called Utanapishtim in the Babylonian epic of the
   great flood. He survives the great rains in a vessel with
   his animals and family. The vessel's description resembles
   closely that of the Ark in Genesis 6.
3. The very strong man who slays a lion is known as
   Gilgamesh in the Sumerian epic, Samson in the Hebrew
   tradition and Hercules in ancient Greece.
4. The trickster god is Ea-Enki in Mesopotamia, Hermes in
   ancient Greece and Satan in the Hebrew tales.
5. The words of the great Biblical prophets are accepted in
   three religions: Judaism, Christianity and Islam.
6. The concept of the survival of the human soul after death,
   and of this soul being judged by the gods of the nether
   world, was first elaborated by the ancient Egyptians. On
   the walls of the pyramids one can see the gods Osiris
   (Pluto) and Thoth (Hermes) weighing the good and bad
   deeds of the deceased on a pair of scales. This episode in
   the soul's life after death survives in Islamic doctrine to
   this day, except that only the one God presides over the
   judgement, assisted by his chief angel Jibril.
7. The concepts of paradise and hell are first described in

Old Persian cosmology. From there it was accepted into Christianity and it is an essential part of Islamic dogma concerning creation and judgement. The word 'paradise' itself is Persian for garden, which is how it is rendered in Hebrew and Arabic. The fire of hell where the evil spirits will have to spend eternity is clearly described in the Book of Revelation from which a great deal of imagery has passed into the Koran, although Muslim scholars would not agree. They would put it thus: 'God has given to John Theologus and to Muhammad fractions of his knowledge concerning the last day. In other words the two visions are similar because they are God's revelation, not because Muhammad read the Book of Revelation. He never did.'

8. Closely connected with this is the concept of doomsday, armageddon, the end of the world, the end of time. In other cosmologies, such as Hinduism or Confucianism, there is no trace of this belief. It is typical of Middle Eastern thinking to regard time as linear, as a long straight thread that begins at creation and ends at doomsday. In Hinduism time is a spiral without end, and history is cyclical without conclusion.

The Christian-Islamic conviction is that each human soul is separately created by God with an individual personality, and is then immediately placed in an embryo in a mother's womb, all this with foresight and providence. After this the soul in its unborn body will be gestated, born and will live on earth until it is separated from its body by death at the time God has predestined for it. After death the body will be buried but the soul will live on until resurrection, when it will be given a new body similar to but better than the first one. Such is the belief of Islam and Christianity. Hinduism teaches that the soul goes through an endless chain of rebirth (*samsara*), each new life being better or worse than the previous one depending on the good or bad deeds (*karma*) of the individual.

In Buddhism this concept is retained in essence but it

is haunted by the question of whether the individual soul survives at all. Indian cosmology sees individual history as cyclical, like world history. The rebirth into a new life happens without judgement, as an event controlled by cosmic law.

All these cosmologies are again quite different from the Far Eastern idea (also found in some central African religions) that the spirits of the ancestors reside underground (like Ulysses' father) or linger near their graves; in any case the spirits live on near their descendants and receive offerings from them as their due. This concept of the life after death is closely linked to that of a collective, familial spirit as opposed to the highly individualized concept of the soul wandering lonely in Islam and Christianity.

In pre-Christian times every person was bound to his and her god(s) by the ties of birth, *natio*, as we have seen. No one can change his ancestors, so no one could change his gods. The ancestral spirits, if neglected, would haunt their descendants demanding sacrifices and threatening to send sickness if the right rituals were not performed soon. In Africa today, in numerous clans, the ancestral spirits still have to be placated. It follows that no such person can convert to a new religion completely. Many missionaries have made their converts very unhappy and even neurotic by prohibiting the continuation of ancestor worship. The frightened new converts did not dare to confess that their ancestors rose from their graves and appeared in their dreams to claim their due sacrifices. Worship *must* continue.

In this context it becomes clear why Jesus did not abolish Judaism and why Buddha did not abrogate Hinduism. Buddha taught that worshipping the gods was not useful, since it could not lead to salvation, but he did not prohibit it. Jesus, likewise, although creating a new religion, did not prohibit, for instance, the slaughtering of a lamb at Passover, but he did not make it part of his own practice. Only three centuries later, when Christianity had become the state religion in the Eastern Roman Empire, could the bishops act more severely against the (already decadent) pagan practices. Islam followed this bad example with a vengeance. It treated all 'old' religions with comtempt, and the new mosques at Jerusalem and Damascus were built on top of the old churches. The first mosque at Delhi (*c.* 1200) was built with the stones from the old Jain temple, just as the churches had once been built on the ruins of Zeus temples.

The result of the religious history of the Middle East over the past 5000 years has been that, of the once numerous religions, only one is now dominant, the youngest, Islam. The number of Jews dwindled over the centuries, then started increasing again about a century ago, and is still growing, mainly through births and immigration. The Christians, once the dominant religious community in the entire Middle East west of the river Euphrates, were dealt a blow with the onslaught of Islam in 634, a blow from which they never recovered. Christianity was reduced to a minority religion by constant attrition until today there are only a few hundred Christians in Turkey, for instance, compared to many millions in 1914. Only in Egypt has the Christian population maintained itself at a constant level of just over 4 million, the same number as in the year 634.

The Zoroastrians once dominated the entire Middle East east of the Euphrates, including Central Asia and Afghanistan, but after 634 they were destroyed in Iran and in most of Asia. Only a few escaped to India, where they have survived and are now called Parsees. Islam, now in its Shi'a form, is becoming ever more dominant in Iran, so that the last surviving Zoroastrians, Christians and Baha'is had to flee soon after 1979 as the Shi'a is even more intolerant than the Sunna.

The three surviving great religions of the Middle East (The Baha'is are a special case) – Christianity, Judaism and Islam – have many features in common in spite of centuries of hostility. Indeed one might argue that their very nature of aggressiveness is unique among the religions of the world.

Other religions – Hinduism, Buddhism, Confucianism – have never been the causes of war. The Chinese and Japanese have waged many wars in their history but they were not wars of religion. Africans and American Indians used to fight wars in centuries past, but they also were never religious. Religion has become a reason for warfare only for the believers in Islam, Christianity and Judaism.

It could be argued that in many cases the conversion of the 'enemies' was only an excuse for conquest, as for instance, in the conquest of Mexico which resulted in the Christianization of the native Mexicans. When the Arab Tariq landed in Spain (711) with the intention of conquering it, he exclaimed, 'This land belongs to Allah so it belongs to us!', which is certainly a concise formulation of faith as an excuse for conquest. The Islamic conquests of the seventh and eighth centuries were undoubtedly nothing more than the natural expansion of the Arab nation, whereas from the late tenth century onwards that expansion was taken up by the Turks, whose overpopulation of Central Asia forced them to make war on the Byzantines in the west and the Indians in the east.

Similarly, the aggressive wars of the Jews too, as described in the books of Joshua and his successors, were wars of national conquest. The Philistines were attacked not because they adhered to their own religion but simply because they were in the way of Israel's expansionism. The original inhabitants of Palestine were not converted to the worship of Israel's God, they were killed. The Arabs (after 634) followed a similar policy: the Christian majorities of Jordan, Syria and Palestine were not converted *en masse* to Islam but were sold into slavery or killed off. Only in Egypt and later in Spain was the Christian population permitted to continue tilling the soil. The Turks were no less ruthless. The totally Christian population of Asia Minor was killed or enslaved between the eleventh and nineteenth centuries. Few escaped.

So perhaps it is true to say that the wars of religion were, in most cases, wars of conquest. The great Tsar of Russia and defender of the church of Moscow, Nicholas I, may have stated that his conquest of Azerbaijan in 1828 was a crusade against Islam, but the same could not be said of his brother's conquest of the Christian kingdom of Georgia in 1803. The number of wars which the many princes of Islam waged against their Christian neighbours is far exceeded by the wars they fought among themselves. Perhaps the concept of religious war in Middle Eastern history needs to be subjected to a thorough revision.

5. GODS AND SPIRITS

Myths are literary descriptions of the 'other world' and what happens there. This is the non-material, non-physical world of the unseen beings. These beings are called spirits and their habitat is the spiritual world as opposed to the physical world of earth. That spiritual world cannot be located 'somewhere else' because only matter takes space. The spirits can be in more than one place, they are not confined in space, they are unseizable. If the spirits so wish they can make themselves visible to human beings, which means probably that they can cause our minds to have visions of them. A spirit can also cause our ears to hear him or her (we are assuming that spirits have gender, although of course they are not physical), so spirits have voices.

Spirits often appear in dreams. One spirit can appear to two people at the same time in different places, irrespective of whether those people are awake or asleep. Thus they can communicate with people and they can hear us calling them even if they are far away. They are free agents wandering at will in the world. They can fly and penetrate doors and walls since they are not material. They do not need human beings, except the spirits of the dead, who need the offerings of their living descendants to survive. If they receive no offerings, no ritual sacrifices, the spirits of the dead may appear to the living as ghosts. A ghost is thus the spirit of one who has died, appearing in visible form, recognizable to the living, even if very hazy and vague; in the dark, a spirit can shine like the moon, or at least phosphoresce like the sea.

The spirits are divisible into numerous species (so called by Arab writers, as if they were species of animals). Spirits can be good or bad, for we must remember that they occur in a moral world. Amoral people do not believe in spirits. The noblest spirits are called angels; they only occur in the three major modern religions of the Middle East — Judaism, Islam and Christianity — since those are the monotheistic religions, and the One God has a need for angels to act as his messengers and to carry out other tasks on his behalf. Very often it is not clear in the Bible or in the Koran whether the Lord himself appeared to Abraham, Jacob or Muhammad, for instance, or whether it was an angel.

At the other extreme of the morality scale there are the satans or devils (in Arabic *shaytan* and *ifrit*), evil spirits who take pleasure in harming and harassing people. The most powerful of them all is *the* Satan, *the* Devil (in Arabic *Iblis*) who is the God of Evil, the old Persian Ahriman. The difference between Iblis and Ahriman is that Ahriman acts on his own whereas Iblis has been created by Allah and acts only with Allah's express approval (Koran 7:14).

In Islam and in most other cosmologies there are also 'intermediate' spirits like the *jinns* of the Arabian tales, of whom some are Muslims who may help people, while others are heathens who will tease and tempt people capriciously.

What is the difference between gods and spirits? In principle the gods are the most powerful category of spirits. However, in the context of a monotheistic religion the gods are called spirits. Thus the American Indians called their supreme being the Great Spirit because the Christian missionaries would insist that there is only one God who is true; the others being false. Likewise in Arabian tales the *jinns* and *ifrits* who can blow themselves up to gigantic size, mow down armies of armed horsemen, lift up castles and palaces and put them down in another country so gently that the household personnel would not even notice, are spirits, not gods, because they are not worshipped. The Great Spirit of

North America, however, *is* a god, because he is worshipped. This makes our definition very simple: a god is what you worship. There is no other definition possible since we can only define the spiritual beings in terms of their relationships to us as human beings. The spiritual world is invisible so definitions by size or weight are impossible. In any case, as we have seen, mere size does not make a spirit into a true god. Furthermore, the opinions of the believers will always differ from those of the non-believers. The Bible and the Koran fulminate against the false gods and idols which are worshipped by foolish people whom God will condemn for their error.

The further we go back in history, the more gods we meet. In the earliest times every family had its own gods. These gods are often identified with their statues or other objects in which they 'live'. These statuettes, figurines or other objects (in New Guinea some gods still live in skulls) were often placed in a box (see *Ark*); even today in some regions of Africa a man can carry his gods with him in a box or pouch. Laban complains that his gods have been stolen in Genesis 31:30. Evidently what matters is not the material they are made of but the spiritual 'charge' which makes the objects magically powerful. Many modern theologians object to these images being called gods, since for them the term 'god' must be restricted to the one God who alone may be worshipped. However, the 'house gods', like the Roman *lares* and *penates*, are certainly worshipped, and so they are gods by our definition. Gods, being spiritual, can make themselves as small as mice or as large as thunder-clouds, as in Canto XI of the Bhagavadgita, where Krishna, who was the size of a man, assumes his true size, filling the sky to the horizons.

The mythologist takes no sides; he records what the religious texts and the oral traditions relate. He describes the rituals in which prayers and hymns to the gods are (or were, in the case of dead religions) performed. His task is not to prove that the worshippers are erroneously adoring false gods, but on the contrary, to show how the people's expression of their veneration for their highest spiritual values enriches our understanding of the deepest motivation of humanity.

6. HOMER AND THE GODS OF ANTIQUITY: EUROPEAN ATTITUDES

Westerners, and Europeans in particular, are so enthralled by Homer's brilliant poetry that they do not realize how he leads them away from the gods into the world of humanity. Homer composed and recited his epic works for the kings and the sophisticated noblemen of eighth-century BC Greece, which then already had a millennium of civilization behind it. An evolution unique in human history had taken place: Homer and his contemporaries no longer took the gods seriously. They had become a target of mockery. Henceforth the arts, poetry and painting depicted the gods as beautiful people, no longer as true, fearsome beings who could demand adoration and strike people down with the plague. The Greek myths had become a collection of fascinating fairy tales, a quarry for symbol-seeking psychoanalysts.

Few scholars have wondered what happened to Greek religion. When Socrates was accused of no longer believing in the gods, his detractors were right: he and his fellow intellectuals have left the real religion behind. It was no more than ritual. Almost 2000 years later the erudite Italians became interested in Greek poetry, philosophy and art again, creating what is rightly called the Renaissance, the rebirth of European civilization, after the long dark Middle Ages when reason was exiled. With Greek philosophy Greek scepticism was revived, an attitude of mind that made the Copernican revolution possible and so heralded the explosive development of science, that powerful daughter of scepticism. Only constant doubting guarantees the progress of science and European thought. This revolution of the European spirit caused a rift with Asia that never healed and is now incurable, as the Asians remained faithful to the gods.

Let us consider as an example the famous Homeric tale

of Hephaistos trapping his adulterous wife Aphrodite in bed with her lover Ares, the handsome young warrior. The gods laughed at the cuckolded husband. Homer himself did not understand the original myth nor its meaning. In his day the Greek people no longer venerated Hephaistos as they had in previous centuries. Through comparison with ancient Greek and Asian popular practices we can restore the original cosmology. Hephaistos ranked with the twelve highest Olympians as ruler of the zodiacal sign of Aquarius, the rain-god. Hephaistos was the original Greek creator, equated with the Indian god Brahma. He had created the gods' palaces in heaven, for which they gave him Aphrodite as his consort. She ruled the sign following her husband's, Pisces, for the sea was her element. She rose out of the sea as the beautiful verdant Greek islands. As such she was created by her husband. As earth goddess Aphrodite is identified with the Biblical Ashtara, the Babylonian Ishtar. She fell in love with the young handsome god Adonis, the Syrian name for Mars, Baal or Tammuz, the god of spring and flowers. Every year he made love to her, then he died when the dry season came. Every spring the rains of Hephaistos revived him, and with him verdure and flowers. Ares (the Roman Mars) was the ram-god of the sacrificial fire (he sacrificed himself in war for the fatherland). He ruled the sign of Aries the ram which follows Pisces at the spring equinox on March 21–22, the ancient new year's day when a young ram was sacrificed in all Middle Eastern countries.

The Biblical prophets fulminated against the 'useless heathen idols' of Baal and Asherah, but we must not forget that the people of Palestine, whether Canaanites or Israelites, were 95 per cent farmers and so preferred divinities of agriculture, vegetation gods to the abstract Jehovah of the animal-breeding Jews whose chief public feast was the sacrifice of the male lamb at Passover, a feast which originally coincided with the spring equinox. Here, as in all the religions of Asia and Africa to the present day, the function of the gods and the annual rural celebrations 'mesh' so precisely that no part of that religious body can be removed without disrupting the very fabric of the culture. The people have continued their pagan ceremonies for millennia, only changing the names of the gods to those of saints or angels. There must be continuity of sunshine, rain and season, to ensure that crops and children will grow as before.

Modern European farmers have left these religious conditions of their life behind. They base their methods on science, no longer on faith and ritual tradition. In Oriental and African cultures this change has not yet taken place. There is, of course, a wide band of cultural transition as one travels east. In Israel most agriculture is ultra-modern, but in Greece many pre-Christian beliefs survive. A well near Athens was once dedicated to the goddess Demeter. Its water must not be drunk by any woman unless she wants a child, because drinking that water will make *every* woman pregnant, whether she is married or not. So I was assured by a local woman. Belief – and therefore faith – is conditioned by a certain mentality which may be individual, but is usually induced by society. When everybody takes the existence of spirits for granted, how can one deny it? This belief in turn is the foundation of magic, spirit possession, prophecy, ghostly apparitions, faith healing and all the other beliefs that are the study-objects of mythology.

7. WHAT IS A MYTH?

Mythology is the collection and study of myths. The English word myth comes from the Greek word *mythos*, 'word or story', first used by Homer himself, who acknowledged that he received his mythic tales from his muse, the 'daughter of Zeus'. This poetic allusion already gives us one meaning of the myth: it must be divinely inspired. Fables and fairy tales are invented stories for amusement and a little education as well, but myths and legends are true.

Legends were originally the histories of the early Christian saints. Sagas were the heroic tales of the kings and warriors of the past, most of whom did exist. Here we hit the essential question of myth: did the gods of antiquity exist? Few people nowadays believe in them, although I know people who still venerate the ancient Celtic gods. India is the one country where all the gods of antiquity are still worshipped. If, however, one asks an Indian scholar whether Vishnu and Shiva exist, he will reply that they are appearances of the one invisible divine reality. Other philosophers have gone further: Buddha taught that the gods need no worship; Marx scoffed that all religion was deceit. Curiously today both Buddha and Marx are themselves venerated as if they were divine.

So can we then define myth as the opposite of reality? Reality can be proven to exist or to have existed, but myth is the description of the unseen reality. This unseen world can be individual, like the world of our dreams, or it can be collective, as a result of a common upbringing in the traditions of a group. Mythology then is the study of the unseen world of a given group or community such as the Greek or Celtic nations of the past.

Only the past? Is the mythologist only concerned with dead religions? Do living religions have no myths? The answer, of course, is that they do. Myth is an integral part of all religions. Religion is the worship of God or of the gods. A religion is thus always based on the acceptance of certain concepts outside reality, a belief in a divine presence, which for non-believers does not exist. The mythologist studies this cosmos but is careful to take no sides. Mythology is a branch of the science of anthropology, especially its subdivision called religiology in America. The anthropologist studies the religion of a contemporary people by observing their common rituals, the ceremonies of the priests, etc. The mythologist studies what people believe, as opposed to what they can see around them. Most of the peoples on earth believe that there is more in the world than can be seen or heard. They believe in a spiritual world. That world is for them a reality but for an atheist it is myth. The mythologist tells no one that he is wrong, that he only believes in a myth. A myth is a collective belief that cannot be proved to be true. But that does not make it untrue. The mythologist, when told that certain people 'live in a dream', smiles, since he is a philosopher who knows that almost all people live (at least part of the time) in dreams, that is, they believe in myths.

These different opinions give rise to endless disputes, and to attempts by the believers to make their beliefs rationally acceptable to the unbelievers who continuously harass them with questions like: Did Eve really come out of Adam's rib? Was there really a great Flood? Did the manna really rain from heaven? Did Lazarus really rise from death? The mythologist should never get involved in these disputations. His concept of reality is much wider than that of the scientist. He does not deny the truth of faith. What people believe is their reality. If others have different beliefs, they are free to have their own faith. The time of the wars of religions is past. Or is that also a pious belief?

These cautionary remarks are necessary lest anyone is displeased to find references in this book to his or her own religion and exclaims: 'There is no myth in my religion! These stories are all historical truths!' No one denies it. All myths are equally true. The mythologist merely describes what people in many countries have said about their beliefs.

The result is that there may be contradictory statements in this book. Mythology is not a logical subject. For example, Aphrodite was married to both Ares and Hephaestos. Impossible? But mythology has its own rules of logic. A god is not one person but many, the gods can divide themselves and reunite, like Krishna dancing with a dozen girls, each one believing that she sees the only real Krishna. Gods are not physical beings, so they are not countable. Jesus tells Mary she must not try to touch him, because his presence is not physical: there is nothing to touch! Yet one must not conclude that he was not there, nor that she only dreamt him. Ghosts likewise can be seen and heard but they are not material, all that a human being can feel when approaching a ghost is a cool breeze. The gods also lead many lives, they die and are reborn every year. In this respect Jesus was only the last of a long line: Tammuz, Dumuzi and Baal were all precursors of the handsome Adonis who rose every year at Easter.

The gods are as elusive as they are powerful. They influence our lives and yet they remain unnoticed. They are numerous and yet there is only one God. The gods are both friendly and terrifying. Elijah experienced God as a gentle dawn breeze (I Kings 19:12) but Ezekiel was terrified by his vision. As for Muhammad, the approach of the divine presence often made him wrap his robe around himself, fearing God's powerful presence. When Arjuna insists that the young god Krishna show himself in his true form, he is suddenly struck down by the immense number of bodies and faces, filling the universe. God is endless, yet he fits in a small body. The firmament cannot contain him, but the human heart can embrace him.

New students of myth will find themselves literally entering Dante's threefold domain of the spirits. Dante had a good guide, so he emerged from that weird world of other beings and lived to write his epic tale. The student of mythology may not have Dante's strong character. Therefore great caution is advised, just as young students of psychoanalysis have to be warned by their tutors to keep their sanity at all times. In the myths of the visitors to the other world, like Eurydice, each visitor is warned to take special precautions, otherwise he or she will never get out. The other world is not only magically dangerous but also powerfully attractive. Persephone had already fallen in love with the king of the other world, Eurydice had eaten a few pomegranate seeds, symbols of love. The other world is the land of the dead, no one ever comes back from it, except in myth. That is why students of myth have to be extra careful that, whenever they wish, they can escape from the mythical world, which always puts a spell on its visitors. They must under all circumstances keep their sanity and be able to stand back at any time to contemplate the other world independently. Many mythologists have been swept away by other people's beliefs, too weak to resist the magic of myth. I myself have more than once felt the voodoo of the spirits while listening to the tales of ghosts and *jinns* in a circle of believers. Visiting a community of believers is already like entering another world, since they live with the spirits as if they were house martins. The student who goes in search of the spirits without special mental precautions may find that he or she has lost the way out of the labyrinth, which is the symbol of the other world; only those who find their way out will have a long life.

Dr C. G. Jung has shown the close links between the world of myths and the world of dreams, the world of our own interior mind or psyche, our microcosmos, and has also warned his readers not to get lost in that world below this world – our subconscious.

Once the student of myths and dreams has learned the numerous symbols in them, he or she will feel like a person who has learned a foreign language: they will suddenly discover that they can 'read' those symbols like a language. It has been known for some time that dreams are messages from the subconscious soul, and that we can regard their symbolism as a language. Likewise, myths are a form of symbolism, a language, and the mythologist is like a language teacher. Remember that the language can only be understood by adults. Those who lose their way in the labyrinth lose their individual identity. Myth is the description of the other world in symbols. The mythologist, like the archaeologist, can decipher the hieroglyphs without losing the way in the pyramids.

8. MYTH AND HISTORY

The majority of the names in this book cannot be dated, beginning with Adam, the first king of the earth and the first prophet of God. According to the Jewish tradition he was born in the year 1, in the first week of that year.

In the Islamic tradition there is also a problem: if Mary the mother of Isa (Jesus) was the daughter of Imran (Amram) then she was the sister of Musa (Moses) and Harun (Aaron), the fourteenth and fifteenth prophets in Islamic history. But Isa was the twenty-fourth prophet, so there was a long period of history between Musa and his nephew Isa (see *Prophets 2*).

After Moses came Joshua, Samuel, David, Solomon, Elijah and all the other prophets until Zachariah, Mary's uncle.

In old Persian history, as it is retold in the great epic of *Shahname*, the *Book of Kings* by Abu Kasim Firdausi, there are many undatable kings, especially Jamshid who reigned for a thousand years, and his successor Zahhak (Dahaka) who had two snake heads growing out of his shoulders, but who could not be killed until doomsday.

Of course in the traditions of Mesopotamia the kings' historicity is even more problematic. Gilgamesh, king of Uruk, is undatable, except that he must have lived before 3000 BC. But when did he visit the immortal Utanapishtim in the Land of Eternal Life?

If a ruler's dates are known with reasonable certainty, they will be given in his entry.

The Periods

The following is a list of the major historical periods in the Middle East, arranged according to the nations whose dynasties ruled parts of the area during that time.

Sumerian	(1) 3600–2528 BC
	(2) 2294–1998 BC
Egyptian	3100–332 BC
Akkadian	2334–2154 BC or 2371–2191 BC
Babylonian	(1) *c.* 2100–1900 BC
	(2) 1894–539 BC
Amorite	2057–1517 BC
Elamite	(1) 1850–1505 BC
	(2) *c.* 1350–*c.* 645 BC
Assyrian	1813–609 BC
Hurrian	1800–1300 BC
Hittite	(1) 3000–2000 BC
	(2) 1975–1650 BC
	(3) 1395–717 BC

Urartu   1300–590 BC
Israel and Judah, kings 1020 (Saul)–587 BC (Zedekiah)
Sabaeic   750 BC–577 AD
Lydian   687–547 BC (Death of Croesus)
Persian   650 BC–651 AD
Hellenistic: Seleucids 305–64 BC
Nabataean   170 BC–105 AD
Roman   64 BC–306 AD
Byzantine   306–1453 AD
Arab   641–1258 AD
Crusader   1099–1292 AD
Mamluk   1258–1517 AD in Egypt and Palestine
Ottoman   1453–1923 AD

9. PRONUNCIATION

I have introduced names and other words from a wide
variety of languages including Arabic, Babylonian, Egyptian,
Hebrew, Hittite, old Persian, middle Persian, new Persian,
Phoenician, Sumerian, Turkish and Ugaritic. Obviously each
language has its own structure and its own phonetic system. It
is impossible to represent these phonetic characteristics without a very sophisticated computer programme and printer to
match. I therefore ask you to excuse the absence of diacritic
signs. As for the stress, most oriental languages have the
stressed syllable at the end of the word. Names like Iran,
Afghanistan, Azerbaijan, Mika'il and Tel Aviv, all have their
stresses on the last vowel. Feminine place names like Haifa,
Mecca, and Medina stress the penultimate vowel. In the case
of dead languages, of course, we have no idea how they were
really pronounced. Most Oriental languages distinguish long
and short vowels, but modern printers have no macrons for
the purpose.
   The Semitic languages are characterized by a clearly
sounded glottal stop called *hamza* in Arabic, as well as
by the *'ayn*, a letter whose pronunciation we know only
from Arabic. In modern Hebrew it is not pronounced, or it

sounds like the *hamza*, as in Ya'kov, the Arabic Ya'kub, in which the *'ayn*, spelt with an ordinary apostrophe, is sounded by a long contraction of the pharynx. In all cases where a 'normal' English word exists, or when there is a common English form for a name, it is used in preference to the exotic forms. We are writing in English, so we write Koran instead of the quasi-Arabicized Qur'an. We write Solomon instead of Shelomon (Hebrew) or Sulayman (Arabic), although the Arabic forms, if they are very common in Islamic literature, will have their own entry.

The *q* is used in Arabic words and names to represent *qaf*, the laryngeally pronounced *k*.

No writer on Oriental subjects can be completely consistent. The English forms for the Arabic name Muhammad, for example, namely Mahomet and Mohammed, have gone out of use, so Muhammad is used throughout this book.

There are numerous variations in spelling in the Oriental languages themselves. For example the Arabic *masjid*, 'mosque', is pronounced 'masgid' in Egypt, the Arabic *ramadan*, the month of fasting, is pronounced 'ramazan' in Iran and Pakistan. In Turkish all Arabic words are entirely respelt. The spelling of Biblical and modern Hebrew words is often different, e.g. Jacob and Ya'kov.

10. THE SOURCES

The sources for myths, legends and all other religious texts are either oral or written. The oral traditions have been collected by individual scholars, the first of whom was Herodotus (480–425 BC). The Middle East has always been a mine of oral traditions, such as the epic songs of Digenis Akritas (in Greek), the Daredevils of Sassoon (in Armenian) and Dede Korkut (in Turkish), all three from Asia Minor. The *Shahname*, the Persian epic of about 120,000 lines, is largely based on oral traditions, and the Arabian Nights Entertainments were entirely based on the wonderful art of the Arab story tellers; they were given their final redaction as *The 1001 Nights* by the end of the Middle Ages. Even during the past hundred years numerous collections of tales, ballads and songs have been recorded in colloquial Arabic, Persian, Turkish, Baluchi, Syriac, Kurdish, Armenian and other languages.

It is fascinating to listen to these contemporary story tellers in Middle Eastern countries. They still enjoy narrating the legends of Adam who was expelled from paradise and had to work in order to eat, of Noah with two of every species of animal in his ark (including two elephants), of King Solomon who ruled the demons, of Joseph in Egypt, and of many other personalities with whom Christian, Jewish and Muslim children are equally familiar. This repertoire of today's story teller in Arabic-speaking countries demonstrates the continuity and the incredible longevity of the oral traditions.

The written sources for the mythology of the Middle East are equally rich. They begin right at the time of the invention

Cuneiform	Semitic	Arabic	European
Assyrian	Aramaic	Arabic	Greek
Akkadian	Canaanite	Persian	Coptic
Babylonian	Coptic	Ottoman-Turkish	Armenian
Eblaite	Edomite	Kurdish	Georgian
Elamite	Egyptian	Berber	Latin
Hattian	Ethiopic	Urdu	Modern Turkish
Hittite-Nesite	Hebrew	Uzbek	
Hurrian-	Himiaritic		
Mitannian	Lihianic		
Luwian	Mandaic-Sabian-Nazaraic		
Old Persian	Meroitic		
Palaic	Moabitic		
Sumerian	Nabataeic		
Ugaritic-	Phoenician		
Shamraic	Sabaic-Minaic		
Urartian-	Samaritan		
Vannic	Sinaitic		
	Syriac		
	Thamudic		
	Yezidi-Kurdish		

of writing by the Sumerians in about 3000 BC, and they continue to the present time. Opposite is a list of the languages in which written documents have been preserved to the present day. The list is divided into four categories on the basis of the type of script that is used: cuneiform, Semitic, Arabic or European.

The oldest known languages of the Middle East all use the cuneiform scripts, the scribes of each language having altered the cuneiform characters to suit the needs of their own language. Cuneiform script has been used for no fewer than fifteen languages over a period of 3000 years. Cuneiform Babylonian actually became a lingua franca in the Middle East during the second millennium BC and was used from Egypt to Iran. Cuneiform scripts are syllabic, which means that each character represents a syllable, like *ba, be, bi, bo,* etc. The Semitic forms of writing on the other hand are consonant scripts which means that each character represents a consonant, like *b, d, f, g, h, k, l, m, n, r, s, t, w,* etc. Naturally the reader has to be thoroughly familiar with the language in order to decipher it. Compare the Londoner who, seeing the sign 'KNGS CRSS STN' on a bus, will not hesitate to read it correctly. Modern Arabic and Hebrew still employ their traditional consonant scripts for daily usage.

Egyptian has to be mentioned as an exception to our rule: its hieroglyphic script evolved into a pure consonant script over the centuries but Egyptian is not a Semitic language. Arabic on the other hand *is* a Semitic language with a Semitic script but it has been given a separate category because, since the spread of Islam to the far corners of the Middle East, a dozen languages have adopted Arabic script for daily use; the most important ones have been given in the list.

The term 'European' covers the languages which have a script based ultimately on Greek, the Romans having developed their script in the pre-Christian era, the others in Christian times. Modern Turkish now uses the Roman script, Uzbek uses cyrillic.

The ancients wrote on clay tablets in Mesopotamia, on papyrus in Egypt, while all the scripts have been used for inscriptions on stone. As soon as these scripts had been deciphered, an incredible wealth of literature became available for the student of mythology. We now have detailed information on the myths of the gods of the Assyrians, Babylonians, Egyptians, Hittites, Hebrews, old Persians, Phoenicians, Sumerians and many other nations, all of whom lived in the pre-Christian era. In addition, other peoples have also written about their neighbours' gods, notably the Greeks, the Romans and much later, the Arabs.

Finally, a great deal of knowledge of the ancient religions has been gleaned by the archaeologists from their excavations of temples, shrines, altars, statues, reliefs and other monuments. Artefacts such as metal objects protecting the wearers against evil, often with inscriptions on them, are also useful sources of data. Negative descriptions can also be informative, for instance the constant criticism by the Biblical prophets of the heathen practices indulged in by the Children of Israel, or the equally critical writings, of the later Church fathers, condemning the 'worship of the devil', all of which we now just call religions, no longer idolatry.

A

Aaron (Hebrew: *Aharon*, Arabic: *Harun*)
1. Elder brother of Moses (Exodus 6:20–3; 7:7) and his mouthpiece appointed by God. For forty years Aaron was Moses' devoted helper and preacher. Aaron's rod blossomed (Numbers 17:8). He was appointed the first high priest of Israel, a function which his sons inherited. If only he had not participated in the worship of the golden calf, he would have been a perfect man (Exodus 32; Hebrews 5:4–5). He died at the age of 123.
2. Byzantine sorcerer during the reign of the Emperor Manuel Comnenus (1143–80). He was in possession of King Solomon's keys, which have since disappeared. Aaron was a famous necromancer, able to control demons and make them work for him.

Aaru
In ancient Egypt the abode of the virtuous dead. It is represented as a vast field of wheat, symbol of life.

Abaddon (Greek: Apollyon)
The angel of war who lives in the bottomless pit of death. The king of the locusts (see *Locusts*) which emerge from the smoke-filled bottomless pit as soon as the fifth angel has opened it with his key (Revelation 9:11). These locusts look like horses but with scorpions' tails, faces like men and hair like women. See *Abyss*.

Abadir
'Mighty Father', a Phoenician name for the supreme diety.

Abatur
In Gnosticism the father of Demiurgos.

Abba Amona (Aramaic)
'Father, Mother', the supreme divine couple in the Cabala.

Abbas
'Frowner', Muhammad's uncle, son of Abd-al-Muttalib, Muhammad's grandfather. He died much later than the Prophet, in 32 AH/654 AD. He was the ancestor of the Abbasids, the dynasty which ruled in Baghdad from 750 to 1258. Legends are told about his life.

Abdullah (Abdallah)
Son of Abd al-Muttalib, father of Muhammad. One night in the year

569 Abdullah, on his way home, was met by a prophetess who begged him to spend the night with her. She, having second sight, could see divine light radiating from his countenance, illuminating his path. She concluded that by God's will in that night the conception of God's last prophet would take place, and she wanted to be his mother. However, Abdullah was a virtuous man, which is why God had chosen him to be the father of his prophet. Abdullah declined politely, went home and in that same night he embraced his wife Amina. It pleased God to transport the *durra* ('seed or pearl') of light (see *Nur*) from his loins to Amina's womb so that she conceived the embryo of the Prophet. Nine months later when she gave birth to Muhammad, Abdullah had already died.

Abdu'l-Kadir (Abdul Qadir al Jilani, Abd al Qadir al Gilani or Djaelani)
Abdu'l-Kadir (1077–1166) is considered by his biographers as the greatest saint of Islam. He was born in Persia near the Caspian Sea. He worked as a teacher and preacher in Baghdad, from where his fame spread. Many wondrous stories are told about his miraculous deeds. After his death he continued to be venerated. His tomb in Baghdad, over which Sultan Sulayman built a fine monument in 1535, is still the goal of many pilgrims. He has become the most universal of all the Islamic saints. It was believed that his spirit had retained the magic power to help poor people in distress. Mystical seances (called *zikr* in Persian,

see *Dhikr*) are held in his honour to this day. His veneration has spread from Iraq to southern Arabia. The main points of his doctrine are as follows:
1. Purify the heart of all worldly desire.
2. Fear God and obey the precepts of the Koran and Muhammad.
3. Be generous and hospitable, care for people with kindness.
4. Be patient; avoid anger, do not quarrel with people.
5. Travel and learn, show people the Way, be independent but humble.
6. Fight the self which worships itself, then you will not fear death.
7. The ideal saint has found his own essential core, and so he lives in God.

It is often difficult to assess in the numerous tales that are told about him, where history ends and legend begins, but the believers are not worried by such details.

Abdu'r-Rahman, ibn Abu Bakr
Son of Abu Bakr, who fell in love with the daughter of Abu Sufyan, archenemy of the Prophet Muhammad, and married her. He joined his father-in-law in raiding Muslim caravans until his father converted him and his wife to Islam. Both then became staunch defenders of Islam against Abu Sufyan who was finally defeated by Ali.

Abel (Arabic: Abil, q.v.)
Second son of Adam and Eve, the first man to sacrifice a lamb to God. It pleased God, so Cain became jealous and killed him.

Abigail

Wife of David (1 Samuel 25:3 ff); sister of David (1 Chronicles 2:16).

Abigor

One of the upper devils in hell, commander of the infernal legions. He is the demon of warfare who knows the secrets of victory which he will sell to the prince who will offer him his soul. He rides a winged horse into battle.

Abil (Habil)

In the Islamic tradition, the Arabic name for Abel, second son of Adam and Eve. Abil was a faithful son and a devout Muslim, following the words of his father, Allah's first prophet on earth. Abil was ready to give his twin sister to his elder brother Kabil (Cain) as his wife, but the latter was not prepared to return the favour by parting with his own twin sister, as God had commanded Adam: 'No son of yours shall marry his own twin sister.' The brothers had to marry the other's twin sister. At that time there were no other women on earth. Then God demanded a sacrifice from each of the brothers. Kabil found a few wild fruits, but Abil sacrificed his fattest ram. Kabil started a quarrel and Satan, who happened to be standing near them, offered Kabil a big stone with which he smashed Abil's skull. Abil was the first human being to die and the first to be buried, by Kabil. See *Cain*.

Abinadab

In I Samuel 7:1, a Levite in whose house the ark of the Lord stood for twenty years.

Abracadabra

A magic formula, probably from the Coptic *abraxas* 'hurt me not'.

Abraham (Arabic: *Ibrahim*, q.v.)

Founder of the Hebrew nation (Genesis 12:1–6). He may have been a Sumerian (Chaldee), from Ur, the oldest city in the Middle East. He had a son Ishmael (see *Isma'il*) by Hagar (see *Hajar*), an Egyptian slave woman, and a second son, Isaac, when he and his wife Sarah (q.v.) were both very old (Genesis 17:1). Thus Abraham became the ancestor of two nations, the Arabs and the Jews. He instituted circumcision (Genesis 17), which is still practised today by both nations. God made his first covenant with Abraham (Genesis 15:18). Abraham entertained the angels (Genesis 18); and is ready to slay his son for God (Genesis 22).

Abraham's Bosom

In Luke 16:22–3, where Lazarus the beggar is carried by the angels, he is comforted after his death in Abraham's bosom for all his suffering.

Absalom

David's jealous and rebellious son, symbol of the handsome but restless young man (2 Samuel 13:22 ff.). He was killed in battle and mourned by David.

Absu

In Chaldean (Sumerian) cosmology the immense space, source of the primeval waters where Ab, the father of the waters, the lord of wisdom lives.

Abu Jahl

'Father of Ignorance'. His true name was 'Amr ibn Hisham of Mecca. (Koran 22:8). He had nothing but scorn for Muhammad.

Abydos

In ancient Egypt, the holy city of Osiris (q.v.), who was buried there himself, as were many pharaohs.

Abyss (Greek: *abyssos*)

'Unfathomable'. In Babylon, the primeval chaos from which the universe evolved. The 'deep' (Luke 8:31; Romans 10:7); 'bottomless pit' (Revelation 9:1–11; 11:17; 17:8; 20:1–3). The abyss or underworld where the dead live. Abaddon or Apollyon is the king of the spirits who live in the bottomless pit. It is filled with fire and smoke and locusts which will emerge on doomsday and darken the sky after the fifth angel sounds his trumpet.

Abyssinia

See *Queen of Abyssinia*.

Accad (Akkad)

First Babylonian city, made his capital by Sargon I in 2475 BC

Ad

A city and its people in southern Arabia (Koran 7:63). Hud (q.v.), the prophet, warned them to convert. God destroyed them all (89:5).

Adad (Hadad)

1. Mesopotamian weather-god, ruler of storms and giver of vital rain. His bull bellowed like thunder; he is depicted standing on its back armed with his lightning. He marked the end of summer.

2. Assyrian god of storms, son of Anu, giver of rain, identified with Baal and also with Hadad.

Adam

The first human being to stand on earth, made of clay by God, who then blew life into his nose or, in other myths, vivified him simply by touching him lightly with his finger. The 'clay' suggests that human beings are clay vessels into which God pours his spirit like wine, this wine being a metaphor for blood, the 'spirit' that makes men live. That is why blood belongs to God (Genesis 9:4). It is his own spirit. It seems that the Garden of Eden was somewhere on earth (Genesis 2:8). Here Adam, who was created after God's image, was placed to live. God then took a rib from Adam and made a woman out of it (Genesis 2:21). No reasons are given for Adam eating the forbidden fruit (Genesis 3:6). It has been said that he and Eve should have left eating the fruit until after they had been properly married by God, but Adam is already called 'her husband'. Evidently, the 'fruit' which Eve 'gave' to Adam is her own pudenda. He 'ate it', a common metaphor for enjoying a woman. When God called him, Adam weakly blamed Eve. 'The woman whom Thou gavest to be with me, she gave me of the tree, and I did eat.' Both the Bible and the Koran make it clear that Adam should have obeyed God, since nothing is more important than that. Instead, he obeyed his wife, unquestioningly, thus starting the chain of generations.

The Islamic tradition gives precise details of Adam's life and birth. When God revealed to the angels that he would create Adam they foresaw that behind his clay forehead Adam would hide lies, something angels could never do. 'Man will hatch hatred, jealousy and sin, he will light the brush-fire of war.' God ordered three angels in succession to bring Him clay from the earth, but the earth refused: 'No part of mine will be used to form a disobedient sinner.' Finally, Azrail (q.v.) tore out the clay because God's command to him had priority. God then moulded a man after his image, which means the shape he had in mind. (Remember that God has no shape.) God had already created Adam's soul in the shape of a spark. This he blew into Adam's nose and from there it entered his heart which started to beat so that his blood began flowing through his veins. When it reached his eyes, he opened them. When it reached his mouth he opened it and praised his maker for the wonderful world he could see. When the blood finally reached his feet he stood up and walked around.

One morning when he woke up he saw a lovely creature, like him yet not like him. He called her Haiwa, 'Life'. God taught him the names of all the plants, animals, stars and angels, in Arabic. God told him not to eat the fruit of one tree (see *Fruit*). However, the serpent Iblis (q.v.) entered the garden and persuaded Eve (Haiwa) to eat from the tree. Adam, knowing that Eve would be expelled from the Garden (see *Janna*), decided to keep her company so that he could protect her in the hard life on earth. Still he should not have disobeyed God at any price, say the Islamic authors. Thus he ate the fruit, after which both of them fell down to earth. Adam landed on a mountain in Sarandib (Sri Lanka), from where he made his way on foot through the forests of India which was not yet inhabited, and through the deserts of Arabia to Mecca. He wept frequently when remembering his sinful disobedience, but Jibril (q.v.) appeared to point him in the right direction.

In Mecca, Adam built the first Ka'ba, instructed by Jibril who also taught him to pray there. Eve appeared to have landed in Arabia. She too found her way to Mecca, also guided by Jibril, who also performed the first wedding ceremony on earth, so they were properly married. They had forty children, twenty sets of twins. Their two eldest sons, Kabil and Abil quarrelled over Kabil's twin sister whom Adam had given to Abil as his wife. Kabil killed Abil. After his death, Adam had to supervise the sinners' journey to hell.

Adam Kadmon
'Man-Preceding'. The original man, the precursor of Adam, who was still a friend of God, according to Jewish mysticism the ideal model for those who wish to be close to God.

Adapa
1. In Babylonian myth, the son of the god Ea, the god of wisdom, and priest-king of Eridu, the Babylonians' oldest city. Ea gave Adapa knowledge but not eternal life. Ea was

also a fisherman and when the south wind broke his boat on the cliffs, Adapa caught him and broke one of his wings. For this deed he had to account before the supreme god Anu in heaven. His own father Ea misled him about the correct behaviour in heaven, so that Adapa did not receive eternal life as he had hoped.

2. One of the seven Apkallu, the wisest of men, a priest in the temple of Ea at the Sumerian city of Eridu. He was a favorite of Ea, but Ea wanted to keep him as a servant so he deceived him about what he would be offered at the court of the chief-god Anu. Had Adapa partaken of the water and the food offered to him in heaven he would have become immortal. He is the forerunner of the biblical Adam, the first man.

Adan
See *Adn*.

Adar (Adrammelech)
The god of the Sepharvites (2 Kings 17:31) from Assyria, for whose worship they burnt their children in the fire.

Adim
One of the ancient Egyptian kings after the flood, son of Budasheer, whose spirit lived on in his subterranean palace. Adim often went in secret to consult his wise (dead) father. Adim built the first installation for distilling fresh water from sea water in a deep vast cave.

Adn (Adan, Aden)
The Garden of Eden in Islam. See Koran 9:72; 13:23; 18:31; 19:61; 20:76; 35:33; 38:50; 40:8. Those who practise good works, patience and purity, will live in mansions in those gardens full of streams and angels. It was from here that Adam fell to earth, landing on Sri Lanka, see *Fall*. It is also called Dar al Thawab 'House of Recompense', where the virtuous believers will reside.

Adonai (Hebrew)
'My Lord'. The common Jewish term of address to God whose name they may not pronounce. Its origin is the Hebrew *Adon* 'Lord', from which we also have Adonis (q.v.).

Adonia
In Byblos, in about 1000 BC, the untimely death of Adonis was publicly commemorated with wailing and mourning, followed by a banquet. The women carried portraits or figurines of Adonis, that most comely youth, and after the meal they united with their lovers, for the love goddess.

Adonis
A handsome young man with whom the goddess of love Venus-Aphrodite-Ashtaroth fell in love. His Babylonian name was Tammuz; he could be identical with the Roman Mars. He was killed while hunting wild boar and changed into an anemone. He was worshipped in Phoenicia as the god of spring. See also *Tammuz* (Tamuz), *Baal* and *Dumuzi*.

Adramelech
One of the superior devils of hell, chancellor of Satan. He was represented as a centaur who would make love to women.

Advent

The second coming of Christ as prophesied by Paul in 1 Corinthians 15:23–8 (see also John 14:3). See *Messiah*.

Aerolith

A meteorite, a stone fallen from heaven. Such a stone was worshipped in Syria in Emesis (Hama), as part of the cult of Baal (q.v.).

Aeshma (Aesma)

In old Persian 'Fury', the Zoroastrian demon of wrath and revenge, the personification of violence, a lover of conflict and war.

Agar

See *Hagar, Hajar*.

Agaures

One of the Oriental devils in hell, commander of legions.

Agla

Ancient Hebrew acronym for the formula that chases evil spirits away.

Agriculture

1. The Egyptians worshipped Ma'at as the god of agriculture.
2. Adam was told that 'the ground is cursed'. Where there was previously lush vegetation, there would henceforth be 'thorns and thistles' (Genesis 3:17–18). Adam was told to eat the 'herb of the field' and bread, that is, corn in some form of preparation, unleavened like flat breads or *naan*. There is no mention of domestic animals. Yet in Genesis 4:2 'Abel was a keeper of sheep', while Cain was a 'tiller of the ground' who brought the 'fruit of the ground' as an offering to God. He, however, had no respect for it. In the days of Jacob and Laban, agriculture was no longer mentioned. Abraham travelled long distances with his cattle (Genesis 13:3), apparently as a nomad with his extended family. No cultivation was mentioned. Wheat is first referred to in Egypt (Genesis 41:22) where the land had been tilled for centuries.

Ahasuerus (Ahasverus)

King of Persia (Esther 1:1).

Ahasverus

A man who was punished by God. When Jesus, exhausted by carrying the cross on his way to Golgotha, leaned against a door to rest, the owner, Ahasverus, chased him away, not wanting convicts at his door. God condemned him to be without a house and to wander the earth till doomsday and Christ's second coming. So he became known as the Wandering Jew. He prays to Christ to come quickly, but Christ is carrying his cross so he cannot walk fast. Christ replies: 'Suffering makes me tarry but thou shalt wander until I arrive.' The Jew is rejuvenated every thirty years, Christ's age at crucifixion. Gradually he becomes a wise man, repenting his sins and urging others to do likewise so as to avoid God's wrath. Some people in the Middle Ages claimed to have seen Johannes Buttadeus, as he was called in Latin.

Ahduth

'Unity, concord'. In Jewish mysticism the act of union with God, the highest goal.

Ahimelech

High priest of Israel, executed on Saul's orders for treason (1 Samuel 22:16).

Ahl Al-Badr

'The people of Badr', the names of the heroes who fought the battle of Badr west of Medina for the Prophet Muhammad. The Arabic word is often corrupted to Halbadiri or Alibadiri in other languages. Reciting all these names will cure the sick and make thieves return stolen property.

Ahmad

The heavenly name of Muhammad whose advent was announced by Isa (Jesus) in the Koran (61:6). According to Islamic scholars his advent was announced in the Bible by Jesus (John 14:16, where the English translation is 'comforter', 15:23). The Greek word is *parakletos*, in Aramaic *menahhemana*, which the Arabs read as Muḥammad. See *Faraqlit*.

Ahriman

In the Avesta (q.v.), Ahriman is the god of darkness, the great evil spirit. The old Persian religion taught that in the beginning, before creation, there was endless light in which Ahura Mazda (q.v.) the god of knowledge, lived. Ahriman was the god of lies (*drug, druj*) and thus of ignorance. He lived deep below in the shadow of darkness. From time to time he attacked Ahura Mazda's fine creation. He might be beaten back but he would not rest from trying to destroy creation, and from trying to make all creatures love him and hate their creator until the last day.

Ahriman's own self was in the form of a toad, black like soot, worthy of hell, sinful like a noxious beast. He made the essence of wickedness from which he created the demons. He created lying speech, while Ahura Mazda created true speech from his great light. Then he created time so that Ahriman lay prostrate for 3000 years, until his own evil kingdom acquired the phenomenon of time and so grew and developed, for without time nothing can grow or decline. Then, like a snake, the evil one attacked the stone sky and penetrated earth. Like a fly he infested all plants and animals on earth. Ahriman created poison which made the plants wither, and pain which made the animals sick. Then Ahura Mazda created medicine which cured the sickness. Ahura Mazda created the bright sparkling fire, but Ahriman created smoke, soot and choking ashes, thus defiling the whole creation. He bored a tunnel through the earth and made Hell in the centre of Earth.

Thus the seven evil demons fight the seven noble gods for ever. Bad thought, word and deed were inspired by Ahriman, as were aimless lust, idleness and sloth, vengefulness, avarice, meanness and discontent. He also created dirt and pollution against the purity of the earth, the noxious insect against the plants, the cold winter against the warm summer, stench against fragrance, sickness against health, poison against food, lions and murderous wolves against sheep, dogs and cows, toads against fishes, whores against women, death against life.

Ahu
See *Osiris*; *Ahura Mazda*.

Ahura Mazda
'Great God'. *Ahura* is the old Persian word for God; *Mazda* means 'great'. The old Persian name for the creator. In middle Persian this becomes Ohrmazd. In the Bundahishn (q.v.) Ohrmazd reveals to Zarathustra (q.v.) his creation: 'I created the sky without pillars . . . I created the earth which bears all life . . . I set in motion the sun, the moon and the stars . . . I created the corn that it might be scattered in the earth and grow again . . . I created and protected the child in his mother's womb . . . I created the cloud which bears water for the world . . . I created the wind which blows where it chooses . . . Could I not raise the dead and make again that which was?'

Ai
'Ruin', a city in Canaan where Abraham camped (Genesis 12:8) when arriving in the promised land. Joshua destroyed Ai after Jericho, including all its people and beasts (Joshua 7:8).

Ailuros
The cat-deity of ancient Egypt, also called Bast, Bastet.

Aiolos
The Indian Vayu, god of the winds, inventor of sails and of astronomy, King of Aiolia.

Aion
The Phoenician god of time and passing life.

Airyaman
God of friendship and healing in Persian mythology. A philosophical concept personified as a god.

Aisklepios
The god of medicine and therapy, the patron of doctors whose temple stood at Pergamon. See *Asclepius*.

Aker
In ancient Egypt, the lion-god, protector of the sun at night.

Akhen-Aton
'Aton is pleased'. King of Egypt 1377–1360 BC His dynastic name was Amenhotep IV. He changed his name when he decided to worship only Aton, the first conception of monotheism. But see also *Zarathustra*.

Akoman (Ako Mana)
From the old Persian *aka manah* 'wicked intention', 'evil mind'. An evil spirit who possesses liars according to Zoroastrians. Chief demon of destruction created by Ahriman.

Al Ait
The Phoenician god of fire.

Alalus
In Hittite mythology, the father of the gods, the eldest god.

Alaq
Usually translated as 'blood-clot', it could also mean 'a drop of sperm'. It is the very beginning of an embryo, from which God causes a human being to grow (Koran 96:1–6). See *Blood*.

Alchemy (Arabic: *al-kimiya*, from the Greek *chymos* 'juice')
Originally pharmacology, the science of extracts from medicinal plants, ultimately for the purpose of discovering the panacea, or the elixir (*iksir*), the medicine that cures mortality, providing good health to its drinker until doomsday (see *Khizr*). Avicenna denied alchemy as a science, calling it a deception. *Al-kimiya al-akbar* 'the greatest alchemy' was the 'philosopher's stone', the secret object which turned base metals into gold. According to others it was a liquid (*chymos*) which would, when someone washed his or her face in it, make them irresistible to others, to love and to wealth.

For the Sufis alchemy is the secret of contentedness. The true Sufi desires nothing except knowledge, in particular knowledge of God. He has emptied his heart of all other things. See *Al-iksir*, *Elixir*.

Aleph
The first letter of the Hebrew alphabet. The word means a bull, sacred animal of the Egyptians, equated with the god Apis. The *A*, if placed upside down, can be seen as a bull's head. In the zodiac, it symbolizes Taurus, the sign of the bull, into which the sun enters around 22 April, at the height of spring. See *Astrology*.

Alethai
Worshippers of Al Ait, the god of fire.

Alexander the Great
See *Al-Iskandar*.

Alexandria
This city was founded by Alexander the Great on the site of the ancient town of Rakuda (Rhakotis) which was founded by King Misraim, son of Baisar, son of Ham, son of Noah.

Al-Ghazali, Abu Hamid
An Arabic author, philosopher, theologian and Sufi master, 1059–111. He was professor at Baghdad, a post from which he resigned to devote his days to meditation upon the wordless state of his soul. He later returned to orthodoxy and wrote his famous work *Ihya' 'Ulum id-Din*, *The Revival of the Religious Disciplines*.

Al-Hallaj, Abu'l-Mughith
'The Wool-Carder' 857–922, an Arabic-speaking Persian mystic and martyr. He spent his last years, after many journeys including three pilgrimages, in Baghdad. Owing to his severe Sufi practices he had risen through all the stages to complete union with the Beloved. He prayed night and day even on the graveyards. He used to preach to the people even in the *souks* (market places) so that he soon had a vast following of devotees who memorized every word he said. Later, these sermons, as well as his numerous hymns, parables and proverbial phrases, were collected. They

were translated into French by Louis Massignon (1913–57). Most famous of all were the emotional utterances of his last days, after being sentenced to death by the weak-minded young caliph, a toy in the hands of the fanatic Shi'a vizier Ibn al-Furat (922). All the sermons of Al-Hallaj radiated the love of God which burnt in his heart, consuming his inner being. It was all that mattered to him. His most famous words were, '*Ana al-haqq*', 'I am the Truth', which was interpreted by his enemies as 'I am God'. His claim to be united with God made him say the impossible, for no man can be God.

Ali

1. Ali ibn (son of) Abu (or Abi) Talib, the first imam. As the son of Abu Talib, Ali was a full cousin of the Prophet Muhammad, who took him into his house when his father fell on hard times. Muhammad, being thirty years older, was like a father to him, and when he received his first revelation at forty in 610, Ali, who was then only eleven years old, believed in him, and so became the first Muslim after Muhammad's wife Khadija.

The tradition relates that God decreed Ali's marriage to the Prophet's favourite daughter Fatima and that the ceremony was actually celebrated in Heaven, with Jibril (q.v.) acting as Fatima's *wali* (guardian). Fatima gave Ali two sons, Hassan and Husayn (Hussein) often known as *al-Hasanayn*, 'the twin Hasans'. The five of them, Muhammad, Fatima, Ali, Hasan and Husayn, are often celebrated in poetry as God's most beloved human beings, who alone could see Jibril, God's angel, when he appeared on earth invisible to other human beings. Numerous miracles are reported concerning Ali.

The Shi'a religion reveres Ali as the one to whom Muhammad gave his *wasia*, 'charge or testament' when he felt death approaching. Thus Ali, the first Muslim, was made the first Imam, legitimate leader of all Muslims; this title transferred by divine right to his son Hasan, the second imam, and to Husayn, the third imam.

When the Prophet Muhammad died in 10 AH/632 AD, Ali was busy comforting the family and organizing the interment, so that he was not present at the meeting of the political leaders in which Abu Bakr was appointed khalifa (caliph, successor to the Prophet) although by right he should have been. This scene was crucial: it sparked off the dispute between the followers of Ali, *Shi'at Ali*, the Party of Ali, normally referred to as the Shi'a, and the much larger group of the followers of Abu Bakr and Omar, who call themselves the Sunna, a term which is erroneously translated as 'orthodoxy'. Ali was murdered in 40 AH/66 AD in Kufa. See *Shi'a*

2. See Zayn al'Alaidin.

Alif

First letter of the Arabic alphabet, formed by a single vertical stroke of the pen, which also signifies the number one, and Adam, the first man, the first creature to stand upright, whose name begins with *alif*. In the Sufi symbolism, *alif* refers to *Allah ahad* (Koran 112:1), 'God is one', both words beginning with *alif*. This signifies that there is no other reality, and that the soul must become one with him.

Aliha (Alihat, Ilaha, Ilahat, Allaha, Allahat)

1. The ancient sun-goddess of the Arabs before Islam, identified with Shams (q.v., see also *Shamash*). She was queen of the world. In battle, the winning side would pray to the sun to linger in the sky so that they could defeat their enemies; the latter, when in flight, would pray to the sun-goddess to set quickly and leave them in the cover of darkness. See Joshua 10:12.

2. Idols, false gods (Koran 21:21; 38:4; 71:23; 7:138–140). Also called *asnam*, 'images'. They are named in 71:23 as Wadd, Suwa', Yaghuth, Ya'uq and Nasr; see also *Manat*, *Allat*, *Taghut* and *Uzza*. Little is known about these ancient gods of the Arabs; some were local spirits, others were apparently equated with the Greek and Egyptian gods like Ammon-Zeus, Hera, Artemis, Isis-Demeter, Apollo-Horus, etc. In Muhammad's time northern Arabia was already Christianized and several other Arabs had turned to Judaism or Zoroastrianism.

Ali Naqi

'The Pure'. The tenth imam of the Twelver (*Ithna'ashariya*, q.v.) branch of the Shi'a, also called Ali Al-Hadi, 'the Guide'. He was a pious man constantly praying and reciting the Koran. He was condemned by the caliph to live in the garrison town of Askar near Baghdad. He died in 254 AH/868 AD allegedly poisoned.

Ali Rida (Reza)

Ali Rida ibn Musa was the eighth imam of the Twelver Shi'a. He was born in Medina in 148 AH/765 AD. He died in Tus in Persia in 203 AH/818 AD. In Medina he led a life of piety and study but in 202 AH/816 AD the caliph Al-Ma'mun summoned him to Marv and appointed him as his successor with the new title Al-Rida, 'God's Pleasure'. Ali adopted a green flag as his standard. On the way back to Baghdad he died and was buried in Tus – which was renamed Mashhad, 'Place of Martyrdom' (now Meshed in northern Iran). It is still a very important centre of pilgrimage for the Shi'a. It is said that Ali was poisoned with an infected pomegranate. His burial in Iran laid the foundation for the Shi'a in that country.

Al-Iksir

See *Elixir*.

Al-Iskander (Iskander, Iskender, Sikandari)

The Arabic name for Alexander the Great, also known in the Islamic traditions as Dhu'l-Qarnayn (q.v.). With Islam his fame and his exploits were told and sung in the far corners, from Indonesia to West Africa. The famous Persian poet Firdausi (q.v.) devotes two of the forty-six cantos of his great epic *Shahname* (*Book of Kings*) to Sekandar, Al-Iskandar, whom he makes a grandson of the Persian king Darius, by contriving to marry Darius' daughter to the king of Yunan (Greece, or Maqedun, Macedonia), whose name is Filibus (or Filiqus in the widely divergent traditions). Their son Al-Iskandar, was taught by the great *failasuf* (philosopher) Aristut (Aristotle). In later versions it is Elijah (Nabii Iliyas) who accompanies the young king on his numerous campaigns. Other, better known, more popular versions make Khizr (q.v.) the companion-sage of Al-Iskandar.

The campaign took Al-Iskandar first west to Rome and Andalus, then south into Africa where they met Queen Kandaka (Candace, Acts 8:27) and visited the Tower of Atlas where the waters of the ocean are pumped down into the earth to become the well water that feeds the rivers – Aristotles' theory to explain why the oceans never rise nor the wells dry up. After numerous adventures in Africa, Al-Iskandar travelled to Egypt, thence to India and China. In every country he was welcomed as the ruler to whom God had given power over all the kingdoms of the earth. In every country he married either the queen (in Amazonia) or the king's daughter. Invariably, Al-Iskandar departed one week after the marriage in order to conquer more countries before his short life ended. Immutably his wives gave birth to sons who later, after their grandfather's death, became kings. Finally he called an eagle which carried him up into the sky from where he saw the earth like a saucer whose rim is the mountain of Kaf (q.v.). Back home at last, Al-Iskandar, still a young man, died suddenly by God's decree, in possession of all the earth's kingdoms but with no time to enjoy his power.

This is the essence of the Islamic traditions of the Al-Iskandar saga; the moral is that even the mightiest emperors should fear death at any time so that all their power is of no avail and all their efforts to conquer are futile – they never conquer death. In addition, the saga gave the people of the Middle Ages an idea of geography as it was then known.

Allat
One of the three goddesses who were worshipped in ancient Arabia before Islam. She was especially venerated by the Thaqif clan in Taif, east of Mecca, in the form of a large stone, a square rock, kept in a wooden structure. Beneath the stone there was a treasure of precious stones which was later taken away by the Muslims. Allat was known to Herodotus as Alilat, and she was called the Mother of the Gods. The valley of Wajj in which the city of Taif stands, was sacred to her and no trees could be cut there without ceremony. Her worshippers placed fine cloths on the stone as offerings. Her priests were recruited from the clans of Urwa and Mughira. The goddess' local name was Lat, Mother of the Sun, which evokes comparison with Latona, the Greek mother of Apollo. Allat protected those travellers who made vows to her and brought sacrifices after a safe return journey.

Allatu
Mesopotamian goddess of copulation, wife of the demon king Nergal.

Allulu
A Mesopotamian bird-man who loved Ishtar, the one who broke his wing.

Aloe (Arabic: *Shubir*)
A plant (*Liliaceae*) from whose bitter juice medicine is made. The leaves were used in ancient times to protect houses against spirits.

Aluqa
A demoness who seduces men, sucking their blood after copulation so that they are totally exhausted and commit suicide. Cf. Arabic *alaq*, 'clot of blood' and *alaqa*, 'To stick to, hang, be sticky'.

Alyasa'
Koranic prophet (6:86; 38:48). This simple mention (by name only) has earned Alyasa' a place among the twenty-five prophets who are recognized in Islam. The Arabic name derives from Elisha.

Aman
1. 'Peace, pledge'. Protection promised by Muslim rulers to non-Muslim citizens who pay *jizya*, a poll tax for the 'unbelievers'.
2. In ancient Egyptian mythology, the devourer of the dead.

Amashaspan
'Holy, immortal' in Persian mythology.

Amathaunta
Egyptian goddess of the sea.

Amber (Greek: *elektron*).
Fossil resin referred to by Ezekiel (1:4, 27; 8:2) to describe God's light.

Amenti
In ancient Egyptian cosmology, the abode of the dead, where the souls of the deceased are judged by Osiris (Hades) and punished or rewarded for their deeds.

Ameretat
Old Persian goddess of water and immortality. See *Amurdad*.

Amesha Spentas
The 'bounteous immortals' or 'holy immortals', in Zoroastrian lore the seven sons and daughters of God. They are Spenta Mainyu, Vohu Manah, Asha, Khshathra Vairya, Armaiti, Haurvatat and Ameretat (Amurdad).

Amethyst
The purple stone that prevents intoxication in its possessor. In Hebrew, *ahlamah*, 'dreamstone'. Associated with Jupiter and thus with the sign of Libra. One of the foundation stones of the new Jerusalem (Revelation 21:20).

Ammon
1. Son of Lot and his younger daughter, Benammi, ancestor of the Ammonites, a peripheral Hebrew clan often vilified by the prophets (Genesis 19:38; Ezekiel 25:3).
2. (Amun) Egyptian god of thunder and lighting, worshipped also at Amman the city named after him in what is now Jordan, where the Romans built a temple for Jupiter-Ammon, god of justice.

Amorites
Sons of Canaan (Genesis 10:16), mountain peoples, proverbial wrongdoers who must be expelled (Genesis 15:16; Deuteronomy 20:17; Joshua 3:10).

Amulet (Arabic: *ta'wiz*, 'refuge' or *hijab*, 'protection')
Preferably a small Koran or one chapter of it, wrapped up or placed in a tiny brass box and suspended around a child's neck, which will protect him from illness. Lion's claws may be added, which will give the wearer strength and protect him against assault. Favourite chapters of the Koran for amulets are: 1, 6, 18, 36, 44, 55, 67, 78. The 'verses of preservation' are: 2:256; 12:64; 13:12; 15:17; 37:7. Amulets are also hidden in houses. See *Talisman, Da'wa.*

Amurdad
Ameretat in old Persian, the deity of the plants, especially the mysterious *haoma* plant, and of all the green life of the earth, of long life and health.

Amurru
Chief god of the Amorites.

An
Sumerian god of heaven, son of Nammu, father of Enlil, spouse of Ki.

Anahit
An ancient Armenian goddess in pre-Christian times, the same as the Iranian Anahita. She was the daughter of Aramazd and was praise-named 'Sculpted in Gold', for her statue was made of gold. She was the sovereign goddess, dispenser of life, the mother of chastity. Her flower was the hyacinth.

Anahita (Anahid)
Ancient Persian goddess of immaculate beauty, of dawn. Aredvi Sura Anahita in old Persian, 'the Pure Mighty Moist One', goddess of the mythical world river and of all the lakes. Her name means 'pure' because water purifies, i.e. it lends spiritual regeneration to those bathed or washed in it, so that they become just and truthful, and thus integrated into the cosmic order. She was rhapsodized as 'Anahita increasing corn, increasing herds, increasing offspring, famed for her justice, immense as the waters flowing over the land, purifier of the waters from the mountains, purifier of the seed of males, of the wombs of females and of their milk as well . . .' Her water blessed marriages and helps the unborn child to grow. Her ritual was the predecessor of the Christian baptism by submersion. Her life-giving strength is cosmic, it is as powerful as all the world's rivers together. She is portrayed as a young maiden, the Greek Kore.

Anat
Goddess of springs in Phoenician mythology. She received the god Baal (q.v.) when he fell from heaven as rain at the end of the dry season, so that she could cause new springs to rise from the earth. She was both his sister and his wife, like Jupiter Pluvius, the Roman rain-god, and Juno, goddess of summer.

Anath
Sister of the Ugaritic god Baal. She slayed all his enemies at a feast.

Anbiya'
See *Prophets*. The *Qisasu'l-Anbiya', Tales of the Prophets*, is an Arabic book (translated into Urdu, Malay,

etc.) containing the lives of the prophets before Muhammad, beginning with the creation, Adam and Eve.

Android

A mechanism that looks like a human being but is constructed and animated by the devil. Pretty boys and girls must be carefully examined: they might be sent by the devil to seduce us.

Anduruna

In Mesopotamian cosmology, heaven, where the gods 'play'.

Angels

From the Greek *angelos*, 'messenger', a translation from Hebrew and Arabic *mal'ak* 'messenger'. God sent messages to his prophets by means of his angels. According to some books they are the sons of God (Job 1:6; Psalms 82:6). According to some mystic philosophers they are the transmitters of God's grace, enlightenment and moral principles to human hearts so that we may be mindful of the straight path to God, by his light. The prophets agree that the appearance of angels is one of dazzling brightness and that they have wings (Isaiah 6:1–3; Koran 35:1) and fine, shining garments. Angels are organized in a huge hierarchy, the seven archangels, including Gabriel, Michael, Uriel and Raphael (qq.v.), at the summit, with access to the Throne of the Most High. In Islam four archangels are usually named: Jibril, Mika'il, Azra'il (the Angel of Death) and Israfil (the Angel of the last Trumpet) (qq.v.). See also *Malik* (Guardian of Hell) and *Ridhwan* (Guardian of Paradise).

The angel of the Lord appears/calls to Hagar (Genesis 16:7; 21:17) announcing the birth of Ishmael, 'The Lord has heard', 'I will make him a great nation.' See also *Hajar*. The phrase seems to mean both God and his messenger (Genesis 22:11). In Luke 2:9, the angel of the Lord announces Jesus' birth. In Exodus 3:2–6, it seems that the angel of the Lord, 'in a flame of fire' is God himself calling, 'Moses . . . I am God.' The three men who share Abraham's meal in Genesis 18:2 are said to be the Lord and two angels. Two angels visit Lot and smite his pursuers with blindness, Genesis 19:11. An angel of the Lord appears to Elijah twice, once in a dream (1 Kings 19:5–7). David saw the angel ready to destroy Jerusalem (2 Samuel 24:16; 1 Chronicles 21:16). A description is given in Matthew 28:2–3, when the angel rolls back the stone, opening Jesus' grave causing an earthquake: 'His countenance was like lightning, his raiment white as snow.'

According to the Islamic tradition, God created the angels before man, out of pure light. They have no sex and no desires other than to love God and people, especially Muslims. They are conscientious, devout servants of the one God. Their daily food is prayer, they need nothing else. Since their substance is light they are completely transparent, they have no hidden parts. As a result they cannot lie, all their thoughts are visible and righteous. They have wings and white robes; they can see, hear, speak, fly, walk, comfort, strike and destroy anything the Lord commands them, but they can also build. They can appear in any size or shape, move mountains or save souls from the fire. Angels are continually being created by God, many for a specific purpose, such as carrying the souls of the men fallen in the holy war up to heaven from the battlefield. Some carry a sword but that is not necessary, because they can destroy all enemies simply by God's will. The mere appearance of such a dazzling figure suffices to stop all wicked men from continuing their evil deeds. In heaven angels are constantly busy working for God. On earth the angels may at any time interfere in the holy wars, dropping rocks on God's enemies and so deciding the outcome. Angels may also live on earth in human form, for the protection of the weak and to stop evil. Angels have no carnal desire, they are never angry, they never disobey God. Their drink is repeating the holy names of God. The *karubiyun* (*cherubim*) are a species of angels.

Angra Mainyu
See Ahriman.

Anjuman (Persian)
A local association of Zoroastrians, later any religious association.

Anointed
Jesus implies that he is the anointed one, by a reading of Isaiah 61:1 (Luke 4:18). See also Acts 4:27; 10:38. Saul and David are the two first anointed kings: 1 Samuel 10:1; 16:13. See *Messiah, Christ*. The significance of the anointed king is in the myth of divine kingship which

has been carried over from Judaism into Christianity.

Anointing Oil
Olive oil (Exodus 30:24–5) for the anointing of priests and later kings.

Antara (Antar)
Antara was an Arab hero whose exploits in North Africa are still sung in Egypt and as far west as Morocco. Antara's father was Shaddad or Shadadi, an Arab who, during his conquest of the Sudan, 'liberated' a young woman called Zabiba ('Raisin'), who later turned out to be the king's daughter. She bore him Antara, a boy who at two was already strong enough to pull down a tent; at four he slew a large dog, at nine a wolf and at fifteen a lion, all with his hands. Antara is the typical model of the poet-hero. Some twenty-seven Arabic poems and fragments about him exist, in several of which there occurs the name of Abla, his cousin whom he loved ardently. However, he had to fulfil many arduous tasks before he was deemed worthy of marrying her. These tasks and the accompanying exploits he performed, were described in ten volumes which were probably composed during the thirteenth century.

One story relates how Antara, whilst travelling up the Nile one day, met Negus (Najus), king of Habashia (Abyssinia or Ethiopia), who appeared to be his grandfather, his mother's father. When he wanted to penetrate deeper into Africa he had to go through a huge tree, which was believed to be the abode of spirits.

He found himself in a palace in the sky surrounded by pomegranate trees in blossom.

In his numerous adventures, Antara discovered a witches' kitchen and the country of the Amazons, the warrior women in the far west of Africa, whom Alexander the Great also met on his conquests.

The 'historical' Antara lived in the sixth century, before Islam. He may even have been a Christian and, according to the saga, he married a Christian princess and had a son called Jufran (Geoffrey).

Antichrist

Before doomsday the antichrist, a demonic figure, will be born as the son of a woman and the Devil before the Messiah arrives. He will deceive all, or almost all believers (see I John 2:18): by extension every person who denies that Jesus is the Christ (1 John 2:22; 2 John 7). The antichrist will make war between all the nations until the destruction of human civilization is complete. The concept took shape well after the gospels were written, and was inherited by Islam where it became the 'anti-Muhammad'. See *Dajjal*.

Ants

One day, King Solomon and his court arrived in the valley of the ants, and discovered to their horror that the ants were as large as wolves. However, the ants were even more terrified when they saw the king's flying carpet with all the people on it, for they had never seen human beings. These ants were governed by a queen who, as soon as she discovered the exalted state of her visitor, ordered her subjects to pay their respects to their king. So when King Solomon had landed, all the ants sang in unison: 'Long live the king of all the animals and insects. Praise the Lord.' The king of people and the queen of ants greeted one another courteously. 'Is there anything you fear?' asked Solomon.

'I fear only God; you see, in case of danger my faithful ants would gladly sacrifice their lives for my security,' said the queen proudly. 'We need no other help.'

The ants once dug a pit so that an elephant fell in, where it was immediately eaten by the ants. The elephants had boasted: 'It is the duty of the ants to avoid the elephants' feet. Ants do not matter.' King Solomon had heard this and had admonished the elephants, saying: 'Watch out for the ants, for you are too proud.'

Antum

Sumerian mother – goddess, consort of Anu and mother of Ishtar.

Anunnaki

In Sumerian myth, the seven judges of Hades.

Anu

Mesopotamian and Hittite sky-god.

Anwar-e- Suheili

Persian translation of the great Indian fable book Kalila and Dimna (q.v.).

Anzu

In a Babylonian epic, Anzu was the valet of the supreme god Ellil. One day when Ellil was bathing, Anzu stole the tablets of destiny and escaped to the desert. The possessor of the tablets of destiny, which Marduk (q.v.) took from Kingu, was ruler of the universe. Ea (q.v.) then persuaded the mother-goddess Belet-Ili to give birth to a divine hero who would be capable of defeating the wily Anzu. Belet-Ili brought forth the broad-chested Ninurta. She sent him off into battle with the words: 'Go, capture Anzu, even in flight. Go, Ninurta my beloved, make a path for the whirlwinds. Inundate the earth which I created. Let light dawn for the gods whom I created.' After a long and terrible battle, Ninurta pierced Anzu's lung with an arrow, and recaptured the tablets of destiny. The epic ends with praises for the son of Ellil.

Ape (Arabic: *qird*)

Some scholars have said that the apes were once people who followed the laws of Moses, but they failed to keep the sabbath so God changed them into apes. King Solomon and later Caliph Omar I recognized the pious apes as fellow Muslims who must be left in peace.

Aphrodite

Greek goddess of love and fertility, the Roman Venus. See *Ishtar, Ashtaroth*. She was closely associated with Cyprus, where her mother Dione lived. Her fruit was the apple, the traditional Greek gift from a girl to her lover.

Apis

1. The bee-god. See *Tammuz, Dumuzi*. See also *April*.
2. The Egyptian bull-god, the golden calf (q.v.). See also *Alif*.

Apkallu

In Accadian mythology, the eight sages serving the kings as ministers. Some of them were poets composing the epics of Gilgamesh and Erra. Others were ministers of the Sumerian god Ea.

Apocalypse

Literally 'revelation', but often used to mean the last judgement, when all our sins will be tried, when all of history and its many secrets will be revealed as well as the total machinery of the cosmos with all the movements of the stars and planets, when even the angels and the devils will be revealed. Even God will reveal himself. All other gods will be shown to be false.

Many miracles are described in the Biblical Book of Revelation, written by John and in the apocryphal books of Enoch I and II, which include descriptions of hell. The Apocalypse of Baruch too gives a description of the cosmos and quotes God's words.

All this literature has heavily influenced the Islamic *mi'raj* traditions, in which the angel shows Muhammad round the seven heavens and hell. The Islamic ideas concerning the last days belong to a separate cycle of traditions usually referred to as *kiyama* or *Qiyama* 'resurrection'. A detailed description is given of the experiences of the souls during and after resurrection, until the final judgement, after which the wicked souls fall into hell, while the good souls cross the bridge Al-Sirat and climb up to Kawthar, Muhammad's refreshing well on the shore of paradise. The Koran gives terrifying descriptions of the end of the world (6:73, 158; 18:47; 20:102; 21:104; 25:25; 26:91; 52:10; 70:8; 73:14; 78:38).

Apostle

From the Greek *apostolos*, 'one sent'. A man called by God or Jesus to preach his message. The apostles were 'filled with the Holy Ghost' (Acts 2:4) so that they could effectively preach to the nations in many tongues: Arabic, Parthian, Egyptian, etc. Muhammad is called the Apostle of God, *Rasulu'llah* (Koran 7:157–8; 69:40; 81:19).

Apple

In the Islamic tradition, apples grow in paradise. God sent Ridhwan down to earth with an apple and with the message for Moses that his time to die had come. When Moses smelled the apple he was so overcome by its paradisiac aroma that his soul left his body and gladly followed Ridhwan to paradise.

Was the 'forbidden tree' in paradise an apple tree? The 'fruit' which the serpent offered Eve was not an apple according to Muslim writers but *qamh*, 'wheat'. The Koran (2:35; 7:19–22; 20:120–1) only mentions the tree of immortality, *shajaratu 'l-khuldi*, not its fruit. The Bible only mentions a fruit (Genesis 2:17; 3: 3–6). See *Eve, Fruit, Tree*. See also *Aphrodite*.

April

The Roman month of spring; the name is related to Aphrodite, and to Apis, the bee-god.

Apsu

'Sweet water', the kingdom beneath the earth in Sumerian cosmology.

Aqhat

Ugaritic champion of archery. The goddess of war, Anath (Athena?) coveted his fine bow and offered to buy it from him. Her price was immortality. Aqhat spurned the offer, so she had him killed by an eagle.

'Aql

'Intelligence'. Three categories of *makhluqat*, created beings, possess intelligence: angels, *jinns* and humans. Sometimes, by God's favour, an animal may become intelligent.

Arabian Nights (Arabic: *Alf Layla wa Layla*, 'A Thousand Nights and a Night')

A famous collection of fairy tales, rogue stories and other imaginative narratives told to the caliph Harun al Rashid (q.v.) during 1001 successive nights by the sister of his latest wife, hoping to save her sister's life. Harun, whose brother had discovered that Harun's chief wife had deceived her husband with a black slave, decreed that all his wives should be put to death after the first night of marriage so that they could never be unfaithful. The vizier's daughter, Sheherezade, suggested to her father that he give her sister in marriage to the caliph and that she, Sheherezade, would make sure that the caliph's latest wife would never be executed. Reluctantly the vizier agreed and so did the caliph. As a special favour he also agreed that her sister, Sheherezade, would be allowed to sleep in the bedchamber with the bridal couple (perhaps a relic from pagan times when a chief would marry two sisters at the same time so that they could keep each other company, taking turns as wives).

On the first night, when the caliph could not sleep, his wife suggested to her sister Sheherezade: 'Tell us one of your many wondrous tales.' Sheherezade began at once with the first story: the Tale of the Merchant and the *Jinn*. When dawn broke she broke off her tale just at the moment when the second merchant is about to slaughter his son who is in the shape of a calf because he has been bewitched by his stepmother, who is now a gazelle held on a rope by the merchant. Naturally the caliph wished to hear the rest of the story, so he decided to suspend the sentence for twenty-four hours: his wife would then live to ask her sister Sheherezade at the beginning of the second night: 'Tell us about the merchant and the gazelle.' And so she did, and went on like that for another thousand nights until the caliph finally decided to annul the sentence and let his wife live.

The 1001 nights tales were not completed in their present form before the end of the Middle Ages. The first European edition was the French translation of Jean Antoine Galland (1704–17). The first printed edition in Arabic was the Calcutta text of 1814–18. It was these tales which first made Europe familiar with *jinns* and caliphs, and all the other characters of Oriental tales. Hans Christian Andersen was deeply influenced by them.

Arabic
Muslims of every nation develop a mystic reverence for the Arabic language as they study the Holy Koran in it throughout their lives. To them it contains the very words spoken by God himself in the original, so Arabic is God's own language, in which he thinks (in so far as it is necessary for God to think). This is why the Koran can never be correctly translated into any other language: it would lose the essence of its contents. The avid student should rather translate his own mind into Arabic in order to become receptive to the Koran. Every word, every letter in it is there for a purpose, and the more we see through this purpose, the more we shall perceive the several strata of hidden meaning in each verse. The Sufis have developed this study into a fine art, contemplating every word, every letter, hoping to find a clue to the *sirr al-asrar*, the mystery of mysteries. An example of this is the mystery of creation, concentrated in a two-letter word (only the consonants are counted), which occurs seven times in the Koran: *kun*, 'be' (q.v.). The mystics contemplate how the *n* (*nun*) joins the *k* (*kaf*) to make the word complete and how by that very fact of completion the thing which God has in his mind, *is*. The Arabic word, if pronounced by God, *is* creation. It follows that the Arabic language itself is not only the

sole instrument of creation but that it, or some of his words, create, if pronounced by the right speaker in the right manner.

A'raf

'Partition' (Koran 7:44). Between hell and paradise there is an *a'raf* (a high wall). There are men standing on this partition who have escaped from hell, but are not (yet?) permitted to enter paradise. They stand there yearning to be admitted to the garden, but their sins and virtues are evenly balanced.

Arafa (Arafat)

'Knowledge'. A hill east of Mecca where Adam at last found Eve after his long wandering through India, Iran and Arabia. When Eve fell from heaven she landed at the fort of Arafa and sat there, weeping with contrition until Adam appeared and 'knew' her, hence the name of the hill, where pilgrims now pray annually.

Aramazd

An ancient Armenian god, the same as Ahura Mazda in Iran.

Archangels

See *Angels*.

Ardashir (Bahman, old Persian: Artakhshathra, Artaxerxes)

According to the *Shahname*, this was the name of several Persian princes.
1. King of Persia whose son, Sasan, lived in the mountains and did not compete for the throne. He had a son, also called Sasan, and so on for five generations. The fifth Sasan was a herdsman in the employ of Papak (Babak), prince of Pars (Fars). The latter saw in a dream that Sasan was a scion of the Kayanid kings, so he took him into his palace and gave him his daughter in marriage. They had a son, Ardashir.
2. The Parthian king of Persia, Ardawan, invited Ardashir to his court but the king's son persuaded his father to send him back to his flocks. The king's daughter eloped with him on two fine horses she had taken from the royal stables. Ardawan pursued them but was stopped by the royal ram which had taken Ardashir's side, a sign from God. Later Ardashir defeated Ardawan and his son, but was defeated by the Kurds. Meanwhile the princess gave birth to a son named Shapur (Pahlavi Shahiapuhar, 'King's Son') who married the daughter of his father's enemy Mihrak. They had a son called Hurmuzd, who was kept concealed. Later, when Hurmuzd shows his skill on the polo field, his grandfather Ardashir recognized him as a true prince. See also *Bahman*.

Aredvi

Great river, arising from Mount Hara in Persian mythology.

Ark (Hebrew: *tebah*, Arabic: *tabut*)

1. The ark is the box that contains life. Exodus 2:3–5 tells us how little Moses survived floating on the water. So did Noah (Genesis 7:1 ff). The ark which Noah built was quite a big vessel for its time: just over 100 metres long, about 17 metres wide and 10 metres high. It had three

levels and a door in the side wide enough to admit an elephant, and high enough to admit a giraffe, which is a very difficult animal to keep! The wood which the Lord prescribed for it was gopher, a tree of the coniferous family, probably cypress. This tree symbolizes the survival of life which is why it is planted on cemeteries in most Mediterranean countries. The cypress is extremely hardy, and survives bad weather and drought, staying green all the time. Its value is symbolic and aesthetic however; it is not very suitable for ship-building.

The ark described in Genesis 6:14 was just a rectangular box, a mere coffin-shaped chest or trunk. It did not even have a rudder, let alone a mast or a sail. It was what we would now call a houseboat, intended for habitation, and safe only while securely moored, floating peacefully on the Euphrates, Nile, Tigris or other wide, quiet-flowing river. When touching down on the summit of Mount Ararat at 5100 metres it must have beached at an awkward angle. In any case, for all the eight people and innumerable pairs of wild animals, including predators, to survive the tossing and turning on the wild waters is nothing short of a miracle.

The ark was the box of life. That definition also applies to the *Aron ha-Berit*, the Ark of the Covenant. Its contents were so heavily charged with magic power that it caused the statue of Dagon (Poseidon) to fall (1 Samuel 5). The Philistines were so frightened that they sent the ark back on an ox-cart with offerings of atonement. The Lord smote 50,070 men in Beth-Shemesh because they had looked into the ark. Later, David, wishing to transport the ark on a cart, put the brothers Uzza and Ahio in charge. Uzza held the ark for a moment to steady it 'for the oxen shook it'. He dropped dead immediately (2 Samuel 6:7). Even David was displeased with this unfair punishment. It shows that the ark was charged with purely magical, blind energy which would kill even good people simply by their touching it and, of course, when they looked inside it.

What was in the ark that made it so powerful that it could topple statues and kill thousands? The simple answer is the Law (Deuteronomy 10:1–5; 31:26). Yet we also learn that God himself was in it, for how else could it be so powerful, and so secret? The Philistines knew that the god of the Israelites was in it, because of the lethal effect it had on whoever came near it.

Could a god be carried in a box no bigger than a coffin? The answer is that that is exactly what it was. The Israelites who had lived in Egypt for generations were certainly familiar with the image of Osiris lying in his coffin. In Spanish churches one can see the adored image of Jesus in his coffin. Rachel stole the images of the gods of her father Laban (Genesis 31:19–34) and put them in the camel's furniture, i.e., the saddle-bags, and sat upon them. Clearly she was hoping that the statuettes would have a beneficent influence on her life if she kept them. It was normal for nomadic tribes before Islam to transport their god(s) in a box or other container on a camel's back. The Egyptian gods, including Osiris as well as the divine pharaohs after their death or resurrection, often travelled on the Nile in a boat. Such boats were built especially for the purpose and one can be admired in the museum of Gizeh. The Greek wine-god Dionysos (who may well have been of Near-Eastern origin) travelled in a boat which, when the god wished to visit the cities to be celebrated, was placed on a cart just like the ark in David's time.

We know that on top of the ark was placed a chair. This was the throne of the Lord. Several such portable thrones have been excavated in Egypt in which not only the kings but the gods were carried during the day of the procession by the priests. Thus when Moses exclaims 'Rise up Lord' (Numbers 10:35), the seated god is believed to rise from his throne 'to scatter his enemies'.

2. In the Islamic traditions the Ark of the Covenant, *Tabut al-'Ahd* (Koran 2:249) was first sent down from heaven to Adam. It was a large wooden box with the images of the twenty-four prophets inside. It was stolen by the Amalaki, the enemies of the Children of Israel, but in a subsequent battle God sent some angels who picked it up, carried it through the air and placed it before Saul (Talut) just when Israel was triumphant, so the warriors acclaimed him king.

Armageddon

In Zoroastrian lore it was taught that one day Ahura Mazda will triumph and deliver all good people from the assaults of Ahriman and his demons in a final doomsday battle, after which peace would reign for ever because all people would speak one language.

In Christianity, the word Armageddon refers to Revelation 16:16, a description of the final battle between good and evil. Armageddon comes from the Hebrew Har Megiddo, the scene of several battles in the history of Israel (see Judges 5:19; 2 Kings 23:29; Zechariah 12:11).

Armaiti

In old Persian 'Devotion' or 'wise', a goddess of justice and earth lore, daughter of Ahura Mazda who sat at his left hand. She ruled and cared for the earth, especially for the green pastures for cattle. She favoured modesty and righteousness, and protected the honour of women, especially devoted wives.

Armiya

The Arabic name for the prophet Jeremiah. He was contemporary, according to the Arabian tradition, with Mu'add, son of 'Adnan, ancestor of the Prophet Muhammad. He is identified by some with Khizr (q.v.).

Aron

The Ark of the Covenant (Exodus 25:17; 37:1; 1 Samuel 6). It was a chest made of acacia wood overlaid with gold (1 Kings 8:3).

Arsaces (Middle Persian: *Arsakis*)

The mythical divine ancestor of the Persians, according to Parthian myth.

He is shown in effigy (on a coin *c*.100 BC) with a bow and arrows.

Arsacids

A Persian dynasty originating in north-eastern Iran, which ruled the Parthian empire from 141 BC to 224 AD.

Arsh

God's throne which stands on eight thousand pillars, the distance between two of these pillars being three million miles (Koran 9:131).

Aruru

Mother goddess in Babylonian mythology. She creates people.

Ascalon (Ashkelon)

The five Philistine cities on the coast north of Gaza.

Ascension

The journey to heaven. This journey has been made, it is reported, by people in their dreams, in a spirit form: they received visions of heaven and its contents while they stayed on earth, or their spirits left their bodies, travelled upwards and came back later to rejoin their bodies to continue to live, unless they stayed in heaven while their bodies died on earth. Finally, body and soul are reported to have travelled together to heaven, as happened in the case of the Virgin Mary after her death, according to Roman Catholic doctrine. Here it is called the assumption, implying that she did not ascend like a divinity, but was invited to join the celestials and raised up. The distinction is academic in a monotheistic cosmology where no one can rise to heaven without God's wish. In a polytheistic world the gods may ascend of their own accord (see 1 Samuel 28:13).

Prophets may ascend to heaven like Elijah (2 Kings 2:11) or the two witnesses in Revelation 11:12. Angels may ascend and descend (John 1:51). Enoch was the first man to be 'taken' to heaven (Genesis 5:24). Elijah ascended in a chariot of fire, pulled by horses of fire, taken up by a whirlwind to heaven (see 2 Kings 2:11). Jesus ascends in Luke 24:51; Acts 1:2–11, 2:31–6; Peter 3:22; Romans 8:34. From Mount Olivet Jesus disappeared from the sight of the apostles, into a cloud. See also *Mi'raj*.

Asclepius (Asklepios)

The god of healing, whose great temple can still be seen at Pergamon (Bergamo) in western Anatolia. The name derives from the plant asclepias, milkweed (*Asclepiadaceae*), a purgative medicine.

Asenath

'Belonging to Nath or Neith', the Egyptian name for the goddess Athena. Daughter of Potipherah, given to Joseph as wife by the Pharaoh (see Genesis 41:45).

Asha (Old Persian: *Rta*)

Deity of the cosmic order, righteousness, truth, virtue. She protects the faithful while they worship her, and gives them immortality.

Ashab (Sahaba)

The companions of the Prophet Muhammad, whose seventy campaigns are celebrated in many legends and praise songs in Arabic and many other languages. The most prominent heroes are Ali, Omar, Uthman, Amr ibn al-'As, Abu Bakr, Khalid ibn al-Walid, Miqdad, Hamza, Abbas and Abd al-Rahman; all are historical but most of their exploits are legendary.

Asher

Fourth son of Jacob and Zilpah, Leah's maid (Genesis 30:13). The name means 'happy' and is related to the Arabic Yasser, 'God has made it easy (to bear)'.

Asherah (Accadian: *Ishara*)

1. A Ugaritic mother goddess, wife of El, mother of Baal. She is identified with the Tree of Life, a fruit tree (fig?), and is depicted as seated between two animals dependent on her for food.
2. A Canaanite goddess, identified with Ashtar, Astarte or Ashtaroth, and Ishtar. She was worshipped in a sacred grove where a big tree represented her as the Tree of Life. Later she was worshipped as a pole or pillar. The name Asherah means 'fortunate', so that she might be identified with the Roman Fortuna, the Greek Tyche. Her tree used to be planted near the altar of the Lord, reminiscent of Indian women worshipping a fig tree near their god's sanctuary, praying for babies.

Ashi

The Avestan goddess of recompense and reward. Originally the goddess of fortune, Ashi became, under the moralizing influence of Zoroaster, a goddess of morality, rewarding the virtuous with her abundant favours.

Ashkanians

The Parthian rulers of Iran whose dynasty ended in 202 AD.

Ashnan

Sumerian goddess of the grain (like Ceres) daughter of Enlil. She was assigned to the fertile land of Sumer by Enki. She is the most powerful deity, supporting the people.

Ashtaroth

Love goddesses (plural of Ishtar, the quivalent Aphrodite (q.v.). In 1 Samuel 12:10, Ashtaroth and Baalim are served by the 'sinful' Israelites. These love goddesses and gods were statuettes, some of which have been found in excavations. They were worshipped by people who hoped for children, cattle and crops.

Ashura

Muhammad observed a fast on this day, the 10th of the month of Muharram. It is related that on that day God created Adam and Eve as well as life and death, the tablet *Lawh*, the pen *Qalam*, heaven and hell. The Shi'a celebrate, or rather, mourn the murder of the Prophet's grandson Husayn on that day. The Sunna commemorate the day when Ibrahim offered his son to God. See *Lawh al-Mahfuz*.

Asiya

One of the perfect women in the Islamic tradition (the others are Maryam, Amina, Fatima and Sarah) (Koran 66:11).

She was the hairdresser of the pharaoh's first queen. She was a Muslim (i.e. a follower of Musa) in secret.

Once when she dropped her comb she exclaimed '*Bismillahi*', and the queen asked her to explain what it meant. She explained that she worshipped Allah the Creator. This was reported to the pharaoh who called her and told her to worship him. When she refused to worship a mortal man the Pharaoh ordered her to be burnt to death with her children.

Asma'

In full, Asmā' al-Husnā, God's most beautiful Names, 99 descriptions of Allah's divine qualities (*sifāt*), though some scholars maintain there are over 400 Names. Many Muslims have a rosary, *tasbīh*, a string of 99 beads by which they recite these Names for themselves. This highly meritorious occupation protects the Muslim against the evil machinations of the Satan.

Asmodaeus

In the Book of Tobit (3:8) Asmodaeus, the king of the demons, caused the seven successive bridegrooms of Sarah, daughter of Raguel, to die before they could consummate their marriage. Finally, God sent Raphael to defeat Asmodaeus, so that Sarah could marry Tobias, son of Tobit. The name Asmodaeus derives from the Hebrew Ashmeday, from the Persian Ashmadaeva. He is sometimes described as having three heads: a ram's head, a bull's head and a man's head breathing fire.

It was Asmodaeus who caused King Solomon to lose his throne when he lost his magic ring, so Asmodaeus sat on Solomon's throne for three days, disguised as the king. Later Solomon compelled him to build the Temple. He is sometimes identified with Samael who seduced Eve (q.v.) and many other women after her. Asmodaeus is an extremely tricky and deceitful character who loves sowing discord. He is the guardian of people's secrets and hidden treasures. See *Azazel*.

Asrafil

See *Israfil*.

Ass

In many languages the proverbial symbol of stupidity but also of devout servitude: Abraham, Jesus and Muhammad rode asses, as did numerous saints, priests and prophets after them. Hell is full of asses, which are the souls of people stupid enough to be tricked by the devil and seduced by worldly pleasures. The ass is also a symbol of sexuality and was even worshipped by a distinct sect in Iraq before it was eradicated by Islam.

Astarte

See *Ashtaroth*.

Astrology

Astrology as it is known in Europe is a Greek invention. The Arab scholars of the Middle Ages eagerly translated the Greek books into Arabic. Extracts of those early works still circulate in the Middle East. The following are the names of the signs of the zodiac as they are known and used in Arabic. The same terms are used in Persian and Urdu. It should be noted that only the name for Taurus is different in Persian. In that language,

Latin	Arabic	Meaning
Aries	Hamal	Ram
Taurus	Thaur	Bull
Gemini	Jauza	Twins
Cancer	Saratan	Crab
Leo	Asad	Lion
Virgo	Sumbula	Ear of corn
Libra	Mizan	Pair of scales
Scorpio	Aqrab	Scorpion
Sagittarius	Qaus	Bow
Capricorn	Jadi	He-goat
Aquarius	Dalu	Bucket
Pisces	Hut	Fish

it is called *Nur*, 'light'. Originally Taurus was the first sign of the calendar year of the Persians and the Egyptians.

There are also names for the signs and the months in other languages, but they have different meanings and are explained in different ways by local scholars. There is a separate series in the languages of India. These have different meanings from the western astrological signs for the lives of the people.

Aries, the ram, is believed to be the most auspicious of all the signs; it is then that the feast of the annual lustration used to be celebrated in Persia. See also *Da'wa*.

Astvat-Ereta
The true world saviour (Saoshyant, q.v.) in Persian mythology.

Atar (Later Atesh)
The old Persian god of fire, son of Ahura Mazda, manifest in lightning. As the offerings to the gods are placed on the fire by the priests, Atar is regarded as the mediator between gods and men.

Atash Bahram
'Fire Victorious'. Ancient Persian fire temple, the highest grade of the Iranian temples. It is regarded as the greatest representative of the cosmic fire on earth, the seventh creation of Ahura Mazda.

Athira (Atheret)
Ugaritic goddess who is depicted sitting spinning at the seashore. She rides a donkey with a silver harness. She intercedes with El on behalf of others.

Aththar
In Ugaritic myth, the god of irrigation, associated with the morning star.

Atlantis (Greek, Phoenician)
A mythical queen who lived in a mountain range surrounded by desert

(the Ahaggar Mountains?). In the centre of the arid circle of rocks there was a green valley watered by numerous clear streams. Here the queen lived with her maidens. Intrepid travellers who had successfully penetrated the desert and the waterless rocks would be received by the beautiful women and become the queen's lovers. No one ever returned; the queen had them all executed.

Atlantis (the name applies both to the queen and her kingdom) was an immortal woman because she possessed the secret of the fire of life (as Rider Haggard surmized); more probably, it was the water of life that gave her immortality, life and health until doomsday (q.v.). She may be identical with the Queen of Sheba or Saba (q.v.). who lived in South Arabia in the time of Solomon (q.v.). The Islamic beliefs concerning the beauties of paradise may be a relic of this Atlantis, or of the Atlantis in the western world.

Atrahasis

1. 'Extra wise', Mesopotamian king of Shuruppak (near the present Tell Fara), father of Uta Napishtim, the Babylonian Noah.
2. Sumerian: 'The Wisest', the only man who survived the great flood because the god Ea told him to build the Ark well in time.

Attar

Farid ud-Din Attar. Famous Persian mystic poet, born in Nishapur some time after 1120 AD. His best-known work is the *Mantiq at-Tair, The Conference of the Birds*, written before 1177. The birds are in search of a king, but the poet says it is better to have nothing to do with rulers. Attar is equally famous for his Arabic prose work on the history of the saints (of Islam). His last mystic work was the *Secret Language*. He died after 1193.

His tenets can be summarized as follows: Only God truly exists, all other things are nothing but shadows. Ordinary religions can bring the believer only part of the way to that ultimate truth. For God there is only unity. The division of good and evil exists only among the lower beings. The human soul, trapped in the body, must look inward to realize its essential affinity with God. Awakened to this knowledge the soul can progress along the way which leads to the self-dissolution into the divine essence.

Avesta

'Injunction', the holy book of the Zoroastrians which has existed from creation. The oldest part of the Avesta, the *Gathas* (hymns) dates from the second millennium BC. These texts were revealed to Zoroaster (the prophet Zarathustra) by Ahura Mazda. The younger Avesta, which is of much later date, helps us to understand the mysterious message of the *Gathas* which are still part of the *Yasna*, the liturgy. See *Zarathustra*.

A'war

'One-eyed'. Son of Iblis, an evil spirit tempting men into debauchery.

Aya

1. A miraculous sign from God. When asked to show a sign from God, Muhammad is said to have exclaimed: 'Every verse in the Koran

is a sign from God.' Some verses cause miraculous healing when recited by a sinless Muslim.
2. The spouse of the Babylonian sun-god Shamash.

Ayatollah

'Miracle of God'. Title of the supreme theocrats of the *Ithna'ashariya* in Iran. These men possess the exclusive authority to interpret Islamic law and what is more, the secret wishes of the hidden living imam.

Ayn

'Eye', very often used as a cautious reference to the evil eye, the destructive effect of an envious glance to which Chapter 113 of the Koran refers as the *hasid*, the envier. The belief which originated in the Middle east centuries before Christ, holds that more people die of the evil eye than of any other affliction: 'It empties the houses and fills the graves.'

The eye of the envier is believed to radiate hatred of such ferocity that it debilitates its object either directly or over a prolonged period, causing pregnant women to miscarry, children to contract any one of the numerous diseases that afflict children in the Middle East (many of which are fatal), livestock to become lean and die of exhaustion, crops to fail, fire to break out in the house, and leading to burglary and loss of wealth and even friends. It is said that women without children, old and sterile women ('old hags') and all men with a defect such as paralysis or leprosy, people ill-favoured by fate and disadvantaged by nature, poor people and beggars – especially women – can cast the evil eye on those who arouse their jealousy (*hasad*), often causing the same defect from which they themselves suffer, and also insanity and sterility, in their intended victims, who are usually happy or lucky people. In addition, persons with deep-set or blue eyes and certain snakes are believed to have the evil eye.

This old fear is the original reason why women of the Middle East wore the veil long before Islam (I Corinthians 11:10); it was a protection against the evil eye. The veil, in Arabic *hijab*, means 'protection'. It is said that the phylacteries of the Jewish people were also originally used to protect them against the evil eye. In Egypt, some women may smear dirt on their children's faces so as to avert the evil eye; some mothers even dress their boys in girls' clothes, boys being the most likely target of the evil eye. Whenever a person sits down to a meal, the name of God must be pronounced over it (Arabic: *bismillah*, 'in the name of God') or else the evil eye might be cast upon the food. Nothing must be openly admired or else its owner will suspect the admirer of the evil eye, unless he adds 'May God preserve us' or a similar prayer, such as the chapter of the Koran mentioned above. A piece of alum, placed in the fire, will melt and take the shape of the envier. It is then pounded and given to a black dog to eat. Numerous other rituals are performed to protect against the evil eye, and charms, talismans and amulets of all types are sold in the streets to those who fear it.

Ayyub

The Arabic name for Job, in the Koran a prophet of God (4:163; 6:84; 21:81; 38:41–4). Ayyub is oppressed by Satan, who takes all his family away from him. Ayyub prays to God, begging for relief from his suffering. God relents and returns his family to him as a reward for his faithfulness and steadfastness.

In the Koran there is no word about the Prologue in Heaven (see *Job*), except in a general way (7:14) when God explicitly permits Satan to tempt people away from the straight path. The popular Islamic tradition, however, is fully aware of the Biblical version (Job 1:12). The battle between Job and the Devil is fought over this single point: that nothing in this world must interrupt the unceasing worship of God. The Devil is determined to persuade Job to leave his prayer mat while Job is even more determined to remain on it, continuing and constantly repeating the adoration of God. Satan believes that Job can be tempted away from this worship. First, he causes Job's goats to die, then his cattle. He tells Job that these disasters happened while he, Job, was worshipping the Lord, that it is futile to remain fixed on the prayer mat while there is work to be done. Job steadfastly continues his prayers without stopping for one moment. Then Satan causes Job's children to die and tells him that it is disgraceful to remain immovable on his prayer mat, but Job carries on worshipping God, undeterred even when Satan makes him ill. As soon as God, relenting, cures him, Job resumes his prayers. Job's wife Rehema deserves mention for her constant faith and support.

Aza'el

Hebrew name for Marut. See *Harut and Marut*.

Azan (Adhan)

The call to prayer which all Muslims must obey five times a day. The call, which is a fixed set of phrases, is itself a prayer. It must be pronounced by an honest Muslim with a clear voice. The first such caller was the first black Muslim, Bilal, who used to stand on the roof of the Prophet's house. The day's prime *azan* is the first, usually before 5 a.m. when dawn is just beginning to show. It is essential for pious Muslims to bathe properly on Thursday night so as to be in a state of purity on Friday morning since it is believed that one Friday the caller will not be a man but an angel, announcing resurrection.

Azar

The father of Ibrahim (q.v.), Terah in the Bible, see Genesis 11:24; Koran 6:74–82; 19:42–51.

Azazel (Zazal)

The spirit of sin, loaded onto a goat, then chased into the desert. Leviticus 16:8–10 deals with the Lord's commandments concerning the two goats that would have to be sacrificed after Aaron lost his two sons. One goat was destined for the Lord God, and the other for Azazel, who is the evil spirit for whom one of the scapegoats is intended. According to the Apocalypse of Abraham XIII, 7, 'Azazel is wickedness [because he has] chosen to live uncleanly.' Most authorities describe Azazel as the devil incarnate. Through him 'retribution and misfortunes fall on the generations of the unrighteous'.

Azazil

Lord of *jinns*. In the Southern Ocean there is a distant island of huge dimensions. Here live the *jinns*, whose king is Azazil, the greatest sorcerer. Azazil often visits the human world for his nefarious work. Some say he is identical with Iblis the king of satans.

Azhi Dahaka
See *Dahaka*.

Azima

Arabic incantation, often written, to chase evil spirits away.

Azrail (Izra'il)

The angel of death. He has the shape of a human being, with large wings. He takes the souls of the old and the young alike. Once King Solomon asked him about his work and his domicile.

'King Solomon!,' he replied. 'Know that my assigned station is on the shoulders of the angel of time. He is the tallest of us all: his head reaches ten thousand years over the seventh heaven, while his feet stretch five hundred years below the earth. In addition, this angel is so strong that he could blow away the earth without effort, with all its mountains and oceans, just sweep it away like dust. He is the one who indicates to me when, where and how I must fetch a soul. You do not rule him since you cannot stop time. He keeps his eyes fixed, century after century, on the lote tree of the end, which the Arabs call *Sidratu 'l-Muntaha*. It grows on the source of the four rivers of paradise and has as many leaves as there are people alive. Every leaf has the name of a person written on it. At every live birth a new leaf sprouts on one of its branches, and when a man or a woman has reached the end of his or her life, his or her leaf begins to wither away and finally drops off, and at that very moment, I am already close by him or her to receive his or her soul.'

King Solomon, whose task in life was to gather knowledge about all God's creatures, and to enlighten mankind with his great knowledge, asked Azrail: 'And having taken the soul out from the body, what do you do next?'

The angel of death, who has a very patient and conscientious character, answered the king: 'Jibril, who is God's messenger and the conductor of souls, is always with me at that moment if the deceased is a true believer, a person who lived in the fear of God, and thus led a virtuous life. He, Jibril, will always bring a sheet of green cloth, silk if the deceased has distinguished himself by devotion, and so the soul will be wrapped in that and gently conveyed to paradise. There the soul will be inhaled by a green bird. The green bird, with the devout soul inside, will live peacefully and happily in paradise until the resurrection. The souls of the sinners on the other hand, will be wrapped in a piece of tar cloth and dropped in a hole in the ground through which the soul will land in the fire, where it will be roasted forever in hell.'

Solomon thanked Azrail for his explanations. See *Death*, *Time*.

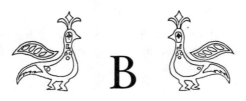

B

Baal (Arabic: *Ba'l*).
A common Semitic word originally meaning 'husband', in the sense of the man who fertilizes the wife. Early in the evolution of Semitic religion Baal came to mean 'the Lord God who fertilizes the land with rain'. In Ugaritic mythology Baal Enet Mahartet was 'the Lord of the wells for the cultivated fields'.

Baal was the son of El and god of storm, lightning and rain. He is depicted as a striding warrior with bull's horns on his helmet, but also standing on waves, possibly indicating the rivers which his rain created, and holding a palm branch, signifying the rising vegetation. In the Old Testament Baal still meant 'husband', but was also the farm-god of the Canaanites and Phoenicians who gave his worshippers rich crops, numerous flocks and fecund farm families.

Each locality had its own *baal*. The *baal* gods were adored with lascivious dances, rites of self-torture and human sacrifices. The religion of Baal was propagated in Israel (1 Kings 16:31-2) and in Judah (2 Chronicles 17:3). Baal was often worshipped as consort of the Canaanite goddess Ashtoreth by means of lewd rituals (see Judges 2:11-17; 1 Samuel 7:4, where altars are built for them). *Baalim* is the plural and since Ashtoreth is identified with the goddess Venus–Aphrodite, Baal may be identified with Adonis the god of the green pastures, who dies every autumn and is reawakened every spring to make love with Venus the goddess of fertility.

Bab

1. 'Gateway'. In early Shi'ism, the senior authorized disciple of the imam. The hagiographical literature of the Twelvers gives the list of the *babs* of the imams. In the Fatimid tradition the *bab* is placed immediately under the imam from whom he received his instructions directly. He in turn instructs the *hujja* (*hojat*) and his colleagues who carry out the duties of administration and preaching to the *umma*, the community of the faithful. The *bab* also has the function of *da'i al du'at*, the preacher to the preachers.
2. 'Gate' was also the title of Sayyid Ali Muhammad of Shiraz, the founder of the religion of the Babis, and, according to the Baha'is (q.v.) the precursor of the new prophet Baha'Allah. He

is also called Nuqta-i-Ula 'the First Point', i.e. the point of departure of the new faith. Sayyid Ali was born in Shiraz in 1819, into a merchant family but soon devoted himself to study and meditation, so impressing several scholars, especially Kazim Rashti, then the Sheikhi leader.

Sayyid Ali's first 'revealed' work was the *Qayyum al Asma*. In *Hurufat al Hayy*, *Living Letters*, Sayyid Ali addressed all the Persians to announce his mission as the Mahdi, the promised Messiah. He was arrested several times and led before a provincial governor, but his charm and religious sincerity won over and converted the governor who then released him. Sayyid Ali was finally arrested through treachery near Tehran, never regaining his freedom. He was condemned to death but when the first shot was fired the bullet hit the ropes which held him but not Bab himself, and so he was freed again. The terrified platoon and its commander had to be replaced. Eventually, on 9 July 1850, the Bab died, but his body disappeared for a while. It was finally laid to rest on the slopes of Mount Carmel.

Babi

A person belonging to the new religion of the Bab (q.v.). The Babis established themselves as a new religious movement when they declared themselves openly to be totally outside Islam (at Badasht, Persia, 1848). There for the first time their most prominent female member, the poetess Zarrin Taj, better known as Janab-i-Tahira or Kurrat ul Ayn, showed herself unveiled, demonstrating her defiance of the *shari'a*. Soon afterwards a group of those present were surrounded by the imperial army. They surrendered on promises of security of life and limb, but were treacherously massacred. The poetess was later strangled after a long imprisonment. This was the beginning of a long history of persecution and massacres of the Babis up to the present day. The Babis split into two groups, the Baha'is (q.v.) and the followers of Subh-i-Azal, 'Eternal Dawn', who adhered to the letter of the Bab's written instruction, *Bayan*. These 'Azalis' number less than 50,000.

Badawi (Bedawi)

Ahmad il Badawi, also known as Sayid Abu Fityanis, is the most popular saint of the Muslims in Egypt. He was born in Fez in 1199 and died in 1276 in Tanta, Egypt. Numerous legends are told about the miracles he performed as a healer. He never married but devoted himself to studying the Koran, fasting for prolonged periods and remaining silent.

Badr

'Full moon'. A well in west-central Arabia near which Muhammad fought the most decisive battle of his career on the Ides of March 624, with the help of the angels, who participated by dropping stones on his enemies, the rich Meccan traders. It was the most important battle in Islamic history. As a result of this victory, all the Muslim men who fought with him there are now considered heroes and the complete list of their names, which are all known, has been printed in a booklet which can be bought in all Islamic bookshops. Its title is *Ahl al-Badr* and its recitation will generate such magic energy that it can sink a ship or guarantee prosperity to the reciter. See *Ahl al-Badr*.

Baha'allah

'God's Magnificence', the praise-name of Mirza Husayn Ali Nuri, who was born in Tehran on 12 November 1817, to a noble family. He never attended school but was a deeply religious boy. In his *Lauh-i-Ra'is, The Chief's Tablet*, he reminisces about his realization of the futility of human life after seeing a puppet show. He was converted to the new religion of the Bab (q.v.) in 1844. There was an attempt on the life of the Shah in 1852, and Mirza was arrested and thrown into the Siyah Cal, 'Black Hole', a notorious dungeon in Tehran, where he was never able to sleep because of the heavy chains on his arms and neck. In the total darkness he had many visions which he later described in his *Book of the Sheikh*. He heard a voice comforting him: 'We will help you . . . Never fear . . . Soon God will raise the treasures of the earth, that is, the men who will help you for the love of you and your name . . .' This experience is considered the beginning of Baha'Allah's mission on earth.

He was sentenced to forfeiture of all his possessions and exiled to Baghdad where he was followed by many of his devotees. For two years (1854–6) he lived in the mountains of Kurdistan as a nomad and dervish. His ever-spreading influence caused the Ottoman government to exile him to Edirne where he openly declared his prophetic mission. Again transferred, Baha'Allah had to settle in Akka (Acre), where he was confined in the castle (1868–77). After this he was allowed to settle in his villa. During the years 1871–4 he wrote his *Kitab-i-Aqdas, The Most Holy Book*. He died on 29 May 1892.

Baha'i

A member of the religion of Baha'iyya, Bahaism, founded by Baha'Allah (q.v.) in 1844. In the same year Baha'Allah's eldest son Abbas Effendi was born, better known as Abd al-Baha', 'Servant of the Baha'. After Baha'Allah's death he was recognized by the majority of the Baha' is as the authoritative interpreter of his father's writings in accordance with his father's will, which, however was contested by his own brother Muhammad Ali.

The first Baha'i group in America was founded in 1894. Abd al-Baha' visited America in 1912 and Europe in 1913. He died in 1920, having appointed Shoghi (Shawqi) Effendi Rabani in his will as his successor; Shoghi was the oldest of his grandsons, the eldest son of his eldest daughter. His title is Wali-Amr-Allah, 'Guardian of God's Cause'. He settled in Haifa in Israel with his family.

The Baha'i religion is entirely based on the works of Baha'Allah and in some cases on his son's interpretations. The theology teaches that God is essentially unknowable except through his creation, which continues forever. God manifests himself also in the prophets, the first of whom was Adam, the last two being the

Bab (q.v.) and Baha'Allah. Faith in the latter, God's manifestation on earth, is the same as faith in God, which is necessary in order for a person to receive the spirit of immortality. There are five sorts of spirits: the spirits of plants, animals, human beings and faithful believers, and the spirit of God, the Holy Spirit.

Bahira (Barich, Rahiba)
A Christian monk who lived in a *deira* (hermitage) in the Syrian desert somewhere on the road from Damascus to Mecca, in the area now known as Jordan, in the last quarter of the sixth century. In that old building, he discovered the books of astrology which had once been dictated by King Solomon and deciphered them, so that he knew the past, the present and the future.

One day, when Bahira was very old, Abu Talib arrived at the hermitage with a small caravan including his young nephew Muhammad, the future Prophet, who was being introduced to the caravan trade between Mecca and Damascus. Bahira's *deira*, was a useful stage post on the road between the two cities. The *deira*, usually a walled monastery, contained a church of which Bahira was the priest; it may have been the abbey of Bosra, near Damascus.

Abu Talib knew nothing about his nephew being the next Prophet at that time, but the learned Bahira did. He saw how he was always shaded from the sun because God moved a small cloud, keeping it above the young traveller's head. When Muhammad dismounted and

sat down on the ground the date palms inclined their proud heads to shade him once again and show their respect. Bahira had read in the stars that the last of God's prophets would be resting under his roof that night. He asked Abu Talib if he could examine the boy. Abu Talib consented, for Bahira was a famous doctor. He had told the monk that Muhammad was his son, but the wise prior spoke thus: 'The books predict that the last prophet will be an orphan at birth.' Abu Talib then had to admit that Muhammad was his nephew. Bahira discovered what he was looking for between the boy's shoulder blades: *Khatam al-Nubuwwa*, the Seal of the Prophets, the Arabic letters forming the words: 'There is no god but Allah and this is my prophet.' (There are variations of these words).

Bahira then revealed to Abu Talib that he had read in the books that about ten years ago the last Prophet of God had been born who would be called to the prophesy in thirty years' time. To which books was he referring? The Islamic writers (Tabari, Waqidi and Razi) explain this as a reference to the 'original' gospel in which they believe Muhammad was announced by Jesus; as Jesus himself was announced by John the Baptist and Isaiah, so there was a need for Muhammad to be announced. An older version of the legend refers to the Books of Solomon. These books were dictated to King Solomon by the condemned angels Harut and Marut (q. v.), in Hebrew, a language which early scholars in Arabia could still read. The Books of Solomon, which contain a complete compendium on the art of magic, as well as a complete set of predictions for all events on earth until judgement day, disappeared soon after Solomon's death, which explains why Israel declined soon afterwards (Chronicles II, 10ff). It is these books which Bahira is said to have discovered in some ruins in the wilderness, where Solomon's palace once stood (perhaps Shechem?).

It appears that Bahira did exist or at least it is the name of the putative author of the *Apocalypse of Bahira* (other writers call him Sergius or Nestor/Nastur). Bahira is also identified by some with the Byzantine scholar Baeira, who condemned the worship of icons or statues. Some even maintain that he was the Christian heretic scholar who taught Muhammad what revelation was. See *Parakleitos*.

Bahman (Old Persian: *Bahumano*, 'Long-Arm')
Bahman, who was also called Kay Ardashir, was the grandson and successor of Bishtasp as king of Persia. It was he, according to Al-Mas'udi, who permitted the Jews to return to Jerusalem, because his wife was Jewish (see the Book of Esther). He finally killed Rustam who had killed his father, Isfandiyar, in a fierce battle. He was succeeded by Humay.

Bahram
From Vahram (Pahlavi), from the old Persian Verethraghna, god of victory in a just cause who became, in later times, the protector of travellers. The famous hymn in his honour (Yasht

14) is still recited for those setting out on a journey.

Bahya Ben Pakuda
An eleventh-century Jewish moralist who wrote *Hovot ha Levavot*, *Duties of the Hearts*, in which he explains that the rabbis have stressed the 'duties of the limbs', but that we must live by our 'inner wisdom', purity of heart, humility and self-examination.

Bakhtiyar-Name
The Book of Prince Bakhtiyar. This is one of the most popular textbooks for young princes, who are supposed to learn good government by reading them. It is also known as the History of the Ten Viziers, and is one of the variants of the cycle of Sindbad (q.v.). It is a framework-tale in which numerous stories are fitted. It begins with the baby son of King Azadbakht whom his parents left on the forest path when they had to flee. Robbers found him and brought him up, but when the king's armed men routed the robbers, young Bakhtiyar was taken to the palace. The king liked him, took him into his service and even made him vizier. The king's ten other viziers slandered him out of jealousy and he was sentenced to death. Each of the ten viziers told a tale to exemplify why a man in Bakhtiyar's position had to be executed at once. After each tale Bakhtiyar tells a story of his own to illustrate why haste leads to disaster. Just before the execution the chief robber, now an old man, arrived and produced the baby's

ornaments, proving that Bakhtiyar was the king's son. There followed a happy reunion and the ten viziers were all executed for lying. Bakhtiyar later became king.

Balan

One of the princes of hell. He is depicted as naked, riding a bear.

Banu Hilal

'The Sons of Hilal', a long series of sagas of Arab heroes who claimed descent from the Yemenite chief, Hilal, whose great-great grandson Barakat, 'Blessings', becomes known as Abu Zayd, the great warrior, who with his friends crossed over, according to legend, into Egypt, Libya and further west, conquering green pastures for the Arabs' camels.

On the way they encountered *ifrits*, *jinns* and other monsters whom they slew, and fair damsels whom they married and had numerous sons by. They stormed many castles full of gold. Their exploits have been published in Cairo in nine volumes.

Baphomet

The idol allegedly worshipped by the Knights of the Temple of Solomon at Jerusalem. It was probably an image of the Prophet Muhammad.

Baptism

Dipping, immersion, originally for purification (Leviticus 11:25). In the most ancient times it signified receiving new life from the life-giving waters.

This Christian ceremony of baptism is thought to be necessary 'for the remission of sins' (Acts 2:38).

Baptism is for, or should be accompanied by, repentance, (Acts 19:4); for washing away one's sins (Acts 22:16); to drink in one spirit and be made into one spirit (1 Corinthians 12:13); in order to rise with the dead and leave death behind (1 Corinthians 15:29 ff); to put on Christ and be one in Christ (Galatians 3:27); to rise with Christ (Colossians 2:12). It is the washing of regeneration. (Titus 3:5). In Peter 5:21, baptism is compared to Noah's ark, which saved those who were in it, and only those. In Luke 3:16, John Predicts that Jesus will baptize with the Holy Ghost, as indeed Acts 2:4 confirms. In Luke 3:21–2 it transpires that baptism has made Jesus pure so that he is worthy of receiving the Holy Ghost.

Baqa'

In Islamic theology, one of the foremost qualities of Allah: Everlastingness. All things perish except God. For this reason the mystic hopes to leave his body, and merge with God.

Baraka

'Blessing', God's favour in Islam.

Baresman (barseman, barsom, barsem)

In Zoroastrianism, grasses strewn for the sacrifice. This plant may be identical with Arabic *barsim* (*berseem*), *Trifolium Alexandrinium*, much used as cattle fodder.

Bariqa

'Effulgence, lightning'. Sufi term for the experience of sudden enlightenment and ecstasy when the divine approaches.

Barker

A person possessed by a dog-spirit. See *Cynanthropy*.

Barqiya

In Islamic cosmology, a region of the first heaven where the angel Ha'il, 'Terrifying', resides. One half of his body is pure fire, from which God makes lightning (*barq*) whenever he wishes to create a thunderstorm. The other half is ice, from which God makes hail (*barada*) as often as he wishes. The fire does not melt the ice, nor does the ice extinguish the fire. The two exist together in one body.

Baruch (Barukh)

'Blessed', trusted friend and scribe of the prophet Jeremiah (32:12; 36:4 ff), son of Neriah, who wrote the words of the Lord from the prophet's mouth. He is also the author (though this is disputed) of the apocryphal Book of Baruch, known as the Apocalypse of Baruch, in which we read what will happen when the Messiah appears: a time of plenty for the survivors.

Barzakh

'Barrier', Koran 23:99: 'There is a *barzakh* behind them until the day they are awakened'. The dead can never go back to life to do better deeds and avoid sinning. In later Islamic literature the word acquires another meaning, translatable as limbo. The soul in the grave is in *barzakh*, in limbo, until the day it emerges from the grave in a new body, for judgement. The good will rest in peace but the wicked will be tormented by black serpents.

Basira

Insight, the heart's secret knowledge (see Koran 12:108).

Batin

'Inside, esoteric, interior'. In Sufi literature, the hidden meaning of the Koran as opposed to *zahir*, the obvious, superficial, accidental meaning of the verses. *Batin* is thus the eternal essence for which every Sufi is searching. It also means 'God' as the one whose presence is hidden inside.

Bats

Bats fly at night because they have no feathers and would be mocked by the birds if they were seen in the daytime. Thus decreed King Solomon. See also *Watwat*. Bats are believed by some to be the spirits of the ancestors.

Batul

'Virgin'. Usually refers to Maryam or Fatima, both of whom are regarded as superior to other women in the Islamic tradition.

Ba'us (Ba'uth)

The Syriac word for Easter. Literally: 'resurrection'.

Bayt-Al-Ma'Mur

'The Inhabited House', the name of a mosque just above the seventh heaven, in the shade of the *Sidrat al-Muntaha* (q.v.). Every morning God creates 70,000 new angels for the special purpose of worshipping him in this mosque. It is also called *al-masjid al-aqsa*, 'the most distant mosque', since there is none higher or farther away. As soon as they arrive in paradise, the virtuous too will be permitted to pray there, since for the faithful there is no greater joy than to worship God. Some saints on earth have, by God's grace, exceptionally fine ears so that they can hear the angel who calls the *azan* (q.v.) enabling these saints to know the correct time for the *salat*.

Baytu-Llah (Bayt-Allah)

'House of God', the name of the great mosque at Mecca, although of course God does not live only there, since he is omnipresent.

Bear

The bear-goddess was worshipped by many peoples of the Russian and north Asian forests from Scandinavia to Alaska. In Asia Minor her name was Artemis (from *arktos*, 'bear'). The Romans called her Diana, 'the radiant one', since she was also the moon-goddess. Artemis, as is well known, was worshipped at Ephesos, but also at many other shrines. Her other name was Callisto, 'the most beautiful', and sacrifices of children were offered to her.

Beasts (Arabic: *dabba*, Koran 27:82)

1. When the word is fulfilled against the unjust, God will cause the beast to go out from the earth. He will speak to them: 'You have no firm belief in our signs.' In the Bible there are four beasts 'full of eyes' (Revelation 4:6–9).

'The first beast was like a lion, and the second beast like a calf, and the third beast had a face as a man, and the fourth beast was like a flying eagle.' These are evidently the four evangelists who 'give glory and honour and thanks to him that sat on the throne'. They are, in the order of the symbolic beasts mentioned above, Mark, Luke, Matthew, and John. In many churches the evangelists can be identified by their sculpted symbols: Mark with his lion (in San Marco, Venice, and elsewhere), John with the eagle hovering above him, etc. These images are originally the four cardinal signs of the zodiac, Leo (August), Taurus (May), Aquarius (February) and Sagittarius (December), in the same order as given above, though that is the reverse order of the time sequence, probably because they can be 'read' from left or right.

2. A lion, a bear, a leopard with four wings, and a horned monster appear to Daniel as personifications of the wicked rulers of the earth. But the saints will triumph. (Daniel 7:4 ff).

Bedouin (Arabic: *Badawi*, plural: *Badawiyin*)

The nomads of the Arabian desert were proud camel breeders. They used to determine Arabian history, since the traders of Mecca and other cities had to pay them 'protection money' for the security of their caravans. Even the Ottoman government paid them to keep the peace. The Bedouins were divided into clans, each one ruled by a sheikh, 'eldest', who was completely sovereign. The clans were frequently fighting one another for the possession of scarce pastures. The Bedouins had a reputation for honour, generosity and hospitality, once one was accepted as a guest and friend. Many Bedouin customs have become part of Islamic Law: vendetta, blood-money, polygamy, etc.

Young Muhammad was brought up by the Bedouins from the age of one week when he was given over to Halima, his foster-mother. During the years he lived there, all the ewes were in milk, and the goats were dropping kids all the time. It was among the Bedouins that he learned the art of managing camels, notoriously difficult animals to handle, which became his profession when he was appointed caravan leader later.

Beer-Sheba
'Seven Wells', a holy place in Israel where the Lord appeared to Jacob (Genesis 46:1–4). Elijah was comforted there by the angel of the Lord (1 Kings 195).

Behemoth
This animal is mentioned in Job 40: 15 ff. The word is translated variously as 'crocodile' and 'hippopotamus'. However, since it grazes, it cannot be a crocodile, which is a carnivorous animal, and it cannot be a hippopotamus either, since it lives in the mountains, and it also has horns. Perhaps, as in so many motifs in the Bible, we have to search for comparable myths in Mesopotamia.

In the great Epic of Gilgamesh we read that the goddess Ishtar (q.v.), when the hero Gilgamesh rejected her invitation to make love to her, sent the heavenly bull to earth, as revenge for the humiliation. It roared so loudly that people died of sheer fright as

soon as they heard it. But the intrepid Gilgamesh, together with his bosom friend Enkidu, set out and attacked this monstrous bull, and after a long battle, managed to kill it. Its feet trampled many people to death, and its mere snorting killed them.

It seems that we may compare, or even equate, this bull to the *behemoth* of the Bible, all the more so since the related Arabic word *bahima*, 'beast', is often used for a cow (it is a feminine).

Bektashi
An order or fraternity founded by Hajji Bakhtash, a native of Bukhara in Uzbekistan. The symbol of the order is their sacred belt which the members put on and take off seven times, saying: 'I tie up greediness, I loosen generosity; I tie up anger, I unbind meekness; I tie up avarice, I unbind piety; I tie up ignorance, I unbind the fear of God; I tie up passion, I unbind the love of God; I tie up hunger, I unbind contentment; I tie up satanism, I unbind divineness.' Thus even dressing is a spiritual exercise.

Belet Ili
The Sumerian goddess of the womb. The gods asked her to create men for them so that they could till the soil and dig canals, and women so that they could continue to bear men. She created seven of each with the result that, after 600 years, the people were already too numerous. The land became as noisy as a cattle paddock, and the supreme god Ellil could not sleep. The people were also sinful, eating their own children, so Ellil

decided to wash them away with a great flood. 'After all, the people have also become too lazy to work for the gods.' Ellil meant to keep this plan a secret from the people but the god Ea (Enki) told his protégé Atrahasis what would happen and how he could save himself by means of a boat. The flood lasted seven days. See also *Anzu*, *Ninurta*.

Belial (Beliar)
Enemy of Christ (2 Corinthians 6:15), who ransoms us from his slavery (*Testament of the Patriarchs*, Zebulon 9:8). From the Book of Jubilees (1:20) we learn that Beliar endeavours to rule the Lord's people and 'ensnare them from the paths of righteousness'. 'Sons of Belial' means 'children of wickedness', hooligans, thugs, criminals.

Belphegor (Baal Fegor)
Originally a god worshipped by the Moabites, seated on a throne. Later the god of inventions, the 'genius', a handsome youth providing wealth. In the Middle Ages the devil of curiosity, exploration and inquisitiveness, enemy of the faith, depicted naked with horns and hairy skin.

Belshazzar
Last king of Babylon, according to the Book of Daniel 5:1 (but he did not know that until it was too late). Historians still dispute his authenticity. He displayed the golden vessels which his ancestor Nebuchadnezzar had looted from the Temple in Jerusalem, while giving a feast for a thousand nobles. While he was thus boasting, 'fingers of a man's hand' appeared and wrote on the wall. 'The king's face changed.' Rembrandt has painted the king's face beautifully: incredulous, yet frightened to death. Daniel, in whom was 'the spirit of the holy gods', was brought in. Daniel accused the king of sacrilege since he had drunk wine out of the holy vessels from the house of God. He interpreted the writing on the wall as Aramaic: 'Thou art weighed . . . and found wanting.' That same night Belshazzar was slain.

Belzebub
Used in Matthew 12:24–7 as the equivalent of Satan (see also Luke 11:15–20). In Mark 3:22 Belzebub is called 'the prince of devils'. The name is spelled Baal-Zebub in 2 Kings 1:2–3, where he is described as 'the god of Ekron', who gives oracles. He is clearly an enemy of the Lord.

Bel- or Baal-Zebub means 'Lord of the Flies', reputedly a Philistine god. It has been suggested that the name was an Israeli mocking pun on the god's real name: Baal-Zebul, 'Lord of the Domicile', i.e. 'Household God'.

Benhadad
A title of the Syrian kings, 'Son of Hadad (q.v.)' (see 1 Kings 19:5).

Berith
The alchemists' devil who could change all metals into gold.

Beth (Arabic: *bayt*)
'House'. Second letter of the Semitic alphabet. The *b* begins the Bible: *Bereshit* is the first word. God granted

the *b* this honour because she was such a modest letter, unlike the boastful *alif* (q.v.). The word 'house' often refers to the house of God, Hebrew *Bethel* (q.v.), where God appeared to Jacob (Genesis 28:19). The Arabic *Baytullah*, 'House of God', refers to the Ka'ba at Mecca. The original meaning of *beth* was 'tent', and the (debatably) oldest form of the letter suggests a tent seen from above. The concept of 'house' implies the number two, perhaps because the nomads' tent stood on two tent poles or because a couple, husband and wife, form the nucleus of a house, i.e. a family or even a nation, as in 'the House of Israel'. Thus the house is the symbol of the habitation of life, the container of the living, from a snail's house to the human body (John 2:19), and ultimately the living spirit. In Islam the grave is often referred to as the 'house of waiting', i.e. waiting for resurrection.

Bethany

'House of Affliction'. A village near Jerusalem, where Jesus raised Lazarus (John 11:18) and from where Jesus ascended into heaven (Luke 24:51). Pilgrims come to pray here.

Bethel

'House of God'. There God appeared to Jacob (Genesis 28:10) who then built an altar there (Genesis 35:7). The Ark stayed there (Judges 20:26–8), and God spoke to Phinehas there.

Bethlehem

'House of Bread'. This name has been explained as referring to the body of Christ (Matthew 26:26). Here, David was anointed as king of Israel (1 Samuel 16:13; 20:6) and so he became the Messiah. Jesus was born there in 'the House of David' (Matthew 2:1; Luke 2:4; John 7:42), as the word of God, which keeps man alive like bread.

Bilal

The first *mu'adhin* (muazzin) or caller to prayer, appointed by the Prophet Muhammad himself. He used to stand on the roof of the first mosque at Medina. It was said by some that he could hear the angels' call to prayers in heaven, so he always knew when to call the prayers himself.

Bilkis (Balkis, Bilqis, Balqis)

Queen of Saba (Sheba), who married Solomon, (Sulayman in the Islamic tradition). Her mother was a *jinna*, her father was the vizier of the king of Saba. Bilkis was a cunning girl who knew that the king wished to marry her. He was a dissolute despot who raped his ministers' daughters. Bilkis however had a dagger hidden in her veil and killed him after their wedding. So she became queen of Saba while her father stayed on as her vizier.

Birds

One day King Solomon received a visit from the eagle, the king of the birds. It spoke to him: 'Great king! It has pleased God to make me your servant with all my fellow birds. Here is a feather from my tail. Take this and whenever you wave it above your head and call the birds, we will come and do whatever you ask us to do.'

King Solomon took the feather, held it above his head and called all the birds. In a few moments the sky grew pitch dark. Only God knows how many species of birds there are in the sky. They all arrived, perching on the trees and stones around the king and asked his pleasure. The king spoke to every bird and asked it to teach him its language. Thus King Solomon learned the languages of the birds, so that he understood what they sang.

Every bird sings a proverb, a word of wisdom, all its days, but we human beings are deaf to such beauty and learning. The peacock's proverb is 'As you judge, so will you be judged.' The nightingale sings: 'Satisfaction is the mother of happiness.' The turtle dove coos: 'Many things are done that should never have been done, many things are left undone that should have been done.' The hoopoe sings: 'He who has no pity on others will not find pity.' The swallow sings: 'Do good and you will be rewarded for it later.' The eagle cries: 'Far from people I live in peace, nearer to God!' The cock crows: 'Praising God is better than sleeping!' The owl hoots: 'The less you speak, the more you gain!' The bulbul, who sings just before sunrise, tells us: 'It is daybreak! Do not linger! Pray to God!'

King Solomon chose the cock as his companion, because it can see through sand as if it were glass, and so find water in the desert, so that the herdsmen can dig a well to water their beasts. Solomon invited the doves to come and live in his temple. They did,

and became so numerous that they provided cool shade for the pilgrims with their wings. The hoopoe would accompany Solomon on all his trips. From the *Qisasu'l-Anbiya'*, the *Tales of the Prophets*.

Birds' Parliament

A long poem entitled *Mantiq at-Tair* by the Persian poet Farid al-Din Attar, based on a treatise by Al-Ghazali, itself influenced by the famous fable-book *Kalila wa Dimna*. The translation of *mantiq* (literally 'speech') as 'parliament' is based on the authority of Arberry and Fitzgerald, following Chaucer. 'Parliament' conveys the idea that the birds not only convened and talked but also took decisions and carried them out.

The birds, assembled by their leader the hoopoe (q.v.) set out in search of the mysterious *simurgh*, the Persian phoenix, whom they wished to become their king. After a long and dangerous odyssey, only thirty birds survived, and they finally recognized themselves as together being the *simurgh*. In the end, the thirty merged together into one bird, the divine *simurgh*.

The poet no doubt wove more than one hidden meaning into this fable. Modern political thinkers can clearly see how sovereignty passes from the king to parliament. However, the poet's intention was more profound. The *simurgh* is God for the birds. Birds are the symbols of human souls which in the end will merge into God.

Bishara (*bushra*)
'Glad tidings'. The blissful message of Islam.

Bishtasb (Bishtasf, Gushtasb)
The modern Persian form of the Pahlavi Vishtaspa (Greek form: Hystaspes, q.v.). The fifth Kayanid king of Persia. He disagreed with his father, and went to Rum (Byzantium) where he married the king's daughter. Later, after various exploits he returned home and succeeded his father Lohrasb as king of Persia. Thirty years later he was converted by Zoroaster to the new religion of Ahura Mazda. The Turanians attacked his palace and abducted his two daughters who were rescued by their brother Isfandiyar, who was later killed by Rustam. Bahman, his son, succeeded to the throne.

Bismillah
'In the name of God'. This formula, with additions, forms the opening verse of the Koran. It must be used when ending life and starting it. When killing an animal one says '*Bismillah Allahu Akbar*'. Likewise the executioner pronounces it when carrying out his duty. '*Bismillah Arrahman Arrahim*', 'In the name of Allah, the Merciful the Compassionate' has to head every book and even every letter written by a Muslim, and has to be pronounced when undertaking any important work. Especially when embracing his wife, a man has to pronounce this formula, lest the child issuing from this union be Satan's child.

Bistami
Abd al-Rahman bin Muhammad Bistami was born in Aleppo and died in 1454. He lived at the court of the Ottoman sultans. He belonged to the Hurufi order of dervishes who attributed a mystic meaning to each of the letters of the Arabic alphabet.

Black Stone (Arabic: *Hajar al Aswad*)
Originally this was an angel, pure and white, whom God sent down in the days of Adam, whom Jibril helped to build the Ka'ba. The angel condensed himself into a stone in the wall, to be kissed by all the pious pilgrims up till the present. Their many sins have gradually turned the stone black. See *Aerolith*.

Blasphemy
Mosaic law sentenced a man to death by stoning for blasphemy (see Leviticus 24:16; 1 Kings 21:10–13). Jesus is accused of blasphemy, and so is guilty of a capital offence (see Matthew 9:3, 26:65; Mark 2:7; Luke 5:21; John 10:33).

In Islam, blasphemy, insulting God, can only be the result of a much worse sin, atheism (*kufr*). In Islam atheists should either be converted or killed.

English Law defines blasphemy as 'the public or criminal libel of speaking matter relating to God, Jesus Christ, the Bible or the Book of Common Prayer, intending to wound the feelings of mankind or to excite hatred against the Church . . .'

Blood
In antiquity, and still in many parts of Africa, it was believed that blood contained, or was, the spirit of a living being, and so its life. With the blood, the life of a wounded animal flows

away. This life spirit was identified with God himself, or with a god. Originally it was believed that sperm was a form of blood, 'white blood', so that one referred to 'children of the father's blood'; blood-relatives were those who descended from one pair of parents. They all owed their blood to those ancestors and so venerated them. The family was inescapably held together by these blood-ties, since that blood was the spirit of their very own ancestors. Blood is inherited through the *linea sanguinis*, the blood line, i.e. the race or lineage. We speak of 'children of the blood' as opposed to adopted children, stepchildren and children of adultery; the ancestral blood, the spirit of the forefathers, is not in them.

If a person is murdered his blood will 'cry revenge'. This must be taken literally: the spirit was in the blood and the spirit has a will of its own. It will haunt those whose duty it is to take revenge. There are myths describing the spirit rising up from the spilled blood in the earth and cursing the slayer.

The reason why the Israelites were not allowed to consume blood was that the spirit of God was in it. Ancient Semitic law dictated that revenge could be 'bought off' with blood-money (Arabic: *dia*), or a young man (later a ram) could be given instead to the bereaved clan, as a ransom for the slain man. It was necessary to demand this, and if no satisfaction was given, to go to war, because once a clan allowed its members to be killed off, it would soon die out. This is why the whole clan was held responsible if one of its sons had slain a man. They were all of the same blood, and that blood had to give satisfaction.

The young man (not necessarily the culprit; a girl might also be accepted) delivered as ransom would become a member of the other clan, having to fight for them or, if a woman, having to bear new sons for them, from their 'blood'. This explains the concept of 'ransom' which runs right through the Bible, from Cain, who was exiled from his homeland (exile was then a punishment as cruel as execution), to Abraham who was allowed to sacrifice a ram as ransom for his son. God had given him a son and so he could claim the boy as his right. Finally, in great love, God sacrifices his own son as ransom for all human sinners, who are collectively guilty of spilling their brothers' blood. The blood of Christ becomes thus the spiritual substance that purifies all the believers of their sins and those of their forebears. Thus ends the great guilt of the world.

Boaz

1. Son of Salmon, scion of the house of Judah, married Ruth (Ruth 4:13) who gave him Obed, father of Jesse, father of King David.

2. One of the twin pillars beside the gate of the temple of Solomon (see 2 Chronicles 3:17). (The other pillar is called Jachin, q.v.) The name Boaz means 'strong'. The two pillars symbolize the two lions flanking the sky-gate through which the sun rises from the nether world into the sky. Likewise, in Egyptian temples the god/king was carried out of the gate on his throne, to be shown to the worshippers; in this way the 'appearance' of the god/king symbolized sunrise.

The Hebrew phrase *Boaz yachin* means 'Boaz established'. Solomon knew this when he called the two pillars thus, and also that Boaz was his ancestor. The two pillars at the gate also have a special meaning for Christians since Jesus was likewise a descendant of Boaz (Matthew 1) and the Temple itself was his body (John 2:22) since it was the abode of the Holy Spirit, and the gate was its mouth from which the word issued.

Books

It is usual among scholars of religions to single out the living religions with a written tradition. For the Middle East these are, in order of inception: Zoroastrianism, Hinduism, Buddhism, Judaism, Christanity and Baha'ism.

The Koran refers repeatedly to books (*kutub*) which God revealed to the prophets before Muhammad, first and foremost the *Tawrat* to Musa, the *Zabur* (Psalms) to David and the *Injil* (Gospel) to Isa. Later Islamic traditions add 'portions' (*suhuf*) of books which have been revealed to other prophets, ten to Adam, the first of the prophets (see *Anbiya'*), fifty to his youngest son Set (Shayth), thirty to Idris (Enoch) and ten to Ibrahim (Abraham), who is mentioned in the Koran as having received a revelation from Allah (2:130). Six prophets brought laws, *shari'a*: Adam, Nuh, Ibrahim, Musa, Isa and Muhammad (Koran 45:17). The law of Islam (*fiqh*) is a later extrapolation by the *ulema*.

Islam recognizes the 'Peoples of the Book' as having a higher status than pagans. The latter must, if they live in an Islamic state, convert to Islam; the former, the Jews, Christians and Sabeans (q.v.) only have to pay protection tax.

Boys

Boys will serve drinks to the blessed in paradise (Koran 56:17; 76:19). Some translators render this word, *wildanun*, as 'children', others believe it means 'servants' or 'youths'. At 52:54, it is *ghilmanun* 'youths, servants, handsome as pearls'.

Bread

Adam had to eat his bread after much hard work (Genesis 3:19); usually a type of flat bread is meant, like Indian or Persian *naan*. The Semites were animal breeders by inclination, preferring to make the agricultural Samarians and Canaanites work for them, and for their bread. So, the Lord favours Abel's animal sacrifice over Cain's vegetable harvest offerings. It was only gradually that bread (and with it, wheat) became sacred, so that only the host and father may break it and share it. See also *Bethlehem*.

Breast Washing

The angel Jibril (q.v.) appeared to young Muhammad one night, laid him down, cut open his breast, took out his heart and squeezed out a clot of black blood. 'This is the Devil's part of you,' he said as he put the heart back in its place and healed the wound so that Muhammad's breast looked as before. According to some writers Jibril washed the heart in water from the well Zamzam.

Bridegroom

The parable of the ten brides (Matthew 25) is a most curious parallel to the Indian tale of Krishna as the bridegroom of the herdsmaids, the images of human souls longing for God.

Brothers

All Muslims are brothers (Koran 49:10; 9:11; 33:5).

Budasheer

King of Egypt, son of Koftarim. When drought threatened, he sent Hermes (Hirmis, q.v.), a famous scholar, to explore the source of the Nile. Hermes discovered several shallow riverbeds where the tributaries were silted up. He dug new canals so that fresh water flowed to Egypt in abundance. King Budasheer also built a huge statue of black granite which is still there. It prevents the desert sand from covering the Nile valley.

Buhayra

See *Bahira*.

Bull

The first (pure white) animal of creation in Persian mythology. The Egyptian bull-god was Apis. The Greek Zeus appeared as a bull to the nymph Europa. The Indian god with a bull was Shiva. The golden calf was a bull calf (Exodus 32). The god Mithra was identified with the bull which he slaughtered, thus offering his own body for the benefit of humanity, as did Jesus in Matthew 26:26. The bull of Mithra's blood became the wine, its spinal chord the grain, its flesh became vegetables and medicinal herbs. As in some African myths, the bull is a symbol of loyalty to a master.

Bull of Heaven

Owned by the Sumerian god Anu. Ishtar, jilted by Gilgamesh sent it to earth to destroy him but he plunged his sword into its back, after his friend Enkidu fought it, but was blinded by its spittle.

Bundahishn

The Pahlavi book of creation as revealed to Zoroaster by the god Ohrmazd. It also deals with the day of resurrection.

Buruj

'The Towers'. Name of Sura 85. In these heavenly towers the angels keep watch. In astrology the *buruj* are the signs of the zodiac (q.v.), i.e. the ecliptical constellations. See *Tanjim*.

Buraq

'Lightning'. The name of a winged female quadruped, taller than a donkey but not as big as a horse. It was created by God to carry the prophets. Ibrahim and Isa rode her to Jerusalem. Muhammad too, rode Buraq, during the night of *al-isra*' and *mi'raj* (qq.v.), through the heavens. Buraq spent the intervening centuries between Isa's death and the call to Muhammad in paradise, longing for Muhammad to ride her, but when he wanted to mount her, she refused to accept him, because he smelled of heathendom. Jibril explained that Muhammad had just broken the heathen statues in Mecca at God's behest. Only then would Buraq allow him to mount her for his heavenly journey. Buraq is depicted with a woman's head and a peacock's tail.

Burda

The cloak or robe of the Prophet Muhammad which he gave to the poet Ka'b ibn Zubayr when the latter recited his famous poem beginning *Banat Su'ad*, by which name it is still known; it is also often referred to as *al-Burda* because it earned the poet the holy Prophet's previous robe, as well as forgiveness for his sins. Ka'b's descendants kept the robe religiously; it is now in Istanbul. *Al-Burda* is also the title of the poem which Ka'b recited. The same title is also given to an even more popular longer poem in praise of Muhammad by Muhammad Al-Busiri in Egypt during the reign of Sultan Baybars (1260–77). This *Burda* is so sacred that keeping a copy will prevent a house from burning down and a ship from sinking. Having written it the poet, who was lame, could suddenly walk again. See *Busiri*.

Bush

The thorn-bush from which the Lord called Moses in Exodus 3 was almost certainly an acacia, the commonest tree in north-east Africa and Sinai. For Muslims this favour bestowed on Moses – that the Lord actually called him – is a reason for long and joyful meditation upon God calling us to his service (Koran 19:52; 20:9–23; 27: 7–12; 28:29–35; 79:15–16).

Busiri

Ashrafu-d-Din Muhammad ibn Sa'id Al Busiri was born in Egypt in 1212 and died there in 1296. He was a famous scholar, calligrapher, religious teacher and poet. Tradition relates that one day when he was gravely ill, he had a dream in which the holy Prophet appeared to him and threw his robe over his shivering body so that the fever ceased. When he woke up he composed a poem of 162 couplets which made him famous. Its title is *Al-Burda*, 'the Robe' (see *Burda*). It praises the Prophet in such extreme terms as to make him semi-divine. The poem is now, seven hundred years later, still so popular that it is recited frequently in Egypt, Morocco, Nigeria, East Africa, Malaysia and Indonesia.

Butifar

See *Zuleikha*.

C

Cabbala (Hebrew: *qabbalah*, 'tradition')

Originally the oral tradition of the Jewish law handed down by the rabbis to their pupils. In addition to Mosaic law, they also developed an esoteric exegesis of the Torah, the first four books of Moses (Deuteronomy was not included) and also of the Psalms and the prophets, especially Daniel, Ezekiel and Isaiah. According to its own tradition the Cabbala was first taught by God to his angels, who taught it to Abraham when they visited him. Finally Moses learned it all during God's conversations with him. It is said that King Solomon, who was well versed in the Cabbala, was the first to have it written down. But this book was lost when he died and it is said that whoever finds it will possess the art of magic. However, the oral tradition was not lost and was finally collected by Simeon Ben Jochai, who wrote it all down after the destruction of the Temple in 71 AD. This became, according to the Cabbala itself, the great Book of Zohar (q.v.).

The Cabbala is characterized by four aspects: law, magic, letter-ciphers and cosmology. The Jewish law, *notarikon*, does not concern us here. The magic part or 'practical Cabbala' enables those who can translate the text into correct action to work magic. The letter-ciphers or *gematria* enable the expert to read the future by translating the letters of the Torah into numbers and then back again. The cosmology comprises interpretations of the Torah and the prophets which enable the scholar to explain the essence of God, the creation, the angels, man's destiny, the demons, the elements and revelation.

The basis of the universe are the three pillars of justice, mercy and mildness. The *rashith ha-galgalim*, the 'head of the revolutions', is God as *primum mobile*, moving the planets eternally. The universe is divided into four worlds containing: the ten *sephiroth* or qualities and the ten divine names; the ten archangels; the ten orders of angels; and the ten heavenly bodies, the ten arch-devils and the ten orders of demons.

Cain (Arabic: *Kabil*)

Eldest son of Adam and Eve, but see *Lilith*. He sacrificed his worst grain to God, so God condemned him. He slew Abel (Habil) because Cain's twin sister was the prettiest of Adam's daughters, and he wanted to keep her for himself and not give her to Abel, as God had commanded Adam.

Cainites
Gnostic sect worshipping Cain in protest against the creator. They therefore considered as good what the Bible calls evil. They declared themselves to be against nature and so in favour of unnatural practices. They would exclaim: 'Glory to Cain! Glory to Judas!'

Calender (Kalendar)
A member of the Qalandariya order of mendicant dervishes founded by Qalandar Yusuf al-Andalusi. The members' duty is to have no fixed abode, so they are known as the wandering Calenders, eternally on a pilgrimage to God.

Calf
Usually a young bull or a heifer, it was worshipped by many peoples in the pre-Christian Middle East. Of course it was not the young animal, often slaughtered, that was worshipped but the deity, male or female, to whom it was sacrificed, and whom it personified. It was the symbol of young life, future strength and health. See *Golden Calf*, *Bull* and *Mithra*.

Caliph (Arabic: *Khalifa*)
'Deputy, successor'. The Caliph was Muhammad's successor as leader of Islam. When Muhammad died his best friend Abu Bakr took the title of *khalifa* in the sense of 'viceregent, vicar' of Muhammad.

The caliph is the only legitimate and accepted ruler of all Islam. He must be a pure Arab and belong to the Quraysh, the clan to which Muhammad belonged. He must also be healthy in mind and body, an adult man and a scholar of Islamic law. The Omayyads and the Abbasids were all sons of Quraysh, but the Ottoman Turks were not Arabs and neither were the Great Moghul emperors of India, in spite of their immense power. So, they were never recognized as caliphs by their Arabic subjects, although they were accepted as rulers, since 'a bad Muslim ruler is better than total chaos'. The ruler of an Islamic state is not only secular head of state but also the leader of the Islamic community. A *khalifa* is also the successor of the founder of a Sufi order. The word is also used of Adam in the sense of 'God's caretaker on earth, his steward'. The Shi'a believe that Ali should have become the caliph; they refer to him as the first imam (q.v.). See also *Shi'a*, *Mahdi*.

Caller (Arabic: *munadi* and *da'i*)
At dawn one day (nobody knows when, only God) a caller will appear on earth and call all the people (everyone will have died by that time). All the dead will then rise from their graves and be restored to life.

Camel Birds (Arabic: *ababil*)
A type of enormous bird which dropped clay bricks on the army of elephants which the king of Yemen had sent against Mecca in the year in which Muhammad was born (Koran

105:3). So God saved the city with his wonderful birds.

Camels

The *Camelus dromedarius* or one-humped camel was first domesticated by the ancient Nubians in what is now the Sudan. The word is of Nubian origin. The culture of the pre-Islamic Arabs was entirely based on the camel, which yielded milk, meat and leather while its bones were made into utensils. The acquisition of camels made it possible for the Arabs to live a nomadic life in the desert.

According to the Islamic tradition, God created the camel out of some of the clay that the angel Azrail had brought him for the creation of Adam. A large lump of clay was left over, so God made it into a camel. Camels are signs of God (Koran 88:17); they may be eaten (6:144); they were once used as sacrifices to the heathen gods (5:103); those who deny God will not enter paradise until a camel passes through the eye of a needle (7:40); a she-camel came out of a rock as a sign of the prophet Salih to the people of Thamud, but they killed it (7:73, 77; 11: 64–5; 17:59; 26:155–7; 54:24–9).

Canaan (Kan'an)

1. Son of Ham, son of Noah, whose descendants occupied the land of Canaan (Genesis 9:18–22; 10:6; Koran 11:44).
2. The country including modern Israel, Palestine, Lebanon and Sinai as well as western Jordan and south-western Syria. The Canaanites spoke a range of western Semitic dialects closely related to Hebrew; they had a highly developed sedentary culture based on extensive agriculture, cultivating almond trees, barley, beans, sugar cane, fig trees, flax, lentils, melons, millet, mulberries, olives, pomegranates, grapes, wheat and other produce. They lived in fortified cities from the third millennium BC and had several scripts to write their languages with, long before the Israelites were literate; the latter adopted most of the Canaanite culture. Canaan was promised to Abraham (Genesis 12:7; 13:14; 17:8); and was shown to Moses by God (Deuteronomy 32:49). Canaan was allotted to the Children of Israel (Joshua 14). See also *Philistines*.

Cancer

See *Crab*.

Candace

Queen of Ethiopia, whose servant is baptised by the Apostle Philip (Acts 8:38). She surfaces a millennium later in the *Romance of Alexander*, when the young king visits her as Queen of Spain or Africa. The Arabic and Persian texts spell her name as Kandaka.

Carpet

Green Carpet, Flying Carpet. King Solomon owned a green carpet so large that his throne stood on it with his two lions and his two armies, the men on the right and the *jinns* on the left. When the ranks were closed the king would order the wind to lift the carpet up and carry it wherever he wished, in such a way that no man would fall, nor pans be upset, because the cooks would be preparing dinner for the soldiers during the flight. The birds had to fly above the king to give him shade.

Castle of Light

The Castle, or Palace, of Light is familiar to students of European mythology (the Castle of the Grail) and of Oriental mysticism (the Persian Koh-i-Noor, the Mountain of Light, where the divine presence is revealed to the persevering pilgrims).

The Castle of Light can be reached only by ship and only a devout and righteous captain will be able to sail his ship to its shore and land safely. There he will find fresh water, fresh fruit, shade to rest in and all his wishes fulfilled by invisible hands.

Other sailors, nearly drowning when their ship was wrecked, were suddenly picked up by white birds and carried to the island with the Palace of Light, which looked like the rising moon just after sunset when the sky has the colour of roses.

The faithful believers are tested before they are admitted to the Island. If a man or a woman shows compassion and takes pity on a wounded dove and carries her along the seashore, the other doves then bring him or her to the Castle of Light, which was previously invisible. It stands high on a rock overlooking the sea, all its arches and windows shining brightly. The faithful live happily in the castle with their brothers and sisters. The fruit trees in the courtyard bend down their branches so that they can pick any fruit they wish; the sea brings them seafood.

The Arabian scholar Maqrizi mentions a citadel in the Sahara built of transparent pillars; it was surmounted by the golden statue of a hurge bird dedicated to sun-worship. The concept of the divine abode of light no doubt originates in the Zoroastrian lore of the High Abode of Ahura Mazda in the limitless light.

Cave

When the emperor Decius persecuted the Christians, seven noble youths of Ephesos hid in a cave in the mountains. The emperor, upon being told of their whereabouts, decreed that heavy stones should be piled up to close off the entrance. However, instead of dying they fell into a deep sleep by God's grace, which lasted for 187 years. When they woke up, the stones fell down. Hale and healthy they walked out, and found to their surprise that Christianity had triumphed. People only remarked about their old clothes, not their religion. The tale is revived in the Koran, Surat-ul-Qahf. See *Kahf*.

Chaldeans

Chaldees, inhabitants of Chaldea or lower Mesopotamia, where Ur (Genesis 11:28) was the ancient city of the Sumerians. They invented writing, astrology and the magic arts in the fourth millennium BC. They were highly in demand until Roman times for their knowledge of divining, oneiromantics (interpreting dreams) and fortune-telling. See *Magi*.

Chariot of Fire,

Elijah ascended to heaven in a chariot of fire (2 Kings 2:11). It is undoubtedly the vehicle of the sun-god as described in Greek and Indian mythology.

Charity

1. Arabic has two words for charity, *mahabba*, which means 'love', and *sadaqa*, which means 'giving to the needy'. See *Hubb*. *Sadaqa* is highly recommended 'to wipe away the sins' of the giver and to 'build a palace in paradise'.

2. Love of one's neighbour, the Greek *agape*, as opposed to love between man and wife, the Greek *eros*. 'Thou shalt love thy neighbour as thyself' (Leviticus 19:18). 'Love ye the stranger' (Deuteronomy 10:19). See also Leviticus 25:35; Isaiah 58:7. These are very old rules for fraternal love, found nowhere else at this early date except in India, where charity has been a rule since before Buddha. See also Matthew 5:44, 18:5, 22:37–40, 25:40; Mark 12:33; John 13:34, 15:12–14; Luke 11:41–2; 12:33; 18:22; and the epistles of Paul and John.

Charm

See *Talisman, Da'wa*.

Cherub

Cherubim are not always the rosy babies seen flying round in European paintings of classical scenes. In Genesis 3:24 they are armed guardians of paradise, keeping out trespassers. In Exodus 3:18–20 they are winged golden statues guarding the 'mercy seat', which was the golden throne in which the seated image of the deity was carried around in the days when the god appeared to the people in ancient Egypt. Ezekiel (1:5–16) had a vision of terrifying cherubim, seen as wheels in charge of the universe (solar system?). They have zodiacal faces (see *Beasts 1*).

Chimera

A terrifying monster, with the head and claws of a huge lion, the tail ending in poisonous snake's head, while a goat's head with long horns rose up from its back. It lived in Asia Minor until Bellerophon killed it.

China

See *Sa'd ibn Abi Wakkas*.

Chinvat

In old Persian mythology the river which the dead souls had to cross before reaching the kingdom of Yima (q.v.); only the virtuous arrived safely. Later it was pictured as a bridge. Centuries after that, Chinvat was thought of as a bridge to paradise for the souls of the blessed. Finally it was incorporated in the Koran as Sirat al-Mustaqim (q.v.).

Christ

From the Greek *khristos*, which translates the Hebrew *messiah* and the Arabic *masih*. The anointed one, i.e. the man who is king by the grace of God. For the Jews this meant the risen David who would come back to put the House of Israel in order. For the Christians it came to mean the risen Jesus, returned again at Judgement. See *Ascension* and *Messiah*. For Islam see *Mahdi*.

Cin (Cinni)

In Turkey, a spirit which may cause *cinnet*, madness. As a result, out of fear, the people often refer to these spirits collectively as *onlar*, 'they'.

The difference between *cin* and *peri* cannot clearly be defined though the *peri* occur more frequently in fairy tales and so are less harmful, one is told.

A *cin* is normally invisible but can make itself visible at any time and in any shape. It may whisper or raise its voice to a thunderous level. These spirits occur in tribes of both sexes, inhabiting old ruins, taverns, mills, bath-houses, inns and cemeteries, but their presence is noticed only at night, although many people take precautions against meeting them even in daytime. In and around Istanbul numerous places are known to be haunted by a *cin* with or without his family. In the Bosporus lives the king of the sea-spirits with his court. Flooded places, lonely dark street corners, big old trees, river-banks and especially latrines and refuse heaps, sewers and dirty gutters are to be avoided, for that is where they live.

A *cin* may appear to humans in different disguises, like a black cat, a black dog, a he-goat, a fox, a wolf, a buffalo or a bird. They have even been seen, we are told, in the shape of dwarfs or giants, or as thin men as tall as minarets, black or white. It is essential to know how to avoid being harmed by a *cin*. The best method is reciting certain prayers or curses.

The *cin* is a tricky creature: he may please a person or punish him for imprudence or lack of respect, but he may also reward good deeds with great benefits or save the innocent from harm. There is a *cin* king who holds council once a year. Initiates know the secret date and can, for a fee, relay a message or request from a petitioner to the king, who gives gifts in gold. A *cin* can inflict diseases, such as paralysis of a limb or insanity. A *hoca* (scholar) can exorcise the *cin* with prayers.

Cloud

In the normally cloudless desert regions a cloud is a messenger from the gods, which can be seen from afar. In Exodus 13:21–2 the Lord appears as a guide in the form of a 'pillar of cloud'. Whirlwinds often have the appearance of a pillar of dust, and are still believed to be caused by spirits. In Isaiah 19:1, the Lord 'rides on a swift cloud'.

Cock

In Islamic cosmology, God created an enormous cock while he was busy constructing the firmament. This cock has its feet in the first sphere (*tabaqa*) of the heavens, while its head emerges in the seventh heaven many thousands of miles higher. There, in the seventh heaven, stands the Masjid al-Aqsa, the Ultimate Mosque, just beneath the throne of God.

Every night, God creates 70,000 new angels, who will gather at that mosque in the morning to worship him. One of them calls the others to prayer, while it is still dark on earth (in heaven the light of God is diffused everywhere). At that moment the great cock of heaven crows. All the good cocks on earth can hear it and imitate it. This is why the cocks crow before dawn, to remind us that it is time for prayer. Only very few people can hear this heavenly cock, fewer still can hear the angel call the *adhan*, the call for the prayers. One day the cock will crow for the last time. Then the angel will call the dead to rise.

Cohen (Kohen)
'Priest', originally a mediator between God and men, related to the Arabic *kahin*, 'fortune-teller, prophet'. The *cohen* was believed to perceive God's will and be capable of teaching his people God's law.

Compassion
Jesus was moved with compassion for a leper in Mark 1:41. Mark 6:34 says: 'He was moved with compassion towards them, because they were as sheep not having a shepherd.' In Matthew 20:34 the two blind men moved him to compassion, in Matthew 15:32, the hungry multitudes, and in Luke 7:13, the poor mother of a dead man.

Copper Scroll
In Cave 3 near Qumran (q.v.), among the manuscripts written on papyrus and parchment, one was found that was written on copper. It was rolled up into a cylinder and badly corroded. It was sent to Britain and 'unrolled' by Professor H. W. Baker at Manchester. It was then sent to Fr J. T. Milik in Jerusalem who translated the Hebrew inscription. The contents are a long list of treasures amounting to a total of 65 tons of silver and 26 tons of gold. Dr John Allegro, who wrote a book about it, arrives at about the same totals. Fr Milik believes that the scroll is a work of fiction. Many scholars agree with him that such a fabulous treasure can only be a figment of the imagination. Many others, however, are convinced that the treasure does – or did – exist, and that it must have been the treasure of the great temple of King Herod at Jerusalem. This treasure, or a large part of it, was ultimately taken to Rome by the Emperor Titus in 71 AD.

However, after Jerusalem was taken by the Romans, small groups of zealots (we would now call them guerillas) continued fighting until their last stronghold, the rock of Masada (q.v.) was stormed by the Romans. We know that there were links, perhaps an alliance, between the zealots and the people of Qumran. Could it be that the zealots had taken the temple treasure with them to Masada to defend it to the last man? Could it be that the Romans knew or suspected that the treasure was there, and could that perhaps explain the Romans' determination and the ferocity of their attack as well as the enormous amounts they were apparently prepared to pay for the preparations alone, including the construction of an enormous sloping road for the infantry to march to the attack and for the transport of their heavy siege contraptions?

Covenant
A mutual promise between two parties each agreeing to fulfil a vow if and for as long as each keeps his word. As soon as one party reneges, the other is absolved from his side of the agreement. God concluded a series of covenants with his favourites on earth: Noah (Genesis 6:18–19; 8), Abraham (Genesis 15:7, 18), Isaac (Genesis 17:19), Jacob

(Genesis 28:13), Phinehas (Numbers 25:13), and David (2 Samuel 23:5). Moses is the instrument of God's covenant with Israel (Exodus 6:4; 19:5; 34:27).

Cow (or heifer)

A cow had to be sacrificed so that a dead man could be brought back to life when Musa (Moses) struck the corpse with a piece of the meat (Koran 2:67–73). It had to be yellow and untrained.

Crab (Latin: *cancer*, Greek: *karkinos*, Arabic: *akrab*)

The zodiacal sign of Cancer, ruled by the goddess Hera-Juno. The crab used to be a regular food for the fishing nations of the Gulf and the Mediterranean. It makes a burrow in the beach and so symbolizes homemaking, collecting food and thus thrift. Its goddess supervises pregnancy, i.e. the formation of fruits, the 'swelling' of the fruits in the wombs and on the branches. Cancer is thus a good sign, bringing fertility and homeliness, saving and expansion of life, as the ears of the corn are swelling.

Crane (Persian: *kurti*, Arabic: *ghurnuq*)

This migrating bird, with its noble gait and fine crest, was once common in the Middle East. It was associated with Apollo the sun-god, since it was believed to be awake very early in the morning saying its prayers. The learned writers in Persian and Arabic have mainly copied what the Greek and Roman authors wrote. The crane's brain and gall bladder are believed to have miraculous medicinal power to ensure a long life.

Creation

1. The Book of Genesis names the skies (*shamaim*) and the earth (*ha-arets*) as the first two things God created. We do not learn what the skies looked like but the earth was *tohu va vohu* (probably, 'chaos') and dark. The spirit of God was hovering above the surface of the water, implying that there was no earth at all, only a waving ocean. The Bible goes further: the spirit of God was *moving* upon the face of the water, creating the image of a large seabird floating on the sea. This type of image would be expected of the nations with a maritime history such as the Greeks, the Norsemen or the Anglo-Saxons, but the Semites reached the sea well after Moses (Deuteronomy 34:2). Perhaps the Hebrews borrowed the concept of the primeval ocean from the Canaanites, who had lived along the Mediterranean coast for a millennium before the Israelite invasion.

The great German lexicographer, Gesenius, translates the phrase *merakhepheth* in Genesis 1:2 as 'The spirit of God was winging above the waters', like an eagle, a common image for a god. The word 'deep' also suggests the ocean, not a temporary flood, (as in Egypt and Mesopotamia), where the river banks slowly rise out of the receding waters each year, suggesting a new creation.

Only after all this was the light created, presumably the rising sun, unless the sky above the ocean was continuously overcast.

2. The Koran stresses the many miraculous aspects of creation (13:2–4; 16:3–8; 67:3). Furthermore, creation is well ordered and perfect (67:3). Numerous books in Arabic and other Islamic languages describe creation as a process which took seven days because God never rested. God created the earth, its layers (*tabaqat*), its 'ornaments', the skies (heavens), their 'ornaments', the sun and the moon with their orbits, Adam, his spirit, Eve, and Iblis, the devil who tempted them. This is the order in which the created beings are described in the numerous popular books.

Some writers add separate chapters on the all-encompassing world-ocean (*al-muhit*), on the plants and trees, the islands and mountains, the animals, birds and fishes, and the clay from which Adam was formed, as well as his soul. Heaven and hell, the angels and the devils were created separately, but first of all the light and the angels' spirits. The spirits of the twenty-five prophets are often mentioned separately, as well as the less luminous human souls created after them. Among some of God's first creations to be named were his own throne (*kursi*), the canopy (*arsh*), the pen (*qalam*), the 'well-kept book' (*lauh al-mahfuz*), paradise with its twelve gates, the eternal fire (*nar*), the 'thin bridge' (*al-sirat*) and the spirit of Muhammad his beloved Prophet. See also *Ahura Mazda*.

Crescent

Often used as a symbol of Islam, probably because the sighting of the new moon, *hilal* (q.v.), by at least two Muslim men of sound judgement is necessary before the new month is announced. Thus the moon regulates the calendar of all Muslims, and with it, their entire chronology.

Cybele

Goddess of Phrygia and Lydia in Asia Minor, daughter of the double-sexed monster Agditis, an earth-god. Cybele (or Kubele) is equated with the Greek Rhea, mother of Demeter–Isis. In the beginning she lived in the pine forests which then still covered the best part of Asia Minor. She fell in love with Attis (Atys), a shepherd-god of springtime, the 'lamb' who was to be slaughtered. Attis died a horrible death for no man can see the goddess and live. Cybele was represented in sculpture as the heavily pregnant earth-goddess with four breasts, riding in a chariot drawn by two lionesses.

Cynanthropy

It was believed that certain people could be changed into dogs when possessed by evil spirits, and then defile themselves by eating unclean things and copulating with other dogs. It was believed by some in antiquity that the Cynocephali, the 'dog-faced' people who lived in India, were the descendants of such unions between men and bitches. See *Dog*.

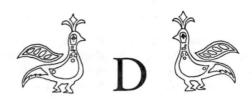

D

Dabur
'West Wind'. In Sufi lore this is symbolic of carnal lust.

Daena (Modern Persian: *din*)
Inner self-consciousness, religion.

Dagon
The fish-god, identified with the Greek Poseidon, of the Philistine fishermen of Ashdod-Azotus on the Palestine coast, 1 Samuel 5:1–7.

Dahaka
Old Persian god of death and demon of deceit and mendacity. He is pictured with three heads, while lizards and scorpions crawl all over his body. He loves destroying life. See also *Zohak*, for which it is an alternative spelling.

Dajjal (Dadjalu)
Short for *Al-mahdi al-dajjal*, 'the false *Mahdi*'. From the Arabic, 'deceiver, liar'. The lord of evil in Islamic cosmology who will appear at the end of times, but before the *Mahdi*. One could call Dajjal the 'anti-Muhammad' in so far as the *Mahdi* will be Muhammad raised by God. When a great famine followed by epidemics afflicts the land, and people indulge in all types of corruption and immorality so that they no longer know the difference between good and evil, then Dajjal will claim that he is God, yet the careful observer will see that he cannot be, for between his eyes Arabic letters forming the word *kafir*, 'infidel', will be clearly visible.

He will be short and missing his right eye. He will command the devils and bring the dead back to life, to make zombies who will work for him. He will be very rich so that many people will follow him. He will cause lovely gardens to grow and be very hospitable. Whenever someone asks him, 'Can you bring my father back to life?', one of the devils will assume the appearance of that person's father so that he or she will believe that Dajjal is indeed God. He will also cause fires to leap up and walk on water. After ruling for forty years, Dajjal will be defeated by the *Mahdi*, chained and banished to a lonely island for ever.

Dalhan
A demon riding an ostrich in the desert. It devours travellers.

Damkina
Sumerian goddess, consort of Enki, ruler of Apsu at Eridu.

Dancing
See *Darwish*.

Daniel
Biblical prophet whose book is chiefly written in Aramaic, the language of Syria which was spreading across the Babylonian empire. Daniel 'taught the learning of the Chaldeans' (Daniel 1:4). This probably meant the art of divining, though the only example of this art we know of is the deciphering of divine writing (Daniel 5:17; see also *Belshazzar*).

He also had an understanding of dreams (Daniel 1:17; 2:4), a function which would now be assigned to a psychoanalyst but which was then part of the diviner's profession. For the ancients, dreams were real messages from some outside spiritual agent, invariably thought to be revelations about the future (see Chaldeans). Daniel was also capable of putting a spell on wild animals (Daniel 6:16–22). That at least is how his contemporaries must have regarded him. In Chapter 7, Daniel himself has a dream, seeing the four beasts (see *Beasts*). These are usually interpreted as the four mighty kingdoms of his time. See also *Danil*.

Danil (Daniyal)
Danil and Daniyal are the two Arabic forms of the name Daniel. Like the biblical Daniel, Danil was a prophet, whose book, *Kitab Danil*, has been translated from Arabic into Turkish and other languages. It gives in a broad sweep predictions about the future of the great medieval empires of the Middle East: Turkey, Iran, India, etc. Much of this literature is apocalyptic, i.e. it reveals 'the signs of the end', the hidden omens which for the wise and perceptive will be clear indications that the end of the world is nigh: earthquakes, volcanic eruptions, diseases, increasing sinfulness and decadence, etc.

In the Islamic tradition the prophet was imprisoned by Bukhtu Nassar, Nebuchadnezzar, until the king had a dream in which he saw a statue with a head of gold and feet of clay. Suddenly a stone fell from heaven, crushing the idol to dust. Then the stone grew and covered the earth. Danil was released from prison to interpret the dream. He said: 'The golden head is your kingdom, the feet of clay are the kingdoms of Iran and Rum (Asia Minor), and in between are the lands of Syria, Palestine, etc. The stone is the great religion that will one day cover all those kingdoms.' Of course, by this was meant Islam.

Daniyal
See *Danil*.

Dar
'House, habitation, country'. *Dar al-Baqa'*, 'House of Eternity', heaven; *Dar al-Fana'*, 'House of Passing', the earth; *Dar al-Ghurur*, 'House of Illusion', this world; *Dar al-Huzn*, 'House of Sadness', this valley of tears; *Dar al-Surur*, 'House of Joy', paradise; *Dar al-Ibtila'*, 'House of Temptation', the Earth.

Dara (Darab) II
Son of Dara I (Darius) and king of
Persia, younger half-brother of Al-
Iskandar (Alexander), who, according to Firdausi (q.v.), replaced him
on the throne of Persia after defeating
him in battle. This 'rewriting' of history 'explains' to the Iranians their
defeat by a Greek king.

Darab
See *Dara*.

Dar-es -Salaam
'House of Peace' (Koran 6:127), paradise.

Darwish (Turkish: *dervis*)
'Poor man'. Like *faqir*, which also
means 'poor man', it has come to
mean 'religious mendicant'. The 'dancing dervishes' were groups of devotees
belonging to the religious fraternity
of the Mevlevis (Mawlawiyya, see
Rumi). They interpreted the poet
Rumi's Aristotelian cosmology according to which the Polar Star (*Al-
Kutb*) is in the centre of the universe, fixed, and rotating only around
its own axis while all the other
stars orbit around it, each along its
own path, at its own speed, in its
own sphere or stratum, at the same
time rotating around its own axis.
The dervishes recreate this sidereal
cosmos in their own fraternity by
dancing around their Grand Master whom they call *Al-Kutb*. Each
dancer rotates round while keeping
a fixed distance from the Master
who stands in the middle rotating
gently, while the youngest dervishes
orbit in the outer circles whirling
round with total abandon, thus signifying their total submission to the
Master's authority.

Dasim
In Islamic tales, the son of Iblis, an
evil spirit causing hatred between
spouses.

Dates
These were Muhammad's favourite
fruits; they are still eaten as a treat
on 'Id al-Fitr. Dates belong to God's
signs (Koran 50:10). Even in paradise
the faithful will enjoy dates (55:68).
When Isa (Jesus) was born his mother
Maryam (Mary) fed him the dates
which sprouted from a dead tree.
This is an often quoted miracle: Isa's
birth caused the dead date tree to
revive.

Daud (Dawud)
The Arabic form of David (q.v.).
David defeated Goliath who is called
Jalut in the Koran (2:251). God gave
him the kingship and the wisdom
he would need. The Koran mentions that Daud learned the art of
forging iron and of making armour
(34:10; 21:80). Daud was also one
of the prophets of God who received
a book, the Zabur, i.e. the Psalms
(only he, Musa, Isa and Muhammad
received books). Daud praised God
together with the birds and even
the hills (34:10; 38:19): 'The birds
were all in tune with him,' and God
was close to him. He even gave him
sound judgement and the caliphate,
i.e. he made him viceregent on earth
(38:26) and he gave him a great son,
Sulayman (Solomon).

David

The name means 'beloved, darling'. David was, and is, more than any historical person, the darling of the Jewish people. Numerous folk tales are told about him and many songs have been composed about him. David was himself a composer and a singer of songs (see I Samuel 16:19) and he is credited with creating the 150 psalms, or a majority of them, the biggest collection of ancient Hebrew poetry. They are very religious songs full of almost mystical faith in God, so he was also God's beloved.

David was the youngest son of Jesse of Bethlehem, and was a simple shepherd boy. God sent his prophet Samuel to Bethlehem, speaking to him all the time. David, though Jesse's youngest son, and not tall of stature, was chosen by God to become king of Israel, because God looks into the heart (1 Samuel 16:7), not at the outward appearance, although that was pleasant enough – David was very good-looking. God said to Samuel: 'Anoint him for this is he' (16:12). Thus David became the anointed of God, in Hebrew *messiah*, in Greek *Christos*.

This is the nucleus of the Judaeo-Christian concept of the anointed kings. The later kings of Israel were anointed; the kings of England, France and Germany were anointed throughout the Middle Ages. The anointing ceremony gave the king God's grace, so that afterwards merely touching him would ensure blessing and good health.

David's victory over Goliath is well known (1 Samuel 17:49). It signifies that a man in battle needs neither great strength nor big weapons. All he needs is God's help, which was ensured by David's continuous faithfulness and obedience to God.

Da'wa

'Call, invitation, claim, supplication, convocation'. The Prophet Muhammad, according to the *Books of Da'wa*, approved of charms and amulets only if they contained nothing but the holy names of God, the angels and the good *jinns*. According to the Wahhabis only God's names may be invoked. The purpose of the *da'wa* is the invocation of God's or the angels' assistance for the protection of the wearers of amulets, charms, etc. The aim of this occult science is to establish friendship and love with others, to cure sickness, to prevent death, to cause fulfilment of one's wishes, to debilitate one's enemies, to secure victory in battle and to become rich.

The practitioner of this occultism, *'amil*, should live an absolutely impeccable life of clean habits, never speak untruth, never eat unclean food or touch unclean things, animals or people. He should be modest and humble, never proud or boastful. He must never speak about his art except with his masters and disciples. Firstly, the letters of the names of the petitioner have to be interpreted according to extensive tables, only a small part of which can be represented here (see table p.102).

For instance, the petitioners are often a girl and a young man, or their parents, wishing to ascertain that the two youngsters will be compatible spouses. The *'amil* will study

Table of Letters of Personal Names with the Qualities they Represent

Letter	Arabic	Roman	Number	Zodiacal Sign	Planet	Divine Name	Scent of Tree, Plant, Fruit or Flower	Element	Quality or Virtue
Greek									
Alpha	Alif	A	1	Taurus	Ceres	Allah	Aloe	Earth	Friendship
Beta	Ba	B	2	Gemini	Mercury	Baqi	Sugar cane	Air	Brotherly love
Gamma	Jim	C	3	Cancer	Neptune	Jami'	Cinnamon	Water	Faithfulness
Delta	Dal	D	4	Leo		Dayyan	Red Sandal	Fire	Fortitude
Epsilon	Ha	E	5	Virgo		Hadi	White Sandal	Earth	Purity
Ypsilon	Waw	F	6	Libra	Jupiter	Wali	Camphor	Air	Justice
Zeta	Zayn	Z	7	Scorpio	Moon	Zaki	Honey	Water	Beauty
Eta	Hha	H	8	Sagittarius	Sun	Haqqu	Saffron	Fire	Truthfulness
Theta	Ta	Th	9	Capricorn		Tahiru	Musk	Earth	Perseverance
Iota	Ya	I	10	Aquarius	Pluto	Yasin	Red Rose	Air	Generosity
Nun	Kaf	K	20	Pisces	Venus	Kafi	White Rose	Water	Love in marriage
Omega	Lam	L	30	Aries	Mars	Latifu	Apple	Fire	Readiness to sacrifice

the meanings of the letters of the couple's names, their zodiacal signs, the accompanying planets, the names of God represented by the letters, etc. On the basis of this data he will decide whether the couple will be compatible marriage partners. The original table is, of course, composed in either Arabic or Persian. There are further columns with, for example, 'negative qualities', such as enmity, hatred, desire, indifference, etc. There is a column with the names of guardian angels and one with those of the protective *jinns*, but their names become increasingly fantastic as one reads down the list. See also *Astrology*, *Heaven* and *Zodiac*.

Day of Judgement

1. In the Old Testament, the words 'the day' in the sense of the day of God's judgement, of doomsday, occurs first in Isaiah 2:1 ff. where the Lord tells the people of Israel, especially of course the women, to behave better, use fewer ornaments, because on this day he will 'wash away the filth of the women of Israel' (4:4). At the same time (or later?) Isaiah says there will be a great war: 'He will judge between nations' (2:3), at the end of which presumably Israel will vanquish all its neighbours just as it did in the time of David. This of course can happen only after Israel has been purified of its sins and corruption, so that it will again be worthy of the Lord's protection. All this will happen in this world, on earth.

2. In Christianity this idea of the nation of Israel triumphing in the end has been replaced by the future triumph of Jesus (son of David) over the evil of all times and all nations. This earth will then be replaced by a new earth (Revelation 21:1). In Matthew 7:22, Jesus says: 'When that day comes', meaning, we may assume, the day when the faithful will enter the Kingdom of Heaven. He will then select those who have been honestly devoted to him to live with him for ever. Jesus refers to Daniel (Matthew 24:15–16), where Daniel says: 'At that time Michael shall appear . . . many of those who sleep in the dust of the earth will awake, some to everlasting life.' When Jesus prophesies: 'The stars will fall from the sky' (Matthew 24:29), we can hear an echo in the Koran 81:2, in almost exactly the same terms. 'No one knows the day' (Matthew 24:36; Mark 13:32; Koran 75:6). It is referred to as the last day in John 6:39.

3. The last day is frequently announced in the Koran as 'the heavy day' (76:27), the 'terrifying day' (6:15; 19:37), the 'difficult day' (74:9), the 'day of decision' (37:21), the 'day of judgement' (13:35; 37:20).

At dawn on the day of resurrection (q.v.), the trumpet (q.v.) will be blown (Koran 74:8) whereupon the sky will start waving (52:9), then it will be split (25:25) and be rolled back (21:104). Mountains will move (18:47; 52:10). The angels will descend (25:22). The caller will call (50:41) close by, and all people will be assembled (6:22, 10:28, 11:103). See *Caller*, *Hour*, and *Qiyama*.

Dead Sea Scrolls
See *Qumran*.

Death

1. The belief that the dead are still alive, only invisible, is almost universal in the Middle East. Death is the separation of the soul from the body: see 1 Kings 17:22, where the soul is called *nefesh*. In the Gilgamesh (q.v.) epic there is no trace of this notion yet. Gilgamesh complains: 'My beloved friend became dust', when lamenting the death of Enkidu (10:5, 21). Eternal life is granted by the gods to Uta-Napishtim and his wife after they have survived the flood in which all other people have perished.

2. Zarathustra (q.v.) was taught by Ahura Mazda (Boyce pp. 80 ff.): 'After a [bad] man is dead . . . the wicked demons rend him completely. At dawn of the third night . . . the demon Vizaresha "who drags away", leads the bound soul of the wicked man, the worshipper of demons . . . The soul goes along the paths created by time . . . The Beautiful One . . . she takes the souls of the just over the Chinvat Bridge . . . from the perilous world to the world without peril . . . Contented, the souls of the just proceed to the golden thrones of Ahura Mazda and the Amesha Spentas, to the House of Song, where the just live.

'When a just man dies, his soul sits at the corpse's head, chanting the Gatha . . . The soul feels as much joy as all that it had felt in life. At the end of the third night, at dawn, it is as if the soul of the just man were among meadows and breathing sweet scents. His own Daena [inner self] will appear to him in the form of a maiden, beautiful, queenly, white-armed. The soul of the just man says

to her: 'What girl are you, the most beautiful in form of all girls that I have ever seen?' His own Daena will answer him: 'Youth of good thought, you worshipped the good Waters and the Fire of Ahura Mazda, you chanted the Gathas [before] the separation of body and consciousness.'

3. In the biblical tradition, Adam brought death into this world as a punishment for his disobedience (Genesis 2:17). The tale is close to the Babylonian myth of Adapa who was deceived by the trickster-god Ea, so that he eventually died. Adam too had to 'return to the ground'. God said: 'Dust you are, to dust you shall return' (Genesis 3:19). The 'breath of life' which God had breathed into Adam's nostrils (Genesis 2:7), Adam had breathed out again. So there was nothing left of man after death, according to this tale, just as Gilgamesh says when lamenting his friend Enkidu's death (see 1. above). Later in the Old Testament there seems to be an idea of survival after death, for it is referred to as 'sleep' (Job 3:13; Psalms 13:3). For sleep a person needs to be alive, and behind that looms the perception that he could wake up one morning, for sleep is not eternal.

4. In the New Testament an entirely new philosophy arises. Jesus promises some of his listeners: 'There are some of those standing here who will not taste death before they have seen the Kingdom of God' (Mark 9:1; Luke 9:27). Does this mean that their souls will survive death to witness the Kingdom of God? The message of the New Testment is that Christ has

vanquished death: 'You must regard yourselves as dead to sin and alive to God, in union with Jesus Christ' (Romans 6:9). 'In Christ all will be brought to life . . . [he] brought resurrection of the dead' (I Corinthians 15:21–3). 'For he has broken the power of death and brought life and immortality . . .' (II Timothy 1:10). It is the devil who through his command of death had all people in his power, but Christ may liberate them (Hebrews 2:15). Christ 'holds the keys of death and death's domain' (Revelation 1:18). Those who believe in the Son of God will not die but have eternal life (John 3:16).

5. In Islam, 'Every soul will taste death' (Koran 3:182). There are several booklets available in the small bookshops of the Islamic countries in which death is described in detail. In the Koran death is announced to the believers as well as the unbelievers (39:30). For all people death has been 'written', i.e. predestined (56:60). Allah has created both life and death (67:2). Death will reach a person anywhere (4:78), so flight is useless (33:16). Death comes with a stupor, *sakra* (50:17), as if a person is drunk. It is not permitted to seek death, said Muhammad.

Once a person is dead and in his grave, it will seem only a short period until resurrection (17:52; 20:103–4; 23:112–14). Before death, a relative or friend of the dying person has to be on watch all the time, and has to repeat: 'There is no god but Allah . . .' until the dying man repeats it. The reason is that when the dead man is in his grave, two messengers from God, Munkar and Nakir, with terrifying aspect, will visit him and demand to know: 'Who is your God?' The correct answer is: 'There is no god but Allah.' The next question is: 'Who is your Prophet?' The correct answer is: 'Muhammad is the Prophet of God.' (This is the other half of the Islamic confession of faith, see *Shahada*). The two messengers will then leave the dead man in peace until the resurrection (see *Qiyama*).

A dying person will suddenly see a man of terrifying aspect, all in white, approaching who will say: 'I am Azrail [q.v.] *Malaku 'l-maut*, the angel of death. Oh pure soul, come out towards God.' He will proceed at once to pull the soul out of the body through the mouth without trouble or pain 'like water out of a bag', since the good soul has prepared itself for this moment. The angel of death will then hand over this soul to two other white angels who will carry it to the first heaven, i.e. the lowest region of the heavens, where the door is opened after the angels have told the gatekeeper whose soul it is they are carrying. After that they arrive at the second heaven and so on until they arrive in the seventh heaven, where they hear God's voice: 'Write the name of this my servant in the Book of Illiyun.' After this the soul is returned to earth and to its body in the grave, because 'I created man from earth.'

Honey or sorbet may be poured into the dying man's mouth, to make it easier for the poor soul to slip out. Once life has gone, the mouth is shut, lest a bad spirit enter it. Perfumes are burnt to fumigate the corpse. It is washed and wrapped in a shroud. If a person dies late in the afternoon, he will be buried before midnight; if later, he should be buried at dawn at the latest, for the Prophet Muhammad said: 'The sooner a good man is buried, the sooner he will reach heaven and be at peace. See also *Mayit*.

Dede Korkut

A collection of twelve stories set in the heroic age of the Oghuz Turks in what is now southern Siberia and the Caspian region. Dede Korkut lived for almost 300 years in pre-Islamic times. The stories as we know them are written down in medieval Turkish, in prose interspersed with rhythmic rhyming passages. The author is anonymous. Numerous chivalrous heroes appear in these stories, wooing beautiful ladies and fighting monsters such as Tepegoz, 'Goggle-Eye', a terrible cyclops. The names of the chief heroes are: Boghach Khan, Salur Kazan, Bamsi Beyrek, Uruz, Dumrul, Kan Turali, Yigenek, Basat, Emren, Segrek, Kan Pudei and King Direk.

Deluge

See *Flood*.

Demons

In ancient Babylonia many demons were mentioned on the clay tablets, e.g. Alu, who crushed men by falling on top of them while they were asleep. The demoness Lamastu, pale-faced with donkey's ears, bare-breasted and with poisonous claws, killed babies at their mothers' breast.

Destiny

See *Qadar, Qisma*.

Dev

Demon, evil spirit of enormous power, a ruthless and immoral god of war in old Persian mythology.

Devequth

'Adherence'. In Jewish mysticism, the constant attachment of the soul to God.

Devils

1. The Devil is Satan in Hebrew, Diabolos in Greek. He occurs numerous times in the Bible as the opponent of God and of all good people. He caused the fall of man by lying to Eve, promising her immortality which he could not give her. Some of the greatest men in the Bible are tempted by the Devil, David, Job and Jesus among them: the latter two resisted him successfully. The Devil is powerful, proud, wicked, subtle, deceitful, presumptuous, cruel, fierce and ruthless. The wicked are called the children of the Devil, obeying his 'lusts'; they are possessed, blinded, deceived and ensnared by him. They will in the end be punished with him. See also *Satan*.

2. There are two terms in Arabic: Shaytan and Iblis. Iblis refers only to Lucifer before and after he became the chief devil. *Shaytan* is used as a generic term; it has a plural, *shayatin*. In Arabic one refers to *the* Devil as al-Shaytan, i.e. Iblis. The devils descend from Jann, a mythical king of the *jinns* who was created before Adam according to some writers. The

original name of Iblis in those early days was Azazil, whom the Christians call Lucifer, the Jews Satan and the Greeks Phosphoros; in all these cultures devils are associated with bad odours, and with suffocating smoke. Azazil was king over the spirits and animals before Adam was created. Iblis and some of the other devils were created out of the element of fire. When Adam was created, the angels and devils were commanded by God to prostrate themselves before him. The angels obeyed, but Iblis spoke out: 'I was created out of the pure and noble fire. Should I humble myself to this little man who was made from mud?' God condemned Iblis to death but Iblis spoke (Koran 7:14): 'Spare me until the day when they will be resuscitated . . . I shall come to them from the front and from behind, from the left and the right [to tempt them].' Thus Iblis, the Devil, with his army of little devils, approaches every man and woman, except those who are determined never to follow him.

Devils are invisible and have friendly but insistent voices which whisper seductively in our ears, to cause desires. Iblis' first (and successful) temptation targeted Adam and Eve, telling them that if they ate the fruit, they would become angels with eternal lives (Koran 7:20). Thus the Devil is a master liar who calls himself a good counsellor (7:21). The Prophet Muhammad said: 'The Devil enters into a man like the blood in his body.' Every person has an angel and a devil appointed for him to accompany him personally. When a child is born and cries loudly, that is when it is touched by the Devil. Only Maryam and Isa were never touched by him. There is a special devil called Khanzab who disturbs people when reading the Koran and praying: 'Spit three times over your left shoulder and recite Sura 113 until he goes.' See also *Shaytan*.

3. Jesus healed those that were possessed with devils: Matthew 4:24; 8:31. Mark 1:23; 5:2 calls devils 'unclean spirits'. In Luke 8:27–9 and 9:42, both terms are used interchangeably. The devils, speaking through the mouth of the possessed man, confess Jesus to be Christ (Mark 3:11; Luke 4:34; 41), because they know more than the feeble persons they possess, whose bodies serve them as places to live in, for without bodies to parasitize, to 'sit' on, they are powerless; they have to beg Jesus to let them move into the bodies of pigs (Luke 8:32) to stay on, but in their madness the pigs run down into the lake. For the Jews pigs are unclean, so their bodies are just the right places for unclean spirits to reside in. All the foreign gods to whom the foolishly apostatical Jews and gentiles sacrificed were called 'devils', *shedim*, in the Bible (Deuteronomy 32:17).

Dhikr (Zikr, jikir, zekr, dhikir, dzikiri)
'Repeating'. God's holy names must be repeated at every moment but especially during nocturnal ceremonies called *dhikr*, the best known of the Islamic devotional rituals. The worshippers are in two rows facing each other, swaying rhythmically to and fro while reciting God's holy names.

Dhu'l Fakar (Zul Fikari, Dhu'l
Fiqar, Zool Fakari and other
spellings)
In the Islamic tradition, a great steel
sword forged by King David. It had
two points, like a snake's tongue, to
put out an enemy's eyes. The famous
ancient sword was captured from the
heathen As ibn Munabbih in the
battle of Badr (March 624). It was
handed to the Prophet Muhammad
by an honest follower; its name
is explained as 'the one with the
grooves'. Muhammad handed it to
Ali who performed miracles of valour
with it. The two-pointed sword was
in the possession of the Abbasids for
many centuries.

Dhu'l-Qarnayn
'He of the two horns'. The Koran
(18:83–94) narrates how God made
him powerful on earth, whereupon he
travelled to the place where the sun
sets in a muddy well, after which he
went east where the sun rises. Finally
(18:95 ff.), Dhu'l-Qarnayn arrived in
the north where he built a metal wall
to protect the world against the invasions of Yajuj and Majuj (q.v.) which
will hold until doomsday. Although it
was Moses who is believed to have
had horns, Dhu'l-Qarnayn has been
identified with Alexander the Great,
the conqueror of the Middle East (see
Al-Iskandar).

Diamonds
The Islamic tradition tells the follow-
ing tale. One day, upon his return to
Jerusalem from an inspection tour,
King Solomon found that its inhabit-
ants were leaving his capital. Loaded

with their possessions, they walked
and rode to an unknown destination.
When Solomon enquired he was told
that the noise of all the saws and
hammers wielded by the builders of
his great Temple was intolerable, so
they had decided to emigrate. King
Solomon persuaded them to return to
their houses in the city, and at once
gave orders for work on the Temple
to cease. He called the leaders of the
jinns and asked if they knew of a
method to cut iron and copper without making noise. One of the skilled
spirits came forward and said: 'Sire,
only the mighty Sahar knows this,
but he has stayed away not wanting
you to see him. He is stronger than
all of us together and much faster.
But once every month, he comes to
a certain well in the land of Hijir to
drink; you may succeed in subduing
him there, wise king.'

King Solomon at once ordered
some of his rapid-flying *jinns* to
find that well, empty it out and fill
it with heady wine. Some armed *jinns*
received orders to crouch near the
well until the giant spirit arrived, then
to inform the king at once. Two weeks
later, the king was standing on his ter-
race when he saw a *jinn* come flying
in from Hijir. 'Sire,' the spirit shouted,
alighting. 'Sahar is lying down drunk
near the well; we have chained him
with steel cables as thick as the pillars
of the Temple. Of course, as soon as
he wakes up from his stupor, he will
break the cables like women's hairs.'

Quickly, Solomon mounted the
winged *jinn*, and was carried through
the air to the well of Hijir, just in time,
for Sahar's eyes were already open.
The king took his seal and pressed it

on the monster's neck. Sahar uttered cries of woe that shook the earth. Solomon comforted him: 'Do not fear, dear demon, I will set you free as soon as you have told me how to cut through metals without making any noise.'

Sahar answered: 'I do not know, but the raven does. All you have to do is take the eggs from a raven's nest and hide them under a crystal bowl. You will see, when the mother raven arrives, how she cuts it.'

The eggs had not been under the crystal bowl for long when the mother raven arrived, and in her bill was a mysterious stone called *samur*. No sooner had she knocked the bowl with it than the crystal split, and the bowl fell in two halves to the floor. 'Where did you get that stone, Mrs Raven?' asked the King. 'From a mountain far away in the west,' answered the raven.

Solomon ordered a squadron of his flying *jinns* to follow the raven to the mysterious western mountain and pick up as many of the *samur* stones as they could carry. When they came back, the *samurs* were handed out to the steel-cutters, the copper-wire clippers, and all the other skilled work-*jinns*, who from that moment worked noiselessly, cutting through thick metal like cheese. Sahar was released, and as the chains were unlocked, the colossus rose up into the sky effortlessly, uttering cries of jubilant joy that echoed in Asia. King Solomon ordered his builders, as soon as the Temple was completed, to construct a golden palace for himself.

Dibbuk (Dybbuk)

Literally 'sticky', because this devil is believed by some to stick to his victims as a parasite. This evil spirit is often mentioned in Jewish folk tales, sometimes as the soul of a dead person, sometimes as a demon who can take possession of a person, making him or her mad and dangerous. Hence the Jewish expression 'a *dibbuk* has entered him' when someone behaves hysterically. Amulets and incantations were thought necessary to protect children and especially women in childbirth against the Dibbuk, the Devil.

The *dibbuks* were spirits constantly in search of bodies to inhabit, so they were a type of vampire (q.v.). A *dibbuk* could be exorcised only by a *tsaddik*, or holy man, who would be asked to recite prayers over the possessed person. He would usually read Psalm 91: 'Thou shalt not be afraid for the terror by night' in Hebrew, then call loudly to the spirit to go and 'relinquish the body of this God-fearing person, in God's name'.

A *shofar* (ceremonial horn) might be blown to frighten the demon away. A bloody spot on the victim's right big toe, and a cracked nail betrayed the *dibbuk's* departure.

Dilmun

A land and a city, probably the Sumerian name for paradise.

Dog

The shepherds who came down from the hills to worship the baby Jesus had Syrian sheepdogs, looking like Scottish collies. The Egyptian dog descended from the jackals in very ancient times; it was called *tjesem* in ancient Egyptian and *saluki* today. It was often mummified and probably worshipped.

Dome of the Rock
See *Sakhra*.

Doomsday
In the Bible, doomsday is the day when God will finally destroy this world: 'he sent his seventh angel to pour out his vial into the air . . . and there were voices, thunders and lightnings . . . and there was a great earthquake . . . and the cities of the nations fell . . . and every island fled away and the mountains were not found . . . and there fell upon men a great hail, every stone about the weight of a talent' (Revelation 16:17–21).

In the Koran likewise, Doomsday is described in vivid detail: the day when the trumpet will be blown (6:73); when the firmament will start moving like molten metal (52:9; 70:8); when the sky will split and be rolled back (25:25; 21; 104); when earth and hills will move (73:14; 18:47; 52:10); when the angels will descend from heaven (25:22–5); when Hell will open (26:91). In both traditions, this destruction will be followed by the resurrection of the dead and their judgement by God. See also *Armageddon, Qiyama, Resurrection.*

Dove (Hebrew: *yonah*)
The messenger bird which Noah sent out through the window in the ark. The first time she found no ground for the sole of her foot (Genesis 8:8). The second time she returned with the leaf of an olive tree, a sign that the earth was greening again.

The dove coos sadly, hence 'mourning like a dove' (Isaiah 38:14). The dove was often used as a sacrifice (Genesis 15:9; Leviticus 12:6). Yet she was harmless (Matthew 10:16). The Holy Spirit has the bodily shape of a dove (Luke 3:22) when descending from the heavens.

The dove is Aphrodite's bird as a symbol of love. Doves mate frequently and visibly and display active courtship and mutual affection. Arab poets often use the theme of the gentle dove (*hamama*) as a messenger of love, peace and good luck. It is the symbol of sweetness, fidelity and attachment between spouses and siblings.

Drac (Draca)
An invisible female aquatic spirit which tempts women and children by means of baubles in order to lure them into the water and there devour them.

Dragon
A red dragon with seven heads and ten horns appears in Revelation 12:3. It wore seven crowns, so it ruled seven kingdoms. Its tail swept a third of the stars from the sky, throwing them onto the earth. Michael and his angels fought against it. It was 'that old serpent called the Devil and Satan and was cast out into the earth and his 'angels' were cast out with him. Three unclean spirits like frogs came out of the dragon's mouth' (Revelation 16:13). They were the spirits

of devils, working (false) miracles. Finally the dragon was thrown into the bottomless pit (see *Abyss*) for a thousand years by the angel with the key and the chain (Revelation 20:2).

Drauga (Drug, Druj)

Demon of falsehood in old Persian mythology. See *Druj*.

Dreams

In Arabic, *hulm* is the word for a bad dream or a sexual dream; *ru'ya* for a vision, and *manam* for a good dream. The Prophet Muhammad said: 'Good dreams are from God. Bad dreams are from the Devil. Tell your good dreams only to your good friends. Tell your bad dreams to nobody lest the evil spread, and pray to God for protection.'

The people of the Middle East have always believed that dreams are true messages if properly interpreted: they are God's signs (Job 33:15; Joel 2:28; 1 Kings 3:5; Matthew 1:20; 2:12). When kings have dreams, empires are at stake (Genesis 41; Daniel 2:4). In the Koran the dreams of the Pharaoh and his two servants are discussed (Sura 12) together with Joseph's interpretation. Muhammad too had a dream (Koran 48:27) in which presumably God showed him the ultimate victory of Islam. See *Ru'ya*.

There are in Arabic literature several hundred 'dream books' to be consulted for the daily interpretation of a person's dreams. Many people in the Middle East lie down to sleep in a mosque or near a saint's tomb, hoping to receive a dream revealing the future.

Druje (droudje, druge, duruge)

Demons (literally 'liars, false gods') who take possession of dead bodies rising from the nether world, unless the correct protective ceremonies have been performed to keep the body pure. The worst of these spirits is called Nasu, 'Carrion Fly'. Originally, Druje was a goddess.

Druze

The name of a religion now mainly found in Syria and the Lebanon, and of an adherent of that religion, plural 'Druzes'. The word derives from the Arabic *duruz*, plural of *darzi* or *darazi*, the servants and followers of the Fatimid Caliph Al-Hakim (996–1021). The Druzes believe that Al-Hakim was the last manifestation of God on earth, so that he was a perfect man. One day he will reappear and triumph over all his enemies, extend his empire over the whole earth and give eternal joy to all his worshippers. God has given superior intelligence to the Druze leaders. There is no better religion.

Dumuzi

A Sumerian god, called Tammuz in Babylonian and Adonis in Greek (qq.v.) The goddess of love and fertility, Inanna in Sumerian, Istar in Babylonian, Venus in Latin, fell in love with him, but he was abducted by the demons of the underworld to the land of death. Inanna decided to go in search of him, so she had to descend to the land of death, which has seven gates. At each of the gates she had to pay for her passage with a piece of garment because we all go to the land of death naked. Every year the goddess had to retrieve her husband from the clutches of death. In some versions of the myth she could only take her lover out of Hades by sacrificing her husband. This is the image of the earth shedding the leaves and flowers of the old season and decorating itself with fresh vegetation at each new spring.

Durra
See *Pearl*.

E

Ea

The Babylonian god of the earth and the waters, the master of wisdom and medical science, equivalent to Hirmis (q.v.). Ea is the oldest manifestation of the universal trickster-god, who deceives man by taking immortality from him. He is shown on the seals with streams of water and fish flowing from his shoulders, attended by a Janus-faced minister, the bird Anzu, and Ishtar as Venus rising.

Eagle

In antiquity, the eagle was the emblem, the personal manifestation, of the god of rain, lightning and thunder whom the Greeks called Zeus, the Romans Jupiter and the Hebrews Adonai. The double-headed eagle was the symbol of the Babylonian god Ningursu, ruler of storm and fertility. The Hittites, too, featured the double-headed eagle as their symbol, looking both east and west, to sunrise and sunset, thus spanning the earth. It remained the imperial symbol in the Austrian and Russian empires.

In the Avesta the eagle is said to perch on the Tree of Light (the Tree of Life), from which the sun rises.

The eagle is often depicted carrying the captive serpent, symbol of evil.

Eanna

The temple of Anu and Ishtar in Uruk.

Earth

The earth, according to the Prophet Muhammad, is composed of seven strata, *tabaqat*, the top one being the surface we call earth. The distance between each layer and the one below it is a 500-year journey (7 million km). It is stretched out like a carpet (Koran 2:20; 13:3; 78:6). It was thought to be a vast plain by the commentators of the Koran, circular and surrounded by *al-muhit*, the world ocean, which in turn is surrounded by the mountains of Kaf (Qaf), so that from God's point of view the earth looks like a saucer filled with water and 'a handful of sand' (Koran 39:67). After doomsday God will create another earth (14:49).

In the centre of the earth lies Jerusalem or, according to others, Mecca. Somewhere above the ocean the throne of Satan is suspended, where it will remain until doomsday.

Hidden deep down, somewhere in the south-western part of the earth, i.e., in Africa, is the Well of Life, from which only Khizr (q.v.) drank, so that he would live until doomsday.

Below this earth is the land of winds, where suffocating desert storms rage all the time. Sometimes they blow on earth emerging through a cave in the mountains. Thus the people of Ad (q.v.) were killed (Koran 69:6) and their land is now a desert in south-ern Arabia. The next layer below is filled with the stones of hell (Koran 2:22; 66:6). The fourth layer is full of sulphur, the fifth crawls with the serpents of Hell, the sixth with black scorpions as big as mules with ven-omous tails like spears. The seventh hell is inhabited by the devils (q.v.).

The earth rests on the shoulder of an angel of huge size, created by God for this purpose. His feet stand on a rock made of ruby stones. This rock in turn sits between the horns of a bull whose name is Kujuta. He stands on the back of a long fish whose name is Bahamut. It swims in an ocean which God created for the purpose. The ocean is supported by nothing; that is by God's will and by his power. To God that ocean is like only a drop of rain floating in the universe. God has created a special angel whose task it is to feed the big fish with smaller fish which have to be created every day. See also *Sandals*.

Earthquake
See *Zilzal*.

Eden
See *Adn*.

Egg
In the old Persian world-view (as related by Plutarch) the sky was a stone vault like an eggshell. Ahriman (q.v.) and his demons broke through this defensive structure and so good and evil are mixed.

Egypt
Numerous legends circulate in the Middle East telling of the wonders of ancient Egypt, which already had an ancient civilization before Noah and the flood. The Egyptian kings kept fabulous wealth in palaces under the ground, where they are still buried. You will be rich if you can find them. To that end one needs the secret code of the hieroglyphs. One also has to be very careful, for the Egyptians knew all about magic, so they could pro-tect those treasures effectively. Any thief approaching the treasures will be struck with total paralysis in the endless corridors of the pyramids. See *Koftarim, Koftim, Philemon*.

Ekur
The temple of the god Enlil in Nippus, Babylonia.

El' (*il*, plural *ilun* or *ylon*)
The ancient Semitic word for God (extended in Arabic to *ilah*, Hebrew *eloh*), found in Bab-El, 'Gate of God'. The chief god of the Canaanites. The Ugaritic is *il*, the Babylonian *ilu*, plural *ilun*, hence Bab-ilun, 'Gods' Gate'. El is especially prominent in the myths of Ugarit and Canaan, as the supreme god, comparable to Anu in Mesopotamia. El is often praise-named 'the bull-god'. We are

reminded of Zeus in Greece and Apis in Egypt. El presides over the council of the gods as the senior god whose blessing is needed for all undertakings. El is the creator of all things who has retired to heaven, remote from all disturbance. From beneath his throne flows the stream which divides into the main rivers of the Middle East. He is praised as the 'kind, compassionate father of men'.

Eleazar

'God Helps', third son of Aaron, first high priest of Israel (Exodus 6:23–9).

Eliah (Elias, Ilyas)

See *Elijah*, *Khizr*.

Elijah

In the Islamic tradition Ilyas or Ilyasin, son of Yasin, son of Harun. Others say he was identical with Idris, one of Noah's ancestors. Others again say he was identical with Al-Khizr (Khadir) who was Alexander's counsellor. Elijah was one of the greatest prophets of Israel (1 Kings 17–22). He predicted a great drought – probably due to over-grazing. When he had to hide from the king, God sent the ravens to feed him bread and meat. Then God provided flour and baking oil for many days in the house where Elijah lived (I Kings 17). Elijah brought the widow's son back to life after he had died. He built a large altar for the Lord and invited him to light the fire, which he did. At last a cloud like a man's hand appeared above the sea, and soon there was wind and rain, as Elijah had predicted.

In the wilderness under a juniper tree, Elijah lived his finest hour: an angel touched him bringing food and water. On Horeb, the Mount of God, Elijah heard 'the voice of thin silence' (1 Kings 19:12) and God was in it. God told him what his task was, and gave him courage. God burnt two companies of soldiers with their captains to ashes because they were not polite enough to Elijah. Elijah predicted to King Ahaziah that he would soon die, and he did (2 Kings 1:17).

Finally, Elijah went up to heaven in a chariot of fire with horses of fire (2 Kings 2:11). There are numerous legends told about Elijah by Jewish people today. See also *Khizr*.

Elisha

A biblical prophet, successor to Elijah (1 Kings 19:16). Elijah left his mantle in his disciple's hand as he took off on his chariot. Elisha whipped the river Jordan with this master's vestment and suddenly the river divided like an obedient servant to let the new master seer walk proudly across on dry feet (2 Kings 2:13). Elisha 'healed' a well by, curiously, pouring a jar full of salt into it. Probably the salt attracted the water. When a gang of bad boys mocked him, two she-bears arrived to tear them to pieces (2 Kings 2:24). To relieve the drought the Lord ordered Elisha to destroy the towns in the valley of Edom; to cut down all the trees; and to dig trenches across the whole area. It is a perfect procedure for obtaining water in an emergency, but it is a predatory policy, causing more desert in the end.

In 2 Kings 4:3–7, Elisha creates olive oil for a poor widow. Elisha was always ready to pray to God on behalf of needy people, and God granted their needs. He caused a woman to conceive and have the child she wanted so much. Years later, when the boy had died, Elisha brought him back to life (2 Kings 4:16–37).

Elixir

This word originates from the Arabic *al-iksir*, which in turn derives from the Greek *xerion*, 'dry substance, powder'. Arab doctors translating the Greek medical works into Arabic adopted the word to denote sprinkling powders applied to sore eyes, a very common illness in desert countries. It was also rubbed into the skin of young men in the hope that it would give them invincible courage and would make them irresistible to women. To this end the elixir was admixed with fox urine and – most effective of all – the sperm of lions: this latter was no doubt originally an African recipe. Skins and skeletons of snakes were likewise added, after drying and grinding them into powder.

It was believed by some of these alchemists that the correct rites and recitations accompanying the process would cause the generation of the *homunculus in vitro*, the image of a little man inside the test tube (see *Alchemy*). This little man was, of course, the spirit whose presence would make the owner powerful, fertile, irresistible and rich. The alchemists, being elderly scholars, were most interested in wealth, knowing that it would buy them power and women. Consequently, the elixir was most frequently pursued in the search

for gold. Numerous books have been written describing the methods by which the alchemists hoped to manufacture the only true elixir, the one that would turn a base metal (e.g. lead) into gold. It was believed that the ingredients should – or could – be vegetable matter including bread or dough, yeast and grain, as well as animal matter. Later, mainly metals were used, the 'right mixture' of which would produce the *metabole*, the transformation of low-class metal into gold. The elixir was added to the inert metal, in the way that a baker adds ferment-starter to dough which transforms the dough into edible bread after baking it at the right temperature for a set time. Some scholars believed that the elixir could also convert infidels to the true faith when taken orally, and give men immortal life.

Ellil

Sumerian god, son of the supreme god Anu, whom he succeeded. See also *Anzu, Ninurta*.

Elohim

In pre-Mosaic times, *elohim* was the collective Hebrew word for the gods, the Latin *di*, Arabic *al-aliha*. *Elohim* is the plural of *eloh*, 'god', already obsolete in Mosaic times. The word occurs in the meaning of 'household gods' in Genesis 31:29. See also 1 Samuel 28:13.

Empusa

A Greek demoness who may appear in the guise of a pretty girl with a donkey's hoof instead of her left foot, but she can also have a terrifying aspect. She enthrals men, making them weak.

Endor

The Witch of Endor was a celebrated fortune-teller who possessed the power of making ghosts appear and speak to her. Her most famous act was evoking the spirit of Samuel before King Saul (1 Samuel 28), after some gods were seen ascending (see *elohim*). We would now call her a shaman, not a witch.

Enki

Sumerian god of creation, wisdom and medicine who could restore the dead to life, for he was the source of all secret and magical knowledge of life and immortality. He was worshipped at Eridu, one of the world's first cities, and was called Ea (q.v.) in Babylonian, King of Apsu. Enki possessed the secret of *me*, 'culture, civilization', which is the genius of progress in knowledge to lead humanity. He invented civilization for the people and assigned to each his destiny. He created order in the cosmos. He filled the rivers with fish. He invented the plough and the yoke so that farmers could till the earth with oxen. He made the grain grow. He is depicted on a relief holding Zu, the storm-bird. Enki rose up from the Persian Gulf, as god of the fish. His wife was Ningursag; she gave him a daughter. He is the father of all plants.

Enkidu

Bosom friend and brother-in-arms of Gilgamesh (q.v.).

Enkimdu

The Sumerian god of farmers, landowners and grain growers.

Enlil

In Sumerian mythology, king of the gods, the lord who keeps his word, the sky-god who also rules the earth. However he did not like people except as slaves. When they became too numerous and noisy he decided to drown them in his great flood. Only Atrahasis (q.v.) survived.

Ennugi

Sumerian god of irrigation, of canals and dykes.

Enoch

1. The Bible has little to say about Enoch, the son of Cain, except that he built a city called Enoch (Genesis 4:17). In the Jewish mystic tradition, he was a righteous man who walked with God until he disappeared (Genesis 5:24). He was actually taken straight to heaven, so he never died. 'God took him to heaven since he was a pious man of faith and a prophet' (Hebrews 11:5; Jude 14). On his way to heaven, God showed him all the spheres of the firmament, and their inhabitants. These adventures have been described in the apocryphal Book of Enoch, which also contains jumbled dreams and prophesies, of which the Hebrew and Greek versions have been destroyed so that the Ethiopic version is the most complete one we possess. This book has had a lasting influence in world literature.

2. Henoch, the Arabic Akhnukh or Hanukj, in the Islamic tradition identified with Idris, (q.v.). The Arabic

Mi'raj (q.v.). is clearly a version of the same tale with Muhammad as the traveller and Jibril as the guide. This in turn has influenced Dante's *Divine Comedy*, in which Dante travels through the universe with his guide. Originally, Enoch's myth is probably an ancient account of the prehistoric shaman's journey to heaven, to receive God's instruction.

Enushirgal
Temple of the moon-god in Sumerian Ur.

Ephod
1. A priestly garment (Exodus 28:6; 39:2; Judges 8:27; 2 Samuel 6:14).
2. An idol, an object of idolatrous worship (Judges 17:5).

Eraj (Iraj)
A king of Iran, son of Fredhon (Faridun) (q.v.). Eraj is the Persian form of the name Arya. Eraj was treacherously killed by his two brothers, Salm and Tur, but was avenged a long time later by his nephew Manush Chithra (Manuchihir), who re-established Iran. All these events occur in epic myths so that it is impossible to date them historically.

Erebos
The Greek name for the land of darkness where the dead reside, under the earth.

Ereshkigal (Ninmenna)
The Babylonian Persephone, spouse of Nergal, the god of the dead in the Underworld. As Mesopotamian goddess of the nether world, queen of the lower regions, she is often praised in hymns.

One day Nergal was sent to her from heaven with an offering of food. They fell in love with each other, and when he had to leave, she was in tears and threatened Anu, the supreme god, that she would revive all the dead, over whom she ruled, and send them back to earth, 'so that they will outnumber the living', unless Nergal was sent back to her, for ever, as a husband. Her minister Namtar had to go to heaven as her messenger, for Ereshkigal felt that she was already pregnant. At last Nergal came storming down the stairs, broke down the seven gates and burst into the goddess' palace straight into her passionate embrace, 'to wipe her tears'.

Eridan
A river in the nether world.

Eridu
A Mesopotamian city, the cult centre of the wise earth-god Ea-Enki.

Erra
Babylonian god of war, death and other disasters. His greatest ally was famine caused by long drought. He may be identified with Nergal, the god of death. He expressed death himself symbolically by his continuous lethargy as he lay in a drunken stupor.

War has always been the major cause of death throughout history. Erra was supplicated to ward off pestilence and other calamities. One of the earliest known epic poems to come to light, written on clay tablets, is the Epic of Erra. At the opening of the epic, Erra sits in his palace while his weapons, which are in reality minor gods called the *sibitti*, complain about his inaction. Erra persuades the old king-god of Babylon to visit his old craftsmen in the land of Apsu beneath the earth. Erra is just on the point of destroying Babylonia when old Ishum, minister of Marduk, warns him: 'Those who make war are the ignorant/War kills the priests and the sinless . . .' Although he has already started devastating the country, Erra is pacified by the wise minister and calls off the hounds of war. Marduk returns to peace. See also *Sibitti*.

Eshm
See *Aeshma*.

Essenes
According to the historian Flavius Josephus (first century AD), one of 'the three philosophical sects among the Jews' (the others were the Pharisees and the Sadducees). Perhaps their name derives from the Greek *hoisoi*, 'saintly people'. They formed monastic groups bound together by oaths of piety, justice, obedience and honesty. They had three main rules: Love God; Love virtue; and Love people. They were ascetics; the majority were celibates, about 4000 people.

The discovery in 1947 of eleven caves in the rocks on the western banks of the Dead Sea, containing ten complete scrolls and thousands of fragments written in ancient Hebrew dating to the beginning of the Christian era, has suddenly shed new light on the Essenes, who were probably the original owners of the scrolls. When Palestine (then called Judea; Decapolis is roughly what we now call Jordan) rebelled against Rome and was crushed by Vespasian (70 AD), the Essenes seem to have hidden their precious manuscripts in a dozen jars in those caves and fled. Their fragile fraternity was no match for the Roman administration. They were devoted to the observance of 'perfect holiness', looking away from this violent world to God's peace in heaven. The teacher of righteousness was the − still unidentified − founder of the community. These Essenes called themselves the only observers of the pure laws of Moses and so the true Israel, who had inherited the covenant with God and with it, salvation. They were the faithful 'remnant' (see 1 Kings 19:18). Some may have fled to Masada (q.v). See *Qumran*.

Etana
Thirteenth god-king of the Sumerian dynasty ruling the city of Kish. Though he was appointed by Anu and prayed daily to Shamash the sun-god, he had no son. Shamash directed him to an eagle who had been snared by a snake. Etana freed the eagle who, in gratitude, carried the king on his back to heaven. There, Etana, in front of the throne of Ishtar, begged for a son. She gave him the plant of birth, which he probably had to eat together with his wife. We know from history that Etana had a son. An incomplete epic in Babylonian about his exploits has been discovered.

Ethiopia

This is the translation of the Hebrew name Kush in Genesis 2:13. However the location of Kush has never been identified, nor do we know who the Cushites were. They must not be confused with the people now called Chushitic, i.e. the Afar-Danakil, Galla-Oromo, Somali and others. The 'Ethiopian' wife of Moses (Numbers 12:1) was called a 'Cushite' in the Hebrew text.

Euphrates (Hebrew: *Perat*, Arabic and Persian: *Furat*)

The western of the two rivers of Mesopotamia. It is also named as one of the rivers flowing down from the Garden of Eden (Genesis 2:14). Likewise in the Islamic tradition it is one of the four rivers whose source is in paradise under the *Sidrat al Muntaha*, the Tree of Life and Death.

Eve

1. In the Bible Eve was created out of Adam's rib, just a piece of bone (Genesis 2:21). It was taken for granted that she must be Adam's wife; her own wishes were not consulted. Eve took the forbidden fruit because it looked good to eat (Genesis 3:6). Adam offered no resistance although he knew he must obey God.

In the apocryphal accretions to the biblical narratives, in the post-biblical period, various characters were added or changed. Best known is the mysterious Lilith (q.v.) who was either Adam's first wife, or his secret sweetheart while Eve was talking to the serpent. Satan gained access to the heavenly garden (paradise was surrounded by a wall with only one gate; Satan was specifically excluded from it by God) by stealth, in the shape of a small snake or even smaller insect (in the Islamic tradition). Once inside (according to a later, apocryphal tradition), Satan took the shape of a handsome angel called Lucifer ('Morning Star') and became friendly with Eve during the hours when Adam was away talking to God or (later) to Lilith.

The reader can see the first human drama developing. Eve fell in love with the dashing Lucifer rather than with the dull and pious Adam. Lucifer taught her how to make love and their first son, Cain, was a devil's child, which explains his murderous character satisfactorily. God did not accept his sacrifice and so Cain slew his younger brother Abel who *was* the son of Adam. Thus Satan's 'temptation of Eve' must be taken literally as a physical seduction.

Cain's murder of Abel and his subsequent banishment was Eve's last punishment for eating the apple. Thus she was punished three times (by expulsion from paradise, by having to give birth in labour without expert assistance, and by seeing her son killed and another removed from her) while Adam was punished only twice – he did not have to bear children.

2. In the old Persian tradition the first woman is called Mashyane. Initially man and woman were one body, growing in the leaves of a plant like a cabbage. Finally God separated them and this part of the myth is parallel to the Biblical tale of God carving Eve out of Adam. God told Mashye (Adam) (q.v.) and Mashyane (Eve) to be good and never to have anything

to do with the spirit of evil, Ahriman (q.v.). Of course Ahriman did 'alter their thoughts' so they began to lie (like Adam and Eve). Finally, God caused them to have children and they populated the earth.

3. The Arabic equivalent is Haiwa. She is not mentioned by name in the Koran, but referred to as Adam's spouse in 2:35; 7:189. God created Eve as a spouse for Adam so that he could live with her in the Garden, but, said God: 'Do not approach this tree.' The tree (or shrub?) had very sweet fruits, the best in the garden, called *qamh*, 'wheat', or perhaps we should translate it as 'seed'. Eve was tempted by Satan who had become her friend by his glib talking, to eat from the tree, because, he said, 'only by eating this fruit will you have children'. Since Eve, according to the Islamic tradition, wanted children (like all women, it is believed), she took the fruit and ate it. Adam followed her, though hesitantly because men are more inclined than women to obey God (so the Islamic writers imply). Eve was told by God that she must henceforth obey her husband and follow him to earth. Earth was a bleak place at that time, nothing but rocks and thorn bushes. Eve learned to make a fire and to cook the food which Adam brought home: animals he had hunted (later they received cattle) and grain he had cultivated and from which she baked bread.

Eve was 'covered' by Adam and gave birth to forty children, twenty sets of twins, each set a boy and a girl. Her eldest son Kabil (Cain) (q.v.) later slew his younger brother Abil (Abel) (q.v.). In this way she was punished for having eaten of the forbidden fruit. Islamic writers always emphasize that women must cover their bodies from head to toe, 'otherwise they would tempt men *again*'.

Exorcism

From the Greek *ex-orkizein*, 'to swear out'. This meant literally that the exorcist swore an oath by his god or other protecting spirit in order to force the evil spirit magically out of the body of a person possessed by such a spirit; compare Luke 8; 2:36–40. The exorcist must have a protecting spirit who is stronger than the evil spirit, otherwise he will be unable to drive it out. Islam forbids all forms of exorcism except by prayer.

Ezekiel

'God will strengthen'. A prophet of Israel in the time of its exile in the land of the Chaldeans. The first chapter of the Book of Ezekiel describes his vision of the universe, the galaxies and the solar system. We owe to Ezekiel the origin of the phrase 'wheels within wheels' (1:6). He had a vision of what seems to have been the signs of the zodiac projected on the firmament. Similar descriptions of the universe have come to us only from India. Ezekiel saw the glory of God above Jerusalem and prophesied what he had seen to his poor exiled people who lived in slavery (Ezekiel 11:24).

F

Fadl (fazl, fazal)
'Grace, favour'. The Islamic word for God's grace, by which we live. (Koran 2:244; 10:58.)

Fakir (faqir)
Literally, 'poor man', the same as *darwish* (q.v.). A fakir is in need of mercy. Many fakirs are men of religion who do not work for money but recite prayers and embrace asceticism for which they receive alms.

Fall
The fall of Adam (q.v.) is described in the Koran (2:36). There is an implication of 'going back' in it (see 2:61) as if Adam fell back onto earth. That is indeed of necessity the reconstruction of the legend. Adam was created on, and out of, the earth, then taken to heaven to live a peaceful life in the Garden. He proved himself unworthy to live in that exalted place so he was told to 'go down'. Thus, for the Islamic mystic writers in Arabic, the word 'fall' takes on the meaning of the fall of the unworthy soul back to earth from heaven. In the process of a human birth the soul 'falls' into its earthly existence. The souls live in a state of bliss before birth. See *Pre-existence*.

Familiar
A spirit that 'belongs' to a witch or sorcerer (Leviticus 19:31); sorcery is strictly forbidden in the law of Moses. According to Deuteronomy 18:11, one person may consult several familiar spirits. In Isaiah 8:19 it appears that in spite of repeated prohibitions the people of Israel still consulted 'those that have familiar spirits and wizards that peep and mutter'. In Acts 16:16, a 'damsel with a spirit of divination' is liberated by Paul who commands the spirit to come out of her. See *Fortune-telling*.

Fana
'Extinction, fading away'. The last stage of the Sufi's long spiritual journey on the way to the divine proximity. No one can see God and live, so the Sufi has to accept that he will die at that moment, but he knows that that momentary experience is well worth a lifetime of asceticism. *Fana'* is also the opposite of *Baqa'* (q.v.). *Fana'* thus expresses the perishable, fleeting condition of this short life.

Faraqlit

Arabic form of the Greek word Para-kleitos, 'famous', which Muslim scholars regard as a reference to Ahmad, the celestial name of their Prophet Muhammad, 'the Praised One'. They believe that by this name Jesus announced the coming Muhammad.

Faridun (Pahlavi: *Fredhon*, Old Persian: *Thraitauna*)

Handsome young king of Iran in the *Shahname*. He chased the evil tyrant Dahhak (Dahaka, q.v.) from his palace and sired three sons with the tyrant's favorite wives, Ahaharnaz and Aranvaz. Their names were Salm, Tur and Iraj or Eraj, among whom he divided his empire: Asia for Tur, the west for Salm, Iran and Arabia for Eraj.

Fate

See *Qadar, Qisma.*

Father

God as the father is a biblical concept, seldom found in other religions except those where the supreme god is originally the first ancestor, usually not a historical person. It is tempting to apply this concept of the primeval ancestor to the father-god of Israel, but there is not enough evidence to sustain it. Nor is it in line with the old Semitic concept of the heavenly God. In any case, the Christians have adopted this relationship of the worshipper to his God as that of a child to his father. Especially when the worshipper identifies relationally with Jesus as the son of God, he feels ready to be sacrificed, just as Abraham's son was ready to be sacrificed, knowing his father loved him. This filial relationship is unknown in Islam. The Koran denies any paternity in relation to God. The worshipper is *abd-allah* 'slave of God', and his worship is *ibada* 'slavery, service'. God has absolute power over all his creatures. He is the master, the owner. See *God.*

Fatiha

The opening chapter of the Koran; Fatiha means 'the opening'. It is recited daily during the regular prayers and so it is the most recited prayer in Islam. Its recital earns great merit.

Fatima (Fatma, Fatuma)

Fatima bint Muhammad was the eldest surviving daughter of the Prophet of Islam by his first wife Khadija. When God commanded Muhammad to marry her to his cousin Ali ibn Abi Talib, the family was very happy. Indeed the marriage was concluded first in heaven with Jibril (q.v.) acting as Fatima's *wali* (legal representative). Jibril was sent down with a basket full of the finest bridal clothes for Fatima and a box full of jewels from paradise as *mahar*, bride-price. However, Fatima would not be happy until God had granted her the favour of being the intercessor for all the women of Islam, just as her father was the intercessor (*Shufa'*) for all the men. God agreed. Thus Fatima was married to her cousin Ali, the first imam, the greatest hero and demon-slayer of Islam.

Fatima had two sons, Hasan and Husayn, often called Al-Hasanayn 'the two Hasans', the second and third imams, who were the apples of their grandfather the Prophet Muhammad's eye. Fatima told her sons many heavenly secrets that she alone knew, because her soul had lived in paradise before she was born, in the shape of an apple hanging on a tree in heaven. She died six months after her father while the angels sang to welcome her to heaven.

Fear (Arabic: *khauf*)

The 'fear of God', should probably be translated as 'respect for God', which in many ancient languages is the same word. 'Shyness' is also often rendered as 'fear'.

In the city of Mecca the annual pilgrimage is often accompanied by an outbreak of disease, in which many die. One day the gatekeeper of the city gate admitted the ghostly figure of fear into the city. She was in the midst of a group of pilgrims. Later he saw the terrifying apparition of disease approaching, closely followed by death. The fearless guard stopped them saying: 'You two will make many victims in the city. I will not admit you.' However, disease protested that she would make only 500 people sick. Thereupon death promised that he would take no more souls than those 500 sick. So the gatekeeper of Mecca admitted them, since death is always God's will.

After the pilgrimage was over, the two horrifying figures left the city. The guard accused them of taking thousands of lives instead of the promised 500. 'We took only 500,' answered disease. 'But thousands died of fear, whom you had already let through. More people die of fright than of disease.'

Fida'i

One who has vowed to give himself as a ransom (Arabic: *fida'*) for the freedom of his loved ones. *Fida'i* is the Islamic equivalent of the Japanese *kamikaze*, the young man who has vowed to lay down his life for his nation, his fatherland or his religion.

Fig

This sweet, fleshy fruit, loved by insects, is undoubtedly a symbol of fertility, so Adam and Eve cover their 'figs' with fig leaves. It may well have been the forbidden fruit itself. The fig tree concealed Mary and her infant in her trunk during their flight to Egypt. See *Fruit*.

Firdaus

'Paradise' (Koran 18:107; 23:11). The word is of Persian origin. It constitutes the highest level of celestial bliss, that is, of spiritual perception.

Firdausi, Abul Qasim

Born in Tus about 940 and died there in or before 1025. He was the greatest epic poet of Persia, who assembled in no fewer than 120,000 lines in his *Shahname* (*Book of Kings*) all the oral and written traditions of the kings of Persia from antiquity to the Middle Ages, before Islam. It is our major source book for the tales of the heroes and mythical kings of ancient Persia. All the later poets of Persia quote Firdausi, mentioning the sagas of his great kings. Omar Khayyam (q.v.), for example, refers several times to the great mythical kings Jamshyd and Kaikobad.

Fire (Old Persian: *atash* or *atesh*)
Worshipped before Zoroaster, as the deity of the hearth which was kept burning, and associated with purity and justice. Fire temples, *dadgah*, were instituted after 500 BC.

One of the first things God created, according to the Islamic tradition was fire. As soon as it existed, the fire raged fiercely, roaring: 'Lord! Send me all your sinners, all those who disobeyed you and I will punish them forever after!' Out of fire, God created Iblis, the Shaytan (q.v.), who was very proud of being a fire-spirit, since the fire was the element of purity. In the beginning Iblis (Lucifer) was God's most faithful servant. He still lives in the hottest part of the fire.

Fir Wood
See *Pine*.

Fish
1. 'The Lord had prepared a great fish to swallow up Jonah.' This theme was taken up by the Koran 37:142. Yunus (Jonah) (q.v.) is called, in the Islamic tradition, 'twice-born', once from his mother, once from the fish. Yunus was thus raised from his grave (the fish) by God, to live a better life.
2. For the early Christians the fish was the symbol of Christ and so of their religion, since the first letters of the words *Iesus Christos, Theou Uios Soter* ('Jesus Christ, God's Son, Saviour') in Greek letters, form the Greek word *ichthus*, 'fish'. A drawing of a fish was a secret sign of the faith. Thus, if we can be reborn in Christ we shall be saved.

Flies
Arab scholars in the Middle Ages wrote that flies, which can be seen copulating in mid-air, give birth to live young; others maintained (as did European writers of that time) that flies just grew in cowdung or in other putrescent substances including human flesh afflicted with disease, or in the bodies of certain animals such as lions, dogs, camels, horses and cattle by spontaneous generation. It was believed that flies lived no longer than 40 days, and that they hunted bugs and gnats in houses, thus making them habitable for humans. Flies were also caught and roasted, then powdered, the resulting black powder being rubbed on the skin against insect bites, and also used by women to draw around their eyes for beauty.

In hell (q.v.) there are numerous flies of enormous size which torture the sinners. For the lord of the flies see *Belzebub*.

Flood
1. Tablet XI of the text of the great Gilgamesh epic describes the great flood which, as George Smith and Friedrich Delitzsch discovered around the turn of the century, is about a thousand years older than the biblical tale of Noah in Genesis. 6. The Babylonian epic introduces the immortal sage Uta-Napishtim (in Sumerian called Ziusudra) (q.v.). The gods decided one day to drown all

human beings because they were noisy. The god Ea (Enki) (q.v.), however, secretly descended to his favourite – Uta-Napishtim – and told him to build a ship, giving him the exact measurements and other instructions: 'Dismantle your house, build a boat, leave your possessions, look for your living ones to save them, put the seeds of all that lives in your boat!' – a remarkably practical piece of advice, such as one needs when disaster is imminent!

Uta-Napishtim did as he was advised, adding gold and silver to his cargo. For six days and seven nights the storm blew. After that, the wind and sea became calm once more. The flood then receded. Silence reigned. All humanity had returned to clay. Uta-Napishtim then sent out a dove followed by a swallow and a raven. The first two returned but the raven did not. The flood had by then diminished and land had become visible.

The description of the great flood in the Sumerian tablets is splendid. It was first published by Arno Poebel in 1914:

All the windstorms, exceedingly powerful, attacked as one
At the same time the floods swept over the cult-centres
For seven days and nights the boat was tossed about . . .

Ziusudra (Zisutra, q.v.) who has built his boat with instructions from the god of wisdom, Enki, 'Opens a window in his boat . . . [until] Utu the sun-god sends his rays of light into the boat.' Ziusudra then worshipped Utu.

2. God sent a flood to punish the people of Egypt for the obstinacy of their ruler in Musa's time (Koran 7:133).

Fortune-Telling (Arabic: *kahana*)
The Prophet Muhammad forbade this practice. See *Geomancy*.

Frashegird
'Making wonderful', restoring to goodness, in old Persian mythology: the dead will be restored to life at the end of time by Astvat-Ereta (q.v.).

Fravashi
Old Persian for 'soul'. The annual festival of Hamaspathmaedaya was the Persian 'All-Souls'.

Fredhon See Faridun

Frog
For the ancient Egyptians the frog represented the gentle goddess of childbirth, Heket, often depicted with a frog's head, an association with the frog's exceptional fertility. With her husband Khnum she was the creator of human beings in the oldest traditions.

Fruit
The fruit, or, in the Islamic tradition, 'the tree', is the forbidden food for Adam and Eve. The identity of this tree and its offensive fruit is still hotly debated among the scholars of Islam. Some think it was the fig tree, the leaf of which supplied the first clothing for the first couple. Others say it must have been the bread tree. In those days wheat still grew on the bread tree, each of whose branches sprouted seven golden ears,

each of which produced five snow-white grains of wheat. Having been tempted, Eve tried one grain and liked it better than anything else. So the forbidden fruit was seed! Later, Adam had to work for his bread.

Fuls
An idol of the Banu Tayy, destroyed by Ali.

Funeral Prayers
See *Khatma*.

G

Gabriel
'Man of God', one of the chief angels in the Bible. He is a messenger from God bringing understanding and enlightenment (Daniel 9:23). He announced to Zechariah the birth of John the Baptist (Luke 1:19) and to Mary the birth of Jesus (Luke 1:24). See also *Jibril*.

Gardens
'God planted a garden eastward in Eden.' (Genesis 2:8; 13:10). No doubt 'eastward' refers to the land of the sunrise. The sun-god in many religions is believed to own a wonderful garden, of which we see only the colourful reflection at dawn.

The Koran refers to gardens as signs and gifts from Allah (6:99; 23:19; 36:34; 71:12; 78:16), especially the vines in them. For the garden of paradise, see *Paradise*, *Janna* and *Adn*.

Gathas
A collection of seventeen psalms in old Persian, composed by Zarathustra (q.v.) in praise of Ahura Mazda (q.v.). They are true poetry, full of zeal and devotion, demonstrating his consciousness of his vocation and of his task to preach God's law on earth.

Gayomard
From the old Persian *gayo*, 'life' and *maretan*, 'mortal', the first man, the first mortal ancestor.

Gaza
A city once built by the Philistines. The strongman Samson unhinged its main gates. Its Palaces will be destroyed by fire, says the prophet Amos (1:7). Gaza was an object of hate for the prophets Jeremiah, Zephaniah and Zechariah, probably because it resisted conquest by the Israelites.

Gazelle
'Swift as the roe' (2 Samuel 2:18) refers to the gazelle, not the roebuck. The latter is a shy forest deer, while the gazelle is the swift desert antelope which outruns the leopard.

Persian poets refer to the 'gazelle', meaning the beloved lady. 'Gazelle-eyed' or 'doe-eyed' is a common English rendering for the koranic *huri-al-'ayn*, see *Huri*.

The lover-poet Majnun kept the

company of tender gazelles in the desert. The English 'gazelle' derives from the Arabic *ghazal*, often a girl's name.

Gehenna

'Place of Torment', just south-west of Jerusalem, where children were sacrificed to Moloch (q.v.), the god of wealth. See Leviticus 18:21; 20:2; 2 Kings 23:10; Jeremiah 32:35. See also *Gehinnom*.

Gehinnom

'Valley of Hinnom' (Jeremiah 32:35) where 'abominations' took place, see *Moloch*. Perhaps many dead bodies were left there, after torture in the flames, so that Gehinnom became another word for hell. The Hebrew word Gehinnom was adopted into Arabic as Jahannam (q.v.). See *Gehenna, Hell, Sheol, Hades*.

Genii

Spirits, see *Jinns*.

Gentiles

The original meaning of this Latin word is 'tribes'. It translates the Hebrew *goyim*, meaning non-Jews. For the Jews all others were tribal people, just as the Romans called non-Romans *nationes*, 'nationalities'. The Muslims refer to non-Muslims as *juhhal*, 'ignorants', and to those who know Islam but have rejected it as *kafirs*, 'infidels'. It is only the Christians who regard the gentiles as their equals who will one day become fellow-citizens of the saints (Ephesians 2:11).

Gentleness

The ideal behaviour for all Christians, as advocated by Paul in 2 Timothy 2:24–25: 'patience and meekness'; Titus 3:2: 'Showing meekness to all men'; 'Wisdom is gentle' (James 3:17).

Geomancy (Arabic: *'ilm al-raml*)

Divination by means of configurations in the earth. The diviner will order his boy to draw numerous lines in the sand in all directions and of all shapes until he has forgotten how many there are. He will then tell the boy to wipe them out two at a time. If there are two left, success will crown the enterprise concerning which the diviner was queried; if one, it will fail. Later, many other forms of geomancy were developed in the Middle East, but this is the original Arabian manner of sand-divining.

Ghaddar

A (female?) demon in the deserts of the Red Sea countries where it catches travellers and tortures them by devouring their genitals.

Ghouls (ghul, ghool)

This Arabic word denotes a creature living in the wilderness where it leads travellers astray by taking on different forms. Some ghouls also devour their victims, others flee when seeing a man. They may be small, riding on hares, or on swift ostriches. If a man meets a ghoul, he has to kill it by a single blow; a second blow will restore it to life. It has the hooves of a donkey, otherwise it can change into any shape, usually to bring misfortune on

---

people. Ghouls can be male or female, the female being called *ghoula* or *si'la*. These females sometimes fall in love with human hunters lost in the forest, and carry them away to their caves in the hills to make love to them. Male ghouls also pick up human girls and carry them off to their caves deep in the mountains, where they seduce them with gold and diamonds and other ornaments. The fruits of these unions are a new race of savages, fierce and fast in hunting and killing, and prone to rape human girls.

One type of ghoul is the *udar*, a male monster which sexually assaults men in the desert. If, as a result of this monstrous rape, the victim develops worms in his anus, he will surely die. The only way to escape these monsters is by reciting the holy names of God unceasingly. Men who are not constant in prayer will be seized by *udars* who play with them like cats with mice.

Ghouls will also hunt people in the marshes of Iraq and eat them. In North Africa they are said to dig up corpses at night, to eat. God condemned them for this sin and made them look as ugly and as black as the carrion they ate. They are not children of Adam, i.e. not human beings.

When the Prophet Muhammad sent his first followers as immigrants to Ethiopia, he sent Ali to accompany them, and there, in the mountains, Ali had to do battle against the ghouls who blocked their path, until he slew their king with his double-bladed sword and drove them away. They still live there in the hills, we are told.

Giants
See *Watchers*.

Gilgamesh
The great hero of a Sumerian epic, the original version of which dates from about 2150 BC. It was the first piece of literature to have been translated into Babylonian, Hittite, Hurrian, Elamite and Ugaritic. Gilgamesh was the forerunner of Odysseus and Enkidu, his friend, of the biblical Samson.

The epic was discovered in 1872 by George Smith, then 32, among the tablets in the Assyriological archaeology section of the British Museum. He first translated the history of the flood (q.v.). The fact that the history of the great flood first occurred in a non-divinely inspired text composed well before the Bible (some thousand years earlier) provoked a storm of protest in which even the German Emperor became involved, threatening Dr Freidrich Delitsch after the latter gave a revelatory lecture, 'Babel and Bibel' in Halle in 1902.

Gilgamesh was king of Uruk sometime before 2500 BC. He was the son of the goddess Ninsun and the god Lugalbanda (or Kullabu). He built the city walls of Uruk, but to do it he recruited all the young men. The discontented citizens prayed to the mother-goddess Aruru, who created a rival hero: the muscular warrior Enkidu (q.v.). This wild man had to be tamed by a strong-willed sexwoman. (The translators describe this woman, whose name was Shamhat, as a *betaera*, a 'wench' or 'harlot'. She was certainly not a prostitute in the modern sense.) Then Enkidu was sent to challenge Gilgamesh. The two wrestled but they were of equal strength so they became friends and decided to go out in search of adventure together. They thought the giant Humbaba of the pine forest would be a worthy opponent. The wise men of Uruk thought it was foolish of them to venture into the deep pine forest, which at that time still covered the mountains of what is now Kurdistan, and which was full of wolves and bears, but the two friends went anyway, slew the forest giant with divine assistance, and came back to Uruk triumphant.

Gilgamesh had a bath and put on fresh clothes, after which he looked so strong and handsome that Ishtar (q.v.) the goddess of love, fell in love with him. She made advances, proposing marriage but he jilted her, knowing how many of her previous lovers were dead in Hades. Deeply insulted, Ishtar flew to heaven and complained to her father Anu, the supreme god, about the indignity she has had suffered from a mortal. Anu sent a pestilence to Uruk, which killed hundreds of people. This plague came in the shape of a bull, but Enkidu and Gilgamesh subdued it and the horns soon decorated the palace at Uruk.

Ishtar was furious that her father's bull had been killed. Enkidu had a dream in which he heard the gods decree that either Gilgamesh or Enkidu would have to die. He fell ill and on the thirteenth day he died. Gilgamesh was inconsolable as he buried his friend. Then he decided to go and ask Uta-Napishtim (q.v.), the only man who survived the great flood, how a man can achieve immortality. After a long and hazardous journey he reached the coast, a beautiful land with colourful flowers. Here he met Sifuri who told him that Ur-Shanabi (q.v.) was the only sailor who knew the sea.

When Gilgamesh finally found Ur-Shanabi, the latter instructed him to build a ship. When it was eventually finished, Ur-Shanabi navigated it across the sea to the land where Uta-Napishtim lived.

He received Gilgamesh courteously and told him the long history of the great flood and how he survived it, so that the god Ellil finally agreed to make him immortal, together with his wife. As a parting present, Uta-Napishtim gave Gilgamesh what he had come for: the plant of life. Grateful, Gilgamesh sailed back to his own coast, guided by Ur-Shanabi. But Alas! The wonder plant, which grew only on the bottom of the sea, was stolen by a snake. Gilgamesh wept as he realized that he had now lost his chance of becoming immortal; the sweet-scented herb of eternal life had eluded him. He did arrive home, however, and proudly showed his guide the walls of Uruk.

So ends the great epic of Gilgamesh, one of the greatest literary works ever written, an example for all the literatures of later times.

Glass

'We now see through a glass darkly, but then we shall see face to face' (1 Corinthians 13:12). 'Beholding as in a glass the glory of the Lord' (2 Corinthians 3:18). It was believed by the peoples of antiquity that in a mirror one could see the other world, and Paul's words are a symbolic reflection of that idea. When the heart is veiled by ignorance and egotism the mirror looks dark but the faithful will see the face of glory.

Gnosis
'Knowledge', especially the mystic knowledge which led to salvation. Gnosticism, the doctrine that gnosis is necessary for salvation, flourished in the first Christian centuries. Human spirits, the Gnostics believed, are sparks of divine light, fallen upon earth. The material world was evil, they thought, while the spiritual world was good and created by the God of truth. See *Ma'rifa*.

Goat-God (Pan)
The she-goat Amaltheia suckled Zeus when he was still a child, on Mount Ida in Crete. Her skin became the Aegis, Zeus' shield which protected Athena. The male goat was widely worshipped in early Middle Eastern religions as the god of fertility. One of the first domestic animals, the goat was often sacrificed as an atonement offering, hence the concept of 'scapegoat'.

Contrary to Matthew 25, the goat-god was a beneficent deity. Women in some tribes let him copulate with them, hoping to become fertile. Some scholars believe the goat-god is the oldest form of the deity who later, in Christian times, became identified with the goat-hoofed Satan. The female goat-deity was also worshipped in the Middle East. The Romans identified her with Juno–Hera.

God
In antiquity most people accepted that there was a multitude of gods. Still today in India the traveller is told that there are hundreds of gods, and it was like that throughout the world until Zarathustra (q.v.) conceived the idea of two gods, one good, one evil. Good people must worship Ahura Mazda (q.v.), the good god and only him.

This belief was adopted by the Alchaemenids when they became rulers of Persia. Among their new subjects were the Jews, both the exiles in Babylon and those who had stayed behind in Israel. Did they take over the worship of the one God from the Persians? They did adopt the concept of paradise, and of life on earth as a struggle between good and evil. Meanwhile the Greek philosophers had come to the conclusion that there was only one supreme being, whom they referred to as *ho Theos*, 'the God'. The Stoics taught this and the Roman intellectuals adopted it.

The religion of the peasants in these countries remained much as it had always been: the ritual worship of local gods. Even in Israel and Judea it is clear from the books of Samuel and Kings that the rural people continued worshipping the ancient gods Baal, Ishtar, Moloch (q.v.) and many others. The theology of the one God was restricted to the upper classes, the priests, scribes, courtiers and kings. Even the kings were often idolators, at the instigation of their mothers or wives we are told, as in the case of Solomon himself. Why the worship of idols, of numerous images, was so much more attractive that even intelligent men found it irresistible, remains a mystery.

The first man to have an intimate relationship with God was Noah (Genesis 6:9; 9:1), but the relationship became continous only from Abraham onwards. Later generations of Jews prayed to the God of Abraham, Isaac and Jacob, suggesting that they had 'inherited' their God from their forefathers. That was the custom among ancient nations. No one could be converted to a god other than that which his father had worshipped before him. From Abraham's day onwards, God remained *the* God of Israel, that is Jacob and his dynasty.

There are theologians who teach that the proper historical worship of the one God began only with Moses; Jacob and his ancestors were just mythical patriarchs. It is certainly only to Moses that God names himself as YHWH (q.v.) (Exodus 3:14–16). This YHWH may have been pronounced Yahweh or Yahuh. In the latter case it may have been an invocation, a call-word or an exultation at experiencing God as a near presence. After Moses the ideal of worshipping the one God remained the true religion of Israel throughout its history, even though many Jews lapsed.

The New Testament introduced a new concept which was hateful to the Jews: Jesus as the son of God (Matthew 3:17; John 1:14; 10:30–38). God begot a son with the Virgin Mary and this son was the word of God (i.e. that which causes creation) dressed in flesh. Muhammad could never accept this concept of God procreating with a woman, so the Koran says: 'He did not beget. He was not born.'

The Christianity of the Middle Ages was even further removed from strict Jewish monotheism. Some 365 saints and the Virgin Mary were worshipped, in addition to Jesus. These holy people had their shrines in numerous places where the pagan gods had previously been worshipped. See also *Aliha, Sanam, Idols, Elohim.*

Gog and Magog
Ezekiel (38; 39:1–16) prophesied that Gog, Magog and other savage tribes would one day invade the peaceful land of Israel and lay it to waste. God would, in his fury, shake the land of Israel so that the mountains were thrown down. There would be terrible warfare, fire and earthquakes, until all the enemies were dead and would have to be buried.

This theme was taken up in Revelation 20:8, when Satan would be let loose from his prison. Gog and Magog, and other nations, deceived by Satan, would gather like sand. God would send fire to devour them, and the Devil would be cast into the fire. In Arabic: Yajuj and Majuj (q.v.).

Golden Calf
Worship of a golden calf was an ancient Egyptian custom which persisted in Jewish habits, like circumcision (Exodus 32:4; Deuteronomy 9:21; 1 Kings 12:28).

Gomorrah (Arabic: *Ghamura* or *Jumurra*, q.v.)
Koran 9:71; 69:9. See Ancient city, probably just north of the Dead Sea which was then not dead. The Lord rained brimstone and fire upon

it, and upon Sodom, for their sins (Genesis 19:24) and overthrew those cities, which probably means that the ground on which they stood covered the ruins, burying them. See *Tibril, Lut.*

Grave

Graves are of great importance in the Middle East. In principle, graves may never be disturbed for the dead must sleep there until resurrection. Every religion has its own graveyards, with inscriptions in its own script. The spirits of the dead are believed to linger in or near the grave, so that no living person should stay in a graveyard after dark when the spirits appear out of their graves to haunt the living. If a daring person goes to sleep there, the spirits will speak to him in his dream and tell the future, or teach him how to heal the sick.

One day the Prophet Moses was walking in the hills when he saw three men digging a grave (they were angels). He asked them: 'For whom is that grave?' They answered: 'The grave is for whom it fits'. (It was for Moses.) This answer illustrates Islamic philosophy which holds that it is no use for a man to build a tomb for himself. God may cause him to die in a distant country and be buried there; someone else will then be buried in his fine tomb.

Numerous graves of saints and prophets are still visited by pilgrims, including the grave of Muhammad in Medina, the graves of Abraham and Jacob in Hebron, and of David and Solomon in Jerusalem; and Moses' grave 20 km east of Jerusalem at Ennebi Musa.

H

Habil
See Abil.

Hadad
Syrian god of lightning, rain and fertility, identified by the Romans with Jupiter.

Hades
The nether world where the dead reside, often named in the New Testament (e.g. Acts 2:31). At the end of time, hell will deliver up its dead (Revelations 20:13); then the souls will be judged.

Hadith
'Tradition'. The words and deeds of the Prophet Muhammad, recorded for all Muslims to imitate as *sunna* (q.v.). The reminiscences of the Prophet Muhammad's contemporaries, which they had told to their children and younger friends, were documented only 200 years after his death. These were recorded in a great corpus of books called collectively the *Hadith-as-Sahih*, *The Correct Tradition*. This record of numerous small events, the acts and words of their Prophet, containing his complete biography in so far as there is no dispute about the historical authenticity of the contents, has been canonized in Islam as law. Whatever the Prophet did, his habits and customs, have become rules of life for every Muslim. His sayings which have been collected in many anthologies are, likewise, as many laws for life and society. Thus the *Hadith-as-Sahih* has become, next to the Koran, a fountain of jurisprudence, overruling society's consensus.

Next to the correct and truthful (*sahih*) tradition, there arose a large body of unproven tales about Muhammad, as well as stories which he purportedly told about previous prophets, creation, Adam and Eve, etc., which are also called *hadith*. To this body belong the legends found in the *Mawlid* (q.v.), the *Mi'raj* (q.v.), the *Wafat al-Nabii*, the vast *Maghazi* literature, as well as the apocalyptic literature in Arabic. The contents of these works belong to the popular beliefs and cosmology. Their contents are largely accepted by Muslims as true history, except by modernists. This book, not being a work of history, refers to them as legends without discussion of their authenticity.

Public recitation of these legends

and their availability in bookshops as printed pamphlets from Morocco to Mombasa in Arabic, in Singapore and Penang in Malay, in Istanbul in Turkish, and in Karachi in Sindhi and Urdu, ensures that probably every schoolchild in the world of Islam knows them by heart. They are the main source for our knowledge of the cosmology of Islam, where the Koran gives only occasional references to the creation of the earth, Adam and Eve, the early prophets and patriarchs, the structure of the universe and the earth.

Many of these legends begin thus: 'Someone asked the Prophet, peace be upon him, "Please tell us about the creation, the prophets, or the last days and the resurrection."' The Prophet's answers to these questions fill many volumes.

Hafaza
Guardian angels who protect the souls of good Muslims after death against the satans (Koran 6:61).

Hagar
In the Jewish tradition, Abraham's (q.v.) concubine, who became the mother of his eldest son Ishmael. Abraham's wife Sarah was so jealous that she persecuted Hagar, until Hagar fled with little Ishmael to the desert where she was comforted by an angel (Genesis 16:10; 21:14). See *Hajar*.

Hail
See *Barqiya*.

Hajar
In the Islamic tradition the same as Hagar, except that she was Abraham's first wife, so Isma'il (q.v.) was Abraham's eldest son by right of law. Yet Abraham (Ibrahim) sent her away at Sarah's insistence. Hajar and Isma'il were comforted in the desert by Jibril (q.v.) who made the well Zamzam for them.

Hajj (Hijja)
The pilgrimage to Mecca, the Ka'ba, Arafat and Mina, undertaken every year by over a million Muslims. For the Sufis, all of life is a pilgrimage, which is the greatest duty in our lives: to travel in search of the divine presence, one's whole life.

Hallaj
First mystic who was martyred in Islam. His union with God was complete. He taught that the searcher (see *Wali*) and Allah love each other with passionate devotion. Later writers have replaced this passion with *mahabba*, 'tender, compassionate love', feeling that emotions like passion were human, not divine.

Ham
Son of Noah (Genesis 9:18–27). He left the ark with his two brothers. While Noah was asleep, overcome by drinking too much wine, Ham saw his nakedness. Noah knew what had happened when he woke up and cursed Ham, simply for seeing him naked. The original reason must have been that one's father's genitals can put a spell on a child. Genitals and even buttocks are still used to put a

curse on a person in the Upper Nile regions. So Ham incurred a magic curse automatically, simply by seeing his father's member of procreation. The political reason for this myth was the justification of the conquest of the people of Canaan by Israel. Canaan was the name of Ham's son.

The Arabic tradition relates that Ham was so strongly sexual that he embraced his wife one night in the ark, in spite of the taboo against sex during the voyage. So God cursed him and made him black. Noah later made Ham king of Africa, so his nine sons became the ancestors of the nine 'black' races of Africa, though we do not learn which.

Haman

In the Koran, the prime minister of the Pharaoh who has to build a tall palace for the king (28:7; 29:38; 40:38). This name is evidently taken from the Haman in Esther 3–7, who hated Mordecai but eventually fell from grace.

Hamd

'Praise'. Repeating *Al-hamdu-lillahi*, 'Praise God, thank God', is meritorious, especially when one is in bad health or even in pain.

Hamoun

The modern name of the Kasavya Lake in Sistan, in which Zoroaster's seed lives on.

Hamza

Uncle of Muhammad who called him the Lion of God. He died at Uhud, 3 AH/625 AD. Numerous heroic tales are told about his extraordinary exploits fighting battles against enemy kings and demons, and about his uncountable love affairs with pretty princesses.

Hand of God

This phrase occurs in the Koran 48:10. The Wahhabis, who take the Koran literally and consider symbolic exegesis the beginning of atheism, maintain that God must have hands because the Koran says so. Human brains cannot understand this.

Hannahannas

'Grandmother'. Mother-goddess of the Hittites. See *Telepinus*.

Haoma

The old Persian name for a secret hallucinogenic herb called *soma* in the Veda. Its yellow juice was drunk by the early Aryans and was believed to render its imbibers immortal. It is supposed by some scholars to have been the *ephedra* of the *Pinaceae* family. The early Iranians believed in its medicinal powers and venerated it as a deity. Drinking it would render a man fertile and pressing the juice out would cause a man to beget a son. Some scholars maintain that it must have been the grape. Wine has always been a popular intoxicant in Iran.

Haqq

'Truth, reality'. For the Sufis this is a name for God who is the essential reality.

Hara

'Peak of the law'. A holy mountain in ancient Persian cosmology, the central mountain of the earth, from whence the pure Aredvi (q.v.) sprang. Hara is an Indian name for Shiva.

Hare

In many mythologies the hare is a symbol of the moon-goddess. The Jews may not eat it. It is believed to be extremely cunning.

Harun Al-Rashid

'The Righteous'. Fifth caliph of the Abbasid empire, commander of the faithful at Baghdad 786–809 AD succeeding his brother Al-Hadi. Harun was born in Rayy near Tehran in 763. He led an expedition against Constantinople in 782, which was so successful that he received the praise name Al-Rashid 'the One who Walks the Right Path'. Harun's expeditions against the Byzantine Empire led to the taking of Herakleia in Anatolia (modern Eregli) in 806.

This triumph over the Christian emperor Nikephoros gave Al-Rashid the aura of a holy warrior so that legends about him began to proliferate. This is no doubt the reason for his being the hero of the Arabian Nights (q.v.).

His mother, Al-Khayzuran, originally a slave girl from Yemen, developed as a woman of strong character and ruled until her death in 789. Harun married a cousin, Zubayda, who gave him his son Al-Amin. He also had a slave girl from Persia who gave him his second son Al-Ma'mun. Both princes succeeded him.

The Arabian empire had been in existence for only just over a century when Harun succeeded, so that its culture was still very crude. It was only in Harun's time that trade and industry developed so that great wealth flowed into the caliph's coffers. This enabled him to indulge in his taste for the fine arts, attracting poets like Abu Nuwas and making his palace at Baghdad into the most fabulous building in the Middle East, where his wife Zubayda ate only from golden dishes studded with gems. The caliph loved music and, of course, story-telling, so that he lives on in legend as the emperor who encouraged Sheherazade (whose Persian name betrays her father's origin) to tell him fairy tales. His nocturnal wanderings in Baghdad, accompanied by his executioner Masrur, actually took place, but history is silent about his encounters with *jinns* and magicians.

Harut and Marut

Two 'angels' who taught sorcery (*sihr*) at Babil (Koran 2:102). Legend relates that the angels, seeing the sins of men, swore to God that they could do better. God told two of them to try life on earth as human beings. Harut and Marut were chosen and sent to live in Babil. They were warned to avoid idolatry, fornication, murder and alcohol, but as soon as they met an attractive woman they succumbed to her charms. Her name was Zuhura (Venus). She persuaded them to taste her wine, which made them drunk. When they were with her in her bedroom, a man entered surprising them *in flagrante*, so they killed him. Then they worshipped Venus and fornicated with her.

Having been watched by their fellow-angels in heaven, they could not escape their punishment. They were hung up by their feet in a well in Babil, where they remain today, still alive. If a man succeeds in finding that well, he can request the two hanging angels to teach him sorcery, which will make him a rich man. See also Genesis 6:1–4, Book of Enoch 7, Jubilees 5.

Hasan (Hassan, Al-Hasan)
Eldest son of Fatima, daughter of the Prophet Muhammad, and of Ali ibn Abu Talib. Hasan was born in the year 3 AH/625 AD and died in 49 AH/670 AD. He became the fifth caliph when his father Ali was murdered in 41 AH/660 AD. After six months he abdicated in favour of Mu'awiya. He was poisoned by his wife, to whom Mu'awiya had promised marriage, although he never did marry her. Hasan had fifteen sons who became the ancestors of the sharifs (*shurafa'*), 'noblemen'. King Hasan of Morocco is his descendant. See *Shi'a*.

Hasan Al-Askari
Hasan Askari ibn Ali ibn Muhammad, the eleventh imam of the Twelver (q.v.) branch of the Shi'a, was born in Medina in 230 AH/844 AD. He was brought to Samarra in Iraq with his father Ali Naqi (q.v.) and died there in 260 AH/874 AD; he was buried near his father.

It has been alleged that he was poisoned by the doctor whom the caliph Al-Mu'tamid sent to him when he was ill. The caliph had tried to dispose of him by having him locked up in a cage with some hungry lions. However, the lions had bowed their mighty heads while the imam prayed

in peace. The caliph had also sent him a horse as a present. The horse was untamed and so fierce that it had thrown all its riders, and the caliph had hoped it would kill Hasan, but when he mounted it, it became completely docile.

He left a pregnant wife when he died so that his son Muhammad, the twelfth imam, was born after his death. It is therefore strictly correct to maintain, as some do, that he left no son when he died. His father Ali Naqi had another son, Ja'far ibn Ali, and some Shi'a scholars recognized him as the last imam instead of Muhammad. They formed the Ja'fariyya sect. They are sometimes called the Nusayris, after Hasan's minister. See *Muhammad al-Mahdi* and *Mahdi*.

Hashim
The great-grandfather of the Prophet Muhammad, ancestor of the kings of Transjordan. He was very hospitable, hence the name *Hashim*.

Hasid (Plural: *hasidim*)
'Pious, righteous'. A member of a scrupulously orthodox Jewish group, often called mystics. The movement originated in the Middle Ages with Jehudah ben Samuel, whose book *Sefer Hasidim* became its standard work. At that time the ataraxia (equanimity) of stoicism was a primary influence: the soul must be moved neither by praise nor by humiliation. The Hasidim centre their lives on the immanence of the divine omnipresence to whom the believer prays, and the transcendent 'hidden' glory to

whom the 'soul of the prayer' travels. In the eighteenth century, Hasidism began to flourish in what was then eastern Poland, Podolia, through the preaching of Israel ben Eliezer. It held that man must be joyful and grateful to God, the soul should be happy to serve the Lord for love and joy.

Hatif (*Hatifu*, plural: *hawatif*, feminine: *hatifa*)

A voice in the desert. Lonely travellers in the desert often hear voices calling to them, or shouting abuse or tempting them to stray from the road by sounding like young women crying for help. The travellers go in search of the damsels in distress and see nothing but will have lost their way. Some *hawatif* may be the voices of angels or of poets who died there and still recite their poems for travellers. The latter in their innocence may recite these poems in the next town and be arrested for slander, unaware of the secret allusions in them, by which the dead poets took revenge on the living. Sometimes a *hatif* will lead the traveller to a hidden oasis where he will meet the owner of the female voice, fall in love with her and live happily on in the oasis, forgetting his home.

Haurvatat

'Wholeness'. Old Persian goddess of water, good health and salvation: Hygieia. Later pronounced Hordad.

Hauzu'l-Kausar (Haud al-Kawthar)

'Pond of Abundance'. Muhammad's pure lake on the shores of heaven. As soon as the sinless faithful arrive at the end of the thin bridge (see *Sirat*

al-Mustaqim, they may drink from it. Its water is sweet and white like milk. It makes the blessed forget all the suffering and unhappiness of their earthly life. They will then proceed on their way to their assigned domiciles, their palaces in paradise (q.v.).

Hawiya

A big fire, one of the departments of hell, the bottomless pit for the hypocrites (Koran 101:6). See *Hell*.

Hayula

'Primal matter'. The Greek *physis*, *prima materia*, out of which all things are created. See *Materia*.

Hazrat

'Presence'. Title given to a Muslim holy man or other religious leader.

Heaven

1. In the Hebrew tradition, the word for heaven is often used in the plural, *shemaim*, as if the belief in the layers of the skies already existed. Heaven is God's abode (Genesis 28:17; Exodus 20:22; 1 Kings 8:27; Psalms 53:2; 73:25). In Jeremiah 23:24, however, God fills heaven and earth, while in Malachi 3:10) heaven has windows from which God can pour down blessings (rain?) on earth. There is no mention of the good souls going to heaven after death as a reward.
2. In the New Testament heaven becomes a place where the good souls will live after death, as a reward, but judgement of individual souls is not yet specified (Matthew 5:3, 12). In Matthew 13:44–6, the kingdom of

Heaven	Prophet	Planet	Metal	Colour	Precious Stone
1	Adam	Moon	Silver	White	Pearl
2	Yahya (John the Baptist) and Isa (Jesus)	Mercury	Mercury	Blue	Sapphire
3	Yusuf (Joseph)	Venus	Tin	Green	Emerald
4	Akhnukh (Enoch)	Sun	Gold	Yellow	Diamond
5	Harun (Aaron)	Mars	Copper	Red	Ruby
6	Musa (Moses)	Jupiter	Iron	Purple	Amethyst
7	Ibrahim (Abraham)	Saturn	Lead	Indigo	Onyx

heaven is explained by many scholars not as the dwelling place of the good souls after death, but as a condition, an elevated way of living, a superior experience of existence, a serene joy for life. That may be the 'many houses in my father's palace' (John 14:1).

In Luke 12:37–8, 'when the master arrives at dawn', one is reminded of the Hindu tradition of the good soul waiting for her divine Lord to arrive before dawn. He knocks on the door (of the heart) and when he is inside, peace and joy reign. Heaven is in the heart. It is only in Revelation that the good men (women are not mentioned) stand before the throne of God who 'will wipe all tears from their eyes' (7:17). It is not only for their good deeds, but 'happy are the dead who die in the faith of Christ' (14:13). The blessed will receive a draught from the spring of life (21:6). No doubt eternal life

is meant – see John 3:16, where it is again faith that is rewarded, not labours. Finally, in Revelation 22:1–5, heaven is described as a place of eternal light, with fruit trees bearing fruits every month, and with the river of light running through.

3. In Islamic cosmology there are seven heavens, although some authors mention even more. Listed above, in ascending order are the strata of heaven as mentioned in the Koran and in other works. Each heaven is presided over by a prophet of the past and has a planet assigned to it.

This table contains in essence the basis of the Islamic astrologers' and alchemists' cosmologies (see *Astrology*), and the basis of the structure of the universe in traditional Islamic literature. It is based on the Aristotelian cosmology containing the planets and metals which were then known.

The eternal life of the blessed in

heaven is described in glowing terms in the Koran, especially in Sura 56. Heaven is described as full of fresh clear streams and shady fruit trees. The good souls sit at laden tables enjoying food and joyful company and being served by beautiful boys and girls with gazelle eyes. See *Huri*.

Hebat

Hurrian goddess of beauty, fertility and royalty, wife of Teshub the supreme god. Perhaps identical with *Hepit* (q.v.).

Hebrew

The language of the book of Genesis, the four law-books of Moses, the historical books, the poetic books, the books of wisdom and the books of the prophets, together forming the Hebrew *tenakh*, which the Christians call the Old Testament. It is closely related to the contemporary languages Canaanitic, Moabitic, Ugaritic (later, Phoenician) and probably Eblaite. All these belong to the northwest Semitic genus of the Semitic language family. Aramaic spread later.

Since God himself is often quoted as speaking in Hebrew, it is believed by millions to be God's own language. The first chapters of Genesis, especially, are often quoted by mystics to demonstrate the powerful language by which God created the universe. In particular the phrase *wa-yehi-or* (Genesis 1:3) is often studied in depth.

Hebrew words and phrases are often used for magical purposes. Small booklets are available in bookshops of the Middle East in which, in the middle of an Arabic text, certain Hebrew letters in secret sequences are printed. Amulet-makers must copy these faithfully when they are producing charms to protect their clients against common disasters like theft, disease or fire. Many of these amulets are sold as love charms. They demonstrate, curiously, that even among some Muslims there is a belief that the Hebrew language and its script have a magic power which the Arabic language does not have. This belief originates in the myth of the magic books of Solomon, which he wrote down from dictation by Harut and Marut (q.v.) and the *jinns* (q.v.). The Arab magical experts are aware that once Hebrew was the language of God's word. See also *Bahira*.

Hebrews

The descendants of Isaac. This includes the descendants of Esau 'who is Edom' (Genesis 36:1). The descendants of Jacob (Isaac's son) were later known as the Children of Israel. Those of them who lived in Egypt under the leadership of Joseph and later of his brother, Judah, were called Judaei, that is, Jews.

Hell

1. In old Persian cosmology hell was called the house of darkness, the house of lies, the house of worst purpose, the house of deep night. In Zoroastrian lore there is no eternal punishment for sinners, since the sinner would have no time afterwards to prove himself corrected. The Zoroastrian hell is a temporary existence. When the good has

ultimately triumphed in all the souls in hell, then all human beings will be resurrected both from heaven and hell, and the living creatures will be reunited with God, the source of all life. See also *Viraf* and *Paradise 1*.

2. In the Hebrew tradition the word Sheol (q.v.) is translated in the English Bible as 'hell', 'grave' or 'pit'. Sheol is the nebulous dark country under the earth, where the dead live their shadowy existence, the equivalent of the Greek Hades (q.v.), which is what it is called in the New Testament. In the later books of the Old Testament the word Gehennah appears, from the Hebrew Gehinnom (q.v.), described as a filthy place of suffocating smoke and torture by burning. Gradually the nether world evolved from a misty land of the shades to a place of punishment for the souls of sinners. The English word 'hell' has undergone a parallel evolution. In pre-Christian times it meant simply the place below the earth where the dead souls existed.

In the the Hebrew books of the Bible this evolution takes place very gradually. Sheol is simply a deep, dark, narrow place, but David the psalm-poet sings: 'Thou wilt not abandon me to Sheol nor suffer thy faithful servant to see the pit, thou wilt show me the path of life; in thy presence is the fullness of joy, in thy right hand pleasures for evermore' (Psalms 16:10–11). There is the division between those who do not deserve God's favour – they will be abandoned in Sheol – and those whom God keeps with him and gives pleasures for ever after. In Acts 2:27, Peter uses this passage to argue that David had foreseen that God would keep him near him to send him back to earth as the living Messiah. In other words, only David of all people was given everlasting life by God.

Still, hell is not a place for punishment but simply the place for the dead. Nowhere in the Old Testament is there even a beginning of the later Islamic system of interrogation of the dead souls and their being sent down to hell for specific forms of torture meted out for specified sins.

3. Hell is a place of punishment in the New Testament (Matthew 5:22, 29–30: only the body is spoken of here). It is a 'furnace of fire' (Matthew 13:42), 'everlasting fire' (Matthew 23:33; 25:41, 46). See also Luke 12:5; Mark 9:47. In Luke 16:23, Jesus describes hell as the place where the heartless rich man is tormented in oven temperatures. He is told that he can never get out. Finally in Revelation 21:8, hell is described as the 'lake that burns with sulphurous flames'. Those thrown into it are 'the cowardly, the faithless, the vile, murderers, fornicators, sorcerers, idolators and liars of every kind', not to be punished but to die a second time, this time forever.

4. In Islam, hell is *an-nar*, 'the fire', the abode for sinners. It has seven layers: Jahannam for Muslim sinners (Koran 19:72); Laza (Ladha') to which the misers who turned their backs on Islam will be dragged (Koran 98:5); Al-Hutama, a fire in which the hearts of the damned, i.e. the pagans, will burn (Koran 104:4); Sa'ir, where the unjust and the embezzlers of the orphans' funds will be roasted (Koran 4:11); Saqar, for those in error, the

fools (Koran 54:47); al-Jahim, where
the idolators, those who deny Allah,
the proud and the blasphemers will
burn (Koran 2:113); and Hawiya,
where the deceivers of the market
place will suffer (Koran 101:8). They
are the hypocrites, the liars who are
not Muslims but devils.

The first hell is just under the earth.
There the suffering is mildest. The
bad Muslims reside here; they may
remember God's name and so get
out one day. The seventh hell is the
deepest, far below the deepest pit of
despair. Here Iblis himself will be cast
and chained forever together with all
his wicked satans, at doomsday, to
burn forever after.

Hepit (Hebat)
Hurrian sky-goddess depicted in sculpture as standing on a lion. The
Romans seem to have identified her
with their war-goddess Bellona, worshipped at Comana in Asia Minor.

Herakles
The Greek god, identified with the
Persian Verethragna, as the god of
triumph, justice and noble duty.

Heraklios (Arabic: *Hiraql*)
Byzantine emperor 610–41 AD. It
was his sad fate to be unable to
stop the destruction of the empire
he had spent 30 years trying to hold
together. Between 634 and 641 he
lost Palestine, Jordan (then called
the Decapolis), Syria, Mesopotamia
and even Egypt to the Arabs. Numerous legends are told about him in
the Middle East, including how he
was warned by God in dreams and

visions that a new prophet would
arise in Arabia whose faith would
conquer the world. When he visited
Jerusalem it is said he received an
embassy of 'circumcised men'. They
brought a letter, we are told, from
Muhammad inviting the emperor to
accept Islam, 'then we shall be of
one *umma*'. The Christian ruler of
Constantinople could not accept, of
course, so he had to face battle with
the Arabs. Their victories are ascribed
to God's decree, since he had decided
that Islam should be the religion
of the Middle East. All the battles
are, in legend, concentrated around
Muhammad's legendary expedition
to Tabuk (q.v.), to take revenge for
the death of his cousin Ja'far (q.v.).

Hermes
See Hirmis.

Hijab
'Protection', a veil or curtain from
behind which the women of Islam
may speak to men other than their
husbands, brothers and fathers. In
Sufi literature the *hijab* is the 'cloud
of unknowing', that which conceals
the face of God (Koran 28:88) from
the apprentice, so that he cannot see
the light (2:256).

Hijaz (Hedjaz)
The central coastal province of Arabia
along the Red Sea, between Najd and
Tehama, which at 37,500 square
miles is larger than Indiana. Its capital is Mecca and it is the Holy Land
of Islam. Muslim poets have exulted
over its exceptionally agreeable cli-
mate. The Pakistani poet Iqbal wrote
longingly: 'Does the cool morning

breeze of Hijaz e'er come back?' It is believed that one day in the future God will send His throne down to stand on earth and from it he will judge all humanity. The place he chooses will be in Hijaz.

Hilal

1. The new moon, the crescent which appears after sunset in the western sky. When it does it has to be observed by two sensible adult Muslims and then the new month will be announced to have commenced. Its first three days are called *hilal*. The moment of the moon's appearance is awaited with particular impatience during the last evening of Ramadan (q.v.) because its appearance will end Ramadan and the fasting with it, and herald *Id ul Fitr* (q.v.). This is believed to be the reason why the crescent is often used as a symbol for Islam.
2. Hilal is also the name of an Arab hero whose sons, the Banu Hilal (q.v.), are credited with innumerable exploits during their conquest of Africa.

Himma

'Resolution, strength'. For the Sufis, the determination of the heart to submit totally to the will of God, and so to gain strength and the ability to act.

Hira

A rocky hill not far from Mecca where Muhammad used to meditate for long spells until, in 610 AD, the angel of God appeared to him and showed him Sura 96:1–5 of the Koran, telling him to read it. This was the beginning of the revelation of the holy Koran, and

of Islam. Every year, many pilgrims come to meditate on Hira, celebrating this joyful event, concentrating their thoughts on the divine presence, as God's word first descended to earth, on that sacred spot.

Hiraql

See *Heraklios*.

Hirmis (Hermis)

Hermes Tresmegistos, the Hellenistic name for the ancient Egyptian god of the nether world, Thoth. The Arabic name is Muthallath bi'l-Hikma, 'Threefold in Wisdom.' This mythical character was incorporated in Islam in three aspects: Akhnukh (Enoch) was identified with him, and he was in turn identified with Idris (q.v.).

This triple prophet once lived in Egypt, in the days before Noah. He built the first pyramid, *haram*, which was named after him (Hirmis is also read as Haramis). Having invented writing he wrote on its walls the achievements of Egyptian technology for posterity. He disappeared in the flood but reappeared in Babel centuries later where he again invented the art of writing and the sciences. He came back to earth a third time, again in Egypt where he wrote his great work on the occult sciences which is still quoted by those who claim to have access to it.

These writings were hidden in a tunnel, *sardab*, from where they were ultimately retrieved by a certain scholar, Balinus, who dug under the statue of Hirmis in Egypt (in Hermopolis in the Nile delta) after he had deciphered the inscription on the statue. It is said that he met Hirmis sitting alive in the tunnel with an emerald tablet in his hand on which he had written his Hermetic secrets. Balinus received it and later passed it on to Aristotle, the preceptor of Alexander (see *Al-Iskandar*), who wrote a book about it which is preserved in an Arabic translation as *Sirr al-Asrar*, and in Latin as *Secretum Secretorum*. It contains numerous proverbs and instructions on how to make magical objects such as talismans.

Hittites

The Hittites in the Bible (Genesis 15:19–21; 23; 26:34; 36:1–3; Numbers 13:29; Joshua 1:2–4; Ezekiel 16:3) were a people living in northern Canaan and Syria. They are not identical with the Hittites whose language has been deciphered from inscriptions in central Asia Minor.

Hoja (Hoga, Khoja)

Hoja Nasredin is a famous character in humorous popular tales in Turkey, Egypt and Iran. He is half saint and half fool, but also a sage with astute insights.

Holy Ghost

The early English translation of *Sanctus Spiritus*, Holy Spirit. The word 'ghost' now means the spirit of a dead person walking on earth, manifesting itself visually or by its voice, etc, but in old English it meant any spirit, alive or dead, like the related German *geist*. Thus 'Holy Ghost' does not mean a spectre risen from the grave but the divine spirit that has always lived. The Revised Version of the Bible renders 'ghost' as 'spirit' in most passages.

The concept is almost exclusively found in the New Testament. See *Holy Spirit*.

Holy Spirit

Isaiah speaks of 'the spirit of the Lord' (11:2; 61:1; 32:15; 59:21) which will lead people in righteousness and will cause the desert to be fruitful. In 48:16 he says: 'And now the Lord and his spirit hath sent me', implying that they are two, but in 40:13 no one has apparently directed the spirit of the Lord. In 63:10 it is vexed.

God's spirit is everywhere (Psalms 139:7); it instructs us (Nehemiah 9:20); the Lord has poured his spirit upon the House of Israel (Ezekiel 39:29); in the form of 'breath' the spirit may make the dead live (Ezekiel 37:9). See Genesis 2:7 for 'the breath of life'.

Revelation 4:5 describes 'seven lamps of fire burning before the throne' as 'the seven spirits of God', referring probably to Zechariah 4:2–6. The spirit of God is a guiding light in the night (Exodus 13:21); a voice guiding 'in his ear' (1 Samuel 10:15--16); it can melt the earth (Psalms 46:6).

Its essence is that it gives life to man (Genesis 6:3); it also confers on men the ability to rule people (Numbers 11:17). It may become fire and burn people (Numbers 16:35). The spirit may be 'in the mouth' of a prophet making him speak either truth or lies (1 Kings 22:22). The Lord can divide his spirit and give parts of it to some of his prophets (2 Kings 2:15). The spirit can make itself felt as a soft breeze (Job 4:15; 1 Kings 19:12). It gives people understanding (Job 32:8). It can 'ride' on the winds (Psalms 104:3–4). It purifies (Isaiah 4:4–5). It has justice (Isaiah 28:6). It makes a man see what other people cannot see (Isaiah 11:3; 1 Samuel 16:7). It 'anoints' prophets so they can prophesy (Isaiah 61:1; Luke 4:18).

In the New Testament the Holy Spirit is the source of power, it causes new birth, it made the Virgin pregnant, it inspired scripture, it is a source of wisdom, it inspires and directs ministers and missionaries, it dwells for ever in the saints; it is sent by Christ from the father, the saints know it and are taught by it; it also imparts the love of God (Romans 5:3).

Jesus received the spirit (Mark 1:10; John 1:32). He was even armed with its power after he had rejected the devil (Luke 4:14). John the Baptist was filled with the Holy Spirit from birth (Luke 1:16). The spirit guided Simeon into the temple and told him who Jesus was (Luke 2:25–30). The term is almost synonymous with God (Luke 10:21). God gives his spirit without measure (John 3:34). The spirit alone gives life (John 6:63), so it feeds the human mind as well as the body.

In Islam, Allah sends the spirit (*ruh*) down with the angels (Koran 16:2), especially during the *Laylat-al-Qadr* (97:4) (q.v.) when the Koran itself was 'sent down' from heaven to Muhammad. Allah fortifies the believers with his spirit (58:22). Isa (Jesus) is a spirit of God (4:171); God fortified him with the Holy Spirit (*biruhi 'l-qudusi*, 2:87, 253). The spirit descended with the Koran (26:193; 16:102) to strengthen, as a

guide, the glad tidings. See also *Spenta Mainyu*, *Ruh al-Quds*, *Ruhu'llah*, *Holy Ghost*.

Hoopoe (Arabic: *hudhud*)
King Solomon gave this bird a golden crest as a reward for shielding him from the piercing of the sun one hot afternoon. But many hoopoes were then killed for their golden crowns by greedy birdcatchers. So the king of the hoopoes begged Solomon to remove the golden crown. Solomon gave them crests of colourful feathers instead.

The hoopoe is a curious bird, it eavesdrops on people, and served King Solomon as a messenger and a spy. One day it reported to Solomon that it had seen the most beautiful woman on earth – Bilkis, the Queen of Saba (Sheba) (q.v.) – while it was spying in her palace, and reported that she wanted him to visit her. The Koran (27:20) says that it carried his letter to invite her to embrace Islam.

Hordad
See *Haurvatat*.

Hormazd
See *Ahura Mazda*.

Horomazes
See *Ahura Mazda*.

Horse
In many cosmologies the horse was the mount of the sun-god who later rode in a golden chariot drawn by four horses. The horse sacrifice was reserved for kings. It was associated with funeral rites and assured the new

king imperial power, symbolized by the rising sun.

Horus

Ancient Egyptian god of the rising sun, son of Osiris, to whom Isis gives birth after Osiris is killed by Seth, god of the dark waters. Horus later vanquishes Seth who has taken the shape of a hippopotamus symbolizing the night. Horus is often pictured as a falcon, or with a falcon's head. The Greeks identified Horus with Kouros, the young Apollo.

Host

In the Bible and the Koran this word means a company of angels, either fighting for God's people (Joshua 5:14) or singing God's praises (Luke 2:13). Allah may send a host of angels to join the battle for Islam (Koran 33:9).

Hour

See *Sa'a*.

House

See *Beth, Dar*.

Hu (Huwa)

'He', meaning God. This is one of the words frequently used in *zikr* (*dhikr*) (q.v.) ceremonies during religious vigils of the Sufi fraternities. It occurs in the Koran 3:1, a verse which is often repeated. '*Huwa Allahu*', 'He is God!' is likewise used, as is '*Huwa Huwa*', 'He is He'.

This last phrase is taken from the philosophers who express by it that everything is identical only with itself. So '*Huwa Huwa*', when referring to God, means he is only himself and

nothing else is him. But for the Sufis it means more: it signifies that God is present in everything, since he is omnipresent (*wasi'*), so the world is one, it is a manifestation of his divine presence everywhere.

Hubal

The heathen god whose statue stood in the Ka'ba until Muhammad destroyed it in 8 AH/630 AD. It received many offerings from the pilgrims until that moment. Hubal was the tutelary deity of Mecca (Koran 17:83).

Hubb (*hubu, tahabbub*)

'Love'. Love in Arabic tales is the devotion to a person or to God which inspires the heart to complete self-sacrifice for the loved one.

Hud

A prophet of God according to the Koran, whom Allah sent to the people of Ad (7:65–72; 11:50–60; 26:123–39; 46:21–8). They tried to kill him when he preached against their heathen practices and worshipped only Allah. King Shaddad of Ad built a famous palace (see *Irama*) thinking he could rival paradise. Allah cursed the city of Ad and only Hud and his wife escaped when a terrible thunderstorm destroyed the city.

Hudhud

See *Hoopoe*.

Hudaybiya

A plain once near Mecca, now well inside the city, where Muhammad made a truce with the city fathers, which ended the war between Islam and paganism (Koran 48:1).

Hukm

'Judgement'. The ultimate judgement belongs to God alone, not to Man (Koran 3:73).

Humay

The daughter and wife of Bahman, king of Persia, mother of Dara I. It was she who first ordered the composition of the 1001 Nights Entertainments in Persian.

Humbaba (Huwawa)

A dangerous giant who, according to the Gilgamesh (q.v.) epic, lived in the great pine forest in the Zagros Mountains (or it might have been the great cedar forest in what is now the Lebanon and the foothills of Cappadocia, or much of Syria which is now desert). Humbaba's face, of which a stone sculpture from Sippar survives, looks terrifying. It seems to be intended that it should give the impression of bark, as if it were itself a piece of a tree.

Humbaba may himself have been a king, or rather a god, of the pine forest, like the bush-lord of the West African forest, to whom the hunters have to sacrifice, otherwise they will see no game or may even perish. The forest god is the natural enemy of the cultivators and of the urban peoples.

Gilgamesh noticed that the paths in the forest were well trodden, where the Humbaba went to and fro, suggesting that he may have been a large ape or primitive man such as one could still find 4000 years ago. Humbaba, in the shape of a fire-spitting dragon, mocked the 'two tiny men, looking like tortoises'. However, the gods intervened on behalf of the two men. The sun-god and the thirteen wind gods joined in the battle against Humbaba so that his face grew dark. He could not escape. He pleaded for his life but the two ruthless men finished him off, and put his big head on a raft.

Hunayn

A field just north of Mecca where Muhammad defeated the Banu Hawazin in 8 AH/630 AD (Koran 9:25). It was the last victory needed before the armistice. See *Hudaybiya*.

Hupasiyas

A Hittite hero whom the gods asked to slay the dangerous dragon Illuyankas (q.v.) and its ugly brood. The goddess Inaras promised Hupasiyas that she would sleep with him if he agreed to kill the dragon. They prepared vessels of wine and other liquor which they set out ready for the beast. Soon the dragon appeared and drank the wine, and so did its young. They then fell asleep so that Hupasiyas could bind them with rope. The thunder-god then arrived to kill off the monsters with his lightning. When it was all over Hupasiyas and Inaras made love.

Huri

1. A woman whose eyes are bright white with jet-black pupils, which is considered very attractive and beautiful in Arabia. In the Koran (55:56–78), these ladies were promised as a reward to the virtuous Muslims, as brides in heaven.
2. Son of Caleb, husband of Miriam, sister to Moses, first builder of the tabernacle, the sanctuary of the Lord.

He fought the Amalekites (Exodus 17:10) and founded Bethlehem.

Husayn (Hussein)

The second son of Ali, cousin of the Prophet Muhammad, and Fatima, the latter's daughter. Born in 4 AH/626 AD, he was only six when Muhammad died. It is said that he could see the angels and understood what they said. In the reign of the caliph Omar, it is said that the victorious Arabs brought to Medina the youngest daughter of the last Persian king, Shahrbanu. She was given to Husayn as a wife and so she became 'the mother of nine imams', Husayn himself being the third imam. She later escaped from the battle of Kerbela and regained her native Iran.

After Ali's death in 40 AH/661 AD, and Hasan's in 50 AH/670 AD, Husayn was the undisputed leader of Islam in the eyes of those who believed that only a descendant of the Prophet should rule. However, real power was in the hands of the Omayyads in Damascus. They were corrupt rulers whose governor of Kufa was especially renowned for his lechery. The citizens of Kufa begged Husayn in repeated letters to come and put things right, threatening that if he did not they would accuse him on judgement day of neglecting his duty to establish justice.

So Husayn set out from Medina with seventy-seven followers and travelled to Kufa. The caliph Yazid sent an army from Damascus to intercept him. Husayn gave battle at Kerbela on the Euphrates. All the male members of his family were slain, except for his infant son Ali Zayn al Abidin, who was sickly. Husayn was treacherously killed after a long fight. The family was taken to Damascus and humiliated but freed when Ali's ghost appeared in the shape of a black knight. Kerbela became the most famous centre of pilgrimage for the Shi'a community.

Naturally, an elaborate literature grew up around the tragic fate of Husayn, in prose and in verse, historical and legendary. Many poets and bards, professionals and amateurs, will recite or chant verses in which the passion of Husayn and his family's sufferings are described in detail, and preachers will admonish their audiences about this irreparable loss, moving them to tears. Songs, eulogies, threnodies and prose works have been composed in Arabic, Persian, Malay, Gujerati, Swahili, Turkish and Urdu, for the purpose of being read or declaimed on the night of Ashura (q.v.). See *Shi'a*.

Hutama

One of the departments of hell (q.v.). It was intended for slanderers and liars.

Hystaspes

1. Son of Aphrodite and Adonis, god of the meadows and green pastures.
2. Greek form of the Persian name Vishtaspa, Zoroaster's patron, king of Iran.

I

Ibazi (Ibadhi)
One of a sect commonly found in Oman and Algeria. The Ibadhis have their own *imam*, spiritual leader; they are dominant in Oman and Zanzibar.

Iblis
Arabic form of the word Devil, from Greek *diabolos* 'slander'. Iblis was created by God from the element fire (Koran 38:76). He refused to prostrate himself before Adam when God commanded all the angels to do so (2:34; 7:11–12; 15:31–3). For this, he was cursed and banned from paradise by God (7:13–18). However, by his clever talking, Iblis persuaded God to give him respite until judgement day, and also permission to tempt and try whomever God will allow among Adam's children (15:36–7; 17:62–3; 38:79–81; 7:16–17; 38:82). After doomsday (q.v.) Iblis' hosts will be cast into Hell (26:95).

Iblis is king of all and father of some of the *shaytans* (satans) or evil spirits.

Ibn (*Bin*, Hebrew: *Ben*)
The Arabic word for 'son', 'son of'. Plural: *Banu* 'sons', 'children'.

Ibn Abbas
Abdullah, son of Abbas (q.v.), and so a cousin of Muhammad, to whom Jibril (q.v.) explained the Koran. He became the ancestor of the Abbasids.

Ibrahim
1. Called *Khalilu'llah*, 'Friend of God', because he was God's host. The Biblical Abraham. In the Koran his father is called Azar. Azar once worshipped a star (Venus?), then the moon, then the sun, until he finally perceived that he must worship only the invisible god, the creator.

In the presence of the tyrant Namrud, Ibrahim took a peacock, a crow, a vulture and a cock, cut them to pieces, then called them one by one and lo, they all revived, once more whole and complete (Koran 2:262). At Mina, near Mecca, Ibrahim threw stones at the devil and to this day the pilgrims throw stones at a stone pillar there every year. Near the Ka'ba the Maqam-Ibrahim, Abraham's Place, can still be seen, where he stood while rebuilding the Ka'ba together with Isma'il. See *Sarah, Nimrod, Isma'il, Hajar*. See also *Abraham*.
2. Only son of the Prophet Muhammad and Maryam al-Qubtiya. He died in infancy.

Idols

The adoration of idols, of graven images (Jeremiah 50:38; Exodus 20:4; 1 Corinthians 8:1–10) is still irresistibly attractive to many peoples. The usual explanation for this is that some people have difficulty realising an unseen, spiritual God, and so carve images to represent him. In reality, it is caused by the way they were brought up. One has to learn to think in abstract concepts, but one also has to learn to venerate wooden statuettes or sculptured stones. Respect and worship are acquired thought patterns. The belief that objects contain spirits ('fetishes') does not grow any more naturally in the human mind than abstract concepts. It was precisely the fact that the people against whom the biblical authors fulminated with such fervour *were* brought up (by their mothers if not by their fathers) in the belief that idols are (or contain) living spirits, that made them 'relapse' into the adoration of what were, in the tradition of their families, true gods, as soon as the severe control of the monotheistic priests and prophets slackened.

Many men have been persuaded by their wives to change their religions. In western countries this is now permitted for commoners but imagine the storm of protest that would blow up if a Christian king became a Muslim or vice versa. Kings do not have freedom of worship. The ordinary people on the other hand, especially those in outlying districts, were more attached to their traditional gods and the rituals accompanying their devotion, such as feasts and dances.

Time and again the Children of Israel and even their kings 'lapsed back' to worshipping idols (in Hebrew *elilim, pesilim, eimim*), often, it seems (as in the case of Solomon) induced to it by heathen wives. These young women had been brought up to worship their ancestors and did not feel happy in a strange environment without their fathers' magic statuettes. See Genesis 31:34, where the word is images, *terafim*.

In the Koran the worshippers of idols are often criticized. Idols are referred to as *aliha*, 'gods'. In later Islamic literature the word is often *asnam* (the plural of *sanam*), 'statue, image', strongly condemned by all Muslim writers, but still widely worshipped, e.g. in Africa. In the time of Muhammad, children were still sacrificed to the gods (Koran 6:137–8), and so were prisoners of war, as Samuel slew Agag before the Lord (15:33). The Prophet Muhammad had 360 idols destroyed in the city of Mecca on the day of his first triumphant pilgrimage. He sent his warriors out to destroy the temples of Al-Uzza, Suwa' and Manat, the famous goddesses of the ancient Arabs.

Idris

1. Idris is mentioned in the Koran as a righteous man, a prophet whom God raised up to a high position and admitted into his mercy (19:56–8; 21:85–6). The Arabic name Idris may equate to the Hebrew prophet Ezrah, called in Greek Esdras (the Christians with whom Muhammad spoke would have called him thus). Other scholars derive Idris from the Greek Andreas, the apostle Andrew, brother of Peter.

Idris was most frequently identified with Enoch (q.v.), called in Arabic Akhnukh, and sometimes even with Elijah (q.v.), called in Arabic Ilyas, or Khizr (q.v.). Other writers have integrated Idris into the genealogy of Hermis (q.v.), the ancient god of the mystics, alchemists and astrologers (see *Sabeans*). Gradually, he became one of the most prominent sages in the Islamic tradition, to whom many wise sayings were attributed, mainly of a mystical nature, so that he was called 'the prophet of the philosophers'.

He is credited with the invention of geomancy (q.v.) and of *zairaja*, the secret art of predicting the future by means of a board containing seven concentric circles along the edge of which were inscribed the signs of the zodiac (q.v.). Along the other circles were inscribed letters and numbers; it seems that the circles were movable in relation to each other so that the whole contraption became a 'machine to predict the future', the first calculator for the sole purpose of forecasting fortunes. Idris was also credited with the invention of writing, which he received from his mythical father Hermis, and of tailoring.

According to the *Qisas al-Anbiya*, Idris was the second prophet after Adam, and before Noah. He entered paradise whilst still alive, because one of the angels felt a special friendship for him and took him up to heaven. On their way, at the fourth heaven, they met the angel of death who had searched the earth for Idris but could not find him. Idris died there and then, in the wings of his angel friend, so his soul is still in the fourth heaven.

2. According to the Islamic tradition, the name of the cook of Alexander the Great (see *Al-Iskandar*). This cook, wanting to clean some fish before cooking them as his master's breakfast, saw them swimming away, revived by the water of the well he was washing them in (see *Water of Life*, *Well of Life*).

Id ul-fitr (The spelling *idd* is incorrect)
'The feast of breaking the fast'. It begins when, at the end of the last day of Ramadan, after sunset, the new crescent is seen. Friends are invited and all eat cakes and dates and drink tea, coffee or fruit juice. For the next twenty-four hours there is a celebration with a fair, visits to friends, meals and wearing one's best clothes, but also prayers in the mosque and giving alms. Especially meritorious on that day is to forgive one's debtors, so that most loans between friends are never repaid. All the books emphasize that God will be equally generous to the lenient creditors and wipe out their sins.

Ifrad
See *Tafrid*.

Ifrits (Efreets and various other spellings)
In Islamic legends, a sub-species of *jinns* (q.v.); the word seems to mean 'wicked, destructive'. It occurs in the Koran only once (27:39–40). When King Solomon (q.v.) expressed a desire to possess the throne of the Queen of Sheba (Saba), an *ifrit*, here described as 'one of the *jinn*',

offered to go and fetch it for his king. (King Solomon was ruler of *jinns* and humans alike). The king agreed and the *ifrit* flew to Saba in South Arabia, a thousand miles in the blinking of an eye. There he entered the queen's palace in the shape of a cloud, and picked up her throne even though it was securely fastened to the floor. With this heavy seat, on which the long line of Sabean kings had sat, the *ifrit* flew back in the twinkling of an eye. He placed it in front of the king and his court, where it was admired by all. It follows from this tale that *ifrits* are enormously strong and fast.

In Pakistan, the ghosts of dead people with vicious characters are sometimes called *ifrits*. In Egypt, *efreet* is the common name for the evil *jinns*, believed to be very powerful, strong, big and malicious. One *efreet* in Cairo was called a Turkish soldier because it was believed that he was the ghost of a dead Turk. It is possible that the Solomon of the above tale was not the biblical king but the *jann al-jann*, the king of *jinns* who lived before Adam when the *jinns* ruled the earth by God's will. See also *Watwat* and *Marid*, a no less formidable kind of spirit. Some scholars maintain that the *marids* are the stronger type, others say that the *ifrits* are more powerful, but that the *jinns* possess the ability to change their shapes. The *ifrits* are capable of carrying heavy objects such as castles or even entire cities, and putting them down in another country without one tile missing from the rooftops. *Ifrits*, when visible, appear as smoke, and when wounded, they emit smoke; this presupposes that they can appear as giants looking like big men. They can also reduce their size to enter a glass bottle. They also have wings like bats to fly at night.

Ifrita
A female spirit, like a *jinna* but bigger and stronger, though not as rough as a *ghoula*. An *ifrita* can assume the shape of a human woman, although with enormous breasts and buttocks, which is very attractive to some men. An *ifrita* can easily seduce a man and keep him enthralled for life while bearing his children. A man who possesses the magic arts can also conjure up an *ifrita* from her hideout in the earth and make her work for him. *Ifritas* are not always wicked; they can even take pity on human beings and help them with their magic powers.

Igigi
Mesopotamian sky-gods, ruled by Ellil (q.v.), also called Anunaki.

Ikhlas
'Sincerity'. In Islamic orthodoxy the word for reform, usually implying the removal of all superstitions and popular practices. In Sufi lore it means seeking only God in total obedience.

Ilham
'Inspiration in the heart' as received by the saints of Islam. See *Wahy*.

Illiyun
The seventh stage of heavenly bliss; the department of heaven where our

noble and pure deeds are recorded (Koran 83:18). The Hebrew is Elyon, 'the highest'. The angels carry the souls of the good upward to Illiyun after death.

Illusion (Arabic: *ghurur*)
In popular Islamic literature, the machinations and deceptions of the Devil (Shaytan, Iblis) cause the weak-minded who listen to him to yearn for wealth, power, status, lust and other earthly pleasures. This leads those who believe him to have illusions, i.e., they 'see' with their mind's eye the things they covet. However nothing stays, and life passes too soon to spend much time on these 'futile games' (Koran 6:91). The Sufis go further in their interpretation of *ghurur*. For them *all* the visual impressions are illusions, leading the human soul away from the divine essence (*dhat*), thus delaying enlightenment. The physical world itself is *ghurur*, transitory sensory visions and feelings, as opposed to *haqq* 'truth, reality' which is one of the names of God. No unity with this ultimate, essential reality is possible until the soul has shed all desire, and with it, all belief in the reality of the physical world. See *Hijab*.

Illuyankas
A great dragon in Hittite mythology. See *Hupasiyas*.

'Ilm
This word is often translated as 'science' but it embraces all forms of knowledge, including poetry, astrology, mysticism, theology, law, medicine, alchemy and history. In the traditional textbooks of Islam, *'ilm* is simply the knowledge that will help a man to enter paradise, by avoiding sin and performing scrupulously all the regular duties of Islam, praying daily the regular prayers, including the supernumerary prayers, and fasting regularly. He should be especially careful not to lose his temper for that is when the Devil gets hold of a man's soul.

Ilyas
See *Elijah, Khizr*.

Image
God created man after his own image (Genesis 1:26); Adam begat a son 'after his image' (Genesis 5:3). The question has never been resolved what the writers (or the compilers of the oral traditions) had in mind. Did Adam look like God in the way that Seth looked like Adam? The text of 1:26 has literally plural forms: 'Let *us* make a man in *our* image.' Were these the gods (see *Elohim*) who are joint creators in most mythologies?

Imam
'Leader'. The word is related to *umma*, 'nation, tribe, community', and *umm*, 'mother', so that *umma* must have meant originally a clan of uterine relatives, and *imam* the chief of such a clan. In the Koran (2:124), God makes Ibrahim *linnasi imaman*, 'a leader of humanity'. We could also translate it as 'an example, a model', on the strength of 25:74: 'Make us an example for the pious.' In 17:71, God says: 'One day we will call together all humanity by their leaders.' The usual

interpretation of this verse is that on the day of judgement every religious community will appear before the throne arranged in ranks and files behind their leaders, the Jews behind Moses, the Christians behind Jesus and the Muslims behind Muhammad. Here, *imam* means 'spiritual leader'.

The imam is the leader of the Islamic community in the village or town, rector of the local mosque. He appoints a preacher (*khatib*) for a long or short time, as well as the *mu'adhin* who calls the Muslims to prayer five times a day. In the poorer regions the imam has to perform all these duties himself.

The main task of the imam is the administration of the moneys given him by the Muslims as *zakat* and *sadaqa* (qq.v.). In the *jami'a* (Friday mosque) of a big city this may amount to enormous sums, giving the imam great power. Like the minister in a Presbyterian church, the imam is sovereign, being responsible only to God. In the past, in the absence of a civilian government, he functioned as an effective administration, like some medieval bishops. The Ayatollah Khomeini reinstituted a national government by the imam in Iran. The king of Morocco is also, in theory, the imam of his country, so that the word often means 'king'.

The ideal imam is the most learned man in his town, for he must be the leader of the prayers. At the start of the prayer in the mosque he stands in front on the left side, facing Mecca, and all the believers join him in neat rows on his right and behind him. They will imitate his movements and repeat his words to make sure their praying is correct and valid. They will also consult him on matters of doctrine and daily life, marriage, divorce, etc. This again makes him the most powerful man in his community, provided he keeps his reputation as a man of sinless probity.

Since mosque and state are not separated and all Islamic theologians are also law scholars, the imam may combine secular with religious power, thus ruling the bodies as well as the souls of his community, the *umma*, which he must guide through a sinless life to paradise. For this reason he enjoys in some communities almost mystic power and popularity, all the more so if his scholarship and asceticism lead people to regard him as a saint. For this reason many communities appoint only a descendant of the Prophet Muhammad (a *sharif* or a *sayid*) as imam, hoping that with the Prophet's blood in his veins he will also have his wisdom and sanctity. All the branches of the Shi'a have made this their doctrine, but they differ over the question of which descendant to appoint as imam.

The Ithna'ashariyya has made the doctrine of the imam its central dogma. These 'Twelvers' (q.v.) believe in the hidden survival of the twelfth imam whom God keeps *maktum*, concealed from unholy eyes in a cave or basement near Samarra in Iraq. This living but invisible imam is visited by numerous pilgrims from Iran, Pakistan and elsewhere. Meanwhile, however, his followers must be advised in matters of faith and practice for their daily lives, so the class of mullahs has arisen, who, the people believe, have precise knowledge of the imam's opinion in all matters of law and custom. They in turn are led, in Iran where the Ithna'ashariyya is the state religion, by an elite of scholars with the title ayatollah, 'miraculous sign of God'. It is not always clear whether they too, are descendants of the Prophet. They represent the prominent clans of Iran, and so are heavily involved in politics. Each of them is a (mortal) imam of a given area.

It is believed that the hidden imam, whose name is Muhammad al-Mahdi, will be revealed by God shortly before resurrection. He will emerge from his cave as a warrior in full armour wielding the Prophet's sword. He will become a military leader (a normal function for an imam), calling the faithful of his *shi'a* (party) to join him in the battle against the sinners and unbelievers, to cleanse the earth and establish his reign of justice.

For the Isma'iliyya community the imam is the Agha Khan.

Imama (Persian: *imamat*)

The imamate, or the doctrine that at any time in history from the death of the Prophet Muhammad onwards, there must be alive, visible or hidden, an imam (q.v.), that is, a leader of the religion of Islam according to Shi'a dogma. This imam must fulfil a long list of conditions. First he must be a descendant of the Prophet through his daughter Fatima and her husband Ali ibn Abu Talib, the first imam. He must be adult, in full possession of his mental powers, and in perfect health. He must be free from sin (*ma'sum*) and infallible (*sadiq*) – he never lies, and possesses

knowledge which no other man has. He can speak not only all the languages of all the nations on earth, but also the languages of the animals and the birds. He must be patient in suffering and intrepid in danger, generous and charitable, ready to help the weak and the poor. He must be steadfast in all the religious duties so that God will answer all his prayers. As a result he will be able to work miracles, by God's favour, so that all men can see that God wishes him to rule. His appearance too will be so bright that all men of discernment will recognize him as the imam. When he does appear – and this may happen tomorrow or in the very distant future, the imam will be the Mahdi (q.v.) whom God will send to restore righteousness on earth, before the day of judgement (q.v.).

Imliq

Son of Shem (Sam), son of Noah, ancestor of the Amaliqah, the Amalekites whom Saul did not exterminate. Israel declared war on them forever (Exodus 17:16; Deuteronomy 25:17).

Imran

1. The Biblical Amram (Exodus 6:18), the father of Moses and Aaron (Koran 3:30).
2. The father of Maryam the mother of Isa (Koran 19:29; 66:12).

Inanna

1. Sumerian earth-goddess, sister of Ereshkigal. She loved Dumuzi.
2. Babylonian mother-goddess, 'mistress of heaven'.

Inannu
See *Inanna*.

Inaras
A Hittite goddess. See *Hupasiyas*.

Incubus
The incubus was believed to be a fallen angel (Genesis 6:1) who begot children with a woman. Later the incubus was a spirit in the shape of a man who had intercourse with a woman in her sleep. Perhaps as a result of the women's dreams the incubi began to take the shape of monsters: dwarfs, giants, ghosts, corpses, male animals or birds.

The daughter of Auf bin Afura lay down one hot day to rest. She had taken off all her clothes and fell asleep. She woke upon feeling a heavy pressure on her breast. There was a black demon, whose name was Lukezi, sitting on her, and his hand went to her throat. She choked and could not even pray. Suddenly the roof opened and she could see the sky from which a leaf of paper descended. It fell on her breast so that Lukezi could read it, for there were letters written on it. No sooner had he read it, than the hideous black devil disappeared through the roof which closed behind him as if it had never opened. The girl took the paper to the Prophet Mohammed and asked him what it meant. He said: 'You should not have uncovered your body while you were having your menses. That made you susceptible to the attacks of devils. Fortunately for you, your father was a devout Muslim, who laid down his life to Islam on the field of Badr. Therefore the Lord intervened on your behalf and sent this devil a letter to warn him that he would not allow the daughter of Auf bin Afura, the martyr, to be plagued by evil spirits. She is impregnable. Now go, daughter, and always remember your father.'

Indar
Old Iranian god of warfare, courage and bravery, the Indian Indra.

Injil
The gospels as given to the prophet Isa (Jesus) by God, according to the Koran (5:110; 9:111; 45:29; 48:29; 57:27). One of God's four holy books, the others being the Tawrat, Zabur and Koran.

Inn (Hebrew: *malon*)
In the Bible (Genesis 42:27; 43:21; Luke 2:7) an inn was not a house with rooms to let but a campsite in the open air near a well, sometimes walled in like a caravanserai, where the draught animals like oxen, mules, asses and horses were usually kept in the centre lest they be stolen. The poor people liked sleeping between the animals, for the nights could be quite chilly. It is therefore quite possible that Jesus was born in a cave as many traditions maintain, rather than a 'stable' which was no more than a littering place with straw for the animals. Joseph may well have preferred the privacy of a cave rather than seeing Mary give birth in public view. The shepherds may have arrived anyway, to draw water from the well, or to sell their wool, mutton and perhaps cheese to the travellers who had

to cook their own food on their own fires. It was not unusual for babies to be born in a caravanserai, although usually women travelled as little as possible. There might even have been a travelling doctor present.

Insan Al-Kamil
'Perfect man', the Sufi ideal of the man who is so imbued with the spirit of God that God speaks through his mouth.

In-Sha'-Allah
'If God wills' (Koran 18:23). No future planning should be done without this phrase.

Inspiration
In Luke 1:67–70 it is 'being filled with the Holy Spirit'; in Acts 2:4 the same phrase is used. See also Acts 2:17 and 4:8; 2 Timothy 3:16; Hebrews 1:1; 2 Peter 1:21. See *Wahy*, *Ilham*.

Irama (Iram)
In the days of the caliph Mu'awiya, a man named Abdullah travelled through southern Arabia in order to trade. Wandering around in the mountains of northern Yemen he came upon a wall that shone in the light of the stars. He rode along it and found the gate, which glittered with a yellow sheen. It was made of gold! Abdullah entered the golden gate and found himself in a city of precious stones, with silver pillars, diamond windows, emerald gardens and palaces of pearl. Abdullah took as many pearls and precious stones as

he could break off, and put them in his saddle bag. Before dawn, he rode out of the gate, but when he looked behind him, the city had vanished.

When he arrived in Mecca the news of his adventures reached the caliph who summoned him. Mu'awiya refused to believe Abdullah's story, but he had to admit that such wonderful jewels as the latter showed him could not be found in his empire at that period of history. So he called Ka'b Ali Habar, the foremost historian of his time. 'Is there,' the Caliph asked him, 'a city of gold and gems in southern Arabia which vanishes at dawn?'

Ka'b answered: 'There is, Oh Commander of the Faithful. It is the City of Irama, never seen in daytime. It was built by the tyrant Shaddad, who robbed all his subjects of their wealth in order to make for himself a paradise, for he did not believe the Prophet Hud whom God had sent to convert him to Islam. Shaddad died before he could live in it, as a punishment from God. The Prophet Muhammed (peace be upon him) has predicted that after his death a man named like his father [Abdullah] would be allowed to see the secret city. What Abdullah says is true.' See the Koran 89:7–8.

Iran
See *Persia*.

Irkalla
A name of the Babylonian god of the nether world.

Isa
The Arabic name for Jesus who, according to Islam was the last prophet (*nabii*) and apostle (*rasul*)

of God until Muhammad, but not God's son. Nor is there a trinity Koran (4:171): God is one God. In the Koran, Jesus is also referred to by other names, such as *Al-Masih*, 'the Messiah' (Koran 3:40) (q.v.). It is assumed by Muslim scholars that the word *masih* describes Jesus' miraculous power, for whoever touched him would at once be cured of whatever ailed him.

In Sura 4:169, Isa is called *kalimat-Allah*, 'the word of God'; this refers to Sura 19:36, where we read that if God wishes a thing to exist he only has to say to it: 'Be' and it becomes (see *Kun*). In Sura 19:35 Isa is called *Qawl al-Haqq*, which can only mean that the word of Jesus was the truth. In 4:169 he is referred to as a spirit from God. He is also an apostle and prophet of God (19:31). He is called 'the man without a father', like Adam who also had no father.

The spirit of God was sent to Maryam (Mary) (q.v.) and she became pregnant and gave birth to Isa (Koran 19:16–27; 21:91) (see *Jibril*). Isa could speak whilst still in the cradle (3:46; 5:110; 19:29–33). He could heal the blind and the lepers: (3:49; 5:30). He could raise the dead, as he did Al-'Azar (Lazarus) (3:49). He prayed to God for food, and a laden table (*ma'ida*, q.v.); it was probably a tray) descended from heaven (5:112–15).

Isa was not slain by the Jews, only his likeness (4:157–8). He was raised up by God (3:55). It is believed in Islamic eschatology that he will come back before the Mahdi (q.v.). Isa was given a sacred book by God, the *Injil* (Evangelium).

Isha'

Islamic prayer, one of the five daily *salats*. The time for *isha'* is about eight p.m.

Ishak

The Arabic form of the name Isaac. God announced the birth of Ishak to Ibrahim (q.v.) (Koran 11:71; 15:33; 37:112; 51:28). Ibrahim was ready to sacrifice his son (not mentioned by name; see *Isma'il*) 37:94–107.

Ishak was himself a prophet (4:163), teaching Islam. Muslims believe that Ibrahim and his sons preached pure Islam and that later generations of Jews altered that doctrine. Ishak was the ancestor of the Jews. He married Ribiqa and they had two sons, Ya'qub (Jacob) (q.v.) and Esau. Ishak stayed with his mother Sara in Falistin, Palestine.

Ishkhara

Babylonian goddess of love, priestess of Ishtar.

Ishmael

'God hears'. The name of Abraham's first-born son, by a handmaid, the Egyptian Hagar (Genesis 16:15). As the son of a concubine (as opposed to a wedded wife) Ishmael lost his right of primogeniture as soon as Isaac was born, so that Abraham gave his entire estate to Isaac and sent Ishmael away (Genesis 25:5). According to the Arabian tradition, Ishmael then went to live in Arabia where he had many sons and became the ancestor of the Arabs, while Jacob became the ancestor of the Jews. To this day the Arabs maintain that Hagar *was* the wedded wife of Abraham, so that Ishmael *was* by law entitled to Abraham's entire estate, and that the text of Genesis has been altered, to 'prove' that Isaac was Abraham's only legitimate son and heir to the land of Palestine. See *Isma'il*.

Ishtar

The Babylonian goddess of love and fertility who seduced men to serve her. Identified with the Greek Aphrodite, the Sumerian Inanna, the Phoenician Astarte and the Canaanite Athirat. 'The brightest star in heaven, queen of the goddesses, wife of Nabu, torch for the earth and the heavens, mistress of the sea, the earth and the wells, daughter of the moon. We have cleaned house and garden oh goddess of the pure sky, we have lit a thurible of cypress wood, oh give us health and wealth!' (From a Babylonian hymn). She was the most worshipped goddess in Babylonia. The lion, bull and dragon were her emblems, the beings dedicated to her. See also *Inannu*.

Ishullanu

Gardener of the Sumerian god Anu, who presented baskets of dates to Anu's daughter Ishtar (q.v.), whom he loved. She however, turned him into a frog after making love to him.

Ishum

Wise minister of Marduk in the epic of Erra (q.v.).

Isis

The Greek form of the Egyptian name Eset, whom the Greeks later identified with Demeter (see also *Cybele*).

She was also worshipped in Syria, the Lebanon and Jordan. She was the wise goddess of magic, especially of antidotes against snakebites. As the mother of the sun-god Horus she is represented with the child Horus on her lap. This makes her a precursor of the Virgin Mary. As goddess of the earth and of the dead she was later identified with the Indian goddess Devi Kali.

Islam

'Resignation'. A state of giving one-self over to God, to serve him for life.

Isma'il

The Arabic name for Ishmael (q.v.). He was the son of Hajar (Hagar) (q.v.) and so the eldest son of Ibrahim (Abraham) (q.v.). According to the Muslim tradition, Hajar was not a handmaiden ('the Egyptian bondwoman', Genesis 21:9–10) but Ibrahim's proper wife. However, he was persuaded by Sara to send her away (Genesis 21:14), and she wandered in the desert until, according to the Islamic tradition, she met the angel Jibril (q.v.), who opened the well of Zamzam for her 'by calling water to the surface' on the very spot where Mecca now stands. Later Ibrahim, overcome with shame and contrition, found her with little Isma'il in the desert while she was feeding the baby, herself fortified by the miraculous water of Zamzam, which the pilgrims drink to this day at Mecca.

Isma'il, who grew up to be prosperous, helped Ibrahim to build the 'house', the Ka'ba in what is now the Haram, Mecca's centre (Koran 2:

124–40). Jibril held up a cloth with the design (we would say the blueprint) for the Ka'ba, showing exactly how God wanted it to be built.

The story of the sacrifice which God demanded of Abraham is elaborately narrated in the Islamic tradition. It is always said that it was Isma'il, not Ishak (Isaac), who was God's chosen victim, although the Koran does not name the boy who said resignedly: 'You will find me among the patient' (Sura 37:102). Then, when 'they had both submitted their wills to God, Ibrahim laid him down on his forehead'. At that moment God called him: 'Oh Ibrahim, you have already fulfilled your vision' (37:104).

The later tradition elaborates on Ibrahim's grief, describing how, while he was placing the knife on his son's neck, tears trickled down his face. Isma'il, however, was patient and peaceful. Then Ibrahim applied pressure but the knife did not cut the tender flesh. In despair, the sad father threw the knife down exclaiming: 'Knife! Do you have to prolong my agony?' Whereupon the knife replied by God's will: 'Prophet of God! The Lord forbade me to cut that flesh!' Thus, Isma'il was saved and a ram, brought by Jibril (q.v.), was killed in his stead.

To this day, pious Muslims will kill a ram every year at Ashura (q.v.), to commemorate Isma'il the son who believed his father blindly when he said: 'My son, I saw in my sleep that I must sacrifice you' (Koran 37:102). It is this filial faith and the mature resignation upon learning that he has to die by his father's hand that is celebrated annually by Muslims, for whom Isma'il has become the perfect son, the ideal young Muslim, ready to die for God at any time, which is the true meaning or the word Muslim.

When God had sent the ram, he said: 'Fadaynahu', 'We redeemed him' (37:107), implying the concept of *fida* (q.v.), 'ransom', which is as fundamental in Islam as it is in Christianity (see also *Husayn*).

Hajar's desperate search for water for Isma'il has resulted in the *sa'y*, the 'running' between the two hills as-Safa and al-Marwa which is now part of Mecca's regular pilgrimage ceremonies. Both Hajar and Isma'il were buried in the *Hijr* (Sanctum) in Mecca.

Isma'il's second wife's name was Saida bint Madad ibn Amar of the clan Jurhum or Jurham. She gave her descendants, and with them Muhammad, pure Arabian blood. Isma'il was half Egyptian since his mother Hajar was given to Ibrahim in Egypt. Ibrahim himself, son of Adhar, was a Persian by origin. Adnan is the first mentioned descendant of Isma'il; after him, twenty generations later, Muhammad was born.

Isma'iliyya

A major branch of the Shi'a with numerous sub-divisions. It branched off from the Imamiyya (the Muslim community which believes there must be a living imam who is a descendant of Husayn) by accepting only the son of Imam Ja'far al-Sadik, Isma'il, as the rightful imam and so, the successor of the Prophet Muhammad as leader of all Islam.

Important sub-divisions of the

Isma'iliyya were the Fatimids who established themselves as caliphs in Egypt in 969–1171; the followers of Hasan al-Sabbah who founded a community in the mountain fortress of al-Alamut in northern Iran. These men became known as the Assassins; they were exterminated by the Mongol invasion of 1256. The Agha Khans claim descent from this line of the Isma'ilis. There are other groups in Algeria, the Yemen, India, Pakistan and elsewhere.

Isra

The nocturnal journey of the Prophet Muhammad. It is, in the popular Islamic tradition, the most important night in the Prophet's life.

The principal episodes of the narrative as it appears in the popular booklets in Arabic and many other languages of the Islamic world are as follows.

It is traditional to open the history of this night of the 27 Rajab with the ceremony of the breast-washing, *sharh as-sadr*: Muhammad was asleep in Mecca; two or three angels arrived and purified his heart with water from the well Zamzam. The moral of this passage is: No one can ascend into heaven if he is a normal, that is a sinful, man. A black clot, *'alaq aswad*, symbolizing sin, has to be washed from his heart first. Only then is the Prophet ready to see paradise. The pure word of God may reside only in a pure soul, to be spoken purely.

Next, Buraq (q.v.) appeared. Buraq was an animal with a human soul; she was the same, says the tradition, as the mount on whom the Prophet

Ibrahim (Abraham) rode when he travelled to the well of Zamzam, where Hajar and Isma'il awaited him. The moral of this passage is that the Prophet Muhammad resumed and extended Ibrahim's mission.

Buraq refused at first to carry Muhammad, but agreed when Jibril, the leader of the three angels (q.v.), told her that it was God's wish, and that Muhammad was the best of men, the pure Prophet of his word. In another version, Buraq smelled the stench of idols on Muhammad's hands, but Jibril reassured her that Muhammad, far from being an idolater, had destroyed the idols in the Kaaba, as God had commanded him. In a third variant of the narrative, Buraq insisted that Muhammad first guarantee her paradise; the request was granted.

Buraq, satisfied, was mounted by Muhammad and, accompanied by the angels, flew through the air to Medina, Jibril remaining on Muhammad's right side as his guide. In Medina, he told Muhammad to dismount and perform the *salat*, for 'this is the place where thou shalt establish Islam, and later die'. For the pilgrims of today, prayers at the site of the first mosque are always advised.

Muhammad continued his journey, landing on the mountain Tur Sinai, where Nabii Musa (Moses) held his conversations with the Lord. The passage of the Koran 20:80 is quoted here, although it did not necessarily take place on Mount Sinai. The burning bush stood, it seems, on a plain; it was there that God spoke to Nabii Musa: 'Lo, I am thy Lord . . .' Muhammad was told to pray there also. A third prayer was required at the birthplace of Nabii Isa bin Maryam (Jesus), whose miraculous conception is referred to seven times in the Koran.

The man, the mule and the angels then passed through a mysterious country where scenes from heaven and hell could be observed. They saw a group of farmers sowing corn and a few moments later harvesting the ripe ears full of grain. Jibril explained that this scene teaches young men the huge profit of the holy war. Just as those farmers reaped ripe corn within minutes after sowing, so the *mujahidun* (holy warriors) would go immediately to heaven when they died in battle.

Next they saw a place where a paradisiac fragrance lingered, although there had evidently been a fire. Jibril explained that it was here that Asiya (q.v.) was burnt to death together with her children in a huge cauldron.

Next they saw people hitting their heads against a rock wall. 'These', said Jibril, 'are the sinners whose heads were too heavy to rise for the *salat* of dawn.' (At the time when Muhammad saw this spectacle, he had not yet preached Islam, so that no one had yet been taught to pray the *salat*. It follows that God showed Muhammad this scene as an example of predestination as well as of retribution in the life to come.) The men who did not pay the *zakat* during their lives were dressed in rags, or had to eat live coals because they had spent all their money on good food and fine clothes while they lived on earth as wealthy men. (Most of the threats of punishment are directed at

men.) They also saw men who were eating raw meat, and others who were eating rotting meat: both were men who left their lawful wives to embrace unmarried girls or unchaste women (while their lawful wives were symbolized by the well-cooked meat which they left untouched). Note the association between 'eating meat' and 'taking a woman', and that between 'rotten' and 'morally corrupt'.

They then saw a usurer swimming in a pool of blood, symbolizing the blood – the sweat and toil – of his victims, who spent a lifetime paying him off. Then Muhammad met a man who carried a burden that was much too heavy for him. He symbolized the pawnbroker who lends money on trust, on people's valued possessions. The Koran says: 'God will wipe out all profit', and 'God orders ye to return the trusts to their owners' (4:58). The moral of these passages is that money is given by God (16:71) and so should be used for charity, to help others and not for making more money. No one should acquire and keep wealth for no one knows how long he will live.

In the next scene, Muhammad met people whose tongues were being cut off because they used their tongues for *fitna*, intrigue, sedition and slander.

Then a woman was seen beckoning to Muhammad with her bare arms, calling him by his name, but Muhammad rode on, looking neither left nor right. The next moment he saw another woman, ugly, old and unattractive (apparently the same woman later in life, but symbolizing the world in which we live). Jibril explained: 'If you had followed that woman when she was beautiful, your community would have followed their lust for worldly pleasures and forgotten the worship of God.'

Next they saw a man trying to pick up a big load which was far too heavy for him. 'This', said Jibril, 'is a Jew or a Christian who is undertaking much more than he can fulfil.' The moral of this allegory is that Islam is an easy religion which all men can understand and follow, whereas Judaism and Christianity are bafflingly complex. Behind this 'surface' interpretation there is hidden the implication that Christians and Jews are pawnbrokers, a specially despicable breed of men for Muslims. For not becoming Muslims they will have to carry heavy burdens in purgatory as a punishment.

Further along the way they met a group of people who were scratching their own faces with iron claws. 'These people', said Jibril, 'defamed their neighbours, fabricating lies about them.' The implication is probably that this is a just punishment for 'defacing' other people.

Next they saw a small hole out of which a cow emerged. It tried to go back but failed. 'This,' said Jibril, 'is the word spoken in haste, the thoughtless promise. It cannot be taken back.'

Further on they heard a voice from below the earth exclaiming: 'Lord, many are my chains and my fierce flames, what wilt thou give me?' And the voice of God was heard: 'For you are all those who forgot my law, my religion and the day of reckoning. Those proud atheists and those who worship false gods will come to you.' The voice was the personification of hell-fire.

They then passed through a lovely green valley with sweet-smelling flowers, shady fruit trees and rivers of milk and honey. 'This', explained Jibril, 'is the valley of the faithful, the worshippers of God.'

Next they met three men along the road who all call to Muhammad, pretending to have urgent messages for him, but Muhammad rode on without looking left or right. Jibril explained: 'That man on your right was a Jew, the one on the left was a Christian. If you had listened to either of them, your community would have followed them, not you. The third one was Satan himself.' The implication of this allegory is clearly that Christians and Jews are in league with Satan.

Finally, after many more encounters, they arrived in Jerusalem where Muhammad was told to tie up his mount to the same iron ring where the Prophet Ibrahim had once tied the same animal, the heavenly Buraq, to the wall of the Holy Temple (believed by Muslims to have been a mosque). They went into the temple and Jibril ascended the stairs to call the prayers (presumably *isha*). At that moment it pleased God to raise and call from their graves the prophets of the past: Nabii Musa, Nabii Isa bin Maryam and Ibrahim are mentioned by name. They came in and stood in a row on Muhammad's right, indicating that he should lead the prayers as their imam. Muhammad hesitated but the spirits of the ancient prophets invited him to lead the *salat* in the Mosque of the Rock. After the prayers, while Muhammad was sitting in meditation (*tafakkur*), three beakers were placed in front of him, one filled with water, one with wine and one with milk. Muhammad chose the milk and Jibril told him: 'If you had chosen the water your community would have drowned, and if you had chosen the wine your community would have sinned. Now your community will follow you in a choice of health and purity.'

The implication of this final passage of the Isra' is that Muhammad was the chosen leader of all the great prophets of the past whom God apparently gave physical form for the duration of the prayers. It follows that Muhammad knows the prayers best of all the prophets so that it is safe to follow him.

Isra'el

The new name given to Jacob by God (Genesis 32:28; 35:10) after he had seen God face to face. The name Isra'el has been variously explained but it seems to mean 'God fights', 'God wrestles' or some similar phrase. It is a very apt name for a nation which has always had to fight for its existence. The consciousness of Israel as a nation, that all twelve million of them descend from this one man, 'have come out of his loins', is the cause of a constant and living mystique. Very few other nations (among them the Japanese and the Kikuyu) have this myth: that they all, as a nation, descend from one ancestor, so they are all cousins. It explains perhaps why they help each other more than members of other nations, and why they mourn the loss of members of their nation collectively.

Israfil

The angel of the trumpet in Islamic eschatology. God created him at the beginning of time. He holds the trumpet (Koran 6:73; 18:99; 20:102; 23:101 *passim*) at his mouth century after century, for at any time God could give him the signal to blow it. At the first blow the stars and the mountains will fall down: the world will be destroyed. The second blast will set in motion the resurrection (*qiyama* q.v.), when all the people will rise from their graves.

Isra'il

Arabic form of Israel. In Arabic it means *safwat-Allah*, 'elite of God', or *safiyat-Allah* 'sincere friend of God'.

Isti'ana

'Begging for help' (Koran 1:5). The Islamic relationship with God.

Izha

'Offering'. Indo-Iranian goddess of the sacrifice.

Izra'il

See *Azrail*.

J

Jabra'il
See *Jibril*.

Jachin (Yakin)
'Certainty, surety, stability'. One of the two pillars near the gate of Solomon's temple. Its twin is Boaz (q.v.).

Jackal
In ancient Egypt, the jackal was the emblem of Anubis, who guided the souls of the dead to the underworld, as did Hermes in Greek mythology. Hence the attribution of wisdom and knowledge to both gods. The jackal was (and still is) admired for its wisdom and cunning in numerous tales told from Africa to India. See *Kalila and Dimna*.

Jacob
Son of Isaac and Rebecca. The secret of his significance for the history of the Jews lies in his great strength of body and his shrewdness: in Genesis 32:24 and Hosea 12:4 reference is made to Jacob wrestling with the angel of the Lord, and winning. His name was then changed to Israel, 'God fights' or 'wrestles' (q.v.).

Jacob did not have a good relationship with his brother, nor with his father-in-law, nor later with his sons. He was probably a self-assertive personality so that even his relationship with God had to be one of fighting. Yet God supported him throughout his life. As a result, the Jews, who had been no more than a small family, became a nation. Jacob was a very fertile man, and had sons with four women. The Jews are, and know they are, the Children of Israel, all descendants of one father, one family. See *Ya'qub*.

Jacob's Staff
The precursor of the magic wand, and of the staff of Moses (see *Matteh*), this staff, made of a branch of a certain tree, forced the spirits in the vicinity to make themselves visible; at the same time it kept them at bay through its powerful radiation.

Ja'Far (Djaafar)
1. Ja'far al-Sadiq, 'the Trustworthy', son of Muhammad al-Baqir, the sixth imam, the last one to be recognized by all the branches of the Shi'a. Born in Medina about 80 AH/700 AD, he

died there in 148 AH/765 AD. He was
a pious, quietistic character with a
great reputation for scholarship, and
he had a multitude of followers.
2. Son of Abu Talib, cousin of the
Prophet Muhammad, who called him
abu-masakini 'father of poor people',
because of his generosity. Ja'far fell
in the year 8 AH/630 AD near Mu'ta
in Jordan. He was carried to heaven
by an angel, where he was given
a pair of wings as a reward for
his bravery.

Jahannam
The Koranic word for hell (q.v.). It
is the place of punishment (Koran
25:65) which is irrevocable. The unbelievers will be driven into it (39:71).
The followers of Iblis (q.v.) will
fill Jahannam (7:18; 38:15), also
the *jinns* (7:179; 11:119; 32:13).
The evil-doer neither lives nor dies
in Jahannam (20:74). This means
that the evil-doer has already died
but that he is conscious and can
feel the torture which his body (or
its remains) undergoes in Jahannam.
Jahannam is a fire – or contains a
fire – which is kept burning all
the time (17:97); those who strayed
from the straight path are its fuel
(72:15), and so are the false gods
they worshipped (21:98). Jahannam
has seven gates which are open at all
times (15:44; 39:71).

Jalal
'Glory, splendour, majesty'. Allah in
his aspect of tremendous power, as *al-
hakim* 'the judge', *al-qadi* 'the ultimate
judge', *al-'azim* 'the tremendous'.

Jalut
The Arabic name for Goliath (Koran
2:251). Nabii Daud bin Isa (David
son of Jesse) heard a voice one day.
'Pick me up!' it said. It was a stone
full of letters spelling God's names. It
said: 'Abraham used me to stone the
devil!' David picked it up and put it
into his bag with his sling. He soon
arrived on the battlefield where King
Talut (Saul) announced: 'The man
who kills this Jalut will marry my
daughter.' David slung the stone at
the giant, killing him and so causing
the entire enemy army to flee.

Jamal
'Beauty, kindness'. Allah in his aspect
of grace (*rahma*), mercy, (*al-rahim*,
'the compassionate'), as the keeper,
(*al-hafiz*), and answerer (*al-mujib*).

Jami, Nur al-Din ibn Ahmad
Persian poet and mystic, born in
1414, died at Herat in 1492. Jami
was the last of the great classical poets
who used the Persian language as it
had been recreated by Firdausi (q.v.).
Most famous are his short spiritual
poems, like the following:

A friend is one who loves you even when
    you harm him.
For every man a man will take his
    place,
But without equal is his dazzling face.

Jamshid
In the *Shahname* the fifth king since
creation. God favoured him with a
thousand-year reign. He introduced
the arts into Persia: the weaving of
wool, linen and silk, the forging of

metal into arms, the masoning of houses and the working of precious stones. In the end he made his courtiers worship him, so God withdrew his favour from him and warlords took parts of his kingdom. He was murdered by Zohak (q.v.). Long afterwards his descendant Manuchihir (q.v.) ascended the throne.

Janna

'Garden'. In the Koran this usually refers to paradise (q.v.). It is described as the garden of delight (5:65; 9:21; 10:9; 22:56); the garden of eternal life (25:15); the garden of refuge (32:19; 53:16); and paradise (18:107). At its bottom rivers flow. There are wells (15:45), and rivers of water, milk, wine and honey (47:15). The garden is as vast as heaven and earth (57:21). It is very high (88:10).

Japheth

Third and 'white' son of Noah who went to live in the Caucasus and became the ancestor of the Europeans, the 'Caucasian' race.

Jashn (Parsi: *jasan*, Modern Persian: jashan)

Religious service in the Parsi Zoroastrian religion. It has to be celebrated on a purified place. Its purpose may be supplication, thanksgiving or worship. It ends traditionally with the Hamazor: the celebrating priest offers his hand to the leading member of the congregation who in turn gives it to the next one in rank. Each following worshipper takes the outstretched hand given to him in both his own and prays: 'Let us be one in strength and in righteousness!'

Jehovah

The Lord God in the Bible. This name originates from the consonant profile JHVH (YHWH, q.v.) 'God', which may not be pronounced by the Jews because it is *ha-shem*, the holy name of God. It is therefore always, when the Torah is recited, pronounced as *Adonai*, 'My Lord'. With that in mind, the Jewish scribes put the vowels of *Adonai*, a-o-a on the consonants JHVH, so that it now looks like 'Jehovah'. It was never so pronounced by the Jews, however, who always said *Adonai*. (Why the vocalization is 'Jehovah' and not 'Jahovah' as might be expected is a philological detail). In the nineteenth century some evangelist scholars took the word as it appears in the English Bible (Exodus 6:3; Psalms 83:18; Isaiah 12:2; 26:4) as the original name of God.

Jerusalem (Hebrew: *Yerushalaim*, Greek: *Hierosolyma*, Arabic: *Maqdas, Bayt al-Muqaddas* or *Al-Quds*)

The name of the city stems from the pre-Hebrew period. It is first mentioned in Joshua 10:1 and 15:8. King David made it his capital (2 Samuel 5:6) and brought the Ark there to rest. Solomon built his great Temple there (1 Kings 5–8; 2 Chronicles 1–7). The city was taken by the king of Egypt (1 Kings 14:25); by Jehoash, king of Israel, when it was the capital of the king of Judah (2 Kings 14:13; 1 Kings 12:21–5; 2 Chronicles 25:23; 36:2; and by the king of the Chaldees (2 Chronicles 36:17; Jeremiah 52:12). It was later taken by the Romans in 71, by the

Arabs in 635, by the Crusaders in 1099, by Sultan Saladin in 1193, by the Ottoman Turks in 1517, by the British in 1918 and East Jerusalem by the Israelis in 1967. This list of conquests is by no means complete, but it illustrates the vital position of this city in the centre of the Middle East.

It is also the religious capital of Judaism, it is a centre of pilgrimage for the Christians, and for the Muslims it is the place from which the Prophet Muhammad rose up to heaven in the night of *mi'raj* (q.v.). Jerusalem was probably a holy city even before the arrival of the Children of Israel under Joshua. It was most probably the 'rock' (now under the Dome of the Rock) and the hidden well of Siloah (Nehemiah 3:15) between the City of David and the Fountain Gate, which were the original sacred places that made Jerusalem a pilgrim centre. Near that 'water gate' Ezra read the sacred law to the people for the first time after the Jews had returned from their Babylonian exile (Nehemiah 8:1).

In old Jerusalem every street and gate, every old house has its legend, its resident ghost, its history of apparitions of those who died in the numerous battles, or as martyrs for the faith in one of the religions. Pilgrims today pay guides to show them the footsteps of Solomon, Jesus or Muhammad, and the graves of numerous holy or famous people. It was in Jerusalem that in the night of the Mi'raj, according to the Islamic tradition, God raised Ibrahim (Abraham), Musa (Moses) and Isa (Jesus) from their graves, so that they could attend the prayers in the sanctuary at Jerusalem, *behind* Muhammad, who thus by implication became the leader of all the prophets. See also *Sakhra*.

Jesse

Son of Obed, son of Boaz and Ruth (Ruth 4:13). Jesse's youngest son was David whom God told Samuel to select and anoint as the future king of Israel and Judea. Through David, Jesse was the ancestor of both Joseph and Mary, and thus the ancestor of Jesus. Jesse's dream, in which he saw a tree grow up from his loins, at the top of which he perceived the glory of God, signified the son of God, who would one day be born from his descendants. This 'Tree of Jesse' is often depicted in medieval churches in stained glass.

Jews

There are few references to Jews in the Old Testament, but they are mentioned in Daniel 3:8–12 as an oppressed minority in exile, being accused at the court of the Babylonian king of refusing to worship his gods and idols. The passage points in the right direction for the anthropologist who hopes to define the Jewish nation. Although the Children of Israel are defined by descent, like a clan or tribe, the Jewish nation is defined by its religion, since proselytes were already welcomed in Roman times (Matthew 23:15).

This religious definition was even applied by the Nazis, who defined a Jew as a person who had at least two grandparents who *visited the synagogue*. There were then people who signed a special declaration on a form, beginning: 'I have been accused falsely. I have never been a Jew . . .' The vast majority of European Jews, however, never denied their Jewishness and so died for their honesty. This fact alone proves that there was (and still is in some countries) a very special mystique about being a Jew which makes it worth dying for one's identity.

Jibril (Jabra'il)

One of the archangels, from the Hebrew Gabriel (q.v.). Sura 2:91 of the Koran shows that Jibril's function was to bring down revelations from heaven to the Prophet Muhammad. In Sura 64:4 he is the prophets' protector. Many scholars identify him with *Ruhalqudus*, the Holy Spirit (q.v.), *Ruh al-Amin*, the Faithful Spirit (Koran 2:81; 5:109; 16:104; 26:193).

He called himself Jibril when appearing to Muhammad when he revealed to him the first lines of the Koran. Jibril also appeared to the other prophets with revelations from God. It is often not clear in the Koran whether it was Jibril speaking to Muhammad or God himself.

When Jibril appeared to Maryam (Mary), his function was different. He looked after her in the Temple, bringing her food from paradise, then he took her to the river bank where he touched her or, in another version, blew upon her side, or under her garment, whereupon she becomes pregnant. Here Gabriel is also identified with the Holy Ghost in the Christian tradition. God also commanded Jibril to destroy the cities of Sudum and Jumurra (qq.v.), where

Lut (Lot) (q.v.) lived, and where the people were Sodomites.

Jihad

Holy war. This Arabic word literally means 'effort' and can also be used in the meaning 'doing one's best in the fulfilling of one's duty'. These meanings however, fall outside the scope of this book.

The holy war has developed into one of the major duties incumbent upon all able-bodied male Muslims. Theoretically it is only intended for the defence of Islam, but that includes attacking any country where Muslims are a minority without the full right to govern themselves. That is the situation, for instance, in Israel, in China and in the former Soviet Union. The *jihad* can be compared only to the mystic patriotism of the Romans, to the crusades and to the Japanese concept of *kamikaze* during the Second World War: the eagerness to self-sacrifice. Especially in Iran, this feeling of being a ransom (see *Fida'i*) for one's country, for the brotherhood of Islam, for one's own family, gives a young man a mystic feeling that his blood will pay for their sins, will liberate his nation, will make the faith of Islam triumphant on earth.

In the modern world this notion is difficult to grasp especially for those who do not remember the war, in which the German SS and Japanese soldiers fought themselves to death. The *mujahids* (those who fight the *jihad*) have likewise dedicated themselves to die on the battlefield. They know that they will soon be in paradise with their families and live there for ever in eternal bliss, close to God.

Jilani
See *Abdu'l-Kadir*.

Jinns (*jann* or *ajnan*. Plural: *junun*)

In Islamic countries we are told of the existence of the following spirits: *jinns*, *shaytans*, *ifrits* and *marids* (qq.v.) of which the latter are the strongest. In Persian the *jinns* are called *deve*, *deev* or *div*, in Pakistan *nara*. *Jann* is also used in the meaning of 'serpent', and Jann is also a jinn king.

The *jinns* (the word may derive from the Latin *genii*) form one of the four classes of sentient and intelligent beings (the other three are angels, *shaytans* and humans in order of creation). The *jinns* were originally created out of the air, like the spirits of whirlwinds, especially the hot air of the *simoom*, the desert wind.

God created them twenty-five thousand years before the earth. For many centuries they observed his law but eventually they became enamoured of their own importance and blasphemed him. He sent his host of angels, who destroyed most of the *jinns*. The survivors were divided into the good *jinns* and the followers of Iblis, Satan, although other scholars maintain that the satans (see *Shaytan*) were created separately, out of the eternal fire of hell.

Jinns are spirits and so mostly invisible. They possess intelligence so they can understand all human languages, and hearing and seeing are within their capacity; they can even feel pity and fall in love. They can also feel hatred, hurt pride, jealousy, resentment and anger. Some are enormously powerful and stronger than elephants (see *Ifrits*), others are as small as beetles or scorpions, who can only crawl and sting, yet they can all do harm and even kill us. Some *jinns* belong to the religion of Islam since they descend from those to whom the Prophet Muhammad preached. Most can assume any shape they wish, including those of animals or birds, and they can all fly at tremendous speed.

Jinns are either male or female, and they procreate and have children, although they live much longer than humans. They can take the shape of men and women and make real men and women fall in love with them, have intercourse with them and have children. If female *jinns* have children fathered by men, these children will have some *jinn* characteristics: long life, good health and the magical arts.

Many *jinns* have ugly and terrifying forms. This is the result of God's curse: When the *jinns* abandoned God's law they began to have intercourse with other classes of creation, especially animals, which is a sin, so God punished them by giving them misshapen children. No person should marry outside his class, nor have intercourse with other species.

Jirjis
The Arabic form of the name George. St George, in the Islamic tradition, became Nabii Jirjis, the Prophet George, with the praise-name Baqiya, 'the Survivor'. Many times God sent him to his people but they killed him. Each time God raised him from the dead and sent him back to his people to preach his true word.

Job

The myth of Job, as we read it in the Book of Job, has influenced many thinkers, from Muhammad to Jung. The Koran (38:42–4) stresses his obedience to God, entirely in accordance with the biblical account. The Biblical Prologue in Heaven (the title is from Goethe's *Faust*) also accords completely with the Islamic cosmology (Koran 7:14 ff.), in which God rules supreme, like the Byzantine Pantokrator, and has the authority to send bliss or suffering to men and women as he wishes.

Man may not criticise God; he has to say, 'I lay my hand on my mouth' (Job 40:4). God is not accountable, he can, if he wishes, turn against his faithful servant and destroy all that he has (1:12). Job (Ayyub) appealed to God (Koran 21:83) lamenting his fate but keeping his faith.

Jung comments on this: Job understood that God is supporting us against God (*Memories, Dreams, Reflections*, London, 1983, p. 373). Jung also perceived that precisely this contradiction, the fact that happiness and suffering seem to come from the same source, so that life at all times is dominated by doubt, uncertainty and instability, is the reason for the popularity and the timeless appeal of Job's history. With Job we all suffer this duality. Yet, as Jung also observes, the tale of Job makes religion whole: it closes the circle to form a complete philosophy. It may not be a 'nice' world-view, but is life always nice? What humanity needs is a cosmology that gives sense to a confusing world and yet explains life's contradictions. The Bible does this, while preserving the one-ness of God, and the Koran has followed it.

Johar

See *Pearl*.

John (Greek and Latin: *Ioannes*)

'God has been merciful'.

1. Apostle of Jesus and evangelist, writer of three epistles and of the Book of Revelation, which in turn has caused theological reverberations through the centuries, and especially influenced Muhammad. We owe John the concept of the *logos*, the word of God by which he created the heavens and the earth. God put flesh on that word and made it live on earth. The word here has come to mean 'spirit', as indeed it is so used in the Koran (19:17; 21:19; 66:12). Jesus (Isa) is identified with the spirit of God (Koran 4:171). We cannot begin here to give a synopsis of John's Gospel, let alone of his Revelation which has inspired writers and artists throughout Christianity. John's vision of doomsday, judgement and the city of God ranks him with the great prophets.

2. John the Baptist, who used the water of the Jordan to wash off the sins of his followers, so that even Jesus was purified to the extent that the Holy Spirit (q.v.) descended on him (John 1:32; Matthew 3:16; Mark 1:10; Luke 3:22). Mark 1:6 and Matthew 3:4 tell us that John lived on locusts and wild honey in the desert. Locusts are still eaten by the Bedouin (q.v.) in times when there is a plague of them. Wild honey could be found in a tree by following the honey-bird.

Jonah

One of God's minor prophets, who was sent to the gentiles but shrank back from his task when he saw the corruption of Nineveh. He incurred God's displeasure when he fled, thinking that he could escape. When he was on a voyage at sea (which must have been a long time later since the sea is a long way from Nineveh) he was thrown overboard in a storm because the superstitious sailors believed that ill luck attached to him. He was immediately snapped up by a fish and, much later, spewed out on the beach. By that time he had more courage and decided to try again to start his job at Nineveh. In fact he was a new man, since he was 'reborn': the depth of the sea is symbolic of the country of death, and the fish is symbolic of the womb. See also *Yunus*.

Jordan

Many tribes must have crossed this river, forced by famine in the constantly desiccating desert, to seek green pastures near the Mediterranean coast. It is the first river one encounters when travelling from Arabia, that never dries up. No wonder that its water was believed to be sacred and life-giving, and thus able to purify a man of his sins (Matthew 3:6).

Joseph

One of the sons of Jacob who had a dream in which he and his brothers were making sheaves of corn, and their sheaves bowed down to him. He also dreamed that the sun, moon and stars bowed before him (Genesis 37:5–11). When he told his brothers and his father about the dreams, they understood it better than he did. The Freudian meaning of the dream can only be interpreted as a desire to dominate his brothers and even his father.

Later, when he was tempted by the wife of the king's officer, he turned her down haughtily (Genesis 39:7). It was quite normal for handsome slaves to be seduced by their mistresses. Indeed, some impotent men bought slaves for the purpose of siring sons for them if they had no heirs. In the Islamic tradition Zuleikha's husband was impotent.

Judah

See *Queen of Abyssinia*.

Judges

The leaders of the Book of Judges were more than judges. They were heads of clans who rose to prominence by winning battles against the Canaanites and later the Philistines. So they were warriors, generals and administrators as well as judges. But they were also religious leaders who took care that the Children of Israel remained faithful to the Lord, who would then give them victory.

Judi

Arabic name for Mount Ararat where Noah's Ark landed (Koran 11:46). From the Greek Gordyai, the name of the Armenian mountains.

Jugular Vein

God is closer to man than his jugular vein (Koran 50:16). This verse is often quoted by the Sufis to meditate by, reflecting that God's spirit is closer to our spirit than our own flesh. All we need is to realize he is there.

Jumurra

Arabic name for Gomorra. Jumurra and Sodom (Sudum, q.v.) were the two proud cities of sin in the Jordan valley. When God commanded their immediate destruction, Jibril arrived, tore the two towns out of the earth, turned them upside down and smashed them down again, after which the clay bricks rained down burying the debris (Koran 11:84). See *Lut*.

K

Ka'ba (Kaaba)

The central sanctuary of Islam, towards which all believers must turn before beginning their prayers. It is also called Bayt-Allah 'House of God'. It is a cube-shaped building, hence its name. However Ka'ba also means 'nipple of a female breast', for it was once, like the Omphalos at Delphi, the centre of a cult for the earth goddess. In pre-Islamic times it housed the statues of the female heathen deities Allat, Manat and Uzza (qq.v.) who have been identified with the Roman goddesses Juno, Ceres and Venus.

In one corner of the outside wall is enshrined the Black Stone, to be kissed by every pilgrim. The pilgrims must make the *tawaf* or circumambulation of the Ka'ba, seven times in a clockwise direction. At its foot are the graves of Hajar and her son Isma'il (qq.v.), and it was believed that it was built by Ismai'il and his father Ibrahim (q.v.), under the direction of Jibril (q.v.), to restore Adam's edifice. Guides point out where Ibrahim stood while he built this structure, the Maqam Ibrahim.

The Ka'ba is surrounded by an open space of irregular shape, called Al-Haram 'The Sacred'. It is bordered by a portico of arches two storeys high, which surround the building. It is surmounted by seven minarets, the last one built by Sulayman the Magnificent. On the Haram is the well Zamzam where the pilgrims drink water from paradise, since it was called forth by the angel Jibril.

It is also said that for a time the Ka'ba was a Christian shrine, since a sculpture of the Virgin and child stood near the gate. Muhammad destroyed all the statues.

Kabala

See *Cabbala*.

Kabil

The Arabic name for Cain (q.v.). In the Islamic tradition, Kabil and his brother Abil (Abel) (q.v.) each had a twin sister. (Eve gave birth to twenty sets of twins, each set consisting of a boy and a girl.) The Lord commanded Adam that no brother was allowed to marry his own twin sister; they had to marry their brother's twin. So Abil and Kabil had to swap their twin sisters when they grew of age and thought of marriage. Kabil could not agree to this.

He loved his own twin sister too much and would not give her in marriage to Abil, in spite of the divine decree. He therefore quarrelled with Abil, and eventually killed him with a stone.

There he stood, with the body of his father's firstborn, the first dead person. What was he to do? Suddenly two male crows descended from the sky, and began to quarrel in front of him. One struck its fellow dead, and without delay began to dig a pit. It then picked up the dead crow and buried it, after saying certain prayers for its soul. Thus God showed Kabil what he must do with his brother's dead body. Kabil dug a pit large enough to accommodate his brother's corpse and buried him in it. That was the first funeral on earth. We learn little about Kabil's later life as a nomad in the desert.

Kaf (Qaf)

The name of the huge circular mountain range which surrounds the (flat) earth, according to popular Islamic cosmology. It is inhabited by *jinns*.

Kafir

'One who hides or ignores God's favours'. An atheist, one who says he does not know God. For this sin there is no remedy, it is *kufr*, 'blasphemy' (q.v.), a capital sin.

Kafur

One of the regenerative wells in paradise (Koran 76:5−6). See *Kauthar*.

Kahf

'Cave'. Sura 18 of the Koran tells of seven pious young men who took shelter in a cave, because they were persecuted for their faith in Allah. Their pursuers searched the cave but could not find them because Allah moved them from one part to another, while they were soundly asleep. When they finally woke up, it was 309 years later, and Islam had triumphed. This chapter of the Koran is frequently recited as a cure against illness. See *Cave*.

Kakka

Messenger of the Sumerian god Anu; he brought the gods' food to Ereshkigal.

Kaksisa

Babylonian star-god: Sirius.

Kalila and Dimna

Two clever jackals who told each other fables in the most popular collection of animal tales in the East. *Kalila wa Dimna* is the eleventh-century Arabic translation from the Persian, which in turn was a translation from the old Indian book *Panchatantra*. Originally this was a textbook to teach princes politics.

Kalimu'llah

'God's Word', praise name for Musa because God spoke to him (Koran 4:162).

Kamrusepas

See Telepinus.

Kan'an

See Canaan.

Karina

Also called Ummu Sibyan, 'Mother of Children'. In Egyptian folklore, a demoness who was greatly feared. It is related that King Solomon, when hunting in the wilderness, met a tall proud woman of great beauty, naked except for her hair. She threatened him, not knowing who he was, so he called his friend the angel Mika'il (q.v.) to his aid. As soon as the woman saw the angel, effulgent with helmet and sword, she was so terrified that her hair turned white and her appearance was suddenly that of an old woman. Solomon asked her: 'Who are you?'

'I am Ummu Sibyan the mother of dead children. I have power over all men's children before they are born, and over their mothers as well. I tie the women's wombs so that they cannot conceive, and if they do, they cannot give birth for the fruit will be lying across the exit, and if it does come out it will be dead. And if it lives I only have to look at it and it will die. For I am Salmas, the evil eye. I can prevent the cows and ewes from giving birth and I can make their milk dry up. I can make a man's pastures dry up, his grain be empty-eared, the seed in his loins die. I was once a woman, but I devoured my children in order to obtain black magic power. God condemned me to have only dead children and any woman to whom I show my accursed pudenda will have dead babies.'

Karubi

Arabic for cherubim (Koran 40:70) (See *Cherub*). They are the highest-ranking angels.

Karun (Qarun, the biblical Korah)

A wealthy merchant who lived in the time of the prophet Musa. His wealth had made him proud. He believed that he owed his success to himself alone without God's help, so God caused him to sink into the earth with his treasures (Koran 28:76–82). The treasure is believed to be still buried in Egypt, and some men have gone in search of it. See *Korah*.

Katanes

A type of vampire, a lean and hairy monster with sharp teeth.

Katib

'Writer'. Every person has an angel assigned to him who follows him wherever he goes, recording all his or her deeds, good or bad. On the day of judgement this *kitab*, 'book of deeds', will be shown to every soul and we shall be judged by it, since we cannot deny a single fact in that book.

Kauthar (Kawthar, Kausar)

The lake of abundance on the banks of heaven, just before the gates of paradise. Its water belongs to the Prophet Muhammad, who may permit his followers to drink from it as soon as they arrive, singed but not incinerated by the fire.

These souls, having spent uncounted hours climbing before arriving at this sacred place are safe from the attacks of flames and satans, and will no longer 'slide back', so they are allowed to rest and quench their burning thirst. The water is sweeter than honey, it cures all illness and thirst for ever. It also cures the drinker from all desire ever to go back to earth.

Kavis
See *Kayanids*.

Kavvana
'Devotion, purpose, meaning'. In Jewish mysticism the heart's intention to unite with God.

Kayanians
Persian dynasty called Akhaemenids by the Greeks, defeated by Alexander in 331 BC.

Kayanids
The eight Kavis (mythical kings) of ancient Persia, from Kay the modern Persian form of Kavi. They were: Kay Kobad, possibly the adopted son of Uzav (Zaw, the last of the Pishdadid kings); Kay Kaus, Kay Khusraw, Lohrasb, Bishtasb, Bahman Humay and Dara (Daral) (qq.v.) who was succeeded by Al-Iskandar (Alexander the Great) (q.v.). The Kayanids, like most mythical kings of Persia, owe their fame mostly to Firdausi's great epic *Shahname, The Book of Kings*.

Kay Kaus
The second mythical king of the Kayanid dynasty, in old Persian Kavi Usa, the son of Kay Abiweh (Abih) or, according to the poet Firdausi, of Kay Kobad. He led a campaign into Mazandaran, a region which was then inhabited by evil demons, who were protected by Diw-e-Safid, the white demon. This great spirit caused stones to hail down on the army of Kay Kaus and took him prisoner. After seven adventures the hero Rustam liberated the king whom he cured of blindness (caused by the stones) by applying the demon's blood to the king's eyes. Later, Kay Kaus climbed the El Burz where some demons had built a palace for him, partly by means of magic machines, partly carried by eagles and vultures. God, wrathful for he saw this alliance between the King and the demons as rebellion, withdrew his favour from Kay Kaus so that the king fell down from the mountain. He survived and later married Sudabe, daughter of the king of Yemen, who later tried to seduce his son Siyawush. After a reign of 50 years, Kay Kaus was defeated and imprisoned by Kay Khusraw who succeeded him.

Kay Khusraw [Khosrou]
The third mythical king of the Persian Kayanid dynasty. In Pahlavi his name was Kavi Haosrovah. He was the son of Siyawush (see *Kay Kaus*), while his mother was a daughter of Afrasiyab. He was born after his father's death and brought up by shepherds in the mountains in what is now Afghanistan. He showed his royal origins by his skill at archery without being taught, and at ten he braved lions and tigers. Gudarz, a nobleman, saw him in a dream as the future king of Persia and sent his son Gew to find him. Gew finally discovered Khusraw and brought him home to Persia with his mother. Kay Khusraw slew a dragon, defeated the redoubtable Turanians in two great campaigns, and killed Afrasiyab, his father's murderer. After a peaceful later reign he crowned his son Lohrasb (q.v.), king, and retired to the mountains, where he disappeared.

Kay Kobad (Qubadh or Kavadh)
King's name in the Persian *Shahname*.
From the old Persian Kavi (king)
Kavata, first of the eight (Kavi kings
or Kayanids of Persia. As a child
he was found by King Uzav floating near a river bank. King Uzav
adopted him and made him his successor. Another legend maintains that
he was a son of Naudhar, a descendant
of Manuchihir (Manushchihir) (q.v.).
Kay Kobad, according to a third version was the son of Zab (Zaw, or Uzav
himself). The hero Rustam (q.v.) was
sent out in search of the lost infant who
was found in a palace on mount El
Burz. Kay Kobad's reign was prosperous even though he had to defend Iran
against the Turanian invaders from
Central Asia. Omar Khayyam wrote:

But come with old Khayyam and leave
    the lot
of Kay Kobad and Kay Khosrow forgot.

See *Kay Kaus.*

Kerbala (Karbela)
A town on the Euphrates. It was near
this town that Husayn (q.v.) fought
his last battle and was killed. When
the country is safe, numerous pilgrims
of the Shi'a persuasion visit the shrine
on his tomb, over which a golden
mosque was erected. This was, however, severely damaged during the
civil war in Iraq. Several previous
mosques have also been ruined by
various attacks. This is the holiest
sanctuary of the Shi'a.

Khadija
The first wife of the Prophet Muhammad, mother of Fatima and so

ancestress of both the Sharifs and the
Sayyids (qq.v.). She was the daughter of Khuwaylid. Widowed twice,
she had two sons and a daughter before she married Muhammad.
When she married him in 595 AD
she was 40 and he was 25. She died
at the age of 65 in 619 AD. She
bore Muhammad two sons and four
daughters. Only Fatima survived him.
Muhammad loved Khadija all her life
and reckoned her among the seven
best women who ever lived. Hymns
are still sung to her in the mosques.

In the story of her life we read
that it all began when she saw a
young man approaching while she
was seated on the flat roof of her
father's house. A cloud hung above
his head sheltering him from the
sun. She perceived that this handsome youth was specially protected
by God, so, being a pious woman she
sent a messenger with a proposal of
marriage. Muhammad answered that
he could not pay *mahr*, bride-price,
since he was a poor orphan. Suddenly
Jibril (q.v.) appeared with a basket
full of precious stones from paradise,
worth a fortune such as had never
even been paid for a queen. The
marriage was soon celebrated and
was very happy. When Muhammad
received his first revelation from God
(Koran 96) he told Khadija first, and
she believed in him as the Prophet of
God. So she was the first Muslim.

Khalifa
See *Caliph.*

Khalilu'llah
'Friend of God', praise-name of
Ibrahim, since God was his guest

(Koran 4:124). Others say God sent Ibrahim sacks of fine flour in a time of famine.

Khannas
'Deceiver'. One of the functions of Satan the Inspirer (Koran 114).

Khanzab
A demon who disturbs Muslims' prayers, causing doubt in their minds.

Kharabat
'Old ruin, tavern'. The 'wine house' in which the Sufis gather at night round their *murshid* or master, who lights the lamp, symbol of the divine revelation. The wine is the symbol of the divine spirit.

Khatam
See *Solomon's Ring*.

Khatimu-n-Nabiyin (Khatm al Anbiya')
'The seal of the prophets'. Every true prophet of God has this seal between his shoulder blades, so that no one can falsely claim the prophethood. It is the hundredth, hidden, name of God in secret characters.

Khatma (Hatima)
'End, conclusion'. Prayers for the dead, usually in the form of a recital of the entire Koran which takes all night and is performed by the *Mu'allim* (teacher) and thirty students, since the Koran is divided into thirty parts, usually one day, forty days and one year after the time of death. It is

said that neglect of this recitation will cause the ghosts of the dead to appear and beg their children for their 'food', which for the dead is the prayer of the living.

Khaybar (Haibara, Kaybar)
A fortified city east of Medina which belonged to a rich clan of Jews, called Al-Nadir, when Muhammad settled in Medina in the year AH 1/622AD. Their chief was Kinana, their field marshal was the giant Jew Marhab. The fortress was besieged by the Muslims under the command of Ali ibn Abu Talib (q.v.), who performed many miracles of valour before taking the steel door of the fortress off its hinges and using his body as a bridge across the moat so that his men could storm the fort. Ali's fight against Marhab was the longest battle of the campaign until he finally slashed the enemy in two. Since that day other fortresses have been called Khaybar, notably the Khyber Pass in Pakistan, the 'Gateway to the Pagans'.

Khilafa
The caliphate. See *Caliph*.

Khizlan
'Abandonment' (Koran 3:154). In Sufism the state of a soul which has fallen from God's grace.

Khizr (Khadir)
'The Green One'. In the Islamic tradition the teacher of Alexander the Great (Al-Iskandar, q.v.) who fell into the Well of Life so that he would live until doomsday. Some people claim

to have seen him. He is referred to in the Koran (18:59–81). He is identified with Ilyas (Elijah q.v.) or Jirjis (q.v.).

Khshathra Vairya

Literally 'the Desired Kingdom' in the old Persian language. In the later Pahlevi texts the name contracts to Shahrevar. Zoroaster taught that before Creation Ahura Mazda, the Great God, created out of Himself seven divine powers or gods by means of which (or by means of whom) he then achieved His creation. Khshathra Vairya is conceptually the most abstract of the Zoroastrian deities, each of whom represents a philosophical concept as well as a god or goddess. In the upper world, Khshathra Vairya represents the kingdom of heaven, whereas on earth he represents God's kingdom of charity and caring for the poor and weak, thus overcoming all evil. Through him God, Ahura Mazda, rewards good and punishes evil afterwards. Khshathra Vairya is thus the god of pure purpose and good thought, the very personification of Ahura Mazda's majesty, power, and goodness, because goodness is the chief weapon for men and women to fight evil in the long struggle to realize God's Kingdom on earth.

Khuld

'Eternal life'. According to Islam, all souls will have eternal life, be it in hell or in heaven. See *paradise*.

Khuluppu

The world-tree in Babylonian cosmology. It stands on the bank of the Euphrates; its wood is medicinal. It is made into a nuptial couch for Ishtar's lovemaking.

Khumbaba

See Humbaba.

Khvarenah (Hwarena)

'Glory, divine grace', a reward from the old Persian gods for truthfulness, which stayed with an honest man for life, unless he lied. King Yima, the first man, was ruler of the earth. This made him proud so he boasted: 'I am immortal.' Khvarenah deserted him at once, and flew away in the shape of a falcon or hawk, evidently a sun-bird (see *Horus*). Yima died sadly.

Ki

Sumerian goddess of the earth, mother of Enlil the god of wind and sky (q.v.).

Kimiya

See *Alchemy*.

Kiramu

See *Katib*.

Kish

A Babylonian city. See *Etana*.

Kisra

Arabic name for the Persian Chosrow (Khusrau), the shah of Persia; sometimes also for the Kaysar, the Byzantine emperor. It is said that both rulers had a vision and heard a warning voice in the night when Muhammad was born.

Kiswa

'Robe, cloak', Muhammad's woollen garment. This was a long wide overcoat which a person, when going to sleep, wrapped around his body. Muhammad's *kiswa* was so sacred that sick people when touching it would feel better at once. Even the angels touched it. It was so wide that even Fatima, Hasan and Husayn (qq.v.) could be wrapped in it when they felt cold.

Kiyama

See *Qiyama*.

Koftarim

Mythical king of Egypt of the dynasty of the sons of Ham. He built the first lighthouse (which the Greeks called Pharos) on the Mediterranean coast. He built an entrance gate which could keep criminals out by means of mechanical staring eyes looking fixedly at the on-comer. This put all the evil men to sleep at once. The king also owned a mirror which showed him what every citizen in his country was doing at any time. It also showed him any approaching enemy armies. The king would then simply activate those 'blazing eyes' and all the enemy soldiers would fall down, fast asleep. The king's treasure house was guarded by a glass statue which turned all approaching thieves into clay statues. These have since been covered by desert sand, and some are still there.

Koftim

King of Egypt, son of Misraim, who lived in the days of the building of the Tower of Babel and the confusion of human tongues, so it is in his time that we first learn of the Egyptian language called Coptic.

Korah

Son of Yashar, leader of the rebellion against Moses (Numbers 16:1). See *Karun*.

Koran (Qur'an)

'Recital, revelation, word'. Its meaning refers to Sura ('chapter') 96, where the angel pressed Muhammad to read aloud the words he showed him, written on a piece of cloth. This at least is what one of the historians has recorded. The angel repeated the word *'Iqra'!'*, 'Read aloud!' 'Recite!'. Other scholars maintain that it was God's presence pressing on Muhammad, and that it was God's voice he heard. Certainly, this and all other words in the Koran are, according to Muslims, in their totality the literal words of God. Every syllable in it was willed by God in its place. (It would take us too long to discuss here the question of the createdness versus the eternal origin of the Koran).

A person who believes that the Koran is the word of God is a Muslim, since by implication he accepts that Muhammad spoke the truth and was God's last true prophet. Islam stands or falls by that belief. A person who does not believe that the Koran is the word of God, believes by implication that Muhammad was a liar and that Islam is an illusion. It is not possible to believe that half the Koran is God's word.

Muhammad's first revelation (*wahy*) (as recounted in Sura 96) took place in the Christian year 610, when

Muhammad was forty. During the subsequent twenty-two years of his life, revelations came to him at irregular intervals, sometimes only one verse, sometimes an entire sura at a time.

These revelations were put together by the caliph Uthman (d. 656) after the war in Armenia, in which many Arabs died, who knew the entire Koran by heart. The final version apparently satisfied most Muslims, for we know of little opposition to this definitive redaction. Some hold that Muhammad wrote down the Koran himself, but a large number of scholars maintain that he was illiterate, so that his mind was not cluttered by the knowledge of writing or any other knowledge. His was a virginal mind ready to receive God's definitive word.

The Shi'a scholars maintain that Muhammad dictated the Koran to his cousin Ali, but that this manuscript is kept secret. Uthman, whose legitimacy as caliph the Shi'a do not accept, tried to destroy it. Uthman's edition omits all references to Ali, the first imam, so that some Shi'a leaders are convinced it has been tampered with. However, the Koran as we know it today in its printed form is accepted by the vast majority of Muslims as the true version.

This means that since it is the literal word of God, it must be obeyed totally and without protest. *'Islam'* means submission. Every rule in the Koran is law. It follows that for Muslims in every country on earth the Koran is the only authority for their behaviour. In countries where Muslims are a majority, they will insist that the government must be based exclusively on the Koran, and not on any man-made laws. (We call such Muslims fundamentalists, a term they do not like). They include in the term 'government' all its branches: legislative, executive and judiciary. In countries where Muslims are a minority, they are unhappy to be ruled by non-Muslims, so they try to change the government to make it a Muslim one. The Koran is not only the sole fountain of divine authority for Muslims, it is also a source of salvation and so of good health. Recitations of the Koran are often organized for the benefit of the sick and of those possessed by evil spirits, much as the Bible was used in former days. It is also used for swearing in court. No book may be placed on top of it, and it must never be put on the floor. Some Muslims will not allow non-Muslims to touch the Koran. See *Revelation*.

Kothar-u-Khasis
Two Ugaritic gods of craftsmen and weapon smiths.

Krsaspa
The son of Thrita of the Sama family. Hero of the old Persian epic tradition. When his brother Urvakhshaya was killed, Krsaspa set out to avenge him. 'He slew the horned dragon, eater of men, the poisonous, yellow-coloured ... He slew the monster Gandarwa with the golden talons whose maw was a destroyer of men, whose hands were stone.' Krsaspa was seduced by the sorceress of Kabulistan, Khnathati, but he escaped. After his 'withdrawal' his sleeping body was believed to be

guarded by 99,999 fairies until the day of resurrection.

Kumarbi

Hurrian and Hittite god equated with the Sumerian Enlil (q.v.), comparable perhaps to Kronos. He was the supreme sky-god, weather-god and father of the gods. He played a major role in the great epic entitled the *Song of Ullikummi*, which has been preserved in the Hittite language. Kumarbi emasculated his predecessor (and father?) Anu and sat on the throne of heaven. Later, the earth gave birth to three mighty gods: one was Tasmisu (a rain-god?), the second the river Aranzakh (the Tigris). The third deity's name is illegible. Kumarbi married the sea-god's daughter, but this part is very uncertain. She gave birth to the giant Ullikummi, the mountain-god, wrecker of towns. Kumarbi was deposed by young Teshub, his own son (q.v.).

Kun

This mysterious Arabic word means 'be'. It occurs seven times in the Koran, always with reference to God creating the embryo of Isa in Maryam's womb (2:117; 3:47–59; 6:73; 16:40; 19:35; 36:82; 40:68). The sentence reads: 'If God wishes a thing, he merely says to it *Kun*, 'be', and it becomes.' *Kun fa-yakunu*, 'be and it becomes' is frequently quoted in the pious Arabic literature on the prophets, saints and other miracle-workers. Often the narrator will say: 'And then it was a matter of *kun fa-yakunu* and their wishes were fulfilled.' In this way Islamic saints, with God's help, can perform any miracle they

wish (see *Wali*). Often the traditional legend will also say: 'It was when the *nun* (the letter *n*) joined the *kaf* (the letter *k*) that their wish was fulfilled.' This implies that even God needs time to pronounce a syllable. He will begin pronouncing the word by the letter *k* (the vowel *u*, though written above the letter, is ignored; the syllable *ku* is treated as a minimum pronounceable unit) and by the time he is pronouncing the letter *n*, the thing which he has in mind is already becoming a reality.

Kurds

The Kurds have lived in the area which they now occupy, east of the Tigris river, along the entire northern and eastern border of present Iraq, for three and a half millennia at least. They speak an Iranian language related to, but distinct from Persian. They have their own culture although they are Islamicized. When the Arabs invaded Iraq in 635, the Kurds kept them at bay, but gradually all the good land was taken from them. When the Turks invaded in the eleventh century, more land was taken from them. Under the Ottoman Empire (1517–1918) they were left to live in their mountains apart from occasional expeditions of armed Turks to collect taxes.

In 1920 the British promised the Kurds independence but the successive Arab governments in Baghdad have never given it to them. Instead it is more likely the Arabs will continue a policy of ethnic cleansing (notable under Saddam Hussein) while the Kurds will go on fighting for their right to a national state. They feel that dying is better than slavery.

Kurnugi

In Mesopotamian cosmology, the underworld, the land of the dead. Ereshkigal was its queen, the mistress of the earth. Ishtar, the goddess of love and worldly pleasure, went down into it and as a symbol of the decay of all feminine beauty and all carnal enjoyment, she was stripped of her jewellery. Ishtar's absence from earth caused dismay because there was no more fertility as no bull mounted a cow, no man embraced his wife. The gods implored Ea (q.v.), the lord of intelligence, to find a way to liberate Ishtar. He did and she rose from the earth, like the morning star, retrieving her crown, and with her, love returned to earth.

Kursi

1. God's throne which is so vast that it stretches across the heavens. Just beneath it is the abode of the most blessed. (Koran 2:255).
2. The Ayat-al-Kursi (Koran 2:256) is the most revered passage in the Koran. Reciting it regularly assures one of reaching paradise.

L

Labuna
In the Islamic popular tradition, the big fish which swims round and round in the lower ocean. On its head stands the earth bull which holds the earth between its horns. Labuna eats 70,000 fish every day; these are specially created for it, each lasting it for three days' travelling. A specially created angel flies daily down from heaven to bring fresh food.

Labyrinth
A maze or 'erring' garden, common in ancient myth. The best known was the labyrinth in Knossos (perhaps the palace itself), where Ariadne (the saving spider-woman from heaven) spun her thread to save her lover Theseus from certain death. The labyrinth is a symbol of the land of the dead: easy to get in, impossible to get out.

Lahar
The Sumerian god of cattle, created by Enlil (q.v.).

Lahut
The divine world, the uppermost stratum of the universe where Allah resides. In Sufism the highest stage to which the seeker can attain; to be immersed in the deity.

Lamb
In the shepherd cultures of the Middle East, the lamb was the symbol of new life. Those people were so attached to their flocks that they regarded the lambs almost as their own children. Thus the prodigal son in the Bible was compared to the stray lamb. The eldest son, who was due to God as a gift to the father, may be substituted by a male lamb (ram: Genesis 22:8,13). Thus the lamb became the stand-in for the first-born whose life was offered to God in the earliest times. In Exodus 12 it is clear that the blood of the male lamb redeems, i.e. frees, the sons of Israel from being smitten by God, like the first-born of Egypt. As a result of these traditions, the concept of the son redeemed by the sacrificial lamb was familiar to the people of Israel. Thus John the Baptist used it (John 1:29) indicating Jesus as the redeemer. In Revelation the lamb of God (5:6–14) is worshipped, being the son of God himself.

Lamp
1. In Islamic tradition King David (Nabii Daud) prayed to God that he would teach him or give him a means to detect the liars in his kingdom. God created a lamp in David's temple telling him that it would go out as soon as a liar swore an oath while touching it. David soon realized how few honest men there were on earth.
2. The stars are lamps (Koran 41:12; 67:5). God is a lamp (24:35).

Lat
See *Allat*.

Lawh Al-Mahfuz
(Lauhu-l'Mahfudhu)
The well-preserved tablet, (Koran 85:21–2). The eternal Koran is written by the pen (*qalam*) on this mysterious tablet, a vast table of green pearl in heaven under God's throne. According to some scholars it contains the complete destinies of all human beings from creation to doomsday so that knowledge of what is written on it would benefit all of us. It is said that God can erase its contents if he wishes and so change the future at any time, but he keeps it secret except for his prophets.

Laylat al-Qadr
'The night of the power'. One of the nights in the last week of Ramadan (q.v.) during which, Muslims believe, God reviews the destinies of men and women. Sura 97 says that the Koran descended on this night, and that the angels descend on it every year to bring peace. Muslims spend this night praying in the mosque.

Letter (Arabic: *khatt*)
A line of handwriting, also *harf*. Letters are often used by exorcists to write incantations which will cure possessed patients. Every letter of the Arabic alphabet has a special meaning apart from its phonetic and numerical values; its meaning also gives it magic power, so letters can be used for divining.

Leviathan
In Psalm 104:26, the poet refers to the *liwiathan*, a creature made by God to play in the ocean. This word is often translated as a whale, but in Isaiah 27:1 and Psalms 74:14 we read that it is a dragon with many heads, writhing like a snake in the sea. Like the behemoth, the leviathan has a function in the apocalypse. The two monsters will ascend, the behemoth from the earth and the leviathan from the sea (Baruch 29) to serve as food for the righteous.

Sometimes the Hebrew *liwiathan* is translated as 'crocodile'; in early biblical times crocodiles could still be seen in some rivers in Israel and in the Nile they were still common. However, the etymology of the word, from *liwya*, 'writhing', rather suggests a snake, a seasnake or the cosmic ocean-serpent surrounding the inhabited land mass.

For the crocodile-god see *Seth* and for the hippopotamus-goddess see *Taweret*. For the hippopotamus as a symbol of nocturnal darkness see *Horus*.

Lice
These were sent to Egypt as God's punishment (Koran 7:133; Exodus

8:16). They could possibly have been sandflies or perhaps bedbugs.

Lightning
See *Barqiya*.

Lilith (Lilim)
Adam's first wife, the goddess of the earth and of the night, equated with the classical Athena-Minerva. The goddess' symbol was the owl, which points at an original identification of the owl with Athena. See Isaiah 34:14, where Lilith, 'the screech-owl' is a symbol of death and desolation. Lilith, like Athena, was originally a goddess of death who lived in the world under the earth, with the dead. As such, she was also a goddess of fertility, since for the antique mind the earth where the dead are buried is also the land that gives us grain and food, hence her function as Adam's first wife (the name Adam also means 'earth'). She revealed herself to him in the night and seduced him, against Elohim's wish.

Perhaps Cain was her son, and Abel Eve's. Being the sons of the rival wives of one man would explain their mutual hatred, fed by their mothers; in a polygamous household this is a common theme.

The name Lilith is derived from the old Semitic word for night, *lel* or *lelath*, Arabic *laylah*. As goddess of the night she also ruled the spirits and ghosts, hence her name also means 'ghost', 'spectre' in Hebrew. She is later identified with Lamia, the Libyan goddess of death and the earth. Lilith is also identified by some

with the witch Empusa, a precursor of the Succubus who seduces men while they are asleep by straddling them. She is also called the queen of Zamargad or Zuburijad, the emerald kingdom of the love-goddess where lovers wander for ever surrounded by verdant meadows. For her role as the goddess of aborting mothers, see *Karina*.

Some hold that Lilith was the goddess of babies; new born boys up to the age of eight days – the time of circumcision in the Jewish tradition, which was a cause of death for some; and girls up to the age of twenty-one days. Other traditions hold that Lilith was hairy; perhaps she was a goat, the totem animal of the city of Athena, Athens, and Zeus' wet-nurse. Hairy forest females often seduced human men in early myths. This is the precursor of the mythical *ghoula* or gorilla in later times.

Lion
Lions occurred, in antiquity, not only in Africa but all through the Middle East and into western India. Kings used to keep them as a symbol of royal power and a method for disposing of unwanted heretics (Daniel 6:16). In Syria and the Lebanon a lion-god was worshipped who killed a bull and devoured it. The scene is often represented in sculpture. Lions licked the feet of saints and prophets, showing that God's pleasure was with those holy men. St Mamas is depicted riding a lion as a symbol of controlling his wrath and passions. In Egypt the goddess Sekhmet (called Sachmis in Greek) (q.v.) was represented as a fierce lioness who attacked men

in battle in defence of her son the sun-god Ra-Horus.

According to the Islamic tradition, God created the lion out of the blood of the Prophet Nuh (Noah). One night, as Noah was busy putting the ark (*safina*) together from large boards, Satan came in the shape of a wild boar, to dislodge a board that Noah had just hammered into position. Noah, upon seeing the plank loose, took his hammer and put it back with double the number of nails. This happened three times, until Noah was purple with rage, but he uttered not a single bad word. The third time, in his haste (knowing that the ark had to be ready before the rains started) Noah hit his thumb. The blood flowed onto the sand and God created the lion out of this noble blood seething with the prophet's justified wrath. The lion then chased away the wild boar. See also *Queen of Abyssinia*.

Locusts

In the Islamic tradition, locusts were among the first animals created by God. They are sensible creatures and were among the first to take pity on Adam when he was expelled from paradise. They were created out of the clay that was left over when Adam's body was shaped by God. They have a king who is as big as an eagle; he receives his orders directly from God. Thus, when the Pharaoh refused to let the Children of Israel go, God commanded the locusts to fly across Egypt, spreading out all over the country, darkening the skies.

Locusts have old Arabic letters written on their wings, which read: 'God is one.' The locusts form one of God's armies which he can use against any heathen kingdom.

Lohrasb (Luhrasb)

In Firdausi's *Shahname*, the nephew and successor of Kay Kaus (q.v.) and fourth Kayanid king of Persia, who lived before Alexander the Great. Lohrasb founded the city of Balkh, now in Afghanistan. He was killed in his palace by Turanians and was succeeded by his son Bishtasb (q.v.). According to some scholars it was Lohrasb who sent his general Bukht Nassar (Nabuchadnezzar) to destroy Jerusalem and disperse the Children of Israel.

Lot

The nephew of Abraham, who lived in Sodom. God sents angels to visit him (Genesis 19:1). Later, God saved him from the destruction of Sodom (Genesis 19:16). See *Lut*.

Lotan

In the myths of Ugarit and Canaan, Lotan is described as 'the primeval serpent', the 'close-coiling one of seven heads'. This monstrous dragon was slain by Baal in a long and fierce battle. The name Lotan is the same as the biblical leviathan. Even the description is the same (See Isaiah 27:1; Job 26:13).

Lotus Tree

Lote tree, jujube tree, Latin: *zizyphus*, Arabic: *Sidrat al-muntaha* (q.v.) The Lotus tree of the end (Koran 53:14–16; 56:29) grows in heaven. In its shade Muhammad received God's revelation. There the believers repose after death. Eating the delicious fruits of this tree they cease all yearning for their life on earth. It is botanically quite distinct from the Egyptian lotus, *Nelumbo caerulea*, the famous blue Nile flower, and the white lotus, *Nelumbo lotus*.

Love

1. Like most philosophers, the great doctors and poets of the Islamic Middle East distinguish two types of love: temporary and eternal.

The love of God will last, once it has been kindled, for a lifetime and even after this life. The love of a person of the opposite sex is usually temporary, since it is based on fine appearance. A famous Persian physician cured a princess of her love for a handsome commoner by secretly giving the latter a poison which made him ugly, so that the princess no longer cared to see him. Death, too, cures such temporary love since only the living can be loved in this way, superficially and capriciously.

The Arabic word for love, *hubb*, is also used for intimate friendship, and this form of love is certainly intended to last a lifetime. This includes the love of the student for his teacher, a filial love. Love between parents and children is prominent in all Islamic tales, as is loyalty between brothers. See *Ishq, Mahabba, Hubb*.

2. Allah loves those who love Him (Koran 3:31; 5:54). God will give love to those who believe in him and do good (19:96). We should love God (2:160). The Sufis live for the love of God (5:59).

Lugulbanda

Father of Gilgamesh (q.v.), king of Uruk.

Lukman (Luqman)

The Arabian Esopus, a story-teller and sage (Koran 31:12–19). Many tales circulate in the Middle East from him and about him.

Lut

Arabic name of the Biblical Lot (q.v.). See Koran 6:86; 7:80; 11:70–89; 15:59–61; 21:71–4; 22:43; 26:160–9; 27:54–6; 29:26–33; 37:133; 38:15; 50:3; 54:33–4; 66:10. The frequent occurrence of Lut's name in the Koran indicates his importance. He was a nephew of the Prophet Ibrahim who was sent by God to warn the sinful cities of Sudum and Jumurrah (qq.v.) that they must repent or face destruction. Their sin was immoral 'lust with men in preference to women' (Koran 7:81). The sinful citizens persisted in their deviant ways in spite of Lut's message from God. Thus the Lord told Lut to take his family out of the city of Sudum. Lut's wife stayed behind for she wanted to buy salt first. Alas! God's commands must be obeyed immediately. She perished when God sent Jibril (q.v.) to tear out the two cities from the earth and smash them down. Afterwards rain descended and the Dead Sea was created, called by the Arabs: Bahr Lut, 'Sea of Lot', or Buhayrat al Mayyita, 'The Dead Lake', or al-Muntina, 'The Stinking Lake', or al-Magluba, 'The Inverted Lake' since there Jibril turned the earth upside down.

M

Macroprosopos
In the Cabbala there is a long description of this vast mysterious phenomenon looming behind all visible beings, behind the most distant stars. It is the face of God.

Madyan (Midian)
The land of the prophet Shu'ayb (q.v.), the father-in-law of Musa (q.v.) (Koran 7:85–93). The people called him a liar (11:84–95; 22:44; 29:37). They were punished with an earthquake (7:91; 11:94; 29:37). Musa also lived there, (20:40).

Magi (Singular: magus)
See *Majus*.

Magic (Arabic: *sihr*)
Magic is permitted in Islam only for curative purposes, and only if the name of God is invoked, and no other deity. This is 'white magic', which uses passages from the Koran. 'Black magic' is called *Al-shaytani* 'devils' work'. This includes fortune-telling by a *kahin* soothsayer who employs a *jinn* to 'steal' the knowledge of the future from the angels in the first (lowest) heaven. It also includes the art of paralysing or even killing a person at a distance by means of incantations, as well as 'charming' a person to fall in love with the magician's client, to go mad, to become unlucky, or to be transformed into a wild animal or bird, or to be unloved.

Mahabba
'Love', intimate friendship, especially divine love purified of earthly passion which the devotee feels for God. Indeed God inspires this love, then returns it. In the Koran (5:59) God describes his love for the blessed in paradise. 'He loveth them and they love Him.' This love is immortal. See *Rida*.

Mahdi
'Literally the one who is guided by God'. In Islamic belief, before resurrection, it is said that God will send his prophet back to earth as Muhammad al-Mahdi, the 'Rightly Guided One'. It is believed that with God's help the Mahdi will finally destroy the wicked and establish his kingdom of justice on earth. Several times in Islamic history men have been known as Mahdi.

1. The most famous of the men known as Mahdi was Muhammad Ahmad ibn Abdallah. He was born in Dongola, Sudan, in about 1840. From childhood he had been deeply religious; he studied with several teachers and was initiated into a Sufi order. For a time he lived at Aba, an island in the White Nile where he acquired a reputation for holiness and magic powers. He was attended by a small company of devout men and many followers. When he turned forty, Muhammad Ahmad, like the Prophet Muhammad at that age, decided that he must fulfil the mission which God had entrusted to him. He wished to cleanse the house of Islam by removing faults and accretions, to re-establish the faith of the Prophet Muhammad, and then to prepare the path of the Lord, i.e., make the world ready for resurrection (*Qiyama*, q.v.) and the day of reckoning.

In August 1881, the government of the Sudan sent an army against Aba, which was miraculously defeated, so that many believed that Muhammad Ahmad was indeed sent by God. A second, third and fourth attempt by the government to defeat the Mahdi also failed. El Obeid, the capital of Kordofan province, capitulated to him in January 1883. In November, an Egyptian army under the Arab governor and a British officer, W. Hicks, was annihilated, including Hicks and all his officers. This ended Turco-Egyptian rule in the Sudan: Darfur, Bahr el Ghazal and other provinces rallied to the Mahdi as their saviour from foreign rule. In January 1885 the Mahdists stormed Khartoum and overwhelmed the garrison. General Charles Gordon was killed. Then, at the height of his glory, the Mahdi died in June 1885 in Omdurman.

Many tales are told about the numerous miraculous signs from God that his followers witnessed, proving that he was indeed God's guided leader.

The Mahdi's state did not die with him. His *khalifa* (successor) Abdallahi, ruled the Sudan until Sir Herbert Kitchener defeated him in 1898. Abdallahi and his helpers, the Ansar, were pursued and killed in 1899. The Mahdi's two sons were also shot, but God, we are told, had his plans. The Mahdi's youngest wife who was known to be pregnant, was hurried to safety by the Mahdi's faithful followers in 1885. She gave birth in that year to a son Sayid Abd al Rahman al-Mahdi who lived to see his country's independence. He became a famous religious leader.

2. It is said in the Ithna'ashariya that the hidden twelfth imam, Muhammad al-Mahdi (q.v.), will return to earth at the end of time, when corruption and immorality are rampant on earth. All the people on earth will hear a clear voice (belonging to the angel Jibril (q.v.)) announcing the advent of the Mahdi and giving a detailed description of his features so that nobody can mistake or ignore him. Even those people who are asleep will hear the voice so that everyone must believe it. The Mahdi will be tall with a handsome, moon-like face, looking much like his ancestor the Prophet Muhammad. His name will be likewise Muhammad ibn Abdallah. He

will be preceded by the following signs, and any man claiming to be the Mahdi without these signs is a liar:

a. Heavy rains will cause worse floods than any before in history.
b. A meteor or comet will appear on the eastern horizon as brilliant as the moon; it will have two curved tails almost touching each other.
c. For three days and nights the sky will be bright red, like fire.
d. There will be war, civil disorder and destruction everywhere, the people will show no more compassion for each other, not even parents and children.
e. Foreign tribes from the Far East will invade the Arabian lands.
f. The sun and the moon will be eclipsed in the same month.
g. The people of Egypt will kill their government.
h. The Arabs and Kurds will invade Iran and Khorasan.
i. The Koran will no longer be followed and the people will be godless.
j. The pilgrimage to Mecca will be prevented by armed robbers.
k. Baghdad will be a city of sin and will be destroyed by an earthquake.
i. Epidemics and famine, plague and poverty will spread.
m. Dajjal (q.v.) will appear claiming to be God. He will command the devils who will mislead the people into sin.
n. Arabia will be totally destroyed by the army of the false imam called Safiyani.

The true Mahdi will be preceded by numerous regiments whose black standards will carry victory to the farthest corners of the earth against the evil forces of Dajjal. Thunderstorms will accompany his arrival, so that Arabia will become a land of many rivers along the banks of which green pastures will stretch where there was nothing but desert, and fruit trees will be heavy with fruit. Previously dumb animals will suddenly speak to the people, showing themselves to be equally intelligent. There will never be any more war, nor hostility among men. There will be no more corruption nor poverty since the earth will overflow with fruitfulness. See also *Imam*.

Mahre and Mahrianag
Adam and Eve in old Persian mythology.

Ma'ida
'The table'. In the Koran (5:114) the disciples asked Isa (Jesus) for a table. After he had prayed a red table descended laden with bread and fish. When they had all eaten their fill, Isa restored the fish to life. Some men declared this to be magic but they were changed into swine. Some say this happened every year. The people who ate from the fish were all cured from diseases. Finally the table rose up again to heaven because the people were ungrateful, ungodly and mocked Isa.

Majus
The Arabic form of the Greek *magos*, 'sorcerer, diviner, astrologer' cf. *magia*, 'magic', *mageia*, 'the lore of

the magi', now known as Parsees, (Koran 22:17). The magi were originally Persian priests but in the time of Christ the word referred to astrologers in general. They followed a star (Matthew 2:1–12) which may have been the conjunction of Jupiter, Saturn and Mars. The word Majus is also used for Zoroastrians in general and even for Brahmins. See Koran 22:17.

Mala'ika (Plural of *mal'ak*)

'Angels', a collective term used very frequently in the tales of the Islamic world. Angels do not reproduce from seed like plants and animals. Each one is created by God for a special purpose and so has a special shape. The largest known angel is the angel of time (q.v.), who rotates the firmament with the stars in his hand, thus creating countable time. Angels are created out of pure light so that they are transparent: they cannot conceal even a single dishonest thought, supposing they could ever think one.

The angels' food is the worship of God, their dearest wish is to help human beings in their suffering. In paradise they wait on the souls of the blessed, but on earth they work for humanity in disguise. God can send angels down at any moment to help his faithful worshippers in distress. Angels bring messages to God's servants; Jibril (q.v.) is specially assigned to carry revelations to the prophets. Angels may wield flaming swords to keep the sinners and devils out of paradise, or to strike disobedient *jinns*. Hosts of angels may be sent by God to participate in the battles between Muslims and unbelievers. They will rain hailstones on the latter who will die in their thousands. See *Israfil, Azrail, Jibril, Mika'il, Ridhwan, Angels, Death*.

Malik

'The Owner' (Koran 43:77). Perhaps the Arabic translation of the Greek Pluto, ruler of the nether world. One of God's gigantic and terrifying servants. He is in charge of Jahannam (Hell) (q.v.), where he supervises the devils who punish the sinners. When Muhammad visited him, Malik treated him rudely until Jibril rebuked him: 'You are speaking to the last prophet of God!' At once Malik became polite.

The tortured souls cry out to him but he tells them: 'You will stay here until God takes you out.'

Mamh

In Baluchistan it is said that in the mountains live exclusively female bears called *mamh*. Whenever one meets a man she will force him to copulate with her, after which she will give birth to another *mamh*. These female bears will even enslave a man and keep him, in their caves, breaking one of his feet to prevent him from running away.

Mammetu

Babylonian goddess of fate and destiny.

Manaf

One of the ancient heathen gods of Mecca, before Islam. The god's statue was caressed by women but when they had their periods they were not allowed to come near it.

Manakib (*Manaqib*, plural of *manqab*)

'Quality, virtue', but used mainly in the sense of miracles performed by Muslim saints as God's signs.

Manat

One of the three ancient Arabian goddesses mentioned in the Koran (53:21; 37:149). The other two are Allat and Uzza (q.v.). Manat was especially venerated in Balqa in northern Arabia, where people prayed to her for rain and victory over their enemies. The sick would come from far and wide to bathe in the hot spring of Balqa (known to the Romans as Peraea) and pray for a speedy recovery.

A statue of Manat was brought to Mecca where the people wanted to worship her; this was done during the annual pilgrimage by means of the well-known jogging between Safa and Marwa. When Muhammad was establishing Islam, he confirmed that those rites must be retained as part of the annual pilgrimage (Koran 2:153). Manat was the goddess of destiny, equated with the Greek Tuche, Tyche.

Manna

'Gift, abundance', in both Hebrew and Arabic. The food from heaven (Exodus 16:14; 16:31; Deuteronomy 8:3). God still keeps hidden manna (Revelation 2:17). Manna is mentioned three times in the Koran (2:54: '[God] sent down manna and the quails'; 20:82; 7:160). It is believed by Islamic scholars to have been a rain of white sugar ('hoar frost' – Exodus 16:14; 'white' – Exodus 16:31). It has been compared to coriander seed (Umbelliferae) but these seeds smell like bedbugs (Greek *kori*, hence the name Coriander), and are not attractive, even for hungry people, without being cooked. It has also been compared to syrupy liquids exuding from the tamarisk or ash tree. Other scholars believe it must have been wheat or some other *Graminaceae*.

Manuchihir (Manochehr)

Persian hero in the *Shahname*, born from a granddaughter of Faridun, King of Persia, who sent him to face the army of Tur, rebellious son of Faridun. Manuchihir slew Tur and his brother Salm in battle, and succeeded Faridun as emperor.

Maqama (*maqam*, plural *maqamat*)

'Station'. The soul travels through a series of stations on its way to God. Each station is also seen as a fixed attitude or stratum between the earth and the throne of God. The spirit (*ruh*) of every good person, saint and prophet has a special *maqam* somewhere between earth and God's throne (see *Kursi*). Even angels have their *maqam* assigned to them in one of the heavens. It follows that every holy soul has its own height or elevation above the earth as a result of the living person's own efforts.

Marduk (Assyrian: *Ashur*; Sumeria: *Enlil*; Greek: *Zeus*)

Babylonian sky-god, and king of the gods, god of storm and lightning. He was son of Ea (q.v.) and his goddess Damkina, daughter of Zerbanitu, and the father of Nabu; his cult centre was Babylon itself, which he founded; he was the national god. Marduk created the winds and storms like the Greek Zeus. He also fought the equivalent of the Titans, the gigantic offspring of the goddess of chaos, Tiamat (q.v.), who were eleven species of demons. When the gods trembled before Tiamat, only Marduk had the courage to take arms and confront her. With bow and arrows, mace and net, as well as the thirteen winds, all mentioned by name, he vanquished the sea-goddess and her monstrous brood.

He divided her vast body into the vault of heaven and the earth with the mountains from which he made the Euphrates and Tigris flow. From the blood of his enemy Kingu, he created people, the slaves of the gods, whom he told to live by his laws. When the god of death, Erra (q.v.), made Marduk rise from his throne in heaven, the sun set, the earth was plunged into darkness and crime ruled among the people, who began to eat each other. As soon as Marduk sat down again, order was restored on earth.

Marid

'Rebel' in Arabic. An evil spirit in Islamic traditions. See *jinn*.

Ma'rifa

'Knowledge, information'. In Islamic philosophy this word translates the Greek *gnosis* of the early Christian mystics. This new perception of the truth is poured into the Sufi's soul by God as soon as he has removed all desire, hatred and vanity from his heart and has made his mind still and peaceful.

Marriage

1. 'A man shall leave his father and his mother to be united with his wife' (Genesis 2:24). It was for Adam's sake that God created a woman and instituted the relationship we call marriage. When Isaac married Rebecca he was consoled for the death of his mother (Genesis 24:67). Proverbs 31 sings the praises of the good wife. Jesus said: 'A man shall be made one with his wife and they shall become one flesh (Matthew 19:5–6; Mark 10:7–8). Jesus condemned divorce.

2. Although plurality of wives is sanctioned in the Koran, the well-known passage in Sura 4:3 would seem to be leaning towards monogamy, since a man can only have more than one wife if he divides his attention and money between them all equally – not easy to do. The Persian work *Akhlaq-i-Jalali, A Code of Morality*, states (p. 135–6) '[a man] is to seek no other wife beside [his first]. With the exception of kings . . . no man is permitted to have a plurality of wives. Even in their case it is more prudent to abstain from it, because a man stands in relation to home as a heart to the body, and as one heart cannot give sustenance to two bodies, so one man cannot manage two homes.'

It should be noted that 'homes' here refers to the Islamic custom (already practised by Muhammad) of having one house or at least one room reserved for each wife. Since polygamy is only for the rich, such a man would have each of his wives in a house or flat by herself, so that many women would not even know their co-wives.

Maryam (Mariam)

The mother of Jesus. She is well known in Islamic legend. Sura 19 of the Koran is actually entitled Maryam. She was the daughter of Amran and Hanna, sister of Harun. She was given a room in the Temple at Jerusalem by her uncle Zakaria. One day when he brought her bread, he saw that she already had fruits of all kinds, fresh and sweet, on her table. Jibril (q.v.) had brought them from paradise. Upon her maturity, Jibril arrived and announced to her: 'The time has come which the Lord has destined for your conception' (Koran 3:45–6). Jibril lifted her garment and blew on her body, so that she suddenly felt pregnant (4:171; 19:16–27; 21:91; 23:50; 66:12). When she expressed her surprise at this, he explained: 'God has decided to create the embryo of his next prophet in your womb by sending you a breath of his Holy Spirit, just through his word, that is.'

Terrified and feeling sick, Maryam walked out of her room and out of the city. In the fields, she suddenly felt the first pangs of labour and had to lean against a withered date palm. She gave birth there and then and washed her baby boy in the well which God had created on the spot for the purpose. The water tasted like fresh milk and was very nourishing for both mother and child. Jibril reappeared and showed her that the old date palm was suddenly sprouting green leaves and fresh juicy dates. When she expressed anxiety about what people would say, Jibril comforted her saying: 'The Lord has looked after you and your son. When people ask you awkward questions, do not answer. Let your son speak, he is his prophet.'

So she ate the dates, fed them to little Isa, and when she came home with him, she did not answer the suspicious questions of her parents but looked at Isa who reproached his grandparents: 'Let your thoughts always be pure. I am a prophet of God.' When her parents heard this they bowed their heads and accepted their new grandson. See also *Isa*.

Masada

When Jerusalem fell to the four legions of Vespasian (an enormous army for those times) in 71 AD, Jewish resistance in Judea was by no means dead, but it was hopeless. It concentrated in two fortresses which soon fell, and in a forest in the Jordan valley, where Bassus, the Roman commander, simply cut down the trees until the Jews tried to escape. He had them all massacred.

The last bastion of resistance, the one place where all the Jews that hated Roman rule had assembled, was Masada, an unassailable citadel on a rock in the mountains to the west of the Dead Sea. There were perhaps 1,000 men in that fortress, with their families, under the able leadership of Eleazar Ben Yair.

Bassus died suddenly and the new

Roman commander, Flavius Silva, surrounded Masada in the spring of 73 so that no one could escape. He knew that all the survivors of the rebellion who persisted in their hostility were in the citadel, so he decided to smoke them out like wasps. He built an ingenious contraption 30 metres high to batter the wall in a place where it was difficult to defend. When the wall was breached, the Romans set fire to the wooden walls of a building, then withdrew to wait for the fire to burn itself out.

The defenders realized that they had no more than a day to live. Eleazar assembled all the men and spoke to them: 'We have the choice between dying in the flames or on Roman swords. Our women will become Roman concubines. Let us rather kill each other. Each man must kill his wife and children and burn all he owns. Ten men will be chosen to kill all the other men. One man finally with be appointed to kill his nine fellows, then commit suicide. Thus we will die with honour.'

That is exactly what happened. The fire burnt all night before finally dying down. When the Romans entered the citadel through the breach the next morning, they were met by an eerie silence. They saw nothing but corpses wherever the smoke lifted. Silva withdrew his troops, their job done. When they had gone, two women with five children who had remained hidden all the time, emerged and returned to their homes, unhurt. They were the only survivors.

Mashia
See *Mahre and Mahrianag*.

Mashianag
See Mahre and Mahrianag.

Masih
The Arabic form of Messiah, identified with Isa (Jesus) in the Koran (3:45; 4:157, 171–2). The Koran denies that the *Masih* is Allah (5:17, 72). In Islamic eschatology it is believed that the *Masih*, i.e. the Prophet Isa, will return to earth before resurrection, and before the Mahdi, but after Dajjal (q.v.) whom Isa will defeat in battle and slay. Terrible famine will visit humanity so that people will have to live on prayer like the angels, with no food available to them. With the descent of the *Masih* from heaven, a golden era will commence.

Masih al Dajjal
the false Messiah, the Islamic 'Antichrist'. His aspect will be monstrous and terrifying when he appears as one of the signs of doomsday. Others say that he will look like a handsome man on whose forehead only the careful observer will notice the word *kufr*, 'atheism'. He will defeat a Muslim army from Medina with his followers, the Jewish army, until the prophet Isa appears to defeat him forever.

Materia
A latin word meaning 'mother-substance', often used for wood. It also translates to the Greek *physis*, 'nature' and is rendered in Arabic as *asas* 'basis'. This basic substance was used by God for his creation according to those philosophers who taught that

God did not create *ex nihilo*, but out of the pre-existing matter.

Matteh

'Staff, rod'. *Matteh Elohim*, 'God's staff', was the miracle-working rod in the hands of Moses and Aaron. The word *matteh* derives from the ancient Egyptian *madew*, 'royal staff, sceptre'. See *Staff of Moses*.

Maut

'Death'. The Koran (2:182) says: 'Every soul will taste death.' This expression is based on the view that at the moment of death the soul comes out through the mouth so that the last thing a dying person tastes is death taking out his soul.

Mawlid

There are three categories of biography of the Prophet Muhammad. The *sira* or 'path' is the official Islamic account. His biography as written by Western historians looks rather different, since it contains accounts of the raids and other undertakings that are played down by his official Islamic biographers. Finally there is a third category of biography, in which the life of Muhammad is embellished ever further, and in which many miracles are narrated that God made him perform. This is the *Mawlid*, 'nativity'.

The many *mawlid* texts that are extant in Arabic, Turkish, Malay, Swahili and other languages, are partly didactic, partly liturgical. They teach the people (as opposed to the educated classes) what everybody is supposed to know about Muhammad's birth and youth. This narrative is usually interrupted by hymns to Muhammad which are sung by Koranic schoolboys (one might say 'seminarians', except that there is no priesthood in Islam) rather than by the congregation. The latter sing only some of the refrains.

A *mawlid* text is recited on the eve of the the nativity of the Prophet, the 12th of the month of Rabi' al-Awwal, and sometimes on seven consecutive nights. The recitation of favourite chapters of the Koran, the singing of hymns to Muhammad and frequent prayers to God for good health, avoidance of evil and admission to paradise are included. The listeners are blessed, it is believed, by simply hearing these devout recitations, which they could not perform themselves since the majority are not educated in classical Arabic.

The contents of the *mawlid* are conventional. It begins with the conception of Muhammad by his mother Amina, which was announced by angels and animals, and accompanied by miracles. The prophets of the past appeared in her dreams to comfort and encourage her. When Muhammad was born he recited his prayers immediately, by divine inspiration. He grew up as an orphan, for his mother died when he was six, and his father had died before he was born. His uncle Abu Talib took him on trips to Damascus for trade and so young Muhammad became a trader and camel driver. A rich young widow named Khadija (q.v.) watched him riding at the head of a caravan and fell in love with him. Their marriage was, of course, arranged in heaven. The *mawlid* recitation and festival is the most popular occasion in the Muslim calendar.

Mayit

'Dead body'. As soon as a Muslim dies his or her body must be washed (see *Washing of the Dead*) after which it is wrapped in its *kafan* (shroud), usually two sheets of white cotton cloth. Only the rich can afford a coffin. Burial takes place within twenty-four hours of death. The living must not be seen or heard weeping; only the prayers for the dead may be heard. Women are not normally allowed to attend funerals, as it is said that they are too emotional. The dead body is carried by the kinsmen (sons or younger brothers) to the cemetery (*maqbara*), where it is placed in the grave in such a way that when rising the person faces Mecca, for that is where the risen dead will all go.

Mecca (Arabic: *Makka*)

The holy city of Islam (Koran 28:57; 29:67). It is also called the 'mother of cities' (6:92; 42:7). The first ever house on earth was built there by Adam: (3:96). Ibrahim and Isma'il built the Ka'ba there. See Ka'ba.

Medina

It was to this city that the Prophet Muhammad migrated (the *hegira*) in 622 AD to escape from the harassment of the Meccans. This migration marks the start of the Islamic calendar. Ten years later he died in Medina on or near the spot where the great mosque with its famous green dome now stands. A mausoleum previously stood on his tomb where thousands came to pray for his intercession with God on their behalf. It is said that his voice was often heard there in answer to the saints' prayers, and even that his hand was seen by some saints.

Melchizedek

(Hebrews 7:1–2) 'King of Righteousness', also called 'King of Peace'. He is identified by some with the archangel Michael. Others hold that he was an archpriest as well as king of Salem. He blessed Abram (Genesis 14:18).

Menog

Old Persian for Spirit, mind, holy spirit.

Mercy

Arabic *rahma* (Koran 40:7), Hebrew *hesed* (Numbers 14:18). Both words refer to God's willingness to ignore transgressions, negligence and other human weaknesses. The Koran calls itself 'a mercy and a guidance' (10:58; 17:84). To live in heaven is to be 'in God's mercy' (3:103). God's mercy embraces everything (7:155).

Merkabah

'Vehicle', the carriage of Ezekiel (q.v.), the four-wheeled throne carried by the four angels symbolizing the four compass points of the zodiac (Taurus, Leo, Sagittarius, Aquarius, with the heads of an ox, a lion, an eagle and a man). Thus the vehicle represents the entire universe which is the throne of God. The *merkabah* later referred to a Jewish mystic sect, which, after the destruction of the Temple, stressed the universality of Judaism in the diaspora. The initiate is guided by the teacher through the seven 'temples' *hekalot*, symbolizing the divine macro-cosmos, while at the same time ascending the ever higher stages of his soul's evolution towards God. See also 1 Kings 19 ff.

Mesha

The King of Moab who triumphed over the Israelites (2 Kings 3:4), whereupon he erected an inscribed stone (now in the Louvre), dedicated to the god Kemosh, as a thanksgiving.

Meshed (Mash-had)

'Place of martyrdom'. The name given to the ancient Persian city of Tus after Ali Rida (Reza) (q.v.) died there, allegedly poisoned on the orders of the Abbasid caliph Al-Ma'mun, in 203 AH/818 AD. He was buried in a corner of the mausoleum where Harun al-Rashid (q.v.) had been interred after his sudden death in Tus nine years previously.

A large mausoleum in central Meshed now commemorates the death of Ali, the eighth imam. His grave was forgotten for centuries until the vizier of Sultan Sanjar was lost there during a hunt and had to spend the night in the old ruins. The spirit of Ali appeared to him in a dream and told him that he must rebuild the tomb and make it a shrine for pilgrims. This was done so that today it is the greatest centre of pilgrimage in Iran.

Messiah

In the Christian tradition, this concept combines aspects of the Jewish tradition, namely the belief in the return of David (Jesus as the son of David) (q.v.), with Hellenistic ideas. Whereas the risen David would only restore Israel to the Jews to live in freedom and peace, the return of the Christian Messiah will create the millennium: peace for all time, for all kingdoms. The deceiver, Satan, will be cast into the bottomless pit upon which the angel will set his seal (Revelation 20:2). The Messiah will ride on a white horse coming down from heaven. He will be called true and faithful, two virtues that are hard to find in human beings. All his soldiers will be dressed in white, riding white horses. They will vanquish by the word of God and the Messiah will be the king of kings, and he will smite entire nations and empires. Thus the Messiah will defeat evil both *in abstracto* ('the beast') and *in concreto* by slaying the evil empires – presumably their governments, since the people are seldom guilty of their rulers' crimes, although many nations have been punished for their evil rulers.

In Luke 4 and Acts 4:27 and 10:38, Jesus is referred to as 'the anointed' (q.v.). This is the original meaning of *messiah*, and *christos* is the Greek translation of this word. The origin of this concept is the knowledge that all self-appointed rulers are tyrants so that the only man who has a right to rule must be the just and honest man whom God has chosen. God chooses such a man for the Jews in 1 Samuel 9:15–17 and 16:1–13. Only God's choice can make a man the legitimate ruler of a nation. Only he will be 'true and faithful'.

The Jewish tradition mentions the Messiah only in Daniel 9:24–6, where his advent is linked to the restoration of Jerusalem after the Babylonian exile, i.e. after the Jews have returned to the land of Israel. He will rule only for a few weeks. It is only much later, in the diaspora, that the Jewish belief in the advent of the Messiah, i.e. the return of David, became widespread, especially in Jewish folklore, in songs and stories. The Jewish scholars were more hesitant about believing in him.

In Arabic, the word for Messiah, *Masih* (q.v.), occurs eight times in the Koran (3:45; 4:157, 171; 5:19, 75, 78; 9:30, 31). In all cases it refers to the past, to Jesus in the Gospels, never to the future. The word is simply used as a second name for Jesus, translating 'Christ'. For the Islamic belief in the future saviour see *Mahdi* and *Muhammad al-Mahdi*.

Micaiah

'Who is like God?' A prophet of the true God, opposed to the false prophets of Israel. He confronted 400 of the latter (1 Kings 22:6–28) including the charlatan Zedekiah with his horns. Micaiah alone prophesied the truth: that King Ahab would die.

Michael (Arabic: *Mika'il*, q.v.)

'Who is like God?' One of the archangels. A mysterious 'prince' who serves God (probably a warrior-angel) (Daniel 10:5–21; 12:1; Jude 9). Revelation 12:7 says that Michael and the angels will fight the dragon, and the dragon will be cast out in the final combat between good and evil, the dragon being the impersonation of the Devil, 'that old serpent' (12:3).

This heavenly battle for the mastery of the world, that is, of the human soul, has often been depicted in art and sung in epic. In the Greek Apocalypse of Baruch (XI:2), Prince Michael holds the keys of the kingdom of heaven, and a deep bowl which contains the merits of the righteous, in the shape of flowers. He supervises all the angels who guard the people and watch their deeds.

Midian

A region in Sinai where Moses' father-in-law, Jethro, lived (Exodus 3:1).

Mika'il (Hebrew: *Michael*, q.v.)

The name only occurs once in the Koran (2:92) but in later popular Islamic literature, especially in the *Tales of the Prophets*, the sacred history of the world, Mika'il appears frequently to defend a prophet of God against his attackers, usually the unbelievers. Even King Solomon had to be defended against Karina.

In Islamic cosmology, he was an archangel of God, second in rank only to Jibril (q.v.). Mika'il is the 'fighting angel' whom God sends where right and justice must be defended against demons and bad men. Usually the mere appearance of Mika'il, effulgent in his shining armour, is enough to disperse the enemies of God, blinded by the light of his wrath. Before the day of judgement (q.v.), Mika'il will fight the world's final battle against Iblis.

Milk

This is considered the best of all beverages for Muslims. One of the rivers of paradise is pure milk (Koran 47:15).

Miracles

1. A prophet who says 'God speaks to me' must show a sign to prove that God does act through him. In most cases, miraculous healings are God's signs to the people (see Acts 3:4–9).

The Prophet Muhammad performed several miracles according to Al-Bukhari and Muslim, two of the famous traditionarians: he cursed his enemy Suraqa, as a result of which the hooves of Suraqa's horse stuck fast in the rocks; he predicted accurately who would die in the battle of Badr and in which place; he healed Abdullah's broken leg; he fed a thousand people with the meat of a kid and a basket of barley; he quenched the thirst of his warriors by giving them water in the desert; the trees always held their foliage over his head in such a way that he was in the shade; he fed 300 men with one cake.

2. The best-known miracles in the Bible are the ten plagues of Egypt, intended to convince its king that the Jews must be allowed to leave (Exodus 7:10–11; 10). Some of these plagues may actually have a kernel of historical truth. Frogs, locusts and maggots do sometimes multiply in their millions. The stench of the Nile and the dying fish may have been the first instance of pollution in that long-suffering river.

Moses turned his staff into a snake, reminding us that some of the gods had staffs with snakes attached to them, a symbol of immortality. Exodus 14:21 tells the famous story of God 'driving the sea away' for the Israelites,

and later drowning the pharaoh and his army. In Exodus 17:6 Moses struck water out of the rock with his staff.

Joshua performed a miracle by stopping the water of the river Jordan, so that the Israelites could walk across (Joshua 3:16). Samson (q.v.) tore a lion to pieces with his bare hands (Judges 14:6); his last act was to push over the two heavy pillars of the Philistine temple so that all his enemies died (Judges 16:30). Samuel (q.v.) caused a great thunderstorm (1 Samuel 12:18). Elijah (q.v.) cured the widow's dying son (1 Kings 17:22). In 2 Kings 1:10–12, Elijah caused fire to fall from heaven so that it destroyed the hundred men sent to arrest him. Elisha (q.v.) struck the Jordan with Elijah's cloak so that the waters divided (2 Kings 2:14), enabling him to cross over on dry feet. Elisha cured General Naaman of leprosy (2 Kings 5:14). Peter cured two lame men (Acts 3:7; 9:32). Philip cast out evil spirits and cured the lame (Acts 8:7). Paul struck a sorcerer with blindness (Acts 13:11). In Acts 14:10 Paul told a crippled man to walk and he did.

The good miracles are the faith-healings, the majority of which are recorded in the Gospels and the Acts of the Apostles. Heathen kings were usually more stubborn, as were the mendacious priests and sorcerers so they needed more spectacular miracles to convince them that only the one God has the power. See *Prophets, Revelation, Manakib, Signs*.

Mi'raj

1. In Sufism, 'ascension' in which the individual soul, imitating Muhammad,

climbs up through the ten spheres of the Aristotelian firmament, at every stratum gaining the virtue in which the prophet ruling that stratum, excelled, e.g. repentance (Adam), compassion (Isa), brotherly love (Harun), readiness to sacrifice (Ibrahim). The final goal of that nocturnal journey (*isra*, q.v.) is to see God (like Musa), to stand facing him at a distance of less than a bow-length, like Muhammad. See Koran 53:6–17. See also *Heaven*.

2. The second (after the *mawlid*, q.v.) part of the popular biography of Muhammad is the legend of the *mi'raj*, the ascension to heaven. It conventionally began with the purification, often referred to as the breast washing (q.v.). Now Muhammad was free of deceit and mendacity so that he was ready to become the messenger of God's word on earth. For this purpose God invited him to come and sit before his exalted presence, to see him with his own eyes, for who would have believed a prophet who had not seen God himself, as did Musa and Ibrahim (qq.v.)?

In order that he could tell his nation about the perils of hell and the pleasures of paradise, Muhammad was given a conducted tour through the seven heavens and hell to see for himself how the souls suffered who had not kept God's commandments and how those who had, enjoyed eternal happiness. In addition he met seven prophets of the past including Musa and Harun who paid him homage as a greater prophet than they were. Even Isa (q.v.) admitted that Muhammad was greater. In this way the excellence of Islam above all other religions was instilled in the minds of the people who listened.

The *Mi'raj* owes its name to the Arabic word for 'ladder', by which Muhammad climbed up to heaven. It is read or chanted as a story or a poem relating all the miraculous things that the prophet saw in hell and the heavens, on the night of 27 Rajab, called *Laylat al Mi'raj*. See *Isra*.

Mirror
See *Glass*.

Mithra (Mitra, Greek: *Mithras*)
Old Persian god of covenants, of friendship and loyalty. One of the most worshipped gods in the Middle East, having been revered from before Zoroastrian times to the coming of Islam. Mithra was the bull-god, Taurus, who was sacrificed annually during April. The Romans identified him with Pluto (Saturn) the earth-god, and worshipped him until Christian times. They developed elaborate ceremonies and symbolisms (all based on Greek and oriental imagery) which continued secretly throughout the Middle Ages. Traces of them can still be detected in the masonic ritual, which has a basic theme common with Roman and Persian Mithraism: an ingrained loyalty to fellow members.

Novices were initiated in seven stages, each stage presided over by one of the planetary deities. Faithfulness and truthfulness were stressed in all the prayers to Mithra 'of the wide pastures', an epithet reminding us that he was originally a god of cattle owners. He has always been a warrior-god, and was carried from the Scythian steppes to Rome where he was popular among the Roman officers until Christianity favoured a different mentality.

Mitra
See Mithra.

Mizan
'A pair of scales'. In the Koran (21:47) it is predicted that: 'A just pair of scales will be set up for the day of resurrection. No soul will be wronged.' Even if a man's good works weigh only as little as a mustard seed it will be weighed. All a Muslim's sins will be written down in dozens of big volumes which will be placed in the left scale. In the right scale will be placed his confession of faith: 'There is no God but Allah and Muhammad is His Prophet', written on a sheet of paper, and that will be heavier. Thus if a man is a Muslim he will be saved from hell-fire provided he has kept the law of Islam: drink no alcohol, eat no pork, commit no adultery, do not steal nor kill except in the holy war, perform the five prayers a day, keep the fast, pay the charity tax, go to Mecca once in a life, and never, never deny God.

The *mizan* will be held by Jibril (q.v.) above the earth somewhere near Mecca. One scale will cover the earth while the other hangs above hell. Muslims are reminded by their learned scribes that they must give generously to the poor for they will find every coin they have ever given away on the right hand scale, and they will need every coin to tip the

scales in their favour against their many heavy sins which lie in the left scale. Those who have suffered much in this life will find their suffering weighing heavily on the right scale. Those who have spent their days in prayer and recitation, will find that their sins have been totally wiped out by their piety. All those whose debts have been forgiven will come and witness for their creditors, whose sins will diminish accordingly on the scales.

Mobad
Chief priest of the Zoroastrian religion.

Moloch (Molech, Molokh, Melech, Melekh, Malik)
'The possessor', the ancient fire-god. The Canaanite god of wealth, probably to be equated with Pluto—Hades and the Roman god Saturn or Mithra (q.v.). The Ammonites (in what is now Amman) worshipped him, and so did Solomon (1 Kings 11:7). King Josiah abolished the burning of children for Moloch in the valley of Gehenna (Leviticus 18:21; 20:2; 1 Kings 11:7; 2 Kings 23:10), which was intended to cleanse Judah. We know little about this ceremony, which Jeremiah condemns (33:35).

Moon
When Habib ibn Malik, one of the infidel Meccans, proposed to Muhammad that he would become a Muslim if Muhammad could perform a miracle, the latter pointed at the full moon which was suddenly split into two halves. The Prophet plucked the

bottom half from the sky and placed it in his left sleeve. Seconds later it came out of the right sleeve, after which he placed it back in the sky so that no crack was visible. The moon rose up normally. This famous legend is known as the moonsplitting, *al-ishtiqaq al-qamar*. One of the signs of doomsday is that the moon will come spiralling down (Koran 75:8).

Mordecai

The uncle of Esther and her guardian after her father's death (see the Book of Esther). The name Mordecai originally meant 'servant of Marduk'.

Moses (Hebrew: *Moshe*, Arabic: *Musa*, q.v.)

The greatest prophet of Israel. His finest hour – and on this all the religions agree – was being called by God and standing barefoot in his presence. By recording God's law, which was called Mosaic law after him, Moses became the central lawgiver for the three religions which are united in honouring him as their earliest great prophet, and from which half the people on earth trace their rules of life and morality. Moses' Ten Commandments (q.v.) are the basis of the moral framework for our societies.

Moses' followers must maintain a spiritual life with God at the centre, a life of respect for other life and for one's parents, and we must curb our desires and our aggression. We must be honest and speak only the truth. These are not easy rules, but they will keep us pure, since in the following chapter God says: 'Ye shall be holy men unto me' (Exodus 22:31).

Moses De Leon

A Spanish Hebrew mystic who wrote a number of works on the Cabbala (q.v.). The *Zohar*, *Splendour*, is believed to be his work; it has had a lasting influence on Jewish mysticism.

Mot (Mowt)

In Ugaritic mythology, the god of death, drought and sterility. The country often suffered prolonged hot summers in which the spring rains ceased early and/or the autumn rains commenced late. People would say 'Baal is dead', as the crops lay withered on the parched ground.

In the myths, Baal's sister Anath went in search of his body, found it and buried it on Mount Zaphon. Then the fierce goddess went in search of Mot and when she found him, she split him in two with her sword, burnt him in fire and ground him in her mill. When the rains arrived, it was believed that Baal had come to life again.

Mother of Scripture

The source in heaven from which the Koran was taken by God and revealed – in part – to Muhammad (Koran 13:39; 43:4).

Mourning (Arabic: *buka*)

Mourning the dead is permitted in Islam if it is of the heart and of the eyes (weeping), but not if it is of the tongue (wailing) or the hands (gesturing). Another tradition says that every tear shed for the dead will become a drop of fire on their faces, causing great pain. The reason for this is that God's justice must not be doubted. If the dead man was bad, his punishment will be just and we may not pity him. If he was good, he will receive joy after death. Angels will precede his bier and so the men must follow it. Women are not allowed to attend the interment since they might be too emotional.

Mu'allim

'Teacher'. Teachers enjoy great respect in the world of Islam. In small Muslim communities in the country, their advice is sought not just in matters of education but also in cases of sickness or possession by a spirit. The teacher will be asked to read the Koran to cast out the demons. The first teacher was Adam, who was also the first prophet since God spoke to him. He was even the teacher of the angels, since he told them the names of the stars.

Mu'azzin (Muezzin, muadhin)

The caller of the prayers five times a day. One Friday morning the caller of the dawn prayer will be the angel of the resurrection.

Muhammad (570–632 AD)

For the Muslims the last and most trustworthy prophet of the one God. To him God revealed the Koran in chapters or in strings of verses, between his fortieth year and his death. The revelation happened when a voice called Muhammad to recite (Koran 96: 1–3). Receiving a revelation was a heavy duty, which left Muhammad exhausted. Often when he felt the spirit approaching, he was frightened and wrapped his cloak around himself. It is possible

of course that he felt cold because the fever of the trance made him shiver (Koran 73:1–4; 74:1–3).

The revelation was exclusively received in the form of verses of the Koran. There are few allusions to visions (17:60; 53:5; 81:23), and two allusions to the 'night journey' (see *Isra*) and the journey to heaven or ascension (see *Mi'raj*), during which Muhammad travelled through the skies (17:1; 53:5–18).

For Muslims it is necessary to believe that Muhammad was *insan al-kamil*, 'the perfect man', first because he never lied, for if he lied just once how could anyone believe whatever else he might have said? Secondly he was perfect because he was chosen by God to be his last prophet, to whom he entrusted his definitive revelation to mankind.

The Sufis revere Muhammad because he experienced the proximity of the divine spirit, who spoke to him (through an angel?). An extensive biographical literature, the *hadith* (q.v.) details every word of Muhammad's that was remembered by his contemporaries. In addition there is an extensive popular tradition relating his numerous miracles. See also *Mawlid*.

Muhammad the Imam

Muhammad ibn Ali ibn Husayn, the fifth imam of the Shi'a, praise-named al-Baqir, 'the One who opens the Source of Knowledge'. Born in Medina, he died there in 115 AH/733 AD, at fifty years of age.

Muhammad Al-Mahdi

The twelfth imam of the Twelver branch of the Shi'a. He was the son of Hasan al-Askari. The Twelvers believe that God concealed the baby so that he became invisible when the caliph's soldiers came to search for him. He was probably born after his father's death in 260 AH/874 AD.

Shi'a writers have drawn parallels between young Al-Mahdi and little Musa, whom the pharaoh wanted to destroy, but whom God protected. Both his conception and his birth were kept so secret that only a handful of devoted servants knew him. The caliph ordered all the wives and slave girls of the deceased eleventh imam Hasan arrested, but to no avail: the child could not be found.

This event inaugurated the period of *ghayba sughra*, 'minor occultation', in which the twelfth imam, though invisible, still communicated with his selected followers. He appointed *safirs*, ambassadors, who would not only communicate his wishes to other countries where his followers lived, but would also be charged with the care of the devotees in Iraq itself.

After seventy years, in 329 AH/ 940 AD, the minor occultation came to an end and the major occultation, *ghayba al-kubra*, began. In other words, God decided that the period of his earthly existence was over, so he no longer communicated with his followers except in dreams and visions, and he may walk upon earth visibly but no one will recognize him except his most devoted followers. They may write him letters which must be placed on the tomb of one of the imams whence it will find its way to Al-Mahdi. One can likewise send a letter floating down a river, or pray to the imam. See also *Mahdi 2*.

Muhammad Taqi

'God-fearing', also praise-named Zaki, 'Intelligent', the ninth imam of the Twelver branch of the Shi'a, and son of Ali Rida (Reza) (q.v.). He was such a great scholar that numerous people visited him to seek answers to questions concerning doctrine and duty. The imam's answers have been recorded and fill 3000 pages of writing. Muhammad died in 220 AH/835 AD and was buried in Al-Kazimayn, near Baghdad, in the same tomb as his grandfather Musa, which is still a centre of pilgrimage.

Muharram

'Forbidden, sacred'. The first month of the Islamic year. The first ten days of Muharram are especially sacred. Many prayers are said to honour the imam Husayn, whose death is commemorated on the 10th, the day of *Ashura* (q.v.). This is the day that God created Adam and Eve and also the day on which Ibrahim had to sacrifice his son, but received a ram instead. Because of this a sheep is slaughtered by all well-to-do Muslim households. The meat is given away to the poor.

The Shi'a, especially, celebrate this day with processions and hymns of mourning. In the first ten days they perform the *majalis*, 'sessions', during which, step by step, the events of Husayn's life are commemorated. Each day an episode is recounted or even (in Iran) performed on the stage: how he went to Kerbela against his family's wishes; how he and his family were ambushed; how they suffered from thirst; how his sons died, with the exception of one who was ill, etc.

Muhyi

'The one who gives life', one of the glorious names of God. 'Look at the signs of God's mercy how he gives life to the earth after she has died. Indeed he will give life to the dead' [at resurrection] Koran 30:49. This passage is used for meditation by the Sufis who await God's moment to give them spiritual life.

Mujahada

'Striving earnestly' for God's sake, from the Koran 29:69. It means overcoming one's carnal desires and other base instincts in oneself. This is the second stage on the Sufi's path to God. A *mujahid* is a man who exerts himself for God, usually in a holy war.

Mulitta

A Babylonian goddess (called Ninlil in Sumerian, Mylitta in Greek) consort of Ellil (q.v.). They were worshipped at Nippur.

Munkar and Nakir

The two messengers in the grave, according to Muslim belief. As soon as the crowd has dispersed from a funeral the dead man in his grave will see Munkar and Nakir, two angels dressed in shining white who will speak to the good man with friendliness. But to the bad man they will look like two terrifying black giants who will speak harshly to him and beat him with red-hot iron staves. They ask: 'Who is your God? What is your religion? Who is your Prophet? What is your holy book? What is your *qibla*?' The correct answers are: 'Allah. Islam. Muhammad. The Koran. The Ka'ba.' If they are given, the man will be left in peace, the grave will become less oppressive and he will see paradise.

Mursal

'One sent', an apostle of God in Islam, who brings his people an inspired book.

Musa

Arabic form of the name Moses, the founder of the Jewish religion. Allah revealed the Tawrat (Torah) to him. The original text was entirely in accordance with the Koran. In the Koran, Musa is the most mentioned of all the prophets after Muhammad. Most episodes related in the Koran are close to the originals in Exodus and Deuteronomy. The calling of the Lord to Musa occurs five times in the Koran (19:52; 20:9–23; 27:7–12; 28:29–35; 79:15–16) demonstrating the central position of Musa and his relation to God in Islam. Sufi thinkers meditate on Musa's blessedness among the prophets because God called him by name to his service. Is there greater joy possible for the soul? The passage in which God calls Musa from the tree, 'Oh Musa, I am Allah!' (28:30) is a sentence for prolonged meditation by the Sufis.

Musa ibn Ja'far

Praise-named Al-Kazim, 'Who Controls his Wrath'. Seventh imam in the cosmology of the Twelvers, not recognized as imam by the Seveners, who maintain that Ja'far's eldest son Isma'il though he predeceased his father, should have been the sixth imam. See *Isma'iliyya*. Musa was imprisoned twice, the last time by Harun al-Rashid, who probably had him poisoned. He died in 183 AH/ 799 AD. Musa was known for his steadfastness in prayer. Some of the Shi'a believe that he did not die but was hidden by God. These followers of Musa are known as the Musawiyya. One day God will cause him to reappear as the Mahdi, they say. Musa is said to have had thirty-seven children.

Muwakkil
'Representative agent'. Guardian angel who acts on behalf of a possessed patient to chase out the devil.

Mysticism
Direct communication between man and God, not through the senses but through the inward perception of the mind, by divine intuition in the soul. The Muslim theologians point at Musa, who held *munajat*, 'conversations' with God on Mount Tur Sinai, and at Adam and Ibrahim, to whom God spoke. The Sufis believe that even now God may speak to his friend (*wali* q.v.). The philosophical elements of mysticism can be summarized as follows:

1. There are two worlds, one being our own material world, the other being invisible.
2. Desire keeps us attached to this world, so its conquest is necessary as a first step.
3. The other world is spiritual and superior. The unknown, unseen, future world is believed to be the true one.
4. Purity is chosen over corruption,

honour over dishonesty, abstract truth over illusion.
5. This choice introduces value: the price one is prepared to pay to obtain or retain a valued thing. This world is regarded as valueless, the sight of God is worth life.
6. The concepts of morality, the weighing of good and evil, and obedience to conscience, are indispensable prerequisites for the achievement of the goal.
7. In daily life the mind is tested for its detachment, until all the desires of the body have gone.
8. This world is finite; the other world is infinite, so the mystic looks forward to living in the universe, 'outside'.
9. The earliest mystic experience is seeing God, at first from a distance, gradually closer, as a dazzling light.
10. The highest experience is the merging of the soul into the deity, the extinction of the self into the self.
11. The soul feels a constant nostalgia to see the other world, heaven, the ocean of light, *nur-darya*, or the mountain of light, *koh-i-noor*.
12. Detachment makes compassion and charity possible. The mystic gives his property away to the poor.
13. The mystic becomes a pilgrim on his way to the promised land. Life becomes a path, leading up the mountain of light.
14. Mysticism has evolved from unity with nature in primitive religions to the unity with God's luminous presence, in a totally spiritual reality.

Nabii (Hebrew: *nevii*)

'Prophet', derived from a verb meaning 'to erupt, boil over'. In some African languages 'boiling' is associated with the activity of spirits. In modern times the word 'prophet' is associated with forecasting the future, but in Arabic and Hebrew the association is more often with the law. The prophet is inspired by God to teach his people the law. Only divinely inspired law will be obeyed by people.

In Islamic theology, a *nabii* is a prophet of Allah, a man to whom God has given *nubuwwa*, the status, task and fate of a prophet. The prophet must enounce in public, *tanabba'a*, what God gives him to say through *wahy*, direct inspiration, or through an angel, *malak*, usually Jibril (q.v.) or by means of revelation inside his heart, *ilham*, by vision, *ru'ya*, or in a dream. The prophet has *nubu'*, 'high status', but he also has to suffer persecution, ridicule, slander, scorn and disbelief. In Arabia before Islam, a man would be called a *nabii* when he started prophesying, *tanabba'a*, inspired by some deity.

Nabu (Nebo)

A Mesopotamian god of speech, language, eloquence and wisdom, patron of scribes, worshipped at Borsippa. Son of Mardu. As messenger of the gods he was equated with the Greek Hirmis (q.v.). He was much worshipped by the Babylonians — witness such royal names as Nebuchadnasser, 'Nabu triumphs'.

Nafs

See *Soul*.

Najashi

The Negus, the king of Ethiopia to whom Muhammad sent a delegation including Ali, who was well received by the Christian king and founded a Muslim community.

Nakir

See *Munkar and Nakir*.

Nammu

Sumerian goddess of the sea who created heaven and earth.

Namrud (Nimrod)

The king who intended to burn the prophet Ibrahim (q.v.) on the pyre but failed since God made the fire cool. Namrud's daughter Sarah (q.v.) married Ibrahim. See *Nimrod*.

Namtar
Mesopotamian god of the plague and other diseases; for this power he was feared by all. He was the chief minister to Queen Ereshkigal in the land of the dead.

Namus
'Law'. The sacred law which Muhammad and before him Musa, received from God through an angel, who is sometimes also called Namus.

Nanna
The Sumerian moon-god of the city of Ur. Also called Sin, he was the son of Ninlil (q.v.). The moon travels through the sky in a boat, a corracle.

Nannar
'Sin'. The Babylonian moon-goddess, twin-sister of Shamash (q.v.).

Nasnas
A type of demon looking like half a man, the child of a *shiqq* (q.v.). It has a head in its chest, one arm, one leg and a tail.

Nasr
'Vulture'. One of the idols worshipped by the people in the days of Nuh (Noah) (Koran 71:23). It may have been the constellation Aquila.

Nathan
'[God] has given'. A prophet of God who anointed Solomon king (1 Kings 1:34). He was also sent by God to David to accuse him of sin and injustice (2 Samuel 12: 1–15), with the parable of the rich man and the poor man.

Nebaioth
Son of Ishmael, according to the Book of Jubilees 17:14.

Necromancer (Hebrew: *doresh el ha-metim* 'investigator of the dead')
A strongly condemned profession (Deuteronomy 18:10), but apparently widespread. The practitioner would closely observe the symptoms accompanying a person's death, such as convulsions and the palpitations of eyelids, in order to predict the future. Others could presage things to come from human bones. A third category of necromancers could 'call up' the spirits of the dead, *ob*, who would be lured into a leather bag from where they would 'speak' (i.e. squeak, since the 'prophet' would squeeze the bag) thus revealing the future to the necromancer (called *yid'oni* in the same passage). See also *Hatif*.

Nephilim
See *Watchers*.

Nergal
Mesopotamiam god of the dead, equated with Mars–Ares, judge of the souls, president of the council of Anunnaki, son of Nunammir and Kutushar the great queen, lord of the battlefield (i.e. the dying), always the victor. Nergal was the strong one among the gods. He was much worshipped with the prayer: 'Thou who art conciliatory, prone to forgive, whose eyes look upon us with kindness, full of compassion, pardon my sins.'

He was also the Babylonian god of the nether world, who held Enkidu, the dead friend of Gilgamesh, in his house. He was originally a celestial god, 'radiant in the pure sky', but the supreme god Anu (q.v.) sent him down to the nether world, Kurnugi (q.v.), with a rich offering of food from the celestials to Ereshkigal (Demeter) (q.v.), queen of Hades. Nergal descended the long stairway which led to the depths of the earth and passed through the seven gates of hell, each one with its own name. Nergal as god of heat and drought was a strange guest in that dark world but he was also a god of death. Once in the underworld, Nergal was seduced by the irresistible Ereshkigal, sister of Ishtar, for a whole week. Then Nergal had to return to heaven to fulfil his mission. However, he was soon back, this time for ever.

Neriosang
Messenger-god in ancient Persia.

Nestor (Arabic: *Nastur*)
A Christian monk who lived in Syria (in Damascus?) during the seventh century. When Abu Talib arrived there for trade, accompanied by his young nephew Muhammad, the old monk recognized the latter as the last prophet of God.

Night Journey
See *Isra'*.

Nimrod (Nimrud, Namrud)
The king of Mesopotamia in the days when the prophet Abraham was born. The Islamic tradition is remarkably close to the Jewish one which is, however, not biblical but talmudic.

The narrative opens when Nimrod's astrologers observe a small star replacing a big one and becoming ever brighter until it shines in the four corners of the universe – or a similar event dreamed by the king himself. The interpretation is that a child born that night would one day sit on Nimrod's throne. The king, enraged, had all the baby boys born that night killed. But little Abraham was hurried away just in time, to the distant hills where he grew up in a cave, suckled by a slave woman, or by the angel Gabriel. The king, informed about this, sent an army but God sent a black cloud which enveloped the soldiers. On seeing nothing, they fled.

Abraham grew up and prospered, studying under Noah and/or Enoch. He then went up to Nimrod's court where he tried to persuade the king to worship the one true God. The king told him to revive his father the old king as a sign. Abraham knelt down in prayer and the old king rose from his tomb and told his son to follow young Abraham and not the worshippers of useless idols. However, the king demanded another sign from the one God. So Abraham cut up four birds, mixed all the pieces, then had a portion of the heap of bones and feathers placed on each of four hills outside the city. He then called the birds and they all sprang to life.

Nimrod, still unsatisfied, his mind blinded by God, sent an army to destroy Abraham, but God created mosquitoes which swarmed all over the army so the men fled in all directions. One big mosquito crept into Nimrod's head through his ear and buzzed there until the king went mad and jumped out of the window to his death.

Nimush
The mountain in Babylonian myth where Uta-Napishtim's (q.v.) boat beached after the great flood.

Ninatta and Kulitta
Two goddesses of music, serving Ishtar. They accompanied her hymns when she sang passionately of her love for Tammuz (q.v.).

Ninawa
Arabic name for ancient Nineveh (q.v.), to which the Prophet Yunus (Jonah) (q.v.) was sent (Koran 37: 147).

Ninazu
Babylonian god of magic incantations.

Ninedinna
Babylonian goddess of the records of the dead.

Nineveh
Capital of Assyria, built by Nimrod on the banks of the Tigris (Genesis 10:11; Jonah 4:11). It was completely destroyed in 606 BC by the Babylonians. God sent his prophet Jonah (q.v.) to preach morality in Nineveh but he found the citizens so immoral that he gave up and walked out, foreshadowing St Peter's experience in Rome. See also *Ninawa*.

Ninhursag (Mammi, Aruru)
A goddess in Sumerian and Mesopotamian mythology, the earth-mother.

She was the wife of the water-god Enki (q.v.).

Ninkarrak
Babylonian and Sumerian goddess of healing who nursed sick humans, like the Greek Hygieia.

Ninlil
The Sumerian goddess of sailors. She was seduced by the sky-god Enlil (q.v.), who was condemned by the gods for this sin to live in Hades. However, Ninlil loved him and insisted on following him to the underworld. The gods decided that she had to postpone her departure until she had given birth because her child must not be born under the earth, as it was to be Nanna the moon-god. When Nanna was born and rose into the sky, Ninlil descended to join her husband and had three more children by him. Ninlil is sometimes identified with Ishtar, i.e. Aphrodite, the sailors' goddess.

Ninmu (Ninsar)
The Sumerian goddess of plants, daughter of Enki (q.v.). She became a wife to her father and gave birth to the goddess Ninkurra, who married her grandfather, Enki, and gave birth to Uttu (q.v.).

Nin-Sun
A Babylonian and Sumerian goddess of the city of Uruk, mother of Gilgamesh (q.v.).

Ninurta
Mesopotamian, Sumerian and Babylonian war-god and patron of hunters, son of the Babylonian god Enlil

(q.v.) and the mother-goddess Belet Ili (q.v.), the goddess of shapes and forms. In the epic of Anzu (q.v.), Ninurta was the great hero who defeated the monstrous usurper Anzu who stole the tablet of destiny so that he could rule the world for ever. Ninurta alone was prepared to confront him, disguising himself as a terrible demon and cutting Anzu's throat after a long battle. Like Mars, Ninurta was also the god of copper and the coppersmiths, the first metal workers on earth.

Nisaba (Nissaba)
Sumerian goddess of the art of the pen, of writing, patroness of scribes, protectress of schools and their staffs and students. Her symbol was the *calamus* (a special hard reed suitable for pressing into the clay tablets then used) on an altar. She was also the goddess of agriculture, ordered vegetation, accountants and magic.

Nisir
The biblical Ararat, where the ark of the Babylonian hero Uta-Napishtim finally beached.

Niya
'Vow, intention'. Compulsory conscious formulation of intention to fulfil any religious duty in Islam. Without this formula beginning: 'I intend to offer to God my obligatory . . .' (morning prayer, noon prayer etc), the act has no validity and has to be repeated. So the word *niya* comes to mean 'conscience, purity of purpose, consciousness'. By silently formulating the *niya*, the believer consciously clears his mind of all thoughts except God whom he is about to serve. The Sufis retain this mental condition all the time, thus conquering all carnal desires and keeping their thinking concentrated on God and nothing else, by repeating his ninety-nine holy names.

Now Ruz (No Roz, Nau Rooz)
'New Light', the ancient Persian New Year's feast which is still celebrated by most Zoroastrians on 21 March, when the sun enters the sign of Aries, the ancient Persian ram-god, equated with the Roman Mars, the god of fire, (in Pahlavi, Asha Vahishta). It is the first day of spring.

Nubara
A tyrant who forced his subjects to worship him as a god. King Solomon (q.v.) flew to his island with an army and slew him. In the tyrant's palace, Solomon met Nubara's daughter Jarada, who was the loveliest girl he had ever seen. He married her at once, but she persuaded him to worship an image of her father. For this outrage God punished Solomon by making him lose his ring, and with it his magic power. God also changed his appearance so that no one recognized Solomon as the king and no longer obeyed him; indeed he was chased from his palace by his own guards. He then wandered to the beach where he became a poor fisherman.

After forty days God decided to end Solomon's period of penitence and he caught a fish, inside which he found his ring. Holding it, Solomon ordered the *jinns* to carry him back to his palace. They obeyed him once again. As soon as he was in his palace,

Solomon went up to Jarada's room, broke the statue of her father and beat the princess until she submitted to Islam. See also *Solomon's Ring*.

Nun

The Semitic word for fish, and for the letter *n*. It alludes to the fish in whose belly Jonah (Yunus) survived, by God's will. It was his grave and yet he came out of it. *Nun* is therefore symbolic of 'belly', and so of 'womb', in which the embryo swims like a fish, to be born from it as a human being, breathing and speaking.

Nur

'Light'. It symbolizes God (Koran 24:35), the true faith (57:28) and the Koran (15:15; 42:52). The first thing created by God according to Islam.

Nur Muhammadi

'The light of Muhammad'. When God had created the light, he saw in its centre a radiance so brilliant that he took it and spoke: 'You are the spirit of my beloved Prophet. I will create the earth and humanity, so that I can send you to it as my last and best prophet to bring the light of my final word.' See *Pearl*.

Nuru'llah

See *Pearl*.

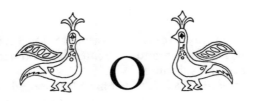

O

Oak

The oak tree was sacred to Jupiter—Ammon and to Baal. Baal's worshippers sacrificed to him under the oak tree (Ezekiel 6:13). Acorns, once human food, were used in the ceremonies for Demeter in Asia Minor.

Occult Science
See *Da'wa*.

Ohrmazd
See *Ahura Mazda*.

Olives (Olivet)
A hill near Jerusalem where Jesus warned of the city's fall. It was there, according to some, that he finally ascended to heaven in a cloud (Acts 1:9).

Olive Tree
Sacred to the goddess Athena, but originating probably in Egypt where its oil was used as an eye medicine from ancient times. An olive tree grew out of Adam's grave, and Noah's dove plucked a branch from it. Jesus' cross was made of olive wood. It was carried as a symbol in the harvest festival procession.

Omar Khayyam
Umar ibn Ibrahim al-Khayyami, Persian mathematical scholar who designed a new calendar for the sultan in 1079. He became famous in Europe when Edward Fitzgerald translated and edited his quatrains (*Rubaiyyat*) in Cambridge in 1859. In these poems Omar revealed himself as neither an orthodox Muslim nor a Sufi mystic, though he was quite familiar with all the philosophies current in his day. He appears to have moved beyond them and become a sceptic, which may explain his attraction for Westerners.

Omen
In Arabic *fa'l* indicates a good omen, *tiyara* a bad omen. The flight of birds was often studied for omens by the Arabs in Muhammad's time, but he forbade it. Meeting a woman first when setting out on a journey is considered a bad omen in India. See *Signs*.

Omnipotence
It is argued in the Islamic catechism that God must be omnipotent, since if anything happened in the universe which God had not caused to happen,

then it must have been caused by another god. But if more than one god existed, they would be fighting and destroying creation. We do not see this happen, so there can only be one God. This is the unitarian principle on which Islamic theology is based. Furthermore it is shown that God can see, hear and speak, since the assumption that he is blind, deaf and dumb is unacceptable.

Islamic scholars thus conclude that there are fourteen divine qualities: existence, pre-existence, immortality, difference, independence, unity, omnipotence, will, omniscience, life, hearing, sight, speech, omnipresence. In each case they take it for granted that people will agree that it is unacceptable to assume the opposite: for example that God did not exist, that he was either born or created by another god, or that he is dependent for his life on, say, the availability of air. Similarly it is unacceptable to assume that there could be anything that God does not know or that he would be dead, like a stone, or that there is any place in the universe where he is not present.

On one crucial question, Islamic scholars have been more consistent than Christian theologians. Basing themselves on the principle of God's omnipotence, they reason that God created evil as well as good and that he wills bad things, because if he does not, someone else must have created evil and still wills its existence against God's will, and without God being capable of preventing it. That would invalidate the principle of unity. (The dualist world concept of the Parsees is rejected.)

The conclusion that God has predestined our fate is inevitable and has been accepted with resignation in Islam (the word *islam* means 'submission'). See *Qadar*.

Osiris

Ancient Egyptian god of the nether world, judge of the dead and husband of Isis (q.v.). He is equated with the Greek god Pluto-Hades and the Babylonian Nergal (q.v.), king of the subterranean world. He was also the god of vegetation: grain grew annually out of his dead body when he mystically married Isis.

Ostriches

The Arabs believed that *jinns* often took the form of ostriches, or rode them. Dalila, Samson's treacherous mistress, rode an ostrich.

Oupire

See *Vampire*.

Owls

The Sumerian goddess of death was depicted on a tablet of about 2200 BC as a nude woman flanked by two owls. The owl is widely believed to announce disease and death with its sad hooting. The owl was dedicated to Athena the goddess of wisdom. Lilith (q.v.), the ancient Hebrew goddess, was identified with the screech-owl (Isaiah 34:14), a female demon associated with infant mortality. Owls' eggs on the contrary would ensure a long life and lasting youthfulness. The contradiction is explained by the pre-classical belief that the deity of death also knew the secrets of life, fertility, rebirth and reincarnation. 'Wisdom' meant 'life'. See *Sophia*.

P

Pahlavi (Pehlevi)
Middle Persian, i.e. the language of Persia during the 'middle' period of that kingdom's history. It was used for official purposes during the Sassanian dynasty (224–642), notably for the documentation of the *Pahlavi Zand*, the great commentary on the *Avesta* (q.v.).

Palestine
Geographical area along the southern half of the eastern seaboard of the Mediterranean, between Egypt and the Lebanon, bordered on the east by the River Jordan and the Dead Sea. It owes its name to the people called Filistines, Falistines or Palestines who lived along the seacoast in the twelfth century before Christ, where even the Pharaoh, Ramses III, could not dislodge them. Gaza and Ashdod were their main cities. Further north and east lived the Canaanites who spoke Canaanitic, a language quite close to Hebrew, whereas the Filistines spoke an unknown language. The Canaanites, like the Eblaites in Syria and the Ugaritians and Phoenicians in the Lebanon, were highly intelligent and advanced peoples with scripts of their own.

The Filistines and Canaanites continued to live in their cities throughout the Hebrew invasions of the twelfth and eleventh centuries BC, under Joshua and the Judges. Long after Solomon (c. 960–922 BC), the Filistines were still there. After Solomon the Hebrew kingdom was divided into Israel and Judah.

The Chaldean emperor Nebuchadnezzar conquered Palestine in 698 BC, laying it to waste. The Chaldeans in turn were defeated by the Persian king Cyrus (called Kores in Ezra I) in 538 BC. The Persians in their turn were defeated by Alexander of Macedonia (333 BC), who initiated the Greek or Hellenistic period; in Palestine, Greek became the language of intellectual intercourse (hence the *Greek* New Testament).

The Romans divided Palestine into provinces: Nabataea (Negev), Decapolis (Jordan), Pentapolis (Gaza, Ashdod), Judaea and Palestina in the centre, Phoenicia and Petraea in the north. These divisions were often changed during the long history of the Roman and Byzantine empire. Then suddenly, under Omar I (634–644), the Arabs invaded and conquered all Palestine.

From 1517–1918 Palestine was a province of the Ottoman Empire.

Until 1948 it was British Mandate Territory. Now it is Israeli.

Each of the inhabitants had and has his or her own religion and today the Holy Land is still strewn with the monuments and graves of the prophets and patriarchs who once lived there, including Abraham, Jacob, David and Solomon.

Papsukkal
Chief minister of the Sumerian gods of heaven, especially of Ea (q.v.).

Paradise
1. The idea of paradise, as well as the vision of an ideal country was first formulated by Zarathustra. The ancient Persians believed that paradise was the state of the world both before the intrusion of evil, and after its destruction by the good God, and this idea was later adopted by both Jews and Christians. The Persians saw the earth as a dish with the sky above it in the shape of a dome of blue rock crystal. The sun stayed in the zenith all day but it was never too hot. Peace reigned on earth as all people lived in harmony together. One ominous day Ahriman (q.v.), the demon of evil, penetrated the frail crystal dome and broke into paradise, causing evil to germinate on earth. Many centuries later the good God Ahura Mazda (q.v.) will have finally executed Ahriman after fierce fighting in which all the good souls must help him. Then the pristine state of the earth will be restored and people will live in peace once more.

In Zoroastrianism paradise is called the 'house of song', the 'best existence', the 'kingdom of Mazda', the 'place of endless light', and the 'dwelling of good purpose'.

2. The Persian word paradise means 'enclosure, walled garden' referring to the crystal walls surrounding the earth-garden. The Book of Genesis speaks of a garden 'eastward' in Eden (2:8) and this could be a reference to the Persian legend of paradise. The garden of Eden is described only by Ezekiel: it was full of the finest trees, cedars, planes, pines and oaks (31: 3–9); it was also full of gemstones: sardin, chrysolite and jade (28:13). Ezekiel (36:35) and Isaiah (51:3) imply that it was a cultivated garden, either a vegetable garden or a park plus orchard for fruit cultivation.

3. For Christians, paradise is where Jesus is. He says so himself in Luke 23:42, promising paradise to a criminal while they are both dying. Only in the Koran do we read descriptions of paradise and the happiness of its inhabitants.

4. The Koran mentions five 'gardens' (*jannat*) and three houses or mansions (*daru*) forming together paradise, although some scholars maintain there must be seven gardens, one above the other (but only God has true knowledge). The two uppermost layers are just spiritual abodes, perhaps above paradise. The following are the names of the gardens, mansions and abodes with the passages in the Koran where they are named: *jannatu'l-khuld*, the 'garden of eternity' (25:16), where the souls enjoy eternal life; *daru'l-salaam*, the 'house of peace' (6:127), where the souls receive salvation and prosperity; *daru'l-qarar*, the 'house of perpetuity' (40:39), where the souls

are assured of security and stability; *jannatu'l 'adn*, the 'garden of Eden' (9:72–3), where the souls are rich in piety; *jannatu'l-ma'wa*, the 'garden of shelter' (32:19), where parted loving souls are reunited; *jannatu'l-na'im*, the 'garden of delight' (5:65–70), where the souls live in bliss; *daru'l-illiyun* (83:18), where the souls of God's prophets live, close to him; *jannatu'l-firdawsi*, the 'garden of paradise' (18:107), among shady brooks and trees; *malakut*, the heaven where the angels and the self-sacrificing souls live (6:75; 7:185); *lahut*, the uppermost heaven where only God lives united with his 'friends' (see *Lahut*).

The lowest sphere, which we call the biosphere or atmosphere, is called in Arabic *Jinan*, where the *jinns* live, or *Nasut* or *Hayawani*, where the animals live (Koran 29:64).

God created paradise with many gates, some say eight, others ten or even a dozen but only God has true knowledge, through which the soul may enter. These gates have the following names: Prayer, Holy War, Almsgiving, Fasting, Repentance, Steadfastness in Faith, Compassion, Devotion, Resignation or Patience, Pilgrimage, Generosity, Vigils. Some scholars maintain that the names are different, but only Allah really knows. What is known for certain is that the gates have names, that the names have meanings and that the souls of the faithful (and only those) will enter paradise through one of them. Furthermore, we know that the souls can enter paradise only if they have been virtuous, that is, without sin; or have performed good works for the eradication of their sins; or

by faith and grace, which are in God's hand.

As soon as the souls of those who are worthy of paradise are within sight of its gates, they will be allowed to rest from the long journey. Some may have walked for many hours or days, some may have had to climb all the way out of the unclean depths of their sinfulness. After many years, with patience and perseverance, they will arrive at a gate, with God's grace. There, near the end of their ordeal, they will be allowed to drink from Kawthar, the lake of abundance, which belongs to the holy Prophet and only his followers and friends may drink from it. Once a man's soul has drunk a sip, he will never be thirsty again, and never be ill. The water is sweeter than sugar, whiter than snow and has such a pleasant smell that no one who has ever tasted it will want to go back to earth. Lake Kawthar is so large that it would stretch from Mecca to the Yemen. There is also the *Tauba*, the tree of remorse, whose fruits are food for every true believer in paradise. Its branches and rich foliage are so large that they provide pleasant cool shade for all the inhabitants of paradise, sheltering them from the dazzling light that shines down from the holy throne above them.

Parakleitos (Arabic: *Faraqlit*)
The Greek name means 'advocate' according to the New English Bible (John 14:16; 16:7). In the Islamic tradition it means 'praiseworthy', and is believed to be a translation of the Arabic *Ahmad* 'most praised', Muhammad's heavenly name (Koran

61:6). The Koran says that Isa (Jesus) announced Muhammad.

Pardon

In Genesis 50:17 Joseph forgives his brothers their wickedness. The Lord is long-suffering and forgives iniquity (Numbers 14:18). We must forgive our brothers seventy seven times: Matthew 18:21. Here Jesus tells his disciples the parable of the unforgiving servant, reminding us that we need God's pardon most of all.

There is frequent mention of pardon in the Koran (53:32–3; 67:12; 33:71; 35:8; 8:29; 4:20; 25:71). God will forgive his debtors more than men do.

Pasargadae

Once a great city in Persia, which is now in ruins. It was here that the first shah of Persia, Cyrus the Great, was buried in a tomb. The tomb, which is still there, is now called the tomb of Solomon's mother by the local nomads. Here Cyrus (Kores of the Bible) lay in a golden coffin at least until the fourth century BC.

Patience (Arabic: *sabr*)

One of the highly praised virtues in Islam (Koran 2:48).

Pazuzu

Mesopotamian monster with four wings and a lion's head.

Peacock

1. Of Indian origin, this bird became the symbol of royalty in Persia. It was associated with rain and hence with the weather-god, Indra. It is also a love symbol.

2. The peacock lived in paradise when Adam was still there. Satan flattered the vain bird so that it permitted him to hide under its wing and carry him into paradise. God exiled it for this sin of vanity.

Pearl

1. In Persian symbolism the pearl is highly admired for its whiteness and purity. Pearls are believed to originate from raindrops falling onto the ocean, where they are 'received' by oysters lying on the ocean's surface with their openings turned upwards 'like waiting brides', hence the expression 'mother of pearl' for the inside of an oyster shell.

The original pearl, also called *durratu l'beiza*, 'the white pearl', because it symbolizes purity, is the *johar*, 'substance' out of which all physical substances were created by God. It is identified with the *nur Muhammadi* (q.v.), the 'light of Muhammad' (see below), out of which God created all things, using an ever diminishing quantity of light as he proceeded from one category of creatures to the next: Muhammad, the angels, the prophets, the first four caliphs (or, in the Shi'a tradition, the seven or twelve imams) and after these the other human beings, animals, plants, stones, etc. See also *Substance*.

2. Creation. In Gnostic philosophy, which has come to us mainly in Greek and Coptic from the second to sixth centuries AD, the pearl is the hidden essence of the substance,

the *natura physica* or *materia*, which God created for the purpose of forming a body in which his spirit could find expression. It is hidden in the deepest region of the universe which is like the inside of a vast oyster shell. This essence of the universe is mystically identical with the human soul which awaits the divine spirit. See also *Sophia, Materia, Creation, Substance, Gnosis*.

3. In popular Islamic legends the pearl is a symbolic reference to a man's seed. This seed, usually imagined as one grain of seed, i.e. one 'pearl', the one which lodges in the womb and makes the woman conceive, is believed to grow *in utero* into the image of its father. It is believed that the mother fosters the embryo but does not give it any of her own properties. The mother has the duty to look after her husband's 'seed', i.e. his child, before and after birth.

The word 'pearl' (Arabic: *durra*; seed: *dhurriyya*) in this context usually refers to the seed of the prophets, *Anbiya'* (q.v.), the koranic–biblical prophets from Adam to Muhammad. This seed of the prophets stayed alive while the men died one after another, because it was transferred by God from each man to his wife during a night appointed by him. It grew in the mother and became a boy who in his turn carried the same pearl in his loins. In this way God kept the pearl alive on earth. This pearl in the special meaning of the seed of the prophets was a fragment of God's Light, *Nuru'llah*, which God implanted in Adam. When God calls (Arabic: *ba'atha*, a prophet 'awakens') to his task of prophesy, the pearl of light will rise to the prophet's forehead where it will shine clearly visible for all who are not blinded by his curse. The pearl-seed passed from Adam via Seth, Anush, Kinan, Mahalail, Enoch, Matushalah, Noah, Sam, Ibrahim, Ismail and Abdullah to Muhammad. See *Nur Muhammadi*.

Persia

The Greek name for Iran, and the name by which that country was known until 1935. The 'good' gods of ancient Persia were the following:

- **Ahura Mazda,** the 'Great God', the supreme deity.
- **Ameretat,** the goddess of immortality and green vegetation.
- **Anahita,** the goddess of love, beauty and fertility.
- **Apo,** the goddess of the waters.
- **Arishtat,** the goddess of honesty.
- **Armaiti,** the goddess of devotion, faith and worship.
- **Asha,** Arta, the god of truth, law and order.
- **Asman,** the sky-god.
- **Atar,** Atesh, the god of fire and purity.
- **Haoma,** the goddess of the secret herb of immortality; the Moon.
- **Haurvatat,** goddess of prosperity, the Roman Fortuna.
- **Hvarekhshaeta,** the modern Khurshid, the many-horsed sun-god, Helios.
- **Mithra,** the god of loyalty, truthfulness and kept promises.
- **Rashnaw,** Rashnau, the god of justice and the last judgement.
- **Rapithwin,** the god of the mid-day time, of summer and warmth.

- **Sraosha,** the god of obedience, fidelity and prayer.
- **Tishtrya,** the god of rain, the Roman Pluvius.
- **Tushnamatay,** goddess of meditation, mother of thought.
- **Vata,** the wind-god, Aiolos.
- **Verethraghna,** Varhagn, the god of victory, equated with Herakles.
- **Vohu Manah,** the god of domestic, 'good' animals.
- **Zam-Armatay,** the goddess of the earth, the Roman Tellus.

Peshdadians
A semi-mythical dynasty of Persian rulers before 600 BC. Their exploits are described in the epic *Shahname* by Firdausi (q.v.). They ruled for many centuries.

Petrel
'Little Peter', a bird so called because it can walk on the ocean's surface.

Philemon (Filimun)
High priest of Egypt in the days of Noah: Noah begat Ham, Ham begat Baisar and Baisar begat Misraim (Mitzrayim), who married Philemon's daughter. They had a son whom they also called Philemon. His grandfather-godfather taught him how to read the ancient Egyptian script as well as the location of ancient ruins in which immense treasures were hidden. Noah made Misraim king of Egypt. The new king built his capital at Rakuda, in Greek Rhakotis, where 2000 years later Alexander built Alexandria.

The learned Philemon built a tower on the coast with a concave copper mirror which could be turned and aimed at enemy ships in such a way that the sun's rays would focus on the ship causing it to catch fire. One unlucky day a huge monster appeared from the sea to devour the citizens. Quickly, Philemon wrote a talisman and placed it on the shore. The monster never re-emerged from the sea. The art of writing such powerful amulets is now lost. Philemon created many other magic machines which to this day protect the graves of the kings, his descendants, against desecrators.

Philistines
The nation that gave its name to the land of Palestine. They lived along the coast in a string of towns including Ashdod and Gaza, and were traders and navigators. The Bible has nothing good to say of them, but in fact they were only defending their towns against the invading Children of Israel (1 Samuel 4 etc). Their language was not Semitic.

Phoenix
The immortal bird of universal mythology, familiar in the arts from Japan to Greece. The Greeks believed that it bred in Arabia once every 500 years and came to Greece to bury its parents, embalmed in myrrh. A better-known myth relates that the phoenix (which is always alone) had neither wife nor young but rejuvenated itself every 250 or 500 years in a fire lit by the setting sun, with spices and herbs in the pyre.

Herodotus saw a phoenix in Egypt, perched on a date palm. Its plumage was fiery red and gold; it was larger than a pheasant or even a peacock but had an equally colourful tail, one golden feather of which would secure its owner wealth, a happy marriage and long life. Young heroes spent years of their lives searching for one.

In Persian literature, the phoenix (*simurgh* (q.v.) or *anqa*) was known in the *Avesta* as *Saena Meregha*, the dragon peacock. There it was the symbol of the human soul before birth (*fravasha*) which was lured by the bait of the pleasures of the flesh into the cage of earthly life. This bait was visualized as the fruit of earthly delight which the serpent gave to Eve and with which Eve seduced Adam when they were still in paradise.

In the Islamic tradition this 'fruit' was grain, which also tempted the birds of paradise, including the phoenix, into the cage of life. The Persian poet adds: 'Even if the cage is made of gold, the bird inside it just wants to escape.'

In middle Persian literature, the phoenix (*senmurv* or *seymorg*) was associated with the Tree of Life and the mysterious Lake Varkash. It had its nest in the 'tree of medicine', according to these texts, the *van-i-yutbesh*, which produced innumerable seeds. When the phoenix perched on its branches it scattered the seeds onto the earth.

The egg was compared by Rumi (q.v.) to earthly life. The bird inside it wanted to escape. For the mystics, the phoenix was the image of the soul yearning to return to the peaceful lake in paradise, or to go up in the flames of rejuvenation, i.e.

the unification with the divine soul for ever. See *Fana'*.

Phylactery
'Protection'. It is a Jewish custom during prayers to wear some passages from the law (Exodus 13:1–16; Deuteronomy 6:4–9) in a small box on the forehead, on the hand or elsewhere on the body, as a ceremonial reminder. In ancient times these passages from the scriptures were worn for protection against evil, hence the Greek name.

Physis
'Nature, the physical world, matter'. See *Materia, Pearl, Substance*.

Pidray
'Mist'. In Ugaritic mythology, a daughter of Baal, the god of rains and clouds.

Pigeon
The messenger-bird of antiquity. The Prophet Muhammad removed a wooden pigeon from the Ka'ba during his first pilgrimage. It was a deity of the Quraysh. Aphrodite's love bird is not the same species.

Pilgrimage (Arabic: *hajj, hijja*)
A journey to Mecca, to be made at least once in a man's life if he can afford it and if the road is safe from robbers, wars and diseases. In many ways, especially for the Sufis, the pilgrimage has become a journey to God, since for weeks on end the pilgrim thinks about nothing but God, whom alone he serves (see *Niya*). For the Shi'a there is also the pilgrimage to the tomb of Muhammad in Medina and those of the first imam,

Ali, in Kufa, the third imam, Husayn, in Kerbela, the eighth imam, Ali Reda (Reza), in Meshed and the eleventh and twelfth imams in Samarra. These visits are called *ziyara*. For the Shi'a they are audiences at the court of the living but invisible imams. For all pilgrims their journey is one of spiritual elevation and of ever-increasing concentration on the divine.

Pine

A symbol of eternal life, also a symbol of a stable marriage (Isaiah 41:19; 60:13; Hosea 14:8). In 2 Samuel 6:5, David plays musical instruments for God which are all made of fir wood. The fir tree was sacred to the goddess Cybele (q.v.) in Asia Minor where it once grew on all the mountains.

Plants

A full discussion of plants in Middle Eastern mythology would fill a separate volume. Almost all Greek and Oriental plants and trees were and are used for medicinal purposes in some way, including acacia, basil, crocus, daffodil, eglantine, fenugreek, lavender, olive, orange, rice, sugar cane, thyme and valerian. Other plants were used for magical purposes, to bewitch one's enemy or to put a spell on a loved one so that he or she would be like a lamb. Certain trees were associated with the dead (the cypress) or were believed to give oracles (the oak). Some plants were themselves deities (basil), or symbolized social life (the pine tree).

Poetry

This is the finest and most widespread literary form for religious expression. Although some prayers are in prose, many have a poetic form. Hymns and dirges, psalms and praise songs are all poetry. Religious feelings are the most exalted emotions that human beings experience, so an artistic expression of these often generates itself in the human mind. Epic poetry describes the exploits of divine beings, beginning with *Gilgamesh* (q.v.) and Hesiodus' *Theogonia*. Mystic poetry is found throughout the Middle East in Persian, Arabic, Turkish and Urdu. It is some of the finest poetry ever written in any culture.

Potipher (Potiphar)

Joseph's owner and husband of the pretty young woman who tried to seduce him (Genesis 37:36–9). In the Arabic tradition his name is Butifar, and his wife's, Zuleikha (q.v.) (Koran 12).

Prayer

For many Western believers, prayer is speaking to God. For most Muslims, it may only be the ritual *salat* (q.v.) which is the daily duty. Even its variations are fixed, and described in detail in the books of *fiqh* (duty). For the Sufi masters however, this ritual form of prayer is unnecessary. The advanced spirit is in constant and intimate conversation with the divine presence, without words but tied with the bonds of living communion. See *Khatma, Sufism*.

Prayer Rug (Arabic: *musalla, sajjada*)

During the time a Muslim spends on his prayer rug or mat, he is safe from harassment by Iblis, the Devil, as the legend of Ayyub (Job) tells us. See *Salat*.

Predestination (Arabic: *qadar*, 'God's power')

In Islamic thinking, man has no freedom to act as he wishes, since God creates even his wishes. Man can create nothing, and there is no freedom without power to use it, including the power to create *ex nihilo*. God has created man and all that he makes (Koran 54:49; 37:94). God guides some to the right path and not others, so God controls our thoughts (16:38; 58:22; 53:44; 6:36, 150). Even the choice of religion is not free (11:120; 6:39).

A modern Muslim scholar explained it thus: 'You think you cut the butter but you don't. It is God who cuts the butter.' This is illustrated by Ibrahim's experience when he pushed the knife down on his son's throat. It would not go in, because God had decided that the boy should live, so the skin could not be cut. This gives a peculiar courage to the fighters in a holy war: the conviction that only God kills means that no bullet can hit them until the moment God has decided that they shall die. Conversely when a Muslim feels his death approaching he will lie down and patiently wait for the end, for he knows that nothing can keep him alive. This conviction also explains why so little is done in the Middle East to save lives after an accident or after a battle. The victims are left to die if it is their hour (*sa'a*). If it is not, they will live on patiently while they await God's decree. It also explains why nothing is done for the environment in the Middle East. As one Muslim commented: 'Don't you know that God can make the desert green tomorrow if he wishes?' See *Qadar*.

Pre-existence

We read in the Islamic traditions that the first thing created by God was the light. In the centre of the ocean of light, *bahr-an-nur*, there was a 'focus' of special brilliance. God was pleased by this brightness. He lifted it up and out of it he created the spiritual substance, pure spiritual light. Then he took half of this spirit-light and out of it he created the soul of Muhammad, his beloved Prophet. He took half of the other half of the spirit-light, and from it he created the souls of the other twenty-four prophets. He took half of the remaining quarter, and from it he created the souls of the angels, thousands of them. Out of the last eighth part of this light, God created the souls of all human beings that would ever live on earth or in heaven and hell, millions of them.

This is the philosophy of the pre-existence of the soul of every person. Some scholars deny it – Allah alone knows the truth. It is clear that some babies are born with brighter souls than others. Some people are destined to illuminate humanity as great 'lights', as scholars, writers, speakers, philosophers, poets etc. Other people have received less light, some are living in the shadows. It is further said by some of the 'Ulama (q.v.) that God took the soul of his beloved Prophet and reduced it to the size of a pearl, *durra*, which he concealed in the loins of Adam. From there it travelled via

Eve to Set and so through the generations until it finally reached Abdullah, Muhammad's father (q.v.).

Promised Land

The land of Canaan was promised to Abraham by God (Genesis 12:7; 13:14; 17:8). See *Canaan 2.*

Prophets

1. The distinction between the 'possessed' and the 'prophet' consists in the quality of the message delivered. 'Possessed' people deliver a message of local importance, but the 'prophet' comes charged with a demand for a new national movement. He calls people to action, to sacrifice, to return to old loyalties. A prophet speaks consciously, deliberately; a possessed person speaks in a trance, involuntarily.

The distinction between false and true prophets has always been hard to make, witness the words of Deuteronomy 13 and 18. How can we know who is the prophet of whom? God said: 'I will put my words in his mouth' (Deuteronomy 18:18). Jeremiah goes even further (23:16): 'The prophets that prophesy unto you; they make you vain, they speak a vision of their own heart, and not out of the mouth of the Lord.' A true prophet 'hears the word of the Lord' in Jeremiah's words. Micaiah sees 'the lord sitting on his throne' (1 Kings 22:19). Indeed, seer was the old word for 'prophet' in Israel (1 Samuel 9:9).

Perhaps 'hearer' would be an equally apt term, for 'the Lord had told Samuel in his ear' (1 Samuel 9:15).

Elijah 'stood before the Lord and heard his word' (1 Kings 17:1). Sometimes the Lord even cried to a prophet (1 Kings 13:21). In Ezekiel's prophesy we read how he saw and heard 'the appearance of the likeness of the Lord', as if he realized that the Lord himself cannot have a physical appearance (Ezekiel 1:28). Then he says, as if to explain how he knew what the Lord wanted even if he could not be heard: 'And the spirit entered into me when he spoke to me, and set me upon my feet, that I heard him that spake to me' (2:2). In Ezekiel 2:10 we learn how a figure holding a written book roll approached the prophet and spread out the roll so that he could read it. A similar experience happened to the Prophet Muhammad many centuries later (Koran 96:1).

In Exodus 4:11–16, the Lord said: 'I will be with thy mouth' so that Moses' mouth is moved by the Lord himself to speak the divine words. One of the most revered passages in the Bible, and repeated in the Koran (26:10; 28:30 from where it is often quoted by Muslims) is the appearance of the Lord in the burning bush, first as an angel of fire (Exodus 3:2), then as a voice from the fire itself (3:4–5; Koran 19:52; 20:9–23; 27:7). See also *Cohen, Angels.* The prominent biblical prophets were:

- Aaron (Arabic: Harun)
- Abraham (Arabic: Ibrahim)
- Ahijah
- Amos
- Balaam
- Daniel (Arabic: Danil)
- David (Arabic: Daud)

- Elijah (Arabic: Ilyas)
- Elisha (Arabic: Al-Yasaa)
- Ezekiel
- Habakkuk
- Haggai
- Hosea
- Isaiah (Arabic: Yisa'yah)
- Jehu
- Jeremiah (Arabic: Yaramya)
- Joel
- John the Baptist (Arabic: Yahya)
- Joshua
- Jonah (Arabic: Yunus)
- Malachi
- Micah
- Micaiah
- Moses (Arabic: Musa)
- Nahum
- Nathan
- Obadiah
- Paul (Arabic: Fulus)
- Samuel (Arabic: Shamuil)
- Zachariah
- Zechariah
- Zephaniah

The Biblical prophetesses were:
- Anna
- Deborah
- Huldah
- Miriam
- Noadiah

twenty-five prophets of the koranic tradition. They are the following, in order of their appearance on earth:

- Adam
- Idris (Enoch)
- Nuh (Noah)
- Hud
- Salih
- Ibrahim (Abraham)
- Lut (Lot)
- Ishaq (Isaac)
- Isma'il (Ishmael)
- Ya'qub (Jacob)
- Yusuf (Joseph)
- Ayyub (Job)
- Shu'ayb (Jethro)
- Musa (Moses)
- Harun (Aaron)
- Dhu'l-Kifli (Joshua)
- Shamuil (Samuel)
- Daud (David)
- Sulayman (Solomon)
- Ilyas (Elijah)
- Al-Yasaa (Elisha)
- Uzayr (Ezra)
- Yunus (Jonah)
- Zakariya (Zachariah)
- Yahya (John the Baptist)
- Isa (Jesus)
- Muhammad

2. In the Islamic popular tradition, God created light first in the form of a pearl (q.v.). This original substance (*jawhar asli*) was feminine in essence like the original matter (*physis, materia*) in Gnosticism. God looked upon this shining pure pearl with so much love that it felt shy, and perspiration 'pearled' on its surface. Out of these droplets of pure light God created the spirits of the

In the Islamic tradition, a prophet is a man who receives a revelation either directly from God or from an angel (Jibril). He is then sent (*rasul*) to his people. Some prophets have become kings, like David and Solomon; this is the ideal condition for an Islamic society, since as a prophet he receives directly from God the laws that must regulate his society, which he rules as king. The Prophet Muhammad was – according to some historians -- recognized as king of Arabia during the last few years of his life. See also *Anbiya'*, *Nabii*, *Books*.

Ptah
Egyptian god of creation who created himself, the sun. The Greeks equated him with Hephaistos.

Pukku
In Babylonian mythology, the sacred drum which Ishtar (q.v.) gave to Gilgamesh (q.v.).

Punishment (Arabic: *azabu'l-qabr, 'adhab al-kabr.*)
The punishment of the grave, in the Islamic tradition. As the dead man lies in his grave, two dark angels will appear and interrogate him about his religion. The dead man's tongue (hoping that he has practised it with endless repetition) will repeat: '*La ilaha illa Allah*', 'There is no God but Allah'. The angels, satisfied, will leave him in peace, first giving him a lamp from paradise. Woe betide the man who does not remember this *shahada* (q.v.). They will beat him forever. See *Munkar and Nakir*, *Death*.

Purim
'Lots'. A Jewish feast commemorating the liberation of the Jews in Persia from persecution by Haman, who had cast the lots (Esther 9:24).

Purity (Arabic: *safaa*)
In Islamic cosmology, heaven and paradise, God and the angels, are completely pure. Angels are sinless, they can neither lie nor think evil. Muhammad never lied, which makes his words worthy of belief. It follows that a person wishing to attain paradise will have to make himself completely pure. This is achieved first by abstaining from any form of dishonesty, so that a pious Muslim is usually very reticent: he wishes to avoid speaking untruth. Secondly, all desire for other men's goods or women must be overcome. All thinking of evil and sin must be banished from the mind, see *Niya*. Thirdly, steadfast prayer and fasting will purify the soul until it becomes worthy of ascending to heaven.

Puzur-Amurri
The navigator of the Babylonian ark.

Q

Qabala
See *Cabbala*.

Qabil
See *Kabil*.

Qada (qazah, kadhaa)
'Decision, sentence given by a judge'. God's decree, i.e. human fate, our inescapable lot.

Qadar (qadr)
'Power'. God's omnipotence. God directs everyone's destiny. God has created good, *al-khayr*, but also evil, *al-sharr*. If he did not create evil, then the Devil must have created it against God's will, which is an unacceptable supposition. So, God is the one who sends us all the things that happen to us: wealth and poverty, feast and famine, sickness and health, good luck and bad. It follows that we should never be proud, but always grateful, since we achieve nothing by our own merit. Happiness is a gift from God. We should share our wealth with the poor, because we owe it to God. He will make new wealth as soon as he wishes, and for whom he wishes, and give it away. Whenever we suffer we should be grateful that God deems us worthy of being tried. It will not last long, for this life is short while patience and faith will ensure us eternal life.

Qadesh
Syrian goddess of sacred love and sensual pleasure.

Qadiriyya
One of the oldest Sufi orders and still very widespread, being revered from West Africa to Indonesia. The term 'order' is misleading since the members of the Qadiriyya are not monks but married men with families. Indeed the descendants of the founder, Abdul Qadir, are among the leaders of the community. They are addressed as 'our Tijanis' in the prayers. The Qadiriyya community is often referred to as *tariqa* (q.v.), 'path', since the ritual prayers of each community are regarded as a path to paradise. The beatific vision (*ru'ya*) and the mystic union (*wasl*) which are the ultimate purpose of every mystic may be attained after years of meditation, concentration and abstinence. See *Salat*, *Sufism*.

Qaf

See *Kaf*.

Qa'im

'The One who Rises'. In the Shi'a religion, this is the term for the Mahdi Al-Qa'im bi-s-Sayf, the 'Riser with the Sword', who will rise against the illegitimate rule of the Sunni caliphs, or, later, against any ruler who does not acknowledge the hidden imam as God's true deputy. The imam must be a scion of the Prophet's grandson Husayn. The Twelvers (the Ithna'ashariya) believe that the Mahdi, the hidden imam, will one day appear and rise against the evil rulers of the time, so he is *sahib az-zaman*, 'the lord of the time'. He will rule the world from his residence in Mecca for a predestined number of years. Others say there will first be many years of holy war, and after that the resurrection. See *Mahdi*, *Shi'a*.

Qalam

One of Allah's first creations, the pen, which has been busy writing since creation – writing our destinies. See *Lawh al Mahfuz*.

Qana'a

'Contentment'. The fourteenth stage on the Sufi path. The Sufi must never complain.

Qarib

'Neighbour'. In Sufi literature a name for God, who is as close as your jugular vein (Koran 50:16).

Qibla (Kiblah)

'Direction'. It is the duty of every Muslim to face Mecca five times a day when beginning his prayer (see *Niya*). In Mecca one may see circles of praying believers surrounding the Ka'ba (q.v.). Muslims like to think that one day the whole earth will be filled with concentric circles of Muslims bending their backs towards the house of God in Mecca. Indeed they believe that on doomsday God will flatten all the mountains and fill in all the seas so that henceforth the whole earth will be a floor for his worship, as indeed it should be, they say. While they wait and pray for forty years in the sandstorm that will blow all the hills into the oceans, the throne (*kursi*, q.v.) and the scales (*mizan*, q.v.) will suddenly become visible. This will be the apocalypse. See *Qiyama*, *Resurrection*, *Salat*.

Qisas Al-Anbiya

Arabic collection of legends of the koranic and biblical prophets and patriarchs, beginning with the creation of Adam and ending with the life of Jesus, son of Maryam.

Qisma (Turkish: *kismet*)

'Part, share, lot'. A person's fixed fate, as decreed by God before his or her birth. It is a person's inescapable destiny, also called *ajal*, literally 'respite'. Whatever God has in store for us, is waiting for us somewhere so that we shall meet it at the appointed time. It cannot be avoided. In Turkey the soldiers say of a dead comrade: 'The bullet with his name on finally arrived'. All our suffering and joy is *qisma*.

Qiyama

'Resurrection' (Koran 75). For the Sufis a man has to die to the world before he can 'rise up' to begin a new life in God, liberated from all earthly attachment. A pious Muslim will take a bath on Thursday night, remembering the proverb 'The purity (q.v.) of Friday begins on Thursday.' It is believed that resurrection will be on a Friday morning at first light when the *mu'azzin* (q.v.) will be the angel calling the dead. See *Resurrection*.

Queen of Abyssinia

In the days of Saul, David and Solomon, a dynasty of queens ruled in Abyssinia (Habashiya) or Ethiopia. In Solomon's time the ruling young queen had a goat's foot. One day she dreamt that King Solomon would be able to heal her, so she boarded a ship and sailed to Aqaba. Solomon knew the date of her arrival and sent some of his *jinns* to meet her and carry her to Jerusalem on a carpet. There he awaited her behind a pond so she would have to raise her skirts to wade through it to reach him. That is how the wise Solomon saw her cloven hoof. It was cured by a piece of hardwood. See *Roc, Solomon, Silk, Saba*.

Qumran

Near the western shore of the Dead Sea is a rocky escarpment with a large number of natural caves. This place is called Qumran, 'The Two Turtle Doves', for reasons now forgotten. In these caves, between 1947 and 1956, a large number of ancient manuscripts in classical Hebrew were found dating from the first century AD and earlier. These manuscripts, called collectively the Dead Sea Scrolls, are of fundamental importance for our knowledge of Judaism and its branches

in the years before and after the birth of Jesus.

Many if not most of these manuscripts appear to have belonged to a community of ascetic Jews who lived at the foot of the escarpment until the reconquest of Israel by the Romans in 70 AD. They considered themselves to be chosen by God for their virtue, their abstemious lifestyle and their strict obedience to the law of God as laid down in the books of Moses. This community believed that the Messiah would soon come, and that only they would be saved.

It has been supposed by some scholars that this community was the sect of the Essenes (q.v.). Others have thought that they may have been some of the earliest Christians. However, since not all the manuscripts have yet been published, no definitive answer can yet be given to this fundamental question in the history of religion.

Qur'an
see *Koran*.

Qusur
Castles or palaces in paradise which are for the blessed (Koran 25:10).

Qutb
The highest saint in a Sufi brotherhood, in whose heart lives the heart of Muhammad.

Qutrub
A type of demon, probably the same as a *ghul* (see *Ghouls*).

R

Ra
Ancient Egyptian sun-god, later identified with the ram-god Ammon. The sun-ram is an ancient African symbol.

Rabbu'l-Nau'
'Lord of the species'. The angel who presides over flora and fauna.

Rahbaniya
'Celibacy, monasticism'. Unwed hermits are not encouraged by Islam. Muhammad forbade 'monkery'.

Rahim
Allah in his aspect of feeling compassion, so one can pray confidently to him.

Rahman
Allah in his aspect of actively helping those who need mercy and giving it to them.

Rain
In the Middle East rain is regarded as a special favour (*rahma*) from God. In antiquity, rain was a god, identified by the Romans with Jupiter Pluvius.

Ramdan (Ramazan, Ramadhan)
The ninth month of the Islamic year. It is devoted entirely to fasting in daytime and feasting and prayer at night. It is a blessed month.

Ramman (Adad or Hadad)
In the Gilgamesh (q.v.) epic, the god of winds, thunder and storms.

Raphael
'God heals' one of the seven chief angels whose wonderful story is told in the apocryphal Book of Tobit, where he cures Tobit's blindness (11:8).

Rasul
'Messenger, apostle'. The Prophet Muhammad is officially called Rasulu'llah, 'the Apostle of God', i.e. the man whom God sent to Arabia to bring the Arabs his message in the form of the Arabic Koran. Other messengers were sent to other nations, e.g. Hud to the Adites, Salih to the Thamudians etc. Four prophets were given holy books to reveal to their nations, Musa (Tawrat), Daud (Zabur), Isa (Injil) and Muhammad (Koran). See also *Books*, *Prophets*.

Raven
An ominous bird, messenger of Hirmis; also one of the seven symbols of

Mithra. It was Hirmis who collected the souls of the dead on the battlefield and it is there that numerous crows were seen. Those sombre black birds with their gloomy calls are associated with death in all mythologies.

In Islamic legends it is related that when Kabil (Cain) (q.v.) had slain his brother he did not know what to do with the body since no one had yet died on earth. So God sent down two crows (created for the purpose) who re-enacted the quarrel before Cain's eyes. Finally one of the crows pecked his brother to death, dug a hole in the earth with his bill and laid him in it, whereupon he covered it with earth. That is how Cain learned that the dead must be buried.

For the Sufis the crow symbolizes the darkness of a period of separation from the Presence.

Rawda (Al-Rauza)

The tomb of the Prophet Muhammad which lies just behind the Masjid al-Nabii, the great mosque at Medina. Next to Muhammad are buried his successors, Abu Bakr and Omar, and Fatima (q.v.) is in the nearby tomb. It is not permitted by the Wahhabi authorities to pray near the grave since no man may be worshipped, but many people believe that prayers said nearby will be effective. It is believed that the Prophet's spirit lives near the grave and answers all prayers.

Re

See *Ra*.

Rehema (Rahma)

The wife of Ayyub (Job) (q.v.) in the popular tradition of the tales of the Islamic prophets. She is honoured and praised for her faith in, and support for, her husband Ayyub during his trial. She remained faithful to him in spite of total poverty and illness, and the loss of all her children.

Reshep

Syrian war-god, with the head of a gazelle.

Resurrection

1. In the Islamic tradition, people will come forth from their graves at resurrection (Koran 36:51; 54:7; 70:43; 82:4; 100:9). God will even know the occupiers of nameless graves. According to the Koran it will be a new creation of every person's body from the very dust out of which God created it before its birth. Even if the body has been devoured by jackals, God will find every atom in their stomachs (13:4; 14:19; 17:49; 34:7 etc) that is to be reunited with their souls. The resurrected will emerge from their graves, which will have risen to the surface of the earth, no matter how deep they were, with downcast eyes, running like scattered locusts towards the great caller (54:7–8).

The day of resurrection is called the day of turmoil, of crying and of rushing, because every risen person will be desperately searching for his loved ones, amidst all the millions of bodies of all the people who ever lived on earth. Every person will be recognizable but if he has spent a lifetime praying to God, his forehead will emit light where it touched the floor often. This light spot will be seen by the angels whom God will send out to find his devout worshippers. The angels will take those believers to the foot of the Sirat al-Mustaqim (q.v.) so they have a headstart on the way to heaven.

All the people will then be assembled and placed in rows, having received new bodies, and they will be told to account for their deeds on earth (Koran 70:44; 84:4; 100:9; 110:2). Their belief in the one God will be especially scrutinized (10:30). Those who followed Satan will not be protected by him (14:22). Those who worshipped other gods will be asked where they are (16:27). They will each be shown a book of deeds in which every one of their sins and virtues is described (18:49). The sinners will see the fire (18:53) for the gates of hell will be opened (26:91). The good people will see paradise (26:90). They will not be terrified on that day (27:89). Allah knows everything that a man hides in his breast (28:69). Those who served God will see him as an ally (34:40-1). Everyone will receive justice. Some scholars say that judgement will begin at once and that it will all be over on the same day; others maintain that it will be forty years after resurrection before the day of judgement (q.v.) arrives. Meanwhile the risen will be waiting in the dark.

2. The first certain reference to resurrection in the Old Testament is Isaiah 26:19: 'Thy dead live, their bodies will rise again.' This passage implies that the dead have immortal souls, so they live, and one day they will be reunited with their bodies. In Daniel 12:2 there is another prediction of

the resurrection when 'the dead will awake' (as if they are asleep). In Ezekiel 37:14 the Lord resurrects a vast field full of dry bones by putting his breath into them. Jesus says that after resurrection people will not marry, but they will be like angels.

The idea of repayment appears first in Luke 14:14. The son will judge the souls after resurrection – a common belief in Jesus' day. The concept of the judgement of the souls was known in Egypt and ancient Persia a millennium before Christ. In a religion where the battle between the good God and the spirit of evil has to be joined by all men and women, the concept of a final judgement makes sense, since all have a free will to take sides for or against the good God. In a theology where God takes all the decisions, judgement of the human souls makes no sense.

There is in most religions an ambiguity concerning individual or collective judgement. Individual judgement takes place immediately after death, after which the soul is assigned a place in hell or paradise. Collective judgement, i.e. the universal hearing of all the souls who ever lived, one after another, has to be preceded by a universal resurrection of all the souls together from their graves. But what happens to the souls between their individual deaths and resurrection is again a question that has caused uncertainty. Does the soul remain with the body in the grave until resurrection? And why is a resurrection of the bodies necessary for judgement? Only Islam makes the answer clear: in paradise the blessed do marry, so they need bodies for the physical enjoyment of their wives.

Revelation

Many theologians have debated the essence of revelation because it is the source of all revealed religions, including all the great Middle Eastern faiths – Christianity, Islam, Judaism and Zoroastrianism. Many branches of Hinduism, such as the followers of Krishna's revelation in the Bhagavadgita, believe in revelation.

Revelation is the causation of knowledge by God in the minds of his prophets. How he does it is the great mystery of all religions.

Islamic scholars have analysed this problem, and have concluded that God can create knowledge in the brain of a prophet simply by putting his words there, or by shining his light there so that the prophet can see more in his mind – things which have always been there, but which ordinary people cannot see since their minds are clouded in darkness. God may also show the prophet things outside him which are invisible to ordinary mortals. For instance God may show him scenes from the past or the future, or events that take place at a great distance. He may also send an angel holding a scroll with letters on it so that the prophet can read aloud from something his companions cannot see. The prophet will also speak to the angel, who is invisible to the others present. They will only see the prophet talking, and then listening to an answer which none but he can understand. God may also speak, call or whisper to his prophet, almost always in the prophet's own language, inside his brain, or from outside – from nearby or from heaven.

1. Revelation and the Old Testament. If we take as our definition of a prophet 'a person to whom God speaks', then Adam, Noah and Abraham were prophets. But some biblical scholars maintain that Samuel was the first true prophet of the Jewish tradition. From him to Malachi there are twenty-four prophets mentioned in the Hebrew Bible, each with his own 'book' containing the revelation he received from God, and the visions which God inspired him to see.

The greatest of all the biblical prophets was without doubt Moses (Deuteronomy 34:10), because God revealed to him the law, contained in the Torah, which is still followed to the letter by orthodox Jews. The concept of a religious law based entirely on God's revelation was adopted in its totality in Islam. The Koran, though it differs from the Bible in many ways, is for Muslims the sole foundation of all Islamic laws.

2. Revelation and the New Testament. Christianity accepted the Old Testament as divinely inspired and added its own New Testament containing the words of Jesus, who as the son of God (though not accepted as such by all Christians) spoke from his own authority, revealing himself to his disciples (Acts 1:9; 2:32) by ascending into heaven before their eyes. God also revealed himself to them as a 'driving wind' (Acts 2:2), sending tongues of flames so that they were 'filled with the Holy Spirit' and could speak in languages they did not even know. In the Book of Revelation

is the great vision of the last things revealed by God to St John, the vision of the new Jerusalem.

3. Revelation and the Koran. Muslim scholars have devoted a great deal of study to the problem of revelation, in Arabic *wahy*. Originally this word meant 'giving a signal to a person which no one else could see'; also 'inspiration', i.e. making a person or an animal do something. The Koran says, 'Thy Lord inspired the bee' (16:68), so that the bee found honey and wax. We call such inspiration instinct, but Islamic scholars are emphatic that *wahy* is distinct from *ilham*, 'intuition', which arises inside a person's mind. *Wahy*, revelation or inspiration, 'comes from a source outside the prophet's soul; it descends upon it from the heavens; it does not emanate from within himself . . .' Muslims believe in the independent existence of a spiritual angel coming from God to Muhammad with the message as described by God:

And verily it is the revelation of the Lord of the Worlds,
Which hath come down with the Faithful Spirit,
Upon thy heart, that thou mayest be of those who warn,
In clear Arabic speech.
(Koran 26:192–5).

See also *Ru'ya*.

Rida (Reza)

'Satisfaction'. The Sufi has to be in a state of satisfaction at all times even if he is hungry. This self-enforced gladness will lead to God being satisfied with his servant. God's satisfaction, *rida*, will result in good fortune and happiness for those who receive it as their reward (see Koran 5:119). See *Qana'a*.

Ridhwan (Rizuan)

One of the archangels created by God, according to the Islamic tradition, especially to guard the twelve gates of paradise. When, on the Prophet's birthday, God commands Ridhwan to open the gates, a cool, sweet breeze from the garden (*janna*) wafts down, refreshing the hot earth's atmosphere. This happened also when the Prophet Muhammad was conceived. Ridhwan has to guard the gates against the satans who are trying to enter paradise secretly so as to learn the future, which the angels know. See *Paradise, Shihab*.

Rim-Sin

A king of the Larsa dynasty of the Sumerian period. Anu (q.v.) the god of kings gave him the city of Uruk, where Anu had his sanctuary. Rim-Sin excavated the river Euphrates with his hands, for he was a great giant.

Ring

See *Solomon's Ring*.

Riwaya (Persian: *dastan*)

A story, as told by a *rawi*, or storyteller. The Middle Eastern storyteller has a literally endless supply of tales and legends from all countries. The Arabian Tales or 1001 Nights are matched by the Persian 1001 Days, also in six volumes. The Arabian quasi-historical *Sirat Banu Hilal* is matched by the Persian *Shahname*; the fables of the Persian Anwar-e-Shuhayli by those of the Arab sage Luqman. Antar, Hamza and Miqdad are Arab heroes about whom numerous adventures are narrated, comparable to the Persian heroes Rustam and Sohrab; Sindbad (q.v.) and Hajji Baba, both adventurers; Nasre-din and Juha, two quasi-saints.

Rizuan
See *Ridwan*.

Roc (Rokk, Roch, Rock, Rukh)
A gigantic magical bird said to nest on an island in the Indian Ocean, probably Madagascar, where so many strange creatures live. It fed on young elephants which it picked up like an owl catching mice. The sailor Sindbad (q.v.) was stranded on its island and discovered a white dome like a saint's tomb. It was the roc's egg. Suddenly cracks appeared and the huge head of the young bird emerged. A vast darkness like a cloud heralded the arrival of the mother roc. While she was 'sitting' on her nest, Sindbad tied himself to her lower leg and when she took off, soaring up into the sky, she did not even notice him. She swooped down on the African mainland to catch a python. Sindbad, grabbing his chance, quickly untied himself, and returned to the civilized world once more.

The roc was known in King Solomon's days. By a ruse, Solomon induced it to bring him a piece of the miraculous hardwood that could cut metal and cure defect limbs.

Rock
See *Sakhra*.

Ruh Al-Quds
The Holy Spirit (Koran 16:104), which is the inspiring agent of the Koran itself. It also fortified Isa (2:81; 2:254; 5:109). The Holy Spirit is often identified with the angel Jibril. See *Holy Spirit, Ruhu'llah*.

Ruhu'l-Jari
'The travelling spirit'. The sentient being that leaves the body during a dream, as opposed to the *ruhu'l-muhkam*, 'resident spirit', which never leaves the body, and the *ruhu'l-haywani*, 'the life spirit', life itself. See *Ru'ya*.

Ruhu'llah (Ruhollah)
The spirit of God which he breathed into Maryam (Koran 4:169; 21:91; 32:8; 15:29; 38:72). Now also a title for the highest mullahs, the ayatollahs in the Iranian Shi'a.

Rumi, Jalal al-Din
A Persian poet, born in Balkh in 1207. He wrote 4000 quatrains but became most famous for his great book of *mathnawi* (*masnavi*) 'distichs', in which he set out his mystic philosophy, often using parables. He became the leader of a Sufi order which was later called the Mawlawi or Mevlevi order, after *Mawlawa* 'my Lord', the common term of reverend address for Rumi. These Mevlevis gradually developed into the 'Dancing Dervishes' of later centuries in the Ottoman Empire. Rumi died in Konya in Turkey in 1273.

He taught tolerance and a peaceful

behaviour towards Jews and Christians. This tolerance was both the root and the result of his great peace of mind, without which the truth cannot be discovered. His many disciples deeply loved him for his kindness and friendliness, his peacefulness and honesty.

Rustam (Rostem)

The most famous hero of the great Persian Epic of the Kings, *Shahname*, by Firdausi (completed in 400 AH/ 1010 AD). He was the son of Zal who was born with grey hair and educated at the court of King Minuchihir (Manuchihr). When he was ten, the shah's white elephant broke loose, but the boy Rustam hit the raging animal with a club so that it fell down dead. He caught and tamed the stallion Rakhsh which stayed faithful to him ever after.

One day Rakhsh was stolen while Rustam was sleeping in the wilderness. He followed the traces and reached a city where he was well received. In the night the king's daughter appeared saying: 'I had your horse taken because I want you as my husband. I am Tamine.' They were married and after Rustam had gone back to his endless battles, she gave birth to a boy whom she called Sohrab.

Rustam served a succession of Persian monarchs: Kay Kobad, Kay Ka'us and Kay Khosrau. He was killed by treachery, perhaps in the sixth century BC, although Rustam is not really dateable as a historical figure. He fought mythical monsters like the dragon and the White Demon. Unknown to him, he killed his own son Sohrab.

Ru'ya

'Vision, dream'. Often prophets and saints claim to have seen God, the angels or the saints in a dream but that is not considered convincing. Muhammad claimed to have seen God 'with the eyes of his body', while he was wide awake. Without that assertion his followers would not have believed him. See *Ruhu'l-Jari*.

 S

Sa'a

'Hour'. The 'hour' is referred to in numerous tales about the latter days. The word occurs often in the Koran (e.g. 22:1–2), always in the meaning of the hour of doom, when Armageddon will begin with earthquakes, thunder and storm. It will be worse than anything else (Koran 54:46) and it will come unexpectedly (6:31). It will happen in the twinkling of an eye (16:77), but it will be preceded by signs (47:18)

'A person's hour' refers to his last hour. 'Each of us has his hour' and many other proverbs refer to death, which also comes unexpectedly, so that we have to prepare ourselves for this hour all our lives, by prayer and fasting. This conduct will also prepare us for the final hour of the world. All the books of Islamic morality agree that working for money is less useful than prayer and fasting, since 'you can't take it with you'. This explains why in Muslim countries there is not the drive for business nor for the environment that there is in the West.

Saba

A city in southern Arabia, capital of the kingdom of Yemen (Koran 34:14). Its inhabitants were ungrateful (*kafir*) to God, so he punished them with a flood. It is identified with the biblical Sheba (Koran 27:21; 1 Kings 10; 2 Chronicles 9), whose queen was called Bilkis (Balqis) (q.v.). She was the daughter of a female *jinn* who had married the last king, so Bilkis herself knew the art of magic. But King Solomon knew more when she came to test him so, within twenty-four hours, she became his wife. At that time she had a splendid palace in Saba and in it a throne which Solomon ordered his *ifrit* to carry to Jerusalem, while she herself was still on her way.

Later kings of Saba neglected its famous system of dams and aqueducts that enabled the citizens to cultivate vines and dates in the gardens, so the dams burst in the flood and the land dried out.

Sabeans (Sabaeans)

1. The people of the city of Saba (q.v.). According to the Koran (27:21) they were sun-worshippers.

2. A gang of robbers (Job 1:15).

3. A nation of traders, Isaiah 45:14, where they are called 'men of stature,' meaning presumably that they were very rich, so they could be identical with 1 above.

4. The Koran (2:50) distinguishes 'believers' (i.e. Muslims), Jews, Christians and Sabeans as the four religions whose members will be rewarded by God; they have nothing to fear (5:73). In 22:17, 'Magians' are added as the fifth religion of monotheists, quite rightly since the Zoroastrians worship only Ahura Mazda (q.v.). All five religions are also 'people of the book', which means they have a written revelation.

Since the Sabeans were the only people of the five who could not be identified, several nations later claimed to be Sabeans hoping to be recognized by the caliph as people of the book and so have the right to claim *dhimma*, 'protection', instead of being forcibly converted like the idolators. It did not help. The only surviving Sabeans lived peacefully in a handful of villages in the Euphrates delta in Iraq. In 1992 Saddam Husayn vented his wrath on all non-Muslims and the Sabeans were completely destroyed. They had a unique culture with an ancient script of their own and spoke Aramaic. They were the last Syriac Christians.

Sacred

Essentially that which belongs to God. In Islam *waqf* property (mosques, cemeteries, schools, land for the maintenance of mosques, etc.) is sacred, i.e. it belongs to God and can never be alienated.

Sacrifice

In all ancient religions, the sacrifice of an animal was a (if not *the*) central ceremony in the ritual calendar. Among the Central Asian peoples horses and also servants were sacrificed to the spirit of a dead king. God's demand that Abraham sacrifice his only legitimate son is probably a last echo of human sacrifice (Genesis 22:2). This sacrifice is commemorated annually by the Muslims by slaughtering a sheep on the tenth day of the month of Muharram.

The first ever sacrifice mentioned in the Bible shows that the pastoral nomads, who were probably the initiators of the biblical tradition, approved only of a sacrifice of sheep (Genesis 4:4), even though the tilling of the soil and the production of grain and fruits was harder work and more hazardous in a country which was totally uncultivated. We must admire Cain for producing any fruit at all, and for following his father's divinely appointed profession as eldest (Genesis 3:23).

The original intention of sacrifice was the pacification of the jealous spirits who envied a man's good luck. The gods were feared and had to be 'bought off'. Jesus never sacrificed anything except himself. The Koran prescribes sacrificing animals (22:36; 108:2). Christians do not sacrifice anything except money, the first fruits at Thanksgiving, and the dedication of their lives in holy orders. Of course the early Church did expect total dedication of its members, as does Islam.

Sadaqa

'Righteousness'. Charity, alms, given to the poor, especially during Id al-Fitr (q.v.). All the alms a person has given will be added up by his *katib* (q.v.) and on the day of judgement (q.v.) they will be weighed against his sins (Koran 2:274–5). Muhammad said: 'Give alms first to your own kinsmen.' See also *Sirat al Mustaqim*.

Saddik (*Saddiq*, plural: *saddiqim*, Also spelled *tzadik*)

'Just'. The Jewish tradition relates that God will always keep thirty-six just men on earth. It is for their sake that he will not destroy the earth – yet. They will not be found among the leaders of men.

Sadducees

A sect of Jews, a religious party in the time of Jesus. Their founder was Zadok (Tsaduk) a 'righteous leader' who lived about 300 BC. They denied the resurrection and had no developed ideas on life after death, since they adhered strictly to the law of Moses, not believing in angels (Mark 12:28; Luke 20:27).

Sa'di

Persian mystic poet born 1185, died 1292 in Shiraz, famous for his two great collections of Sufi poetry, the *Gulistan, Rose Garden* and the *Bustan, Garden of Fragrance*, which are wise tales interspersed with gnomic verses many of which have become common proverbs in Persian, such as 'Curse not the ant who stores the golden grain. He lives in joy.

Let him not die in pain.' This verse expresses the Sufis' compassion for all creatures.

Sa'd Ibn Abi Wakkas

It is related in the Islamic traditions of China that the T'ang emperor T'ai Tsung (Tai Cong) had a dream in 628 AD in which he saw a tall turbaned man slay a dragon. T'ai Tsung sent an embassy to the west, after consulting his diviners. They arrived at the court of Muhammad in Arabia, and he agreed to give them his uncle Sa'd ibn Abi Wakkas, his mother's full cousin, as his envoy to the emperor of China.

The Chinese ambassador hung a sheet of paper on the wall, the Prophet stood before it, and the radiance from his face imprinted an image on the paper. This was taken to China, so that the emperor could recognize Muhammad as the tall man of his dream. The picture, however, disappeared one day when it was worshipped. In addition, the emperor asked for an army from Arabia to defend his western borders. So the Prophet sent 800 young men who settled in China and married Chinese brides. Their descendants are the present-day Muslims of China.

The Prophet had told Sa'd: 'When you arrive in China, pick up some of its earth and smell it. Then, through my power and blessing, you will be able to speak the language'. And that is what happened.

Sadum

See Sudum.

Safura
Arabic for Zipporah, wife of Moses (Musa), daughter of Jethro (Shu'ayb).

Sahaba (Asháb)
The companions of the Prophet Muhammad who accompanied him on his seventy-two campaigns, and to some of whom he promised paradise.

Sahibu-z-Zaman
'Master of the time'. The hidden Mahdi. See *Mahdi 2*, Muhammad al-Mahdi.

Sahifa
'Book, epistle'. A portion of scripture believed to have been given to Adam, Shayth (Seth), Idris (Enoch) and Ibrahim (Abraham) as well as to Musa (Moses) (Koran 87:19). Also, the book which every guardian angel keeps of the deeds (*a'mal*) of every man and woman on earth, and which every recording angel sitting on the left shoulder keeps of a man's sins (Koran 50:16; 17:14). See *Lawh al-Mahfuz*.

Saint (Arabic: *wali*, q.v., Persian: *pir, peer*)
A holy person, referred to in the Bible as *hasid, kados* or *hagios*. Sainthood has two aspects, one moral and one spiritual. A saint never sins and desires nothing. As a result he or she is morally pure, since sins cause contagion with immorality and desire prevents the mind from concentrating on higher thought. This latter freedom is the spiritual aspect of the saint's life. Gradually their ever purified thinking may come closer to God. Thus a saint becomes *waliullah*, 'friend of God'.
A saint in Islam is a person who devotes his life entirely to prayer and to teaching the Koran, lives frugally and has been to Mecca on the pilgrimage. Normally, Islamic saints are married and have children. They may spend most of their time in the mosque. The Sufis use the word *salik*, 'traveller, pilgrim', for one who has renounced the world for the path, *tariqa*, to holiness; also *faqir*, 'poor', for a man who desires no earthly goods. *Sheikh* is used for the leader of a *tariqa* or community of Sufis. *Zahid* means a hermit or ascetic. See *Sufism*.

Sa'ir
'Flaming fire'. A stratum of hell preserved for non-Muslims (Koran 4:11). See *Hell*.

Sajjada
A prayer mat or rug for Muslim worship, also called *musalla*. It is believed that a Muslim praying on it is safe from harassment by Satan. See *Ayyub, Salat*.

Sakhr
'Rock'. The wildest and most evil of all the *shayatin* (devils) in Solomon's kingdom. Solomon took him prisoner by means of the seal with God's secret name on it. He tied a millstone round the devil's neck and threw him into Lake Tiberias. From that time crime and sin were banned. It was only when the rope had rotted many years later that the devil broke free and emerged from the lake, resuming his nefarious work.

Sakhra
'Rock'. *The* rock is the stone excrescence on the square where the Temple

of Solomon once stood. It is now hidden by the Dome of the Rock, one of the finest buildings in Jerusalem, an octagonal mosque which was built in the late seventh century entirely in the Byzantine style. It is called Qubbat al-Sakhra. It is believed that this rock was the foundation stone of earth when God started building it. All the prophets are said to have prayed on it, from Adam to Ibrahim, Isa and Muhammad.

It is said that the rock was originally twelve miles high, reaching halfway up to heaven, until King Nebuchadnezzar destroyed it. On it grew aloes, medicinal plants. The people of Emmaus walked in its shade. The Temple of Solomon was built around it. Henceforth the place was called Bayt al-Muqaddas, 'Sacred House'. It is said that when the Greeks conquered it and placed their idols on it and worshipped them, the rock fell down on them. (This must have been after Alexander's conquest). After that it seems that it re-erected itself. It was on that same spot that an old man (St Peter?) appeared to the Greek emperor (Constantine?), urging him to build a great church on the spot to commemorate the resurrection. He did, and it stood there until Justinian built a bigger basilica in its place. That stood until the Muslims under Omar destroyed it, in 637 AD.

It is also said that the emperor Heraklios met another old man there who prophesied that a race of circumcized men would conquer the rock 'within ten years'. And so it happened. The Prophet Muhammad is said to have alighted there from his steed, Buraq, during the night of Isra' (q.v.) and before his Mi'raj (q.v.). He was hailed by the other prophets (Musa, Ibrahim, Isa) whom God had called from their graves for the purpose, as the imam of all the prophets. He prayed with them at that spot 'in the mosque', though the mosque was not yet there.

On doomsday, God will destroy the earth except for this rock; from it he will create a new earth, extending the rock to form a bridge to heaven so that the faithful can travel across it to paradise, whereas the infidel sinners will fall from it into hell-fire. No trace of evil or evil men will remain and a host of angels will be sent to wash all men white. Before Islam it was believed (and is still believed by some) that after resurrection God will place the scales (mizan, q.v.) here and that His exalted throne (kursi, q.v.) will be visible straight above it. See Sirat.

Saki (Saqi)

The cup-bearer (literally 'pourer') often employed by kings (e.g., the 'butler' in Genesis 40:21). The saki was often invoked by the mystic poets of Persia to pour wine for them. This 'wine' is, of course, a symbol of the divine spirit. Thus the initiates know that the mysterious saki is God himself.

Sakina

'Security, tranquility'. In the Koran (2:248) it is a reference to the Hebrew shekina (q.v.), 'divine presence, immanence' (Numbers 14:10; 1 Kings 8:10). In the Koran (2:249) it says: 'There will come to you the ark [tabut] with the sakina in it.' In other passages the word seems to mean 'spirit, faith, courage' (Koran 9:26, 40; 48:2).

Salaam

'Peace, good health, salvation'. It is the greeting for Muslims. Daru'l-Salaam is part of paradise (q.v.). *Salaam* is also one of the names of God, upon which Muslims, especially the Sufis, meditate.

Salat

The ritual prayer in Islam, the only formal way of enjoying spiritual contact with Allah, apart from reciting the Koran. *Du'a* or individual prayer is more developed in Shi'a Islam, but even that is only permitted as the recitation of prescribed texts. The *salat* is bound by fixed rules which regulate the minutest details of the ceremony. It is the second of the 'pillars' (fundamental duties) of Islam, after the *shahada* (q.v.), 'testimony of faith'.

Every Muslim has to perform the *salat* five times a day, wherever he or she is, except when very ill, dying or giving birth. The duty begins at the age of seven, except for the insane. Neglect has to be atoned for by extra prayers. It has to be preceded by washing, *wudu* (*woozoo*). It begins with the *niya* (q.v.), the formulation of one's intention, and is accompanied by recitation of the *fatiha* (q.v.) and some other passages of the Koran.

The power of the *salat* is tremendous: during its performance Satan has no power over believers. On Fridays at noon there is, in the cities, a collective *salat* in the *jami'a* (Friday mosque), usually followed by a *khutba*, sermon, in which the legitimate ruler of the country must be prayed for. It is at that moment that the imam (q.v.) professes by implication who is and who is not the country's legitimate ruler. Imams, as a result, collectively have political power. Some have started rebellions, some have lost their heads for inciting their congregations (*umma*) from the pulpit. Religion and politics are inseparable in Islam. Separation of the sexes in the mosque is a duty.

Sufism cannot be understood without the *salat*. The Sufis, with the exception of some extreme spiritualists, insist on the performance of the five daily prayers, because it is the necessary condition for making the soul submissive (*muslim*) and so rendering it closer to God. After the *salat al-'isha*, at about 8 p.m., the Sufis will go on reciting passages from the Koran and certain *du'a* prayers prescribed by the founder of the *tariqa* (q.v.). These are followed by *dhikr* (*zikir*) (q.v.), repetition of God's holy names (see *Asma*) and set phrases from the Koran, (such as 112:1–2; 110:3; 6:18; 30:27; 42:9; 43:84; and 6:91 and 28:88, which contain the core of Sufi doctrine). These prayers and recitals go on until dawn when it is time for the *salat as-subh*, dawn prayers. The approach of daylight is awaited and watched with keen attention by the Sufis since light is the representation of God's presence. God's most essential manifestation is light, *nur* (see Koran 2:4; 24:35–6).

Salbatanu

Babylonian planet-god: Mars.

Salih

A prophet of Allah, sent to the people of Thamud in Arabia (Koran

7:73; 11:61; 26:141; 27:45; 91:11). However, the Thamudians refused to accept Islam and even plotted an attempt on Salih's life. They demanded that he show them a sign of God. So Salih prayed to God, whereupon a rock opened and out came a huge female camel which at once gave birth to a fine youngster. But the wicked Thamudians killed both the camels, whereupon God destroyed them by means of thunder and earthquake. Salih escaped to the hills with his wife.

Salsabil
One of the wells, fountains or rivers in paradise from which the faithful may drink (Koran 76:18).

Samael
Seducer of Eve (q.v.).

Samson (Hebrew: *Shimshun*)
A word derived from Shamash (q.v.), the sun-god. The history of Samson can be found in Judges 15. He lived in Zorah, near Beth Shemesh, where the sun-god was once worshipped. In premonotheistic times Samson was himself the sun, victorious in his youth but ending his days in darkness.

Samson killed a lion with his bare hands; he was betrayed by his mistress; he decided on his own death by descending into the darkness or the underworld. His exploits are probably based on the tales of Heracles, which were brought to the coast of Palestine by Greek settlers from Mycenae, who colonised Tell Abu Hawam near Haifa. Both heroes perform hard labours for the good of their fellow citizens.

Samuel
Prophet to whom God spoke (1 Samuel 3:11), and who anointed the two first kings of Israel (1 Samuel 10:1; 19:18). In Arabic Shamwil or Ishmawil (Koran 2:246–7).

Sanam (plural: *asnam*)
'Images'. The idols worshipped by the heathens (Koran 7:138). No statues have survived in Arabia but many have come to light in Israel and Syria. See *Shirk*.

Sandals
In the Middle East, Africa and India, no one used to wear shoes. Sandals are easy to slip on and take off. They are usually left at the door of the house. They may not be worn in a mosque because it is holy ground. That is why God said to Moses: 'Put off thy shoes' (Exodus 3:5; Koran 20:12). On holy ground, that is the parts of the earth where God's presence is concentrated, the worshipper must have direct contact with the earth for his own benefit, so that his feet may be touched by the divine proximity.

The importance of touching the divine presence is demonstrated by the story of the woman with the issue of blood (Luke 8:43–4). Just touching Jesus' garment cured her. In contrast, unholy ground must not be touched at all, so the disciples had to wear sandals when going out on their mission to the heathen countries (Mark 6:9), and even shake the dust off their sandals when they were not welcomed in a place. 'Dust', in a time when streets were not paved, drained or sewered properly, meant all the dirt of the people who lived there. Those who could afford to wore sandals to protect their feet against religious impurity.

Saoshyant (Soshiant)

'Saviour', literally 'the one who will benefit'. The world saviour who is to come, according to Zoroaster's prophecy, to conquer the wicked and stop cruelty by evil, bloodthirsty men, and who will bring the teaching of good purpose. He will come to uphold truth, and will teach us the straight path of salvation.

Saqar

'Scorching heat'. A division of hell reserved for the sorcerers and diviners (Koran 54:48; 74:26), 'blackening the skin of man'. Whoever enters it will be totally burnt.

Saracen

This word which was used for the Arabs during the Crusades, comes from the Greek *sarakenos*, which is from the Arabic *shariqin*, 'orientals', or perhaps from *sariqin* 'robbers'. The latter meaning probably originates from the Nabataeans.

Sarah

According to the Islamic tradition, Sarah was the daughter of Namrud (Nimrod) (q.v.), king of Nineveh (Genesis 10: 8–12), who was mentioned in the Koran (2:258) as a ruler who argued with Ibrahim (Abraham) (q.v.). The Islamic legend relates that Princess Sarah was so exhilarated by the paradisiac fragrance wafting from the well God had created inside the huge fire which Namrud had ordered to burn his enemy Ibrahim, that she asked permission to go and see Ibrahim. Namrud refused, of course, but Sarah went anyway. Through the flames she could see Ibrahim sitting peacefully near a well in a garden that God had likewise created inside the enormous blazing pyre. She saw that the flames did not burn Ibrahim because nothing happens if God does not wish it to happen, even when the laws of nature demand it. She spoke to him through the flames: 'Does it not hurt?'

'No,' answered Ibrahim.

'Can I join you?'

'Yes, just repeat after me: 'Whoever has God in his heart and his holy name on his tongue cannot be burnt.'

She did and was able to walk through the flames to join him. She spent the day with him, drinking the sweet water from the well. When she came home and told her father, he ordered her execution, but God sent an angel to rescue her. The angel lifted her up and carried her to Ibrahim's house in the hills. Ibrahim was already there and the angel joined them in holy matrimony. Sarah became the mother of Ishak (Isaac) (q.v.), although she had to wait many years for this son. She may have had daughters but that is not mentioned. She was jealous of the Egyptian bondmaid Hajar (q.v.), who gave Ibrahim a son Isma'il (q.v.).

It was on their way to Egypt that Ibrahim thought it prudent to hide Sarah in a trunk because she was a very beautiful woman. Unfortunately the customs officer at the Egyptian frontier insisted on opening the trunk, even when Ibrahim offered its weight in gold if he could keep it locked. The officer opened it and saw the most beautiful woman he had ever seen. He reported this to the king who ordered the trunk confiscated and transported to his castle. Ibrahim followed but was unable to pass through the high walls. Suddenly, by God's favour, the stone became glass so that Ibrahim was able to see his wife seated with the king of Egypt on a sofa. The king stretched out his hand, but it withered, for God struck him with leprosy. The king called for a physician who could cure him, but none came. Finally, Ibrahim came in and laid his hand calmly on the king's arm, which was cured instantly. The king gave him a fee in the form of a slave girl called Hajar, who became the mother of Isma'il. Later, when Ishak was born to Sarah, she claimed for him the rights of the firstborn because she was a princess and Ibrahim's first and legal wife. However, the Muslims disagree: Isma'il was, according to Islam, the legal first born son. Through Ishak, Sarah became the mother of the Jews. Ishak looked exactly like his father, so much so that no one could deny he was Ibrahim's son, even though he was born when both Sarah and Ibrahim were very old.

Some scholars have said that the Saracens were so called because they were descendants of Sarah. She is referred to only once in the Koran (and then not by name), in Sura 11:74, when she laughed with joy upon learning that she would have a son and a grandson, Ya'qub, a reference to Genesis 21:6.

Sassoon

A fortress town south of Mush and west of Lake Van in what is now Turkish Kurdistan, but was Greater Armenia until the late Middle Ages. *The Daredevils of Sassoon* is the collective title of a vast complex of epic tales and songs in Armenian. The central theme is the wooing of the beautiful princess Khandoot (Handut) by the chief hero David, son of Meherr, Lord of Sassoon, and Armaghan the proud princess, who, when her husband Meherr left to have an affair in Egypt, swore that she would not admit him back to her bed in forty years. She had to break her oath because Sassoon had to have a king, so she died soon after David was born and so did Meherr.

David was brought up by his uncle Ohan Thundervoice, a splendid character. He gave David his finest horse Jalali, so that he could go and defeat his half-brother Misra Melik, the son of his father's affair, in Egypt. Famous singers visited Khandut with their lutes and sang the praises of David. She sent them to David to sing *her* praises to him, which they did in the most beautiful songs in the epic.

David jumped on his horse and went to court Khandut, but her father the emir demanded the head of Shapur, shah of Persia. David set out to Tehran, challenged the shah, slew him and laid the head at the emir's feet. However, the latter had a few more enemies (mostly Turkish names) that David had to slay before he could marry Khandut. Nine months after the wedding, Khandut gave birth to Meherr, David's big, strong son.

There is much Persian influence in the epic – Shapur, for example, occurs in Firdausi's *Shahname*. There is also some Homeric influence: before David's arrival, Khandut had forty suitors who spent their time eating and drinking, like the suitors of Homer's Penelope. However, as soon as she had decided to marry David, Khandut threw all forty of them out of the castle window, one after the other, breaking all their bones. The epic is full of such unexpected scenes, which make it a lively oral tradition full of folk wisdom and piety, and is also great literature.

Satan

The god of evil, the powerful demon of wickedness, the charming seducer who leads to ruin all those with insufficient strength of will; the Devil. The original meaning of the word *satan* is probably 'false accuser', that is, someone who accuses others, behind their backs, of invented misdemeanours, hence the Greek translation of Satan, *Diabolos*, 'slander, calumny', from which the word 'devil' derives.

Satan does just that when he accuses God of withholding immortality from Adam and Eve (Genesis 3:5). There, in the Garden of Eden, Satan takes the shape of the snake, symbol of lascivity, poison and sure death. He offers knowledge and pleasure of the flesh in exchange for disobedience, that is, lawlessness. This is still the dilemma of modern people: some

keep the law and live in ignorance of material satisfaction, but once broken out of that rigid obedience, they find no moral support. This makes the biblical story so popular in all times.

In Luke 4:1 ff. we read how Satan tries to tempt Jesus with divine power to rule the world, to create food, to be carried by the angels. Jesus refuses; for a man must not try to be God. See *Serpent, Snake*.

Saviour

According to Zoroaster, Aushedar the first saviour will be born from a virgin who in turn will be a descendant of Zoroaster (just as Mary was descended from David). His birth will be heralded by a shower of stars in the sky. At thirty he will begin to restore the laws of Zoroaster which will have been neglected, so that he will establish a better world. The second saviour will be born from Zoroaster's seed which lives on in a lake and will make a virgin pregnant when she comes to bathe. People will become vegetarians, proof of their gradually increasing virtue. See also *Saoshyant*. For saviours in other religions, see *Christ, Messiah, Masih, Mahdi, Muhammad al-mahdi*.

Sayfu'llah

'Sword of God'. Praise-name of Ali as the destroyer of pagan *jinns*. It is still used as a praise-name for warriors in the *jihad* (q.v.).

Sayhun

The river Jaxartes in Asia. In Islamic cosmology, one of the four rivers that flow down from the roots of the tree *Sidrat-al-Muntaha* (q.v.) in paradise.

Sayyid

A descendant of Husayn, the third imam, grandson of the Prophet Muhammad through his only surviving son Zayn al-'Abidin. The Sayyids, it is believed, are gifted with learning and sanctity from birth.

Scapegoat

A male goat which was selected by lot once a year from each village in ancient Israel and many other communities in Asia and Africa. In a solemn ceremony all the sins committed by the community during the past year would be magically 'laden' on this goat and the animal was then 'sent out' with the people's sins as evil spirits sitting on it. It would be left outside the village on the crossroads where many travellers passed. This is why crossroads bring ill luck: they are haunted by evil spirits. If a stranger found it and took it, he would be 'infected' with all those sins. The ceremony was officialised by Moses. See *Azazel*.

Scholars

According to Islamic tradition, which honours scholars, whenever King Solomon gave a feast, the invited dignitaries would be served from silver dishes by the chief stewards; however, scholars would be served from golden dishes by the king himself.

Scorpion

In Sumerian mythology the guardian of the land of the immortals. In Asia Minor, the scorpion was dedicated to Artemis, the goddess of the moon and of wine. It was thus associated with the grape harvest in October, which is when the sun goes through the sign of Scorpio. In Mithraism (as can be seen on many sculptures) the scorpion devours the bull's testicles. The bull signifies Mithra (q.v.) as god of life and summer, and the scorpion autumn, the season of destruction and fall, when the moon appears through the bare branches, and the grapes are crushed.

Script

Writing was taught to man by the Sumerian goddess Nisaba (q.v.).

Cuneiform inscriptions, scratchings on stone, were discovered by a German expedition in Warka (Uruk, Erek) in 1936, and dated to about 3700 BC. Before 2200 BC clay tablets came into use, and at the same time the style of writing changed to the true cuneiform, 'wedge-shaped', writing. This script originally contained some 1700 different characters (no doubt including personal variations), but was reduced to about 800 around 3000 BC. It was used until about 100 BC.

The Sumerians deserve full credit for the invention of writing, well before the Egyptians and the Chinese, who adopted several characters from them. Cuneiform was adapted for Babylonian, a Semitic language, after 3000 BC. It was also used for the old Persian, Hittite, Elamite, Ugaritic and Urartean languages.

The letters of the Hebrew alphabet were sacred, as were the Egyptian hieroglyphs and also the Arabic written in the Koran.

Scroll

Isaiah 34:4, Revelation 6:14 and the Koran 21:104 and 39:67 refer to the heavens being rolled up like a scroll. It is an old Semitic or Bedouin idea that the night sky is like the black canvas of a tent ('roof', Koran 52:5) with tiny openings in it through which the light can be seen behind. This light is of course the divine upper heaven where darkness never reigns (Revelation 21:25–6).

The idea that the starry sky is like a vault with mysterious hieroglyphs on it in the form of constellations, is equally old (Koran 41:53). For these 'signs' (*ayat*) the same word is used as for the verses of the Koran itself. Whoever can read the signs will perceive their 'interior' meaning, i.e. what is behind the 'scroll' on which they are written, so he can foretell the future. The Sufis in particular have taken this concept as a subject for long meditation. The signs of the zodiac and other stars can all be 'read' by astrologers wishing to tell people's fortunes.

Seal of the Prophets

See *Khatamu-n-Nabiyin*.

Sea of Glass

This lay in front of God's throne, shining brightly (Revelation 4:6; 15:2). Angels stand on it singing hymns. This may be the origin of the myth of the mountain of glass which the mystic has to climb in his yearning for God.

Seed

A man's seed (i.e. semen) was regarded equally as precious as his blood (q.v.). This is why both the Koran and the Bible condemn adultery, because a man must keep his seed for the women of his own house, his wives and those women 'whom his right hand possesses' (Koran 4:3). This also partly explains the objections against Jews marrying foreign women (see Nehemiah 13:23–4). Only women of equal nobility are worthy of a man's seed. The pharaohs had to marry their sisters, who alone matched their nobility.

Sefira (plural: *sefirot*)

'Spheres'. One of the (seven or ten) spheres of the Aristotelian universe (see *Merkabah*) each of which represents a divine attribute, the fine tuning or conjuction (Greek: *syzygia*, 'connubium') of which effects the *harmonia*, the felicitous progress of the soul. The Arabic is *tabaqat al-samawat*, the 'layers of the heavens', each one ruled by one of the seven prophets: Adam, Isa, Yusuf, Idris, Harun, Musa and Ibrahim. See *Heaven 3*.

Sekhmet

The Egyptian goddess of war and passion. Her animal was the lion (q.v.).

Serpent

A mythical being having the form of a snake (q.v.) but much larger and longer, with a thinking mind and a vicious nature. In the Bible (Genesis 3) it is the Devil himself who takes the shape of a serpent. Curiously Eve is not frightened of him, which has given some writers reason to suppose he must have appeared in the shape of a handsome man, called Lucifer, another name for the Devil. There is an apocryphal tradition saying that Lucifer had an affair with Eve, whereupon she gave birth to Cain. This would explain Cain's treacherous character. The mythological predecessor of the Serpent is the Sumerian god Enki 'Lord Earth' (q.v.), the Babylonian Ea (q.v.), the god who rules the earth and with it the lives of all creatures.

The ancient Semites associated the serpent with the Moon-god, perhaps for its power to rejuvenate itself.

Seth
1. In Egyptian mythology the crocodile-god, ugly brother and slayer of his twin Osiris, who was later avenged by his son Horus, who emasculated Seth (or blinded him) so that he remained the god of darkness, as Horus is the young sun-god. The Greeks equated Seth with Typhon, their god of storm and darkness.
2. The biblical Seth, third son of Adam and Eve, father of humanity. In Arabic Shayth father of Ataush.

Shabah
The spirits who live in the earth.

Shaddad
In the Islamic tradition the last king of Ad (q.v.) (a wealthy state in southern Arabia) who when the prophet Hud (q.v.) told him about the palaces in paradise replied: 'I can have that here.' Forthwith he built the finest palace ever seen, but when he entered it, death met him on the steps, so he dropped dead before he had time to

live in his palace. It became the empty palace of Irama (q.v.), which was visible only at night.

Shadhili, Abu Al-Hasan Ali ibn Abdallah Al-Zarwili
Born in 1196 and educated in Tunis, Al-Shadhili soon became known as a devoted mystic. He taught that a man must be in constant spiritual contact with God, and be devoted to his service at all times. A man should ideally pray at all hours of the day and night, in all circumstances, since prayer is more important than anything else in life. He forbade mendicancy and taught his disciples to exercise a regular trade, as the people among whom he lived were poor enough. He enjoined his followers to adhere to the Sunna, the strictly orthodox Islamic way of life.

Al-Shadhili reportedly performed many miracles, healing the sick and making the blind see. On a visit to Ethiopia he became acquainted with the use of coffee, which he perceived to be a useful remedy against somnolence during the night vigils (*tahajjud*).

Shafa'a (Shufa'a)
'Intercession'. The Prophet Muhammad will be asked by God on the day of judgement (q.v.) what he would like most. He will reply: 'May I lead my community into paradise?' God will grant that request, the Prophet will then be given a banner or a flag (*liwa'*) and, thus visible from afar, he will be led by the angels across the bridge *Sirat al-Mustaqim* (q.v.) to *Hauzu'l-Kausar*

(q.v.), the first station in paradise. All his faithful followers will be permitted to follow him across the narrow bridge so that it will swing under the weight of millions. For many Muslims this prospect of Muhammad's intercession is the reason for their faith in Islam. The other prophets, Musa and Isa, only asked for their own salvation. See *Standard*.

Shafan (Xaphan)

A fire demon who once threatened to set fire to heaven. He is in charge of the fires of hell which he keeps burning. See *Malik*.

Shahada

'Testimony'. Saying sincerely before Muslim witnesses 'There is no God but Allah and Muhammad is his Prophet' in Arabic makes a man a Muslim. Without it no other ritual (prayer, fasting, pilgrimage) is valid. A man's sincerity may not be questioned.

Shahid

'Witness', especially a witness of the faith, a man (seldom a woman) who died for the faith of Islam, usually on the battlefield, a *mujahid* (see *Jihad*). These martyrs for Islam do not have to wait long lying on the battlefield. Soon after one has died, a bird-angel will descend from paradise, take the soul lovingly in her arms and carry him to heaven, where she will marry him.

Shahname

Firdausi's great epic in Persian (over 100,000 lines) completed before his death in 1020, in which he describes all the heroic deeds of all the many kings of Persia, from Jamshid to Yazdigerd.

Shamash (Sumerian: *Utu*, Hebrew: *Shemesh*, Arabic: *Shams*, Old Persian: *Aftab*)

Babylonian sun-god, protector of justice and truth, judge in heaven and earth, patron of Gilgamesh (q.v.). He was the son of the moon-god Sin, brother of Ishtar (Venus) (q.v.) and husband of Aya. He was worshipped first at Sippar and Larsa but his cult spread to Canaan and Palestine, Arabia and Persia. Shamash was depicted on reliefs with flaming rays rising from his shoulders, leaping up from behind the mountains, with a tiara of flames on his head and a serrated sword. It was under his authority that King Hammurabbi composed the first ever code of law. In Egypt he was identified with Ra.

Shapash

The Ugaritic sun-goddess, often called the 'torch of the gods'.

Sharif (plural: *shurafa'*)

Arabic nobleman who traces his descent from Hasan ibn Ali, grandson of the Prophet Muhammad.

Sharuma

Hurrian god, son of Teshub and Hepit, in Asia Minor.

Shauq

'Yearning'. The passionate longing for God. The Sufi is always yearning for God's proximity.

Shaytans

A race of evil spirits created by God to try men and women for their steadfastness in Islam. There are many types. They are made of fire so that liquid fire flows in their veins. When a hero manages to wound a *shaytan* the fire flows out and consumes the body. A *shaytan* may look like hot smoke, or like a dog, a snake, a scorpion, a wolf, a jackal, a lion, a man or a woman.

Once long ago the *shaytans* were in possession of the earth but God sent an army of angels to drive them out. Some scholars say that they are a species of *jinn* who refuse to submit to God and become Muslims. As many *shaytans* look like human beings it is difficult to identify them except by what they say and do. They are very dangerous since they are strong, unpredictable, versed in witchcraft and vicious. They will teach sorcery for the price of a soul. They can frighten people by taking the appearance of monsters of gigantic size with long teeth, claws and horns, with fiery eyes and making a terrible noise. God created shooting stars (see *Shihab*) especially for the angels, as rockets to destroy *shaytans* with. See *Satan*.

Shekina (Shechina)

'In-dwelling'. The proximity or even the presence of God's spirit and glory in the tabernacle and later in the Temple (Numbers 14:10; 1 Kings 8:10–13). The Arabic equivalent is *sakina* (q.v.).

Sheol

The underworld where the dead reside, often translated as 'the grave'. 'Let the dead be silent in Sheol' (Psalms 31:17); 'Like the sheep they are laid in Sheol' (Psalms 49:14); 'I will ransom them from the power of Sheol' (Hosea 13:14); 'Oh that thou wouldst hide me in Sheol' (Job 14:13). Here Sheol is a refuge from God's wrath and Job's suffering on earth, until such a time as God's grace returns and Job can live in peace and good health again. The word is related to the Arabic *su'al*, 'interrogation'. See *Munkar and Nakir*, *Hell 2*.

Shezbeth (Xezbeth)

A devil who invents lies and untrue tales. In Arabic Al-Kazzab, 'The Liar', Satan.

Shi'a

'Party', short for Shi'at-Ali, 'the Party of Ali'. Ali ibn Abu Talib (q.v.), son-in-law and cousin of the holy Prophet, was the obvious choice for becoming his successor, according to many Muslims. They believe that Ali was the only legitimate heir to Muhammad as the ruler of Arabia and all Islam, caliph, and commander of the faithful. After Ali, his sons and one of their sons ought to have inherited the caliphate, the succession to Muhammad's mystic kingship. The Shi'a (as they are collectively known), who are mainly concentrated in Iran, reject the caliphate of Abu Bakr (who was chosen by a more powerful group), Omar, Uthman and the Omayyads.

When Uthman was murdered, Ali was finally made caliph by his party in 656 AD. However, Uthman's kinsman Mu'awiya, governor of Damascus, accused Ali of complicity in the murder. This led to a split in the ranks of Muslims and so to the first civil war, which ended in the battle of Siffin (660) in which the wily Mu'awiya was victorious through trickery. Ali was murdered in 661 and his eldest son Hasan (q.v.) was poisoned in 670, so that the Shi'a, Ali's party, set all their hopes on Husayn (q.v.), but when he was killed in 680 at Kerbela, turned to his only surviving son, Zayn al 'Abidin, the fourth imam (after Ali, Hasan and Husayn). This began the series of seven (or twelve) imams (the Shi'a do not recognize any caliphs) whose exclusive legitimacy is the central doctrine of the Shi'a.

The question of 'who has the right and the duty to rule Islam, to be commander of the faithful' has haunted the world of Islam from Muhammad's death to the present day. No ruler of Islam has ever been recognized by all Muslims, and many have been murdered (from Omar in 644 to Anwar Sadat in 1981) because their assassins thought they were not legitimate. Since Muhammad, who was sole ruler of all Arabia, had not appointed a successor at his death, there has always been uncertainty. The Shi'a insist that the ruler of the Islamic state must be a scion of the House of Muhammad – a condition which at this time is only fulfilled by the king of Morocco, who claims descent from Hasan ibn Ali. The Sunni scholars insist that the ruler of Islam must be of the House of Hashim, Muhammad's great-grandfather (q.v.). This condition is fulfilled only by King Husayn of Jordan. This condition also explains why the Ottoman sultans were never recognized as caliphs by the Arabs; they did not belong to the Meccan nobility. The Shi'a of Iran maintain that the rulers of Islam must reign in the name of the twelfth imam, the hidden Mahdi (q.v.) who, it is believed, inspires the ayatollah with the Ruhu'llah, the spirit of God.

Since there is no distinction between religion and state in Islam the general rule is that the leader of an Islamic state can legitimize himself only by administering Islamic law in every detail. That is precisely the root of most of the friction in the Middle East, because in our century it has become impossible to apply all the laws of Islam. Only in a few countries like the Sudan and Saudi Arabia is it attempted.

The Shi'a maintain that the Prophet Muhammad, at God's behest, revealed to Ali that he must become the heir to the kingdom of Islam. This episode is known as the *wasia*, the last charge. When Muhammad died, Ali was busy with the funerary ceremonies, prayers and the burial of his father-in-law, so that Abu Bakr was made caliph by his friends, they say. The conflict has never been resolved and lay at the root of the Iran–Iraq war of 1980–8.

Shihab (plural: *shuhub*)

A rocket or fiery missile launched by the angels from heaven against the *shaytans* who are spying on them. A falling star.

Shiqq

A type of demon appearing to travellers as half a man.

Shirk

'Idolatry', literally: 'giving companions' (to God). This is the worst
sin in Islam, just as it is sinning
against the first commandment in
Judaism (Exodus 20:3). *Shirk* is often
translated as polytheism. That is correct, except that the term polytheism
is neutral; 'paganism' reflects more
accurately the Islamic attitude to the
'idol-worshippers' which includes the
Hindus of India as well as the ethnic
religions of Africa. It also includes
soothsayers and fortune-tellers who
have a *jinn* (a 'genius') as the satanic
source of their knowledge. *Shirk* also
includes worshipping or adoring a
human being. No man may bow
down to a man, nor may a man
require others to bow down to him. It
follows that the Prophet Muhammad
may not be worshipped; no one may
pray at his grave; no one may pray to
him anywhere.

Shoes
See *Sandals*.

Shu'ayb
Arabic name of the biblical Jethro,
father-in-law of Moses. The thirteenth prophet after Adam in the
Islamic tradition.

Shukr (Shukran)
'Gratitude, thanks'. The sixteenth
stage on the Ṣufi path. See Koran
14:7.

Shullat
The Babylonian equivalent of Hirmis
(q.v.), a divine messenger.

Shutu
Sumerian god of the south wind in
the Gulf, and of illness and sicknesses,
which he puts into human bodies.

Sibitti
In Babylonian mythology, the infernal
gods, the servants of Erra the god
of death (q.v.). They were the gods
of warfare and battle; they loved
the clash of arms and hated the
quiet life in the city. Erra persuaded
Marduk, the god of order (q.v.), to
rise from his throne on earth for a
holiday in heaven. As soon as he was
gone, all hell broke loose on earth,
literally. Morality disappeared, sons
hated their fathers, mothers hated
their daughters and criminals ruled.

Sibzianna
Sumerian star-god: Orion.

Siddiq
'The Believer' praise-name of Abu
Bakr, the first man who believed that
Muhammad had had a real revelation
from God. He was a true friend.

Sidrat-Al-Muntaha
'Cedar of the end' (Koran 53:14).
The word *sidra* has also been translated as 'lote tree', or as 'jujube tree'
(*zizyphus*). It stands in heaven on the
seventh stratum, just under God's
throne. Each of its leaves has a name
written on it. When the leaf falls, the
bearer of that name must die. The
angel of death will catch the leaf,
read the name on it, then descend to
earth to take the soul of that person
without delay.

Siduri (Siduru Sabatu)
The Babylonian equivalent of Hebe, the goddess of divine wine, who is depicted seated in heaven in the shade of her vineyard.

Signs

Essentially, signs are miracles by means of which God shows that a prophet or saint who claims to speak in his name is indeed speaking the truth. A sign from God therefore is an unusual event intended to make even the most obstinate onlookers believe that the performer is speaking God's word.
1. Jesus showed many signs by his miraculous healings, but many who witnessed them still would not believe in him (John 5:16). Moses had to show ten signs from God, the ten plagues of Egypt, before the pharaoh believed that he must let the people of Israel go free (Exodus 8–11). In 1 Kings 18:38 Elijah demonstrated to the assembled priests of Baal that his god was more powerful than any other. The Lord caused fire to fall from heaven and burn water. See *Miracles*.

Many people believe that one day Jesus will come back to earth (the second advent). He will look like an ordinary man except for certain signs on his person by which the devout will recognize him as the Christ. Many Christians also believe that God will show signs to announce doomsday so that the sinners may repent in time before judgement.
2. Signs will precede the day of judgement (q.v.) (Koran 47:18). The Shi'a writers emphasize that the coming of the Mahdi (q.v.), the reincarnated imam, will be preceded by clear signs – the appearance of an angel and a loud thundering in the sky.

The holy Prophet explained to his followers what would happen at the end of time and how one was to foresee this:

In those days people will no longer study the holy Koran nor keep the law; everybody will be interested only in satisfying his own greed and lust. There will be an epidemic in Jedda, famine in Medina and the plague in Mecca. There will be earthquakes everywhere in North Africa, thunderstorms in Egypt and all over Europe so terrible that entire regions will be laid waste. Iran and Iraq will be destroyed by murderers and vandals in great numbers. Floods will cause the rivers to rise and sweep away thousands while disease will exterminate the Asians of the East. There will be no more morality or discipline. Then God will cause a monster to appear, created from the people's bestiality. It will be ugly and horrifying to see. Its name is Dajjal, whom the Europeans call the Antichrist. He will ride on a giant ass and subject all the people of the earth to his will, causing even more filthy behaviour than is already there. He will rule for only forty days with terror and force. Then God will send the Prophet Isa down from heaven on a white horse with a lance in his hand. His throne too, will descend from above and he will seat himself on it, so that the faithful believers will rejoice. From them Isa will recruit an army and ride out against Dajjal, who will be defeated but escape and run for his life. Then God will intervene and command the earth to hold the monster. Suddenly, Dajjal's feet will be glued to the ground so that Isa can approach and kill him with God's lance. The army of sinners and godless men will be annihilated by the followers of Isa, who will become king at last and rule with justice for forty years. Each year, however, will be as long as two years and two months are at the present time, so that there will be a long period of peace and righteousness, following the second coming of Isa. At the end of his period of reigning for eighty-four years, Isa will return to Jerusalem and pray to God in the Dome of the Rock to surrender his soul again to God, and die there. Seven days later Yajuj and Majuj, Gog and Magog [Revelation 20:8] will finally break through the brass wall that Alexander built to contain them [Koran 18:89]. Waves upon waves of barbarians will come tumbling down from the mountains of the east where they breed in their millions and destroy civilization, especially all the waterworks, so that the people will perish of thirst. The earth will become dry and dusty except for the filth of the barbarians.

This quotation, attributed to the Prophet Muhammad, may have been edited at a later date.

Sijil

The angel in charge of the scrolls in heaven until doomsday (Koran 21:104).

Sijjin

(Koran 83:7–8). This word may have one of two meanings: a deep pit, part of hell, or the register of the sinners.

Si'la

A demoness who catches travellers in the wilderness and plays with them like a cat with a mouse. She may also tempt men with gold. She will play the flute and make a man dance till he dies. Wolves devour *si'las*.

Silili

In Babylonian mythology, the divine mare, mother of all horses.

Silk

1. The discovery of silk happened as follows. King Solomon received a diamond from the Queen of Sheba with a crooked hole in it. She challenged him to find a needle to thread the diamond, certain that he could not. However, Solomon possessed a tiny worm which crept through the tunnel in the diamond, leaving a thin thread behind: the first silk thread.
2. The blessed will receive silk garments in paradise (Koran 22:23).

Silsila

'Chain'. The line of succession of the teachers of a religious community, a *tariqa* (q.v.).

Simon

The Magician of Samaria (Acts 8:9), who bewitched the people with his magic. St Peter condemned him for wanting to buy the power of the Holy Ghost so that he might pass it on to his followers, believing that the gift of God could be purchased.

Simurgh

In Persian myths the immortal phoenix (q.v.) rising from its ashes annually, which may be an indication that he is the god of vegetation. In Attar's *Parliament of the Birds*, Simurgh is the secret name for God. Simurgh the god-bird is called in old Persian *Saena Meregha*, the dragon peacock, symbol of the Persian king.

Sin

Also called Zuen or Nanna, the moon-god in Sumer and Babylon, the ruler of the calendar. His symbol was the crescent, his cult centres were Ur in the south and Harran in the north, and he was depicted with horns and a long beard of lapis lazuli. His temple was Enushirgal, where Gilgamesh (q.v.) prayed to him. He gave oracles containing commandments which even the gods had to keep. A moon eclipse was believed to be a sign of imminent disaster on earth.

Sindbad

The name seems to mean either 'Indian Spirit' or '*Jinn* Born from a Human Woman'. In Persian tales, he was a fabulous magician, sage, statesman and traveller, to whom numerous fables and myths are attributed. He is best known for his tall sailors' tales incorporated in the Arabian Nights (q.v.) stories. See *Roc*.

Sirat Al-Mustaqim

'The straight path' (Koran 1:6; 2:213; 3:101; 4:68 etc.). From the Latin *strata* 'street', it has acquired the meaning of *stricta* 'narrow'. It is usually explained as the narrow bridge. It is qualified only in Suras 19:43 and 20:135 as *sawii*, 'even, straight, correct'. It is the path of God (42:53;

34:6). In the later traditions the sirat is described as no wider than a rope 3000 miles (or hours) in length, 1000 upwards, 1000 across and 1000 downwards. Others describe it as a ladder which the dead souls have to climb into paradise (q.v.) and safety. Beneath it rages the fire of hell (q.v.), which scorches the sinners, so that they fall into it. They can only be saved by repeating God's name. God will hear them and send an angel to rescue them. The good souls will find their good deeds converted into a white horse waiting for them at the ascent. Riding it, they will traverse the *sirat* in three minutes because their good deeds will carry them to paradise. See *Hauzu'l-Kausar*.

Snake

This legless reptile was feared for its swift, deadly bite and admired for its sloughing, leaving behind its old skin and appearing rejuvenated, so leading people to believe that it was immortal. Because it lives in a hole in the ground the snake has become a symbol of the earth-god – or the earth-goddess, for in many cultures the snake is feminine.

In Asia Minor the god of healers, Asklepios, carried a snake curled around his staff (or two snakes, as can still be seen in the symbol of the medical profession) because he had the power over life and death. This staff was no doubt identical with the staff of Moses (q.v.), which he could change into a snake (Exodus 7:9) and which could produce life-giving water (Exodus 17:6). See also *Serpent*.

The Egyptian deity Buto (Per-U-Ajit) was a snake-goddess worshipped at Buto in the delta, protectress of lower Egypt, nurse of Horus. She was represented as a cobra, *uraeus*, and worn by the pharaohs for protection.

Sodom (Arabic: *Sudum*)

Ancient city just north of the Dead Sea, near Gomorrah. The inhabitants of Sodom, the Sodomites, were sinful in the eyes of the Lord (Genesis 13:13; 18:20; 1 Kings 15:12) so the Lord destroyed their city (Genesis 19:24), saving only Lot.

Solomon

King of Israel and Judah 961–922 BC. He asked God for wisdom (1 Kings 3:5) and, according to later legends, this included knowledge of magic. Known in the Koran as Sulayman, this king-prophet has become the chief hero in a vast popular literature of miraculous-moralistic tales about his long reign. He is particularly noted for succumbing to the seduction of 'strange women' who persuaded him to worship 'other gods' (1 Kings 11:4).

A popular tale among Islamic storytellers tells how God permitted the Devil to get hold of Solomon's ring (q.v.), which he had forgotten in the bathroom, so that he lost all his power and the Devil sat on his throne. Solomon became a humble fisherman and repented. God relented and one day Solomon found his ring in the belly of a fish. With it, his royal power came back. The moral of this tale is that all power is from God so that no king should be proud of his power: God can take it away at any time. Anything, but anything

can happen at any time when God wishes it. Nothing, good or bad, should surprise us (Koran 38, 34–5).

The *Book of Solomon* (1 Kings 11:41) is not identical to the 'wisdom of Solomon'. Somewhere, say the Arab storytellers, is this book, the *Book of Magic and of Prophesies*, dictated by Solomon himself. If any man can find it and read it, he will rule the world.

Solomon's Ring (Solomon's Seal)

When King David died it pleased God to make Solomon not only king of Israel but king of the earth, to rule not only all human beings and their domestic animals but also all the wild animals, birds, fishes and reptiles. To signify this mandate of heaven, God sent the four kings of the animal world – the lion, the eagle, the python and the whale, representing the walking, flying, creeping and swimming creatures respectively – to pay him homage as their sovereign. Each animal offered the king a precious stone by means of which he could rule them. Each stone had a secret character (*harf*) inscribed on it.

After this ceremony, four spiritual beings appeared – an angel, a *jinn*, a *shaytan* and an *ifrit* – each of whom also gave Solomon a precious stone with a divine monogram engraved on it, which would enable him to rule each of the four kingdoms of the spirits. After this the angels of the four elements appeared – earth, fire, water and wind – and they too gave Solomon the engraved stones which would give him the ability to rule over them. Thus he possessed twelve jewels, each with a secret sign on it.

Together they were placed in a bezel, which was fixed to a golden ring. The owner of this signet ring can rule the world, the spirits and the elements. When Solomon died, his most faithful servant hid it under a copper dome, where it remained for a long time until the dome rusted and the ring became visible. Someone found it, but they did not know its power – which is just as well. The Arabic word for seal is *Khatam* or *Khatimu*. See *Khatimu'n-Nabiyyin*.

Sophia (Hebrew: Hakhma, Chochma)
The Greek word for wisdom. In Proberbs 8 she speaks as a goddess. She was like the Hindu Devi Shakti assisting Shiva the creator. Later, the Gnostics conceived Sophia as a saintly spirit. The emperor named his great cathedral in Constantinople *Hagia Sophia*, 'Holy Wisdom'. The name survives in Arabic as *safiyya*. Some thinkers identify Sophia with Siduru Sabaut, the Mesopotamian goddess of paradise. See *Pearl, Sufism*.

Sorcery
The *shaytans* (q.v.) taught sorcery in the reign of King Solomon (Koran 2:102). Much sorcery was practised in Egypt (Koran 7:116; 10:81; 20:58). Harut and Marut (q.v.) taught sorcery (2:102).

Soshiant
See Saoshyant.

Soul (Arabic: nafs, q.v.)
That by which men and animals live. Whereas the spirit is the source of energy and life power, a masculine concept of strength and optimism, the soul is a feminine concept of tender sensitivity: the gentle breath of life itself, the *anima* or female innermost living being of the human psyche, the hearth of feelings, the fountain of loving devotion and also the ultimate seat of wisdom and decision-taking. That is why the soul will one day be judged for the body's sins. This image of the soul as a lovable tender woman is almost universal in human thought from Western Europe to Indonesia, although some, perhaps more ancient, peoples have more complex images of a multiple soul.

Originally the soul was identified with the last breath, that which leaves the body when it dies. In a majority of languages the original meaning of the word for soul was breath or breeze. Gradually in the course of human thought, this 'last breath' was given a life of its own; it became that which survives when the body dies, so we now speak of 'my immortal soul'. With a lasting life, the soul also, gradually, developed a character of its own. It loves God while the body loves itself. It searches for wisdom, the body for satisfaction. It was left to the inimitable artistic genius of the Greeks and the Indians to create, in painting and sculpture, the image of the soul as a loving girl, Psyche in Greece, Radha in India, the fountain of devotion for the divine spirit.

Islamic philosophy distinguishes between different souls. *Nafs al-hayawaniya* is the animal soul. Animals can perceive (see, hear, smell); they can also move at will towards their goal. *Nafs al-nabatiya* is the vegetable soul, which can select its food and grow upwards, spreading its branches, opening leaves and flowers. *Nafs al-insaniya* is the human soul, which, in addition to the preceding two, possesses the faculty of reason, *'aql*, both practical and speculative. *Nafs al-lawwama*, the soul of self-accusation dictates our moral behaviour and honesty. It is our conscience. *Nafs al-mutma'inna* is 'the soul at peace'; after completing its spiritual growth the serene soul has peace with God (Koran 89:27). *Nafs al-falkiya* is the celestial soul; all the stars have intelligence. *Nafs al-kulliya*, the universal soul, includes all individual souls.

In the Islamic tradition, God blew Adam's soul into his nose. He had created it many centuries before creating the earth. The soul was afloat in the ocean of light, *bahr al-nur*, in perfect bliss. It did not wish to enter a body made of clay. God rebuked it for this, predicting: 'One day you will be as reluctant to leave this body as you are to enter it now.' Once inside the body, the soul spread with the blood first to the eyes which opened and saw the light, then to the ears which opened and heard the angels singing hymns, then to the mouth which opened and to the tongue which moved, then to the voice which spoke: 'Praise God the sole creator, the eternal one.'

When death comes (see *Azra'il*), he will pull the soul out of the body through the nose, without any delay. A soul full of desires will not want to leave its body, but a soul devoted to God will come flying out to go to God.

The Koran (79:1) implies that there are numerous death-angels (*malaikat al-maut*) who will violently tear out the souls of the wicked or gently release the souls of the good. There is a great diversity of opinion among Muslim scholars regarding what happens to the spirit or soul after death. Some say the good souls live under God's throne in the shape of white doves, others that green birds pick them up like seeds and keep them in their crops.

In the Bible God breathes life into man's nostrils (Genesis 2:7) so that man becomes a *nefesh*, living soul. Here 'soul' seems to have the meaning of a living being as opposed to the dead earth from which he is formed. Man is his soul, not his body. In Leviticus 17:11, God says that the life (*nefesh*) of the flesh is in the blood. That life, given by God to man, may not be eaten for that reason: the soul is life itself which we owe to our creator, and the soul lives in the blood. It has to flow back into the earth and to be covered with dust as a proper burial.

Later, when the blood of Christ was spilled by the Romans, it was collected by Joseph of Arimathea in a cup, later called the grail. Thus that cup contains the soul of Jesus. Whoever drinks Jesus' blood will have eternal life (John 6:54), because that blood contains the soul of the son of God.

Spendarmad (Old Persian: *Spenta Armaiti*)

The Avestan goddess of the earth, especially the holy ground where the ceremonies took place, and of devotion and piety.

Spenta Mainyu (Spenag Menog)
In old Persian, the holy spirit of God which is both one with him and active on his behalf. This spirit of truth enters into the just man, God's best creation who will lead humanity to truth. (See *Ahura Mazda*).

Spider
The spider is regarded as a god by many African peoples. They believe it can hang in the air without falling. The female is believed to eat her husband after copulation, although in reality he normally gets away.

In the Koran (29:41) the spider (*ankabut*) is the symbol of a polytheist, because the spider makes a 'house' that is easily destroyed. During his flight to Medina the Prophet Muhammad survived persecution by his enemies because they could not find him: a spider had quickly woven a web across the mouth of the cave where he was hiding, so obscuring him from view.

Spirit of God
See *Holy Spirit*.

Spirits (Arabic: *ruh*, Hebrew: *ruah*)
In the Old Testament it is not clear what is meant by spirits. Sometimes the translators write 'gods' where modern writers would use 'spirits' (Genesis 31:30–2; 1 Samuel 28:13, 'gods ascending'). Spirits can be represented as statues or figurines for worship. This practice was unanimously condemned by the prophets of Israel, but it was ineradicable.

In Luke 8:26–33 the words 'spirits' and 'devils' are used interchangeably. Those beings could not be seen, but they were apparently evil spirits which needed bodies to live in, to 'possess'.

The belief that spirits can 'possess' persons is widespread in Africa, Greece and all across Asia. The possessing spirit will speak through its victim's mouth, so that it is often believed that a schizophrenic patient is possessed by a spirit. People will try and make sense of what the patient says, thinking that it may be the spirits' oracle, as indeed was the case in Luke 8, when the spirits proclaimed Jesus as the son of God. Far from raving like a lunatic, the possessed man reveals the truth, so he has to be taken seriously in the biblical context.

At all times the peoples of the Middle East believed, and believe still, that the world is full of invisible spirits flying through the air or living in trees, hills, houses, wells and many other places. Whereas the soul is always human, frail, weak of morality, swayed by its many emotions like a reed in the wind, but lovable and often loving, the spirit can be independent of the body and travel around in space. Many spirits are not human at all; they may be nature spirits, animals or even *jinns*, evil spirits, satans, etc.

In no language, however, can the distinction between soul and spirit be sharply defined, nor can we easily equate the words of different languages, each of which represents the expression of a unique culture and way of thinking or cosmology. Natural phenomena, such as plants and trees can be defined scientifically, but souls and ghosts will always be subject to the personal experience of the speaker. It is the genius of a language that it provides words with vague meanings for individual speakers and writers to express their personal experiences and feelings.

According to the Islamic tradition, the kingdom of the spirits is much larger than the lands of men and animals together. It fills almost all the space between heaven and earth. A certain number of these spirits are faithful believers in the one God, but others are infidel demons, some worshipping fire, others the sun, the moon, or some star; there are even those who adore water as if it were a deity. The God-fearing spirits will always stay near people of like minds in order to protect themselves against sin and misfortune. The other types of spirits will always try to tease and taunt people or try to tempt them. This is easy for them, since they can make themselves invisible to human eyes.

Having been given command of all the spirits, Solomon expressed the wish to see his new subjects in their natural shapes. The king soon saw a host of spirits, *shaytans* and *jinns*, who showed themselves to have such monstrous appearances that even their human king was frightened. He had never known that such hideously ugly and misshapen creatures lived in the universe. There were horses with human heads, camels with strong eagles' wings fastened to their humps, peacocks with things like horns or antlers on their heads, men with donkeys' legs. Since Solomon knew that Jannu was the ancestor of all the spirits, he asked the commanding angel why there was so much variation in the physical features of these descendants, all of them cousins, who ought to display some family likeness. The angel answered: 'Oh king, these spirits have often sinned against God's laws, by mating with creatures of different kinds, so their offspring became monsters. Every species of God's creatures may only marry its own kind.' See also *Cin, Death, Jinn, Resurrection, Shaytan, Soul*.

Sraosha

'Obedience, discipline'. Zoroastrian god who is present at every ceremony as a divine personification of the prayers and hymns that the faithful people recite. He is the god who carries the message of this devotion to heaven. The prayer ritual destroys evil, so Sraosha helps the faithful to destroy the demons of evil and defeat the god of lies. Obedience to the divine word will ultimately determine the soul's destiny. Obedience is an active, victorious quality of mind, protecting the soul which Sraosha will carry to heaven when it finally leaves the body. Discipline is a strong virtue.

Sri Lanka (Arabic: Sarandib)

Where Adam (q.v.) alighted after he fell from heaven in the Islamic tradition (see *Fall*). He wept with contrition until Jibril arrived to console him and to lead him over the rocky bridge to India and on to Arabia, where he met Eve.

Srosh

In Middle Persian myths the messenger of the Gods, who was sent down from heaven to announce to a king that his last hour had struck.

Staff of Moses

This staff was very powerful because God was in it. It became a snake (Exodus 4:3); it blossomed and brought forth almonds (Numbers 17:8); it decided battles when held high (Exodus 17:9–14); and it made water come forth from the barren rock to slake the thirst of the Israelites (Exodus 17:6). It was also the 'staff of bread' (Leviticus 26:26; Psalms 105:16; Ezekiel 4:16; 5:16). In the Koran, the staff of Moses (Musa) is referred to repeatedly: it changes into a snake to confound Pharaoh and his magicians (7:107, 117; 20:17–21; 26:32; 26:45; 27:10). In Numbers 17:10, where it was called Aaron's rod, the staff was placed in the ark, proving that the latter could not have been shorter than a coffin.

Standard

After judgement, the Prophet Muhammad will unfold his standard, *liwa'*, raise it high and march towards the Sirat al-Mustaqim (q.v.), the narrow Bridge to paradise. All the good Muslims, all his faithful followers, will rush to come with him, making the bridge swing like a reed.

Star of David

A six-pointed blue star made up of two triangles on a white field. The coat of arms of the state of Israel. This star was shown by God above Bethlehem when Jesus, son of David, was born.

Substance

The basis of matter (see *Materia*) out of which God created the physical world. See also *Sophia*.

Succession

See *Caliph*, *Shi'a*, *Pearl*.

Sudum (Sadum, Usdum)

The Arabic equivalent of the biblical Sodom. See *Lut*, *Jumurra*.

Sufism (Proper spelling: Sufiism, Arabic: *Sufiyya*)

The Arabic word 'Sufi' is usually translated as 'one dressed in wool'. Other scholars maintain that its origin is *safi*, 'pure', since the Sufis seek spiritual purity. Others again say the origin is the Greek *sophia* ('wisdom') (q.v.) and it does seem that there are several comparable features between Sufism and the sophia as it was seen by the Byzantine philosophers. Recent discoveries in Egypt (the Nag Hammadi scrolls) have revealed the incredible flourishing of Christian mysticism there, as well as in Syria. It is attractive to think that this mysticism resurfaced in an Islamic guise after the Arab conquest, because there was a vacuum in Islam, which is a religion of hard discipline, a strict legal system and cold relentless formality compared to the warmth and gentleness of Christianity. Perhaps then, it was into this vacuum that the *Sufiyya* grew, almost in spite of Islam, creating a cosmology that was more universal than that of Islam, free and direct in its openness towards God and loving in its yearning for his nearness.

For Islam there is only God's distance, which human souls will never bridge, there is only the complete submission (*islam*) by physical bowing and prostrating. God remains apart from the world; his difference from us (*khilafa*) is often stressed by the theologians. The relationship between God and man is one of *rabb*, 'master' and *'abd* 'slave'. God is often called *al malik*, 'the owner', who may do as he wishes with his creatures – and does. He causes life and kills (*yuhyi wa yumitu*). The Sufis on the other hand teach that he is in us, and that all souls are in him, in a loving togetherness, as opposed to the threatening omnipresence of the orthodox theologians. They teach that all visible and invisible beings are emanations from him and are not distinct from him. This doctrine sounds very un-Islamic and may well have been influenced by Indian thought.

The Sufis teach that Islam is only for beginners. It is a good introduction to the *Sufiyya* but no more than that. The Sufi master is no longer fenced in by the rules of regular prayer since he is in direct and daily contact with God. Indeed the Sufis teach that the ultimate aim of the *talib*, the seeker, is the union with God (*wasl*) when all differences will have ceased to exist. This, too, seems very un-Islamic. It is this loving attitude to God who in turn pulls his lover (*'ashiq*) towards himself that is the essence of Sufism.

For the Sufi, life is a journey (*safar*) and the traveller (*salik*) is a seeker (*talib*) after God. The seeker cannot attain his goal without knowledge (*ma'rifa*) of the divine secrets. Man's soul is an exile from heaven, and he must learn to recognize the scattered signs of God's secret presence in his creation where his love is diffused. The seeker has to become filled with ardent yearning (*'ishq*) to

join the beloved in heaven. The soul is locked up in its body like a bird in a cage, hoping to fly out to heaven. The purpose of Sufism is to provide the seeker with a way of reaching his goal, leading the soul step by step.

The first step is out of this world, the second leads out of the self. Ambition and agreed, the desire for respect from society, must be left behind. Egotism too is a barrier to liberation. Most human souls live in the *nasut*, the 'natural state' of human beings in this world which is not much better than chickens in a run, fighting for food and females. The law (*shari'a*) regulates life in our society. Everyone has to obey its rules or be punished: there is no freedom. Sufism provides a way (*tariqa*) out of this prison. The seeker needs *jabrut*, a stage in which he has the power to control his desires and follies. Only after he has gained this control can he achieve extinction (*fana'*), the complete liberation of the self, the evaporation of the ego. Then the soul will receive *ma'rifa*, the secret knowledge, the vision of the hidden reality, just as the mountaineer on the summit can see more than the traveller down in the valley.

But all these stages are only steps in the direction of the real goal, the *wasl*, 'arrival', the complete union with God's own spiritual reality, *haqiqa*. The stages are not set out by all the authors in the same order, nor do they all list the same number of *manazil*, stations on the path to heaven (heaven itself is seen as a state of mind, a condition rather than a place in space). This discrepancy is explained by the veil of secrecy that hides the higher stages from the disciples at the lower levels. Those who speak about them do not know them, and those who know them do not speak about them.

Each stage enables the disciple (*murid*) to understand the next stage above. The level above that is still too high to be comprehended. Again, the image of the mountaineer is apt: until he is on the summit of the first foot-hill, he cannot see the lofty mountains beyond and only when he has climbed the highest of those mountains will he be able to see the yet higher Himalayas beyond and far above. That is the awe-inspiring experience of the advancing Sufi, and the further upwards he progresses towards the cloudless light, the less he is able to describe in human language what he experiences and how he achieved that altitude.

Only a few poets have succeeded in moulding their language to express their exalted state of mind. Experience is individual, and so is its expression in language. The traveller who has left his individual self behind is no longer interested in poetry or publicity. He is lost in contemplation of that vast beauty before him. Unfortunately by that very advance he has also lost contact with his followers. One thing is certain: the true mystic has also left the law behind, the rules that imprison mankind. He is free to commune with God. At the highest apex all mystics meet and all religions meet. There are no more dogmas. All is unity, bliss and light.

Sufism is not just a doctrine which one can accept or reject. Once a person has perceived it to be true, he has to follow the path of asceticism to its end for life through the stages of search, yearning, perception, detachment, independence, fulfilment and annihilation (i.e. dissolving the soul in the divinity). For the Sufis themselves, Sufism is not only entirely within orthodox Islam, it is *the* true inner form of *Islam*, it is what Muhammad really meant when he preached to his people. They claim, for example, first that God is the absolute agent (Koran 8:17) and secondly, Muhammad was not anti-Christian, as were his successors, but was prepared to learn much from them, including their Gnosticism.

However, many orthodox scholars distrust the *Batiniyya*, those mystics who interpret the Koran according to its *batin* or esoteric meaning, with the result that most Sufi masters will discuss their esoteric theology only among their own advanced and trusted students. This exclusivism was and is necessary in any case, since many Sufi doctrines cannot be properly understood without severe prior training and discipline which will weed out the dishonest mental sloths. See *Ikhlas*, *Mahabba*, *Suhba*, *Taqua*, *Wali*, *Wilaya*.

Suhba

'Companionship, intimate friendship'. The Sufi ideal of life in a religious community. It also refers to friendship with God.

Suhrawardi

1. Shihabu'd-Din Yahya Umar ibn Abdallah al-Halabi al-Maqtul, Sufi philosopher who lived in Aleppo (Halab) where he was born in 1155. He studied in Baghdad, but returned

to Aleppo when he had learned the Sufi path. He wrote *The Philosophy of Illumination* and *The Temples of Light*, in which he shows the influence of Plotinus. He was executed for heresy by Sultan Saladdin in 1191.

2. Shihabu'd-Din Abu Hafs Umar (1144–1234), Sufi master, founder of the Suhrawardiya order which flourishes especially in India. Author of *Awarif al-Ma'arif*, 'The Knowers of Knowledge'.

Sulayman

See Solomon.

Sun

The sun was worshipped by the Zoroastrians as Hvar-Khshaeta (old Persian; modern Persian: Khorshid) in the famous hymn from Yasht 6: 'A hundred gods stand [worshipping] the sun when he brings light and warmth. When the sun rises the Ahura-created earth is purified, the streams are purified. If the sun did not rise, then demons would invade the seven regions. The shining sun, life-giving, bountiful, chases the demons . . .'

Sunna

'Custom'. The customs and manners of the Prophet Muhammad which were carefully observed by his admiring contemporaries. They told their children all these details of their leader's life including all that he had said and more. These memorable tales were written down by scholars 200 years after Muhammad, and compiled into an enormous body of literature called the *hadith* (q.v.). From this the *sunna* has been distilled. All the acts that the Prophet committed or omitted must be imitated by every Muslim. These are now the model of correct behaviour for all Muslims; all his words and deeds together are the correct custom. So today *sunna* means 'duty'.

Since the rise of the Shi'a (q.v.) which has its own books of law and duty, the word *sunna* and its adjective *sunni* have been used to subsume all Muslims who do not belong to the Shi'a. This is misleading, since the Shi'a also adhere to the *sunna*, with very little differences. They differ only over cosmology, a few customs and the political framework of the state, which they say must be based on the concept of *imama* (q.v.), the interpretation of the will of the hidden imam by the Ayatollahs.

The word *sunna* is often translated as 'orthodoxy', and *sunni* as 'orthodox'. This again is misleading, since it implies that the Shi'a is a sort of heresy.

'Orthodoxy' in Islam depends on the consensus (*ijma'*) of the law scholars (*ulama'*) in a given community. For this purpose most Islamic states have a council of top law scholars called *muftis*, 'advisers, counsellors', who form what would be called in Europe a supreme court, plus a legislative assembly (*majlis*). In Islamic culture there is no tradition of local or numerical representation, least of all by political parties, to decide the law by a majority vote. Islam does not leave law-making to fallible mortals. The law was created by God as codified in the Koran and exemplified by the Prophet's inspired words. There is no need to decide on new laws, since God's law was created for all time and for all people. No mortal can ameliorate it. All that remains in our time is to find new interpretations of existing laws to suit the needs of everyday life. So all an Islamic government needs is a council of scholars who are thoroughly familiar with the Koran and the *hadith*, where they will find (they trust) a phrase, a line or a sentence that will appear to be miraculously applicable to the present time. This application is called *qiyas*, 'analogy'. However, numerous disagreements arise as a result of this practice. For instance there is no law in Islam against smoking, since tobacco was unknown in Muhammad's day. So, most Muslims smoke freely, even hashish. However, many *ulama* maintain that any intoxicating habit is *khamr* (usually translated as 'wine' or 'alcohol'), and therefore strictly forbidden (Koran 2:219; 4:43; 5:90–1).

According to the *sunna*, animals must be slaughtered with a knife, while the butcher says '*Bismillahi. Allahu Akbar.*' This has led to protests, from animal-lovers in the west, who see the practice as cruel. Moreover, the blood must be left to flow away, which has in its turn led to protests on health grounds.

Sura

'Sign'. A miraculous sign from God. One of the 114 chapters of the Koran. See also *Signs*.

Sut

In Islamic tales, a son of Iblis, an evil spirit inspiring clever lies.

Suwa'

The idol of one of the false gods worshipped by the Arabs in the days of Nuh (Noah) (Koran 71:23). It was destroyed in Islamic times.

Syriac

The language of the province of Syria in the Eastern Roman Empire. Although we have inscriptions from the first century AD, the important development of this language began when it became the vehicle of Christian literature about 400 AD. It was one of the oldest languages into which the New Testament was translated. The literature contains many documents of early Christian Gnosticism as well as apocrypha not preserved elsewhere.

The language continued to flourish until long after the Arabic conquest of 637 AD, but it gradually died out as the Christians fled or were persecuted. It survived in the delta area of Iraq and in a few villages in Turkey until a few years ago when the Christians were bombed and driven away.

T

Taaziya (Ta'ziyat, taziyet)
'Consolation'. A ceremony on Ashura (q.v.), the tenth day of the month of Muharram, when the Shi'a faithful visit each other to commemorate the death of Husayn. Preachers in the mosques and other meeting places provoke the tears of their audiences by describing how Husayn was killed and how his family was humiliated. At night a model of Husayn's tomb, also called *taaziya*, is carried through the town amidst prayers and hymn singing. This ceremony is often accompanied by self-flagellation by the men.

Tabernacle
A portable shelter carried by the Jews in the wilderness, from the Latin *tabernaculum*, 'hutment, tent'. The Hebrew word used in Exodus 25:9 is *mishkan*, which the dictionary translates as 'habitation, dwelling, hut, tent, tabernacle, sanctuary, temple, grave, haunt'. All these meanings are relevant for explaining this vague term since the Lord told Moses to 'Make me a sanctuary that I may dwell among [the Israelites]' (Exodus 25:8). The word *miqdash* 'sanctuary', literally 'holy place', is here used almost synonymously.

Exodus 25:10 says it was made from *shittim* which has been identified as *Acacia nilotica*. The Nomadic peoples of the desert possessed no linen because that required an elaborate industry and labour-intensive agriculture. Their tents were therefore made of plaited grass, reeds, twigs and branches, and were always temporary shelters. Even today many people in Africa can erect a small hut in an afternoon. This is what the Children of Israel did while wandering in the desert, every evening before sunset, and in Sinai for forty days while watching the cloud.

After dictating the Ten Commandments, the Lord told the Israelites that on the fifteenth day of the seventh month each year, they must celebrate the Feast of the Tabernacles or Booths (Leviticus 23:39–43). They had to make themselves booths from palm trees and willow branches. For a week they had to live as if they were still in the wilderness, in the natural, unpolluted countryside, to remind them of the hardships of their ancestors. It is in the desert that God reveals himself to his prophets, not in the rich cities.

Table

1. One of two stone slabs on which the law of Moses was engraved by God himself (Exodus 32:15–16).
2. The table of the Lord made of *sittim*, wood, on which the show-bread was placed (Exodus 25:10).
3. See *Ma'ida*.

Tablet

1. A perfume box which also contained talismans written on tiny scrolls, worn by women round their necks (Isaiah 3:20).
2. See *Lawh al-Mahfuz*.

Tabor

A mountain in Israel where Jesus was transfigured, according to Mark 9:2–8.

Tabuk

A valley in northern Arabia where according to the Arabic tale entitled *Ghazwat Herqal*, 'The Expedition against Heraklios' (q.v.), the Prophet Muhammad defeated several Greek armies. Hence the alternative title, *Ghazwat Tabuk*, which is found in numerous printed booklets in the Middle East.

The question of whether Muhammad did reach Tabuk in his last campaign can be left to historians. The few sentences that his biographers devote to the raid have been expanded into a holy war of epic proportions. Numerous miracles took place demonstrating God's wish that the Christians should be defeated: Muhammad fed the army from one bowl of rice and one cup of milk. A few hundred Arabs defeated a million Greeks (in reality the Greeks never had large armies), after which they made them choose between Islam and the sword. A few obstinate bishops clung to Christianity but the vast majority of Greek soldiers and their wives submitted and became Muslims under the threat of death, thus setting the pattern for the later wars between Islam and Christianity, as sanctified by the presence of the holy Prophet himself, who spoke as God commanded him.

Tabut

'Chest, trunk, coffin'. The Ark of the Covenant (Koran 2:248), containing the *Sakina* (q.v.). See *Ark*, *Tebah*.

Tafrid

Literally 'making lonely'. This self-isolation of the soul is a necessary preliminary stage on the path (*tariqa*) of the soul towards God. The Sufi has to sever all links with the world so as to be free. This stage precedes the *fana'* (q.v.) or 'extinction' of the self, or rather its being absorbed into the *baqa*, the eternity of divine existence, the true purpose of the Sufi.

Taghut

Name of a demon who was worshipped by the Quraysh before Muhammad (Koran 2:257–9).

Taha

The name of Sura 20 of the Koran. One of the names of the Prophet Muhammad.

Taklimtu

An Assyrian ritual during the month of Dumuzi (late June) when the god

Dumuzi (see *Tammuz*), still young and handsome, was laid in state and anointed at Nineveh. This symbolized the end of spring. Dumuzi was Adonis, lover of Ishtar, goddess of life.

Talay
'Dew'. In Ugaritic mythology a daughter of Baal, god of rains, who is preceded by cool dew.

Talisman
This English word comes from the Arabic *tilasm*, which is from the Greek *telesmena*. In the Middle East numerous talismans are on sale at high prices. They are scraps of paper with passages from the Koran and other letters written on them, which are believed to protect the wearer against illness. See *Da'wa*.

Talut
King of Filistin (Palestine); the Arabic name for Saul. See Koran 2:247–50.

Tammuz (Dumuzi)
Babylonian god of spring and flowers, of green plants and young animals of the herd. See also *Adonis*.

Tanit (Tanith)
This goddess was carried by the Phoenician (Punic) sailors across the Mediterranean to Carthage, the ruins of which can still be seen near Tunis. Another etymology links Tanit to *tanin*, the old Semitic name for a marine monster like a gigantic seasnake.

Some scholars have compared Tanit

to Ashtaroth (q.v.) in the Bible, which would equate her with Aphrodite the sea-goddess, whose lover Adonis (q.v.) was equated with the Phoenician Baal (q.v.). One of Tanit's symbols was the crescent which was also associated with Aphrodite–Venus as Stella Maris, the goddess of the Mediterranean fishermen, later absorbed into the virgin and child seated on the crescent. (The planet Venus appears as a crescent twice during its 225-day orbit around the Sun.)

Tanit's bird was the dove, like Aphrodite's, the symbol of love and peace. Her fruit was the pomegranate, another symbol of marital love: the Romans called it *punica*, the Phoenician fruit. Tanit's fourth symbol was the fish, in accordance with Venus Anadyomene. See also *Ishtar*.

Tanjim
Islamic astrology, largely based on Hellenistic models. See *Buruj*.

Taqiya
'Caution'. As a result of endless persecution in Iraq, Syria and elsewhere, the Shi'a sects learned to protect themselves by hiding their identity.

Taqua (Takwa)
'Awe, fear of God'. The Sufi will meditate on God's power to punish the wicked and by so doing he will develop a great terror of God's omnipotence, realizing how insignificant and helpless we humans are. The Shi'a, especially the Isma'ili branch, have used *taqua* in the sense of 'fear of the world'. If there was a reason to fear persecution (as there frequently

was in their history) they were permitted to conceal, disguise or even deny their true allegiance, in order to survive.

Tariq

'Traveller by night' (Koran 86:1), which probably refers to a comet seen by Muhammad in the sky. Tariq was the name of the first Arab to land in Spain and conquer it in 711 AD. Tariq was also the ancestor of a tribe now widespread in Libya, Algeria and West Africa. They call themselves *Tariqi*, the plural of which is *Tawariq*, which has become Tuareg.

Tariqa

'Path', the method by which a Sufi (or other religious Muslims) attains his lofty goal. It now means a religious brotherhood of Muslim mystics.

Tasawwuf

'Purity; the habit of wearing woollen garments'. This is the normal Arabic term for being a Sufi. Only pure men can be Sufis.

Tasmisu

See *Kumarbi*.

Tauba (Towba)

Literally 'turning towards', said of both God and man. God may turn his face to a person as a sign of special favour. If God turns away (*tawalla*) then that person will suffer misfortune. He will then have to demonstrate repentance, *tauba*, i.e. turn his soul to God and so convert.

This is the first station on the Sufi path: the total and humble repentance of one's sins, the firm decision to abandon the vain life of this profit-seeking world and to devote one's life to God. *Al-ta'ib*, the penitent person begins his onward journey to God from *Tauba*. *Tauba* is also the name of one of the twelve gates of paradise (q.v.) and also a shady tree which grows there, signifying that repeated repentance on earth nurtures a shady tree in heaven.

Tavern

See *Kharabat*.

Taweret (Thouart)

Ancient Egyptian mother-goddess of the Nile and the primeval darkness who, like the night sky, gives birth to the sun.

Tawhid (Tauhid)

'Making one'. Proclaiming the uniqueness of God ('*Allahu Ahad*', Koran 112). Also used for Theology, i.e. the discipline which studies and describes God's unique being. In Sufism, it describes the zealous efforts of the soul to unite itself with God's essence.

Tawrah (Tawrat)

The Arabic form of the word *Torah*. The book that God gave Musa as his revelation (Koran 3:3; 5:43; 9:111).

Tawwab

'The one who turns, relents' (God). It is believed that God turns away from a man when he sins, so the man perishes. Then, if he shows repentance (*tauba*, q.v.), God may relent, literally turn towards him again and so rescue him from perdition, giving him joy.

Tay (Tai, Taiy, Ta'iy)

Name of a southern Arabian tribe in the days before Muhammad. Its most famous king was Hatim Tay, who is still famous as the embodiment of the old Arabian ideal of boundless generosity. He once slaughtered forty camels to feed his numerous visitors, all of them poor. Having thus ruined himself he had only one fine horse left. It was so swift and elegant that its fame came to the ears of the king of Rome, who sent an ambassador to Hatim Tay to buy it. Before asking the emissary what the purpose of his visit was, Hakim ordered the horse slaughtered since he had nothing else to offer his guest. It was only then – when it was too late – that his guest told him the king of Rome was offering a fortune for the horse. So Hatim Tay had nothing left except his reputation which has survived to the present day.

A film, *Hatim Tai*, was made in India in the 1960s, in which Hatim Tay asks all his subjects whether they are happy. They all are, thanks to his generosity, except one, whose bride has been kidnapped by a demon. Hatim Tay owes it to his honour to go in search of the girl, whom he liberates, after numerous adventures, by slaying the demon.

Tebah

'Ark', from the Egyptian *teb*, 'box, coffin, reed-boat'. This was the 'ark of bulrushes' in which little Moses was entrusted to the Nile by his mother (Exodus 2:3), hoping that the Lord would look after him. This reed cradle was no more than a waterproof basket such as the people of the delta can skilfully plait, even today. Bigger ones are made with paddles to be used as boats for fishing. See *Ark*.

Telepinus

The Hittite god of youth, agriculture and spring flowers, who could cause blight simply by leaving the land. One sad day he became lost in the desert, where he fell asleep. Soon there was blight and famine in the land, and the cows and ewes had no more milk for their young. Telepinus' father, the storm-god, was worried and sent out his eagle to search for him, but it returned without having seen him. Telepinus' house was empty.

Finally the goddess Hannahannas sent out the bee and she found him. She tried to wake Telepinus, but he was so seriously ill that she could not rouse him. So Kamrusepas, the goddess of healing, was called, and performed the ceremony of purification (since death is a condition of ritual impurity). Thunder and lightning (signifying impending rain) accompanied the god's return to the inhabited world. Having revived him, Kamrusepas comforted him and sacrificed twelve rams for him. Once he was well again, Telipenus ploughed, harrowed, irrigated the fields and made the crops grow.

Temple

The holiest Jewish sanctuary is the temple on Mount Moriah in the south-eastern corner of the old city of Jerusalem, next to Mount Sion (Zion). King Solomon built this Temple (1 Kings 6–8) on the site of a much older sanctuary. It was destroyed by the Chaldeans (2 Kings 25:9). It was later rebuilt by Herod, but destroyed yet again by Vespasian in 71 AD.

Ten Commandments

1. The simple rules for daily life given by God to Moses (Exodus 20:2–17; Deuteronomy 5:6–22). Jesus came to confirm these laws (Matthew 5:17; 19:17–19; Mark 10:19). In Luke 10:25, however, he revealed a new commandment by means of the parable of the good Samaritan. In simplified form they are:

1. Worship God alone.
2. Worship no idols.
3. Do not swear.
4. Keep one day of rest weekly.
5. Have respect for your parents.
6. Do not kill.
7. Do not have sex except in marriage.
8. Do not steal.
9. Do not slander or lie about anyone.
10. Do not covet anything that belongs to other people.

Of course even today we are still debating these rules of life. In those days they were an innovation. Time and again in the course of history when the people's morality slackened, disasters have struck, like Aids today, and people realized: we must go back to the Ten Commandments to have an orderly society.

2. The Ten Commandments of Islam are to be found in the Koran (6:151–2):

1. Join nothing as equal to God.
2. Be good to your parents.
3. Kill not your children because of poverty.
4. Do not approach unclean things.
5. Do not kill life that God has made unlawful for you as food, unless it is justified.
6. Do not touch the orphans' property but look after it until they are adult.
7. Give correct measure and weight.
8. When you speak, speak justly, even concerning a relative.
9. Fulfil the covenant with God.
10. Follow no other paths except God's.

Tent

See *Beth, Tabernacle.*

Teraphim

This word derives from the Hebrew *terafim*, 'images', household gods, *penates* (Genesis 31:19), and is perhaps related to *refa'im*, 'shades, ghosts'. The curious episode in this passage reveals that Laban is not an Israelite, but worships his own ancestor gods, represented by 'craven' (carved) statuettes which he kept in a box. These household or family gods served two purposes: they provided protection for their descendants, and they could predict the future, often through a medium or shaman (see 1 Samuel 28). These images were believed actually to be possessed of spirits. No wonder that Laban was extremely angry when he discovered that they had been stolen. A man's security and his family's health depended on the gods' goodwill. A thief could perpetrate black magic with those images.

Teshub

The Hurrian god of the weather, son of Kumarbi (q.v.) whom he dethroned, as Zeus dethroned Kronos. He was the husband of Hepit (q.v.). Teshub rode a bull over the mountains, like Shiva. In his right hand he held the thunder-axe, and in his left the storm clouds. His sister was Ishtar (q.v.), and his son Saruma. Teshub is equated with Baal and Adad (qq.v.). With his brother Tashmish he fought the monster Ullikummi, which was a huge mountain ridge.

Thamud

In the Koran the country to which Salih (q.v.) was sent.

Thorns

The crown of thorns, which the mocking Romans pressed on Jesus' head, was made of the jujube tree, *Zizyphus spina christi*, which resembles the ivy wreaths which crowned Roman emperors. However the *Zizyphus* tree is also the eternal tree that grows in paradise, according to the Koran. See *Sidrat-al-Muntaha*.

Thraitauna (Thraetaona)

See *Faridun*.

Throne (Arabic: *kursi*, q.v.)

God's throne was his first creation; after its completion he seated himself on it (Koran 7:54; 10:3; 13:2; 20:5). During creation it was on the water (11:7). On the day of judgement the angels will stand around it (40:7; 69:17). See *Ark*.

Tiamat

In Mesopotamian cosmology, the goddess of the sea and of creation. She (the salt water) and Apsu (the fresh water of the rivers) (q.v.) were the only beings when existence began. Tiamat, the female of the two beings is also sometimes represented as a primeval dragon and as a mother-animal. She gave birth to Lahmu and Lahamu, who in turn generated Anshar and Kishar, who in their turn had Anu (q.v.), the sky and Ea (q.v.), the earth, also called Nudimmud, and in Sumerian Enki. Ea then begat Marduk (q.v.), called Enlil (q.v.) in the Sumerian original and Ashur in the later Assyrian version.

Apsu was disturbed by the noise of those four generations of gods but Tiamat was more tolerant of her offspring. Apsu plotted war but Ea forestalled him and with his magic power put Apsu to sleep. Apsu was slain but Tiamat's numerous (mostly unmentioned) children urged her to punish Ea. She ordered her son Kingu to take command, while she gave birth to a host of monsters to assist him, including the centaurs and the dangerous scorpion-men, as well as the *ugallu* demons, men with eagle's claws, lion's heads and bull's horns. She gave Kingu the tablet of destiny on which everyone's fate was written. She brought forth gigantic sharp-toothed snakes full of venom and dragons radiating lethal rays, while the gods sat in silent terror.

Then Marduk came forward as the champion of the gods. He offered to combat Tiamat's monstrous children on condition that the gods agreed to make him their ruler. They had little choice. Marduk approached Tiamat cautiously, armed with mace, lightning, net, bow and arrows as well as the storm winds. He used the net to encircle Tiamat, suggesting that she was a big fish. The arms he wielded are reminiscent of the Indian gods' weaponry. He rode in his 'storm-chariot' drawn by four horses.

The storm filled Tiamat's mouth and belly, blowing her up, and arrows pierced her skin, until finally Marduk stood on top of her, slicing her in half.

The gods made the earth out of one half, and the roof of the sky from the other; thus Tiamat became the visible world. Her breath became fog, her spittle (foam) became the clouds, her eyes the two rivers. Tiamat's body, like Brahma's, created the world out of itself. All her children were likewise caught in Marduk's net.

This myth, which was regularly recited in ancient Mesopotamia, is open to more than one interpretation. Politically, it could symbolize the conquest by the cattle-keeping, male-dominated, Semitic-speaking peoples from the north, of the more gentle agricultural and fishing communities settled in the delta area, where the Sumerians' heartland lay. In the delta there was a constant threat from the invading tribes of the north, patriarchal nomads jealous of the wealth of the simple fishermen and the matriarchal cultivators.

The protagonists of the goddess who believe that female deities were worshipped long before the male gods, will see in this cosmic battle the victory of the latter over the primeval female principle of creation. Or perhaps it was the sky gods vanquishing the gods of the nether world.

Time

God created the angel of time (*waqt*) according to the Islamic tradition, to hold the newly created earth in his hand. The angel's other hand holds the sky above the earth like a blue cloth over a dish. The cloth moves above the dish, and through the holes in it the earthlings can see the divine radiance. They call the holes 'stars', not knowing that they receive glimpses of the 'outside' world through these holes. The movements of the cloth cause what we call the movements of the stars, by means of which we measure time. The angel is so tall that his head reaches up to the throne of God, while his feet are 'standing' on the 'bottom' of the universe. He will stand there, untiring, till doomsday. See *Azrail*.

Tir

'Bird'. Son of Iblis, an evil spirit causing disaster, loss and injury.

Tishtrya

In old Persian, the god of the dog star Sirius, the annual rise of which announces the rainy season. Tishtrya was thus the radiant god with the triumphant forces of life on earth. He is depicted as a white stallion, in which shape he defeated the demons of drought sent by the evil Ahriman (q.v.) to keep the rain clouds away. Tishtrya confronted the chief demon of drought, Apaosha, in the shape of a black horse and, after a fight of three days, was defeated and fled. Then the people had to sing hymns to give Tishtrya new strength so that he could come back, defeat Apaosha and fill the happy rivers with rain. Thus every faithful worshipper could help the good gods win the war against the forces of evil, by constant prayer and the singing of praise songs.

Tomb
See *Grave, Rawda*.

Tophet
A kind of oven in which human victims were burnt in heathen days (2 Kings 23:10). Tophet stood in Gehenna (q.v.), near Jerusalem. See also *Moloch*.

Transmigration of Souls
The belief that the soul, having lived one life, leaves its body and enters the womb of a woman, who gives birth to a child with an old soul. Very few people can remember their previous lives, many mistakenly. Some sages can recognize a person who has an 'old' soul, by his or her noble conduct and kindness. A divine spirit may also be born as a child, but such a child will always know his or her divine nature. There are numerous stories of human souls living in animal bodies, the best-known of which are the werewolf tales.

This concept is anathema to Islam which holds that every soul lives only once and after death lives on near its body in the grave, until it is united with a new body at resurrection, and goes to paradise or to hell after judgement.

Trees
1. It has been suggested that the forbidden tree in the Garden of Eden was a fig tree, which is associated in India and Pakistan with fertility, because Adam and Eve make themselves loincloths from fig leaves. It may also have been the *Ficus sycomorus* whose fruits were eaten by the spirits of the dead at the edge of the desert of death in the Egyptian *Book of the Dead*. They received them as food for the long journey through death-night to the dawn of a new life. See also *Apple*.

2. The Lord said to David that when he heard the sound of 'a gong' in the tops of the mulberry trees, he must attack, 'for then the Lord shall go out before thee to smite the host' (2 Samuel 5:24).

3. The ancients planted cypresses on and around their graveyards to signify resurrection. The cedar tree was dedicated to Artemis the moon-goddess of the mountains, in Asia Minor. The olive tree was owned by Athena, the Egyptian Neith. It produced the oil for anointing kings. The oak tree belonged to the God of the Israelites (Joshua 24:26) as it did to Zeus in Greece. See also *Dates, Fig, Jesse, Oak, Olive Tree, Pine, Plants, Sidrat-al-Muntaha*.

Trickster-God
In most mythologies there is a trickster-god, deceiving the hero. In Greek mythology Hermes Psychopompos leads the souls in their dreams to other countries where they see visions, 'illusions'. In the Bible, the serpent, Nahash, deceived Eve (Genesis 3:5) saying 'Ye shall be as gods', implying a promise of immortality. In Sumerian

mythology Ea (q.v.) deceived Adapa by telling him not to accept the food and drink that Anu (q.v.) would offer him in heaven, knowing it would be the food and water of immortality. In the Koran, Iblis became the terrifying trickster (7:14–18).

Trumpet (Arabic: *sur*)

This will be sounded on the last day (1 Corinthians 15:52; 1 Thessalonians 4:16). In Revelation 8:2–11, 15, there are seven angels with trumpets.

The Islamic tradition (Koran 74:8) relates that God created a special angel Israfil (q.v.), whose task it is to hold the trumpet to his mouth without sleeping, century after century, until God gives him the sign to blow. The first blast will destroy all buildings on earth and all people will die. The mountains will collapse, the seas will dry up, the stars will fall down. The second blast, forty years later, will raise the Prophet Muhammad. On the third blast all people will rise, having received new bodies.

Tur

Tur Sinai is a mountain in Sinai where God spoke to Musa (Moses) (Koran 2:60), made his covenant with him and gave him the scriptures to which Sura 52:1 alludes. It was here, according to the popular tradition, that God answered Musa's many questions in their *munajat*, conversations; a subject of profound meditation on God's nearness for the Sufis.

Tuwa

The valley where Allah called Musa and where he had to take off his sandals (Koran 20:12; 79:16).

Twelvers

The largest group of the Shi'a, concentrated in Iran with scattered communities in Iraq, Lebanon and India. They follow the twelfth *imam*. They are known in Arabic as Ithna'ashariya. See *Muhammad al-Mahdi*.

Typhon

Ancient Greek god of storms, hurricanes and whirlwinds. Born from the earth, he had a hundred heads and frightened even the gods until Zeus hit him with his thunderbolt. From this word comes the Arabic *tayfun*, 'typhoon' and *tufan*, 'deluge, cataclysm'. Typhon was identified with the ancient Egyptian god Seth who was represented as a crocodile devouring his brother Osiris.

U

Ubelluris
A Hittite mountain god who, like Atlas, carried the edge of the sky, where the sun sets, on his shoulders.

Udar
See *Ghouls*.

Ufir (Uphir)
The demon which possesses the secret knowledge of medicines. He knows the human body which he dissects in the graveyards. Magic doctors serve him. See *Vampire*.

Uj
A giant who lived in Noah's days. The Flood rose only to his waist, so he survived.

Ukobach
Demon of the oil who is always burning. He is in charge of replenishing the cauldrons of hell.

'Ulama (Ulema)
The scholars of Islamic law. They form a close group in each Islamic state and out of their midst there arises a small group of influential lawyers whose *ijma'*, 'consensus,' has the authority of law. As preachers in the Friday mosques they have a huge influence on the people, since their words are believed to be divinely inspired. The result is, curiously, that often the congregation takes the law into its own hands and rebels against the government.

Ullikummis
In Hittite mythology, the son of Kumarbis (q.v.) (the son of the sky-god Anu) and the sea-goddess. Ullikummis grew and grew and rose up from the sea like a mountain, 1000 fathoms (?) high, a thousand leagues in girth, and made of diorite. His head touched heaven, upsetting the temple of the goddess Hepit (q.v.), the storm-god's spouse. The latter arrived in his chariot and overturned the tall statue (?) of Ullikummis. This may well have been a myth describing the separating of heaven and earth. Ullikummis was thus the earth rising out of the sea.

Umma
The mystic community of Islam. In the popular literature, Muhammad will pray to God for the salvation of his *umma* and God will grant his prayer, so all the Muslims who ever prayed to God will

walk into paradise, following his standard. One day, many Muslims believe, God will make all men Muslims. Then the *umma* will pray daily to him, using the entire earth as the *haram*, the floor of Mecca's mosque. These future events are a subject of meditation for the Sufis since prayer is the first step towards communion with God, all the more so when all humanity prays together.

Ummanu
Seven sages, who wrote the great epic poems such as those of Erra and Gilgamesh (qq.v.).

Uqba
'End'. Name of a Muslim fighter who reached the end of the known world, the Atlantic coast of Morocco. He drove his horse into the waves but it would go no further. Then Uqba prayed: 'Allah, if it were not for thy ocean I would conquer the whole earth.'

Urian
The satan who rules the witches and copulates with them.

Uriel
'My light is God'. The Jewish angel of light, lamps and justice.

Urim
'Lights'. Ornaments (precious stones?) worn by the Israelite priests.

Ur-shanabi
The Babylonian *Charon*, the ferryman on the Sea of Hades in the Gilgamesh (q.v.) epic.

Uruk
The high-walled capital city of King Gilgamesh (q.v.) in Sumer, now called Warka, in southern Iraq.

Urvan
'Soul'. In old Persian tradition the souls of the dead were cared for by the living through offerings of consecrated food and clothing to benefit them in the underworld kingdom of the dead ruled by Yima (q.v.).

Usdum
See *Sudum*.

Uta-napishtim
The Babylonian Noah; the name means 'he found life', i.e. immortality. He is the hero of the great flood in the epic of Gilgamesh (q.v.).

Uttu
Sumerian goddess of earth and plants, daughter of Enki (q.v.) and Ninkurra. Enki wanted to marry her, and Uttu demanded a present of cucumbers, apples and grapes. Enki created the desired fruits, then ate them, as he was a god of both creation and destruction.

Utu
The Sumerian sun-god, created by the sky-god Enlil (q.v.).

Uzair (Uzayr)
Possibly the Arabic form of the name Ezra (Koran 9:30; 2:259). One morning after the fall of Jerusalem, Uzair was riding his mule on his way into exile with nothing but a basket of figs for food. Gazing at the ruins behind him, he exclaimed: 'How will God

ever put life into it again?' At that moment God put him to sleep by the roadside. He woke up a hundred years later to find his figs still fresh enough to eat, but his mule's bones white and dry. Then God asked him:

'How long have you been asleep?'

'Since this morning Lord,' replied Uzayr, as the sun was setting.

But God said: 'One hundred years. But lo! I will restore the bones of your mule and put flesh on them.' And thus it happened. God revived Jerusalem and sent Uzair to the Children of Israel to teach them the *Tawrat* (q.v.), the book of Musa (Moses), because they had lost it during their long exile.

Uzza

'The Powerful One'. The third of the three ancient Arabian goddesses mentioned in the Koran as the 'daughters of Allah', also called Kaukabat, 'the Stars'. This would equate Allah with Uranus, father and grandfather of the goddesses. Uzza was equated with Venus-Aphrodite. In ancient times girls and boys were sacrificed to her.

She was especially popular among the women, who used to bake cakes for her and worship her on the roofs of their houses. She had a temple at Elusa in northern Arabia where a golden statue of her was venerated until Christian times, preferably at dawn as the morning star, Eosphoros. See also *Manat, Allat*.

V

Vahagn (Old Persian: *Vrthragna*)
Ancient Armenian god of war, praise-named Vasapaklal 'The Dragon-Slayer', like Indra. Vahagn was born of water and fire. His queen was Astlik, goddess of the stars. Vahagn was the god of victory, the conqueror of obstacles, and creator of the Milky Way, which is the straw his horse left behind while running across the sky.

Vampire
A dead man or woman who rises from the grave to suck the blood of the living at night, lying with them in bed to get warm, because the dead feel very cold and hungry, and thirst for warm blood. When a person disappeared it was often believed that he or she had become a vampire. If there was fear that a dead person might become a vampire, a nail would be driven into their skull, or the body was cremated. In 1730 an epidemic of vampirism raged in the Ottoman Empire and Hungary.

The word originates from the Bulgarian *vapir*, which in turn derives from the Turkish *ubir*, 'sorcerer'. The vampire looks like a handsome gentleman. He is courteous, well dressed and very popular in society. He can only be recognized by his sharply pointed canine teeth. He cannot be killed because his body has already died. He travels in a coffin in the hold of a ship, but he can also just 'materialize' in a place, even in a crowd at a party. There he will select a female partner, take her to a solitary place and 'seduce' her by biting her (pretending it is a love-bite) in her neck. There he draws blood and sucks it out. From that moment she is his slave. She will surely die unless she finds a male victim to satisfy her own growing bloodlust.

Var
'Enclosure'. In early times, Ahura Mazda (q.v.) told Yima (q.v.) the first ruler on earth, to build a *var*, literally 'a place to keep', for his cattle so that the animals would be safe during the severe winter. Thus the *var* was the first stable to keep the cows warm. Or perhaps it was a walled homestead — the first castle. Here people and animals would be safe from predators.

Varuna
Ancient Persian sky-god of rain and storm, protector of oaths. He rewarded truthfulness, virtue and lawful behaviour. He was referred to as

'lord of the truly spoken word', and also as creator, since creation happens by means of the divine word.

Vayu

Old Persian and Indian god of the winds, the Greek Aiolos (older form, Vaio-los), who carried the souls away to the nether world. Vayu was much feared in Persia as the bringer of storm and lightning. He helped Ahura Mazda (q.v.) in the cosmic war against the evil hosts of Ahriman (q.v.). He was born from the breath of the giant Zurvan (q.v.). He is depicted in full armour with a spear and a golden sword. He may cause death and destruction to his enemies.

Verethraghna

See *Bahram*.

Viraf

In old Persian mythology, a writer who, in a vision, was miraculously carried to heaven and hell. Sraosh himself (q.v.) led Viraf across the Chinvat Bridge to heaven, where he was met by the blessed Fravashis who conducted him to *Hamestagen*, the Persian purgatory. From there he travelled upwards through the successive storeys of heaven, where he saw the souls of good people shining brightly like stars, seated on thrones. He even met Ahura Mazda himself (q.v.). Viraf then descended into hell, where he was shown round by an old hag. There he saw the souls of the wicked suffering intense heat and cold, stench and suffocation, loneliness and boredom. See *Enoch 1*, *Mi'raj*.

Vishtaspa

King of the Persians, son of Arvataspa (1200 BC?), protector of the Prophet Zarathustra (q.v.). Vishtaspa battled victoriously to defend the new faith. He had two sons, Spentodata (Sfendidad) and Pishishyauthna.

Vohu Manah (Pahlavi: Vahman, Bahman)

In old Persian (Zoroastrian) religion the good spirit, Ahura Mazda's (q.v.) first-born who sits at the right hand of his father. He is the god of cattle, the sacrificial animals, and protector of the good animals. He appeared to Zarathustra in visible form; he keeps the records of men's deeds, words and thoughts. He greets the souls of the righteous after death. Through 'good thinking' he leads people to the 'right religion', as god of good thought and pure purpose.

Vohu Mano

'Good sense'. Avestan deity of morality who guides good people towards worshipping Ahura Mazda (q.v.).

Vouruskasha

The world ocean in Zoroastrian cosmology.

Vulture

The bearded vulture or lammergeier, *Gypaetus barbatus*, in Persian, *huma*, is the largest bird of prey in the Old World. It lives in the high mountains of Iran and consumes mainly animal skeletons. It was believed to be the royal bird sent by God to announce the next ruler to the people. Its large shadow is believed to be very auspicious: if it falls on a man he will become king. The Persian kings once used to decorate their crowns with the bird's feathers.

Wafat an-Nabii

Wafat an-Nabii, The Death of the Prophet, is the title of a common collection of legends about the death of Muhammad. Even prophets must die, but God granted Muhammad an hour's delay. Numerous tales have gathered around this central theme, describing in detail how all his friends and followers wept at hearing that their great leader was dying, but how the angels rejoiced that he was coming to join them in heaven. They also tell how he could guarantee paradise to his devoted followers, and, most important of all, whether he asked Ali or Abu Bakr to take over the imamate (leadership) from him, thereby setting in motion one of the two separate lines of succession, that of the Sunna and the Shi'a (qq.v.).

Wadd

'Love'. One of the gods worshipped by the people in the time of Nuh (Noah) (Koran 71:23). It is related that when Adam died, Set (Sheth) buried him in a hillside in India called Nod. A statue called Wadd was carved and placed on the hill. Nuh pleaded with the people to worship only the one God, but they continued to worship Wadd, and so the flood destroyed both them and the statue.

Wahda

'Unity'. For the Sufi, the ultimate goal of life: the unity of love consumes the duality of nature of God and man into the *wahdat al-shuhud*, 'the unity of testimony', i.e. into one consciousness.

Wahy

Inspiration from God, usually via an angel who spoke to Muhammad, who heard it with his ears and knew with certainty that it was the word of God. Only words so received by Muhammad are in the Koran.

Wajh

'Face, presence'. 'Wherever you turn there is the face of God' (Koran 2:109). This verse is often meditated upon by the Sufis, together with 92:20: 'Reward for those who yearn for their Lord's face', and 55:27: 'All things perish but not his face.' See *Macroprosopos*.

Walafar (Valafar)

The demon of criminals who organises crimes and raids. His appearance is that of a lion with the head of a murderer.

Wali (Vali)

Short for *waliyu-llah*, 'friend of God' in popular Islamic theology. It is usually translated as 'saint' in European languages, but there are fundamental differences between a Christian saint and a *wali*. Saints are witnesses of the faith who have died and been sanctified by the Church authorities. An Islamic saint may still be alive, performing miracles by God's will. Moreover there is no central authority in Islam that sanctifies people and makes their sanctity known. Many *walis* are therefore unknown, which is how they want to be, since fame causes the danger of vanity, self-praise and pride. Many martyrs in Islam (see *Shahid*) have never been called *walis*, yet they would certainly qualify for the title; for example Husayn (q.v.). In the Christian tradition a saint is always a celibate, whereas the *walis* of Islam (always men) are usually married.

What *walis* and saints have in common is that they both fit into the traditional sets of beliefs of the common people, although neither the educated classes nor the religious authorities in both Europe and the Middle East are keen to encourage saint worship; the churches because they will be accused of canonizing fairy tales, and the Islamic authorities because saint worship smacks of idolatry.

Numerous believers, especially in Egypt and North Africa, but also in Pakistan and Turkey, spend a night near a *wali's* tomb, expecting the holy man's spirit to appear in a dream and give the solution to the believer's problem; often a cure for some sickness.

Walis are believed to possess the arts of flying, of curing the sick, of punishing evil-doers even from a distance, of rescuing the victims of fire or flood, of making crops grow, of removing spells, of casting out evil spirits, of appearing unexpectedly in distant places both before and after they have died, of living without food, and of bringing dead animals and people back to life, although the revived people usually appear to be ghosts. God seldom revives a dead person once he has decided on their death. Every miracle is an act of God, the texts are unanimous about that, and even a *wali* is powerless without God's help. The very fact that God causes the miracles for him proves that he is God's friend.

Washing of the Dead (Arabic: *ghusl al-mayit*)

In Islam, the deceased's body has to be washed from head to foot before burial. The reason is that the dead man will not have another chance to perform *ghusl* (the required ceremony before prayer) before he has to face his maker on the day of judgement (q.v.). It is therefore necessary to prepare the body for that event by giving it the required state of purity. See also *Mayit*.

Waswas

'Whisperer'. The deceiver, the Devil, who whispers deceitful temptations (*Waswasa*) into our ears (Koran 114:5).

Watchers

In the apocryphal book of Enoch, a race of giants, the children of the angels who married human women. God appointed them as his guardians on the frontiers of his universe, one at every level.

Water of Life, Well of Life

The peoples of antiquity realized that without fresh water they and their animals would perish. Many wells have been sacred from time immemorial. Somewhere on earth, they believed, there is a well which gives its drinker life for all the centuries until doomsday, and good health as well. One drop of it placed on the lips of a dying man will bring him back to life. One draught of it will make a barren woman pregnant. One vial full of it, carefully kept, will make a man a famous doctor.

Watwat

'Bat'. In Egypt and elsewhere in Africa, it is believed that the bats which live in dark caves and which can be seen flying out at nightfall in their thousands, are the spirits of the deceased. Like all the creatures of God, they have a king, the *sultan al-watwat* (*watawit*), who lives in a very deep and old well in Cairo, under an ancient house. No one ever dares to go down there, but the inhabitants present regular offerings to the king of these spirits. They are not harmful unless they are insulted; indeed they are the keepers of the fresh water in the city.

Weather-God

A powerful deity commonly worshipped by the peoples of Asia Minor and northern Syria (Hurrians and Hittites). The Romans identified him with Jupiter Pluvius.

White Elephant

In the *Shahname* (q.v.), King Zal owned a huge white elephant which one morning broke loose. Rustam (q.v.), aroused by the guards, took his mace and stopped the raging beast with one blow on its head causing the great animal to fall down dead.

Wilaya

'Protection, protectorate'. The saint (see *Wali*) is protected by God against Satan, so *wilaya* comes to mean 'sainthood' (Koran 10:63).

Worm

A worm gnawed its way through King Solomon's staff (Koran 34:14). As a result, the staff broke, and the body of the king, which was still leaning on it, although he had died weeks before, fell down. The servants then finally dared to come close to him, and saw that he was dead. The *jinns* and *shaytans* who served him (38:38) then considered themselves free and flew away, leaving the Temple unfinished, and resumed their wicked work, tempting people to do evil again. So suffering, deceit and poverty returned to earth – and all because of a worm!

Wormwood (Hebrew: *ia'anah*, Greek: *apsinthos*)

Perennial herb, *Artemisia absinthium*, unanimously abhorred by all the biblical writers for its bitter taste. It was nevertheless made into a beverage, absinth, to which many people became addicted. What is more, the plant may be the oldest cure for malaria, usually described as headache, shivers and fever.

Wujud

'Existence'. Existence can either be necessary (God's existence), possible (man's existence), or impossible (the existence of other gods). It follows that whereas man's existence is accidental, i.e. dependent on circumstances such as the presence of air, water, food and earth, as well as being created by God, only God's existence is necessary since all other beings depend on him. The Sufis have developed this thesis into the concept of God's reality, *haqiqa*. Only God is real, whereas his creation is shadow-play, a game (*la'b*) of illusions (*ghurur*). The Sufi master sees through this 'veil of illusions', behind which he will perceive the reality of his face (*wajh*).

Y

Yabbok (Yabbuq)
A river which forms the frontier between Jordan and Syria. Here the Byzantine emperor Heraklios I was defeated by the Arabs in 635 AD, and Jordan and Palestine were lost to Christianity. It was at this river that Jacob met numerous angels and at night wrestled with God, so he named the place Peniel, 'God's Face'. God called him Israel, 'God Fights' (q.v.) (Genesis 32:1–28).

Yaghuth
An idol in pre-Islamic Arabia, worshipped on a hill in Yemen. Probably a clan ancestor (Koran 71:23).

Yahuda
In the Islamic tradition, the one son of Ya'qub (Jacob) who survived his younger brother Yusuf (Joseph) when the latter died as king of Egypt (or, according to others, as vizier). Yusuf made Yahuda his *khalifa* (successor) on his death-bed. Thus Yahuda became leader (*imam*) of the Children of Israel in Egypt, who were henceforth called *Yahudi*, 'Jews', after him. Yahuda was well loved as a just, wise and kind leader.

Yahweh
See *Yhwh*.

Yahya
Arabic name for John the Baptist. He was given as a child to his old father Zakariya (Koran 19). He was humble before God, loving and fearing (21:89) and became God's twenty-third prophet.

Yajuj and Majuj
In the Koran, the theme of Gog and Magog (q.v.) comes back as the savage tribes of the northern mountains (presumably the Caucasus). Alexander the Great (Al-Iskandar, q.v.) built a huge metal wall to contain them (18:94–97). When this wall breaks down and the savages overrun the civilized world, that will be one of God's signs that the end is nigh (18:98; 21:96): when the trumpet sounds, the savages will come.

Yama
Ancient Indo-Iranian god of death who accompanies the souls of the deceased to his kingdom of darkness. He was the son of Vivahvant (Sanskrit: Vivasvant), the Sun-god

who created the secret herb of immortality, *haoma*, exclusively for the gods. Yama was also the ruler of the Chinvat, the mysterious bridge across the abyss that separates this world of life from the world of death.

Yam-Nahar
'Sea-river', Ugaritic god of the waters, arch-enemy of Baal (q.v.).

Ya'qub
The tenth prophet since Adam. The Arabic form of Jacob (q.v.) whose arrival as a grandson for Ibrahim was announced by God: (Koran 11:71; 19:49). Ya'qub features in the Koran mainly as the father of Yusuf (Joseph) (q.v.). In 2:133 he urged his sons to follow his grandfather Ibrahim's religion, Islam.

Ya'qub told Yusuf not to talk about his dream of power to his brothers (12:5). When the brothers lied to Ya'qub and told him that a wolf had devoured Yusuf, Ya'qub demanded to see the wolf. The brothers went into the desert and caught a wolf, but when it was brought before Ya'qub, God gave it the power of speech so that it could plead its innocence. Yahya, (John the Baptist) was a descendent of Ya'qub (Koran 19:6). See *Jacob*.

Yasawi (Ahmet)
The greatest ever Turkic Sufi sheikh of Central Asia. His life is shrouded in legend. He studied in Yasi with the famous Arslan Baba; later he went to Bukhara, which was then a great centre of learning, and studied with Sheikh Yusuf Hamadhani, whom he

succeeded as master when the latter died in 1160. Eventually, Ahmet returned to Yasi where he taught for the last few years of his life. He died in 1166. His tomb soon became a place of pilgrimage even for kings and princes, visited by devotees from all over Central Asia. The emperor Timur erected a mausoleum on his grave which is still visited by pilgrims.

Yasht
A hymn, a song of praise for one of the ancient Persian gods.

Ya-sin
The name of Sura 36 of the Koran. This chapter is the heart of the Koran, which, when read or recited, will give much *baraka* ('blessing') because of verses 33–44. It is often recited for dying people so they may remember it on their way to the other world, and for sick people, as it is believed to bring good health to all.

Yathrib
The city later called Medina-t-un-Nabii and so Medina, 'the Prophet's City', once full of date palms.

Ya'uq
An idol worshipped by the people in the days of Nuh (Noah) (Koran 71:23). In Muhammad's time he was still worshipped in southern Arabia.

Yekum
One of the fallen angels who procured terrestrial girls for his fellow angels who had come down to enjoy carnal pleasures. See Genesis 6:2.

Yezidi

One of a group of Persians who worshipped the Devil by being possessed by him during all-night dances.

YHWH (JHVH)

In Exodus 3:14–16 God, at the request of Moses, calls himself YHWH, which is vocalized as Yahweh, but it may not be so pronounced. The usual pronunciation is Jehovah (q.v.).

The four consonants are called by the Cabbala (q.v.) writers the *tetragrammaton*. They conceal the name of God, which no one may attempt to pronounce because if he accidentally pronounced it correctly, there would be an earthquake, since God's real name can move mountains. It is said that King Solomon knew God's true name, which is what enabled him to perform magic and to rule the demons.

Yid'oni

See *Necromancer*.

Yima

The first man in the myths of the ancient Persians, and the first king of the earth. Yima reigned for a thousand years during which peace and happiness prevailed upon earth, the golden age in the history of humanity. Yima taught his people to domesticate cattle for which purpose he built a *vara*, the first stable to keep cattle warm in the cold winters. He ruled the demons and sorcerers so that none of them could do any harm, but as soon as Yima lied he lost Ahura Mazda's (q.v.) blessing and protection, so that the demons got power over him and one of them, Dahhak or Zahhak, a three-headed evil demon, took power over Persia. In Firdausi's *Shahname*, Yima appears as king Jamshid.

Yunus (Yunas)

The Arabic for Jonah, and in the Islamic tradition the twenty-first prophet since Adam. Like Jonah in the Bible, Yunus has a whole chapter of the Koran to himself. Later writers in Arabic have added details which may originate from the Talmud.

In the Islamic tradition, his story is told only from the time he set sail. God wanted to teach him a lesson, so the sailors threw him overboard and he ended his first life in the belly of the great fish. God said to the fish: 'Oh fish, Yunus is my beloved prophet, not your food! I have given him your belly as a prison to stay in for a while. Do him no harm, for one day I shall want him back!'

God made the skin of the fish transparent, like glass. The fish feared the Lord and neither ate nor drank for forty days. From his glass prison Yunus could see all the fishes of the ocean. By God's favour he understood their language and could hear what they said. He listened to them all praising God in their quiet languages, and did the same. Upon hearing this, all the fishes swam towards the fish that contained Yunus and listened to his prayers.

His beautiful voice rose up to heaven from the depths of the ocean and the angels felt pity for the Prophet Yunus. They begged the Lord to set him free. At last God ordered the fish: 'Fish, swim to the beach and let Yunus go!' The fish beached itself and opened its mouth. Yunus walked onto the beach and praised God (Koran 68:49). He is often referred to as the man whose grave moved before he rose from it.

Yusha'

The Arabic for Joshua. He led the Banu Israil, the Children of Israel, into Filistin (Palestine) which was then inhabited by a race of *jabbar*, giants. The Israelites, however, rushed in, shouting '*Allahu Akbar*', 'God is great', and all the city walls fell down. That is how Palestine became a Muslim country.

Yusuf

The eleventh prophet since Adam, the biblical Joseph. He is one of the most popular prophets in Islamic hagiography. Sura 12 of the Koran describes his history, upon which Firdausi based an epic poem. Poetic versions of Yusuf's life have been composed in Berber, Swahili, Arabic, Urdu, Malay and Javanese.

The Islamic narrative differs in several respects from the biblical story; in the course of the centuries it has been embellished with moralistic motifs. In Islam, Yusuf is a prophet of God, and as such he shares in the virtues of all the prophets of Islam: perfect moral conduct, perfect purity of heart and mind, endless patience and stoic resignation to whatever trials God's will causes him to suffer. Yusuf never loses his temper, never speaks harsh words, never stops being kind to those who have treated him unjustly.

The chief difference between the biblical and the later Islamic version of the story is the happy ending: Yusuf, as chief minister to the pharaoh, became king when the latter died, having married the pharaoh's only daughter, Beryl. Many years later, after a very long life, Yusuf met an old widow who lived in dire poverty. She was Zuleikha (q.v.), the woman who had falsely accused him of assaulting her. (Genesis 39:7–19; Koran 12:23–35). God made her young again so that at last she could marry Yusuf, whom she still loved.

Z

Zabur
The Book of Psalms, which God gave to Daud (David) as part of his revelation (Koran 21:105; 17:55; 4:163). Details of the book are not given, except that it is in complete accordance with the Tawrat and the Koran.

Zagam
The demon of the forgers of money. Zagam could change copper into gold, lead into silver, blood into oil, water into wine. He had huge bat's wings and a bull's head. His food was human blood.

Zahak
See *Zohak*.

Zahori
In Spanish-Arabic tales, a sorcerer who could see through walls as if they were glass, enabling him to find lost objects.

Zaim
A nocturnal manifestation of the Devil. He enslaved King Nimrod (q.v.) so that when he pointed at some evil, Nimrod was forced to do it.

Zakar (Dzakar)
Babylonian god of dreams, which were messages from the gods.

Zakariya
In the Koran (21:89–91) the twenty-second prophet of God, the biblical Zecharaiah, who prayed for a son. God gave him Yahya (John the Baptist) (q.v.) who also ranks as a prophet. When Zakariya asked God: 'How can I have a son since I am old and my wife is barren?' God replied: 'This will be your sign: you will not speak to people for three days except by gesture' (Koran 3:38–41; 6:85; 19:2–11).

He was a temple priest, and was instructed by God to look after Maryam, daughter of Imran and mother of Isa (Jesus) and to teach her in the temple.

Zakat
In Islam, the annual tax collected by the imam from every family head, amounting to 2 1/2 per cent of annual income.

Zal
In Persian mythology, the father of the hero Rustam. Zal was brought

up by the bird Simurgh in the mountains.

Zalambur

An evil spirit, a son of Iblis who causes quarrels and makes people cheat.

Zamzam

The sacred well in the sanctuary at Mecca. Its water is believed to be more health-giving than any other. It was 'called forth from the earth' by Jibril (q.v.), so that Hajar (q.v.) could feed the baby Isma'il (q.v.).

Zamzummims

A race of giants who once lived in Ammon (Deuteronomy 2:20–1).

Zand (Zend)

'Interpretation'. The exegesis of the *Avesta* through glossaries, commentaries and translations from old Persian into Pahlavi or middle Persian.

Zanjabil

One of the fountains in paradise. Also ginger (Koran 76:17), a special beverage for the blessed.

Zappu

Babylonian deity of the Pleiades.

Zaqqum

An accursed tree in Jahannam (q.v.), which provides the food for the inhabitants of hell (Koran 37:60–4; 44:43; 56:52–3). Its fruits are like the heads of *shaytans* but the sinners are forced to eat them, though they burn in their bodies.

Zarathustra (Zoroaster)

Persian prophet of the god Ahura Mazda (q.v.), who lived perhaps 3000 years ago in north-western Persia. Even his date and land of birth are disputed and nothing else is known of him except the seventeen magnificent *gathas* or hymns which he composed. When he was twenty, according to the tradition, he left his parental home and sought solitude. He confronted Ahriman (q.v.), the Devil, who wanted to kill him, but he was protected by Ahura Mazda. He prophesied to Ahriman the long war against the good gods and Ahriman's ultimate defeat against the Saoshyant (q.v.), the saviour from the east. Ahriman tempted him: 'Abandon Ahura Mazda, I will make you ruler of the world, you will live a happy life.' But Zarathustra refused: 'Never will I abandon the good Ahura Mazda, my life. I will defeat you with God's word, with my faith and with the truth.'

When the prophet died, his *quareno* (vital spirit) escaped and survives to this day in a lake in the east. One day a virgin will bathe there, become pregnant and give birth to the saviour Saoshyant.

Zardusht

See *Zarathustra*.

Zariadres

King of the Caspian countries. In a dream he saw Odatis (Persian: Hudata, Indian: Sujata), the lovely daughter of Homartes king of the Marathes. On that very same night Odatis saw him in her dream.

Zariadres travelled to the court of Homartes to ask for his daughter's hand in marriage, but the king would not give his daughter to a stranger. Instead the king invited all the young noblemen of his realm and told Odatis that she must offer a cup of wine to the man she wanted to be her husband. She secretly invited Zariadres to come as well, and he arrived dressed as a local nobleman. She gave him the cup and he eloped with her.

The name Zariadres originates from the old Persian Zarivari or Zarer, a Persian hero whose love for the Greek princess Katayun was much sung about by epic poets in ancient Persia. Zariadres was a brother of Hystaspes who often takes his brother's place in later versions of the romance.

Zariran
See *Zariadres*.

Zat (Dhat)
'Essence'. God's essence as opposed to the *sifat*, his attributes. For the Sufis, God's *zat* is the very core of their goal, that with which they hope to be united.

Zauba'a
An evil spirit which appears like a whirlwind.

Zayn al-'Abidin
Full name Ali Zayn al-'Abidin. The only surviving son of Husayn ibn Ali and Shahrbanu, princess of Persia, daughter of Shah Yazdegird III. Zayn al-'Abidin means 'Ornament of the Worshippers'. When his father Husayn (q.v.), the third imam, was killed in Kerbela, Zayn was still a sickly child.

He was transported, with his sisters and aunts, on foot all the way to Damascus by the Syrian soldiers of the Omayyad caliph Yazid. They also brought the head of Husayn, kept in a box, to present it to their master.

When the prisoners were led before Yazid, he insulted the head in their presence, defying the lips to speak. Zayn protested loudly: 'Do not abuse those lips once kissed by the holy Prophet.' Yazid ordered Zayn killed, but the ghost of Ali ibn Abu Talib intervened, appearing suddenly as a knight in black armour to defend his grandson.

Later Muhammad ibn al-Hanafiyya defeated Yazid and liberated the prisoners with the aid of Husayn's ghost. The whole family then returned to Mecca. There the miraculous Black Stone spoke in a clear voice announcing Zayn al-'Abidin as the living fourth imam and successor of the holy Prophet, by God's will, thus preventing any dispute. His health, however, was frail and he died in 95 AH/715 AD.

Zawaiya (Zawiya)
An Islamic abbey where Muslim scholars devote their days to prayer, to the study of the Koran and to religious exercises. It should not be called a monastery, since many of these scholars are married and have families.

Zealots
A Jewish sect at the time of Jesus, who actually chose one of their number to be his disciple: Simon Zelotes (Luke 6:15). The Zealots (the Hebrew word is *Qanai*, which may be the evangelists' reason for calling Simon the

Canaanite) were Jews who hated the Romans and their lackey kings, Herod the Great and his successors, and hoped to recreate the independent state of Israel by force. Inspired by this hope they were eagerly awaiting the miraculous return of David the anointed king of Israel. (See *Anointed*.) Finally the Zealots and their allies the Essenes took arms against the emperor Vespasian and were defeated in the famous battle of Masada (q. v.).

Zedechias
Cabbalist who lived about 800 AD. He could summon the extraterrestrial sylphs.

Zedekiah
A false prophet (1 Kings 22:11; 2 Chronicles 18).

Zepar
A devil which seduces men to commit paedophilia.

Zeus-Ammon
Later Jupiter-Ammon, the combined deity of thunder and retribution, whose worship was concentrated in Ammon (now Amman in Jordan) during the Hellenistic and later Roman periods. The god was represented as both a ram (Ammon) and a bull (Zeus).

Zikr
See *Dhikr*.

Zillullah (Dhillu'llahi)
'The shadow of God'. It is believed that God's light would dazzle us all if he had not interposed a cloud between himself and us. In the Arab countries shade is regarded as beneficent. Thus a good ruler is sometimes addressed as 'shadow of God', that is, the one by whom God protects his people. The Sufis use the term to denote the *insan al-kamil*, the perfect man whose wisdom protects the people.

Zilzal
'Earthquake'. The Koran announces that doomsday will begin with earthquakes.

Zion
'Sunny place', called Sion in the New Testament. A hill south-east of Jerusalem. Zion was a sanctuary of the earth-goddess in pre-Canaanite times. It was in an ancient pond there that the sky-god fertilized the earth-goddess whenever he descended, hence the reference to Zion as 'God's bride'.

Mount Zion was occupied by David, who built his palace there (2 Samuel 5:7; 1 Kings 8:1). During the exile of the Jews it became a focus for their yearning for Israel. In Revelation 14:1, John saw the lamb standing on Mount Zion accompanied by 144,000 ransomed souls who understood the angels' songs.

Its final apotheosis comes in Revelation 21:10–24, where it is described as the new Jerusalem, the bride of the lamb, the city of God where all souls yearn to go eventually. According to the tradition, John was standing on Mount Zion when he saw this vision. The spirit of the Lord was (and still is by some) believed to be present on Zion, since David brought the Ark to rest there (2 Samuel 5:9; 6:12). St Paul promised: 'Ye are come to Mount Zion and the city of the living God . . .' (Hebrews 12:22).

Zisutra
A Sumerian priest-king during the great flood.

Zizyphus
A thorny shrub of the *Rhamnaceae* family with juicy fruits from which the lotus-eaters obtained perpetual bliss. A crown was made from its thorns for Jesus. See *Sidrat-al-Muntaha, Thorns*.

Ziyara
'Visit', i.e. to the tomb of an imam or saint. Although discouraged by the Wahhabis in modern times, who also destroyed Muhammad's mausoleum, there are numerous Muslims who still pray at the tombs of saints. The Shi'a of Iran in particular encourage pilgrims to visit the tombs of the imams (now impossible because most are in Iraq).

Zodiac (Arabic: *mintaqat al-Buruj*)
The twelve signs (*buruj*) of the zodiac are much used by Muslim astrologers to tell people's fortunes, especially when a marriage is being contemplated. They will for instance advise against the wedding if the signs of the bridal couple are water and fire. There are numerous books on astrology in Arabic and Persian. See *Astrology, Da'wa*.

Zohak (Zahhak)
King of Arabia, according to the *Shahname* (q.v.), who fell into the net of Iblis so that two serpents' heads grew out of his shoulders, which had to be fed human brains. He killed King Jamshid, who had reigned for a millennium, after Jamshid had made his people worship him. Zohak also killed his father and many other people until God warned him in a dream. Zohak fled his palace in Jerusalem and found refuge in Mount Demavend, where he will stay until doomsday. He was succeeded by Faridun (q.v.).

Zohar
'Splendour'. In Jewish mysticism the 'glory and inner light' of God towards which the human soul forever strives. It was first described in the *Sefer Zohar*, the *Book of Glory*, the classical work on Cabbala (q.v.).

Zoroaster
See *Zarathustra*.

Zu
In Babylonian mythology, a bird-god who was an enemy of the gods. One day Zu stole the tablets of destiny. The gods were dismayed because no one was prepared to recover these vital records of the future. Finally, King Lugalbanda, father of Gilgamesh (q.v.), was able to retrieve the tablets after slaying Zu. In Assyrian myths it is Marduk (q.v.) who 'crushed Zu's skull'. In another myth it seems that it was Ninurta (q.v.) who overcame Zu. Perhaps Zu was the ancestral bull.

Zuhd
'Renunciation', of all pleasures, even those which the Koran permits. Zuhd

is sometimes translated as 'monasticism' (see *Zawaya*). This is misleading since several Sufi masters were married and had families.

Zuleikha (Zulaykha, Zuleha, Zelikha)

In the Turkish-Persian Islamic tradition, Zuleikha was the daughter of Taymus, king of the Maghrib. She was happy until she saw a handsome youth in a dream, whose face she could not forget. In a second dream he told her that he loved her and that he knew her love for him was sincere. He fortold that they would meet in Egypt. She begged her father to let her go to Egypt, where the young man was vizier. The king wrote letters to the king of Egypt, who agreed to marry Zuleikha to his vizier Butifar (Potipher). When she finally arrived in Egypt she was disappointed to see that Butifar was a white-haired old man, and a eunuch (Hebrew: *saris*, Genesis 37:36). However, she had to marry him as arranged; it was quite normal for eunuchs of high rank to be married.

One day a merchant called Malik arrived from Palestine offering for sale exquisite merchandise to the rich vizier and his young wife. The wares included some young slaves, among whom Zuleikha recognized the man of her dreams. She persuaded her husband to buy the young slave for her; it was not unusual for rich ladies to own slaves, even young males. However, this young slave, who was none other than Yusuf (Joseph) (q.v.), knew that God had destined him to be his prophet, so he timidly but determinedly declined her invitation to make love to her. Enraged by his rejection she slandered him and he was imprisoned.

In the Islamic versions Zuleikha devised a ruse, putting a hundred lovely slave girls in a room and telling them to try and seduce Yusuf. Instead, Yusuf converted them all to Islam through his sweet words. All Zuleikha's stratagems failed and the women of Egypt mocked her for falling in love with him. She then organised a festive meal, at the end of which she served an orange (for good digestion) to each lady, with a knife. Suddenly she called Yusuf and when he appeared all the women cut their fingers since they could not keep their eyes off him. They mocked no more.

The story of Yusuf's years in prison follows the biblical narrative closely. The two royal servants told him their dreams which he correctly interpreted. The one survivor forgot Yusuf as soon as he was released, but remembered him when pharaoh dreamt his dreams. Yusuf was called out of prison, interpreted the dreams and made vizier, since Butifar had just died. Yusuf asked to be rehabilitated. Zuleikha was summoned to court and confessed that she alone was to blame for his humiliation. Disgraced, she had to live in poverty in a hut by the roadside, where she could watch Yusuf whenever he rode past on his fine horse. She prayed to God until he forgave her. Then one day Yusuf heard her praying loudly and told his aide to fetch her. He did not recognize her but pity moved him to pray to God on her behalf. God heard the prayer and made Zuleikha as beautiful as she had been before. Yusuf now recognized her and married her because God told him to do so.

Zu'l-Qarnayn (Dhu'l-Qarnayn)
'The Horned One' (Koran 18:83–95). Usually identified with Alexander the Great, (Al-Iskandar, q.v.). Some scholars maintain, however, that he was not the same person but a King Sakandar in the days of Ibrahim.

Zurah (Dhurah)
'Far away'. The *Bayt al-Maʿmur* (Koran 52:4), 'busy house'. The great mosque in heaven to which, every day, 70,000 newly created angels come to pray.

Zurvan
The old Persian god of primeval time. Some Persians believed that Ahura Mazda (q.v.) and Ahriman (q.v.) were twin brothers who were both born from the 'body' of Zurvan, one from each side. It is a curious attempt to reconcile two hostile deities, by showing their common origin, comparable to Brahma being the father of all the gods.

BIBLIOGRAPHY

AHMAD, Shaikh Mahmud, *Pilgrimage of Eternity (Iqbal's Javidnama)*, Institute of Islamic Culture, Lahore 1961.

ALBRIGHT, William Foxwell, *Yahweh and the Gods of Canaan*, Athlone Press, London 1968.

ALEXANDER, David and Pat, *Handbook to the Bible*, Lion Publishing, Berkhamstead, England 1973.

ARBERRY, A.J., *Tales from the Masnavi*, Allen & Unwin, London 1962.

ARBERRY, A.J., *More Tales from the Masnavi*, Allen & Unwin London 1963.

ARBERRY, A.J., *The Koran Interpreted*, Oxford University Press, London 1964.

ARBERRY, A.J., *Classical Persian Literature*, Allen & Unwin, London 1967.

ARBERRY, A.J., *Sufism*, Allen & Unwin, London 1968.

ARBERRY, Arthur John (ed.), *The Legacy of Persia*, Clarendon, Oxford 1968.

ARNOLD, Edwin, *Pearls of the Faith or Islam's Rosary*, Ashraf Publications, Lahore 1967.

'ATTAR, Farid al-Din, *Muslim Saints and Mystics*, translated by A.J. Arberry, Routledge & Kegan Paul, London 1966.

BEYERLIN, Walter (ed.), *Near Eastern Religious Texts Relating to the Old Testament*, Westminster Press, Philadelphia 1978.

BLACK, Matthew, *The Book of Enoch or I Enoch. A New English Edition*, E.J. Brill, Leiden 1985.

BORGHOUTS, J.F., *Ancient Egyptian Magical Texts*, E.J. Brill, Leiden 1978.

BOYCE, Mary, *Textual Sources for the Study of Zoroastrianism*, Manchester University Press, Manchester 1984.

BRANDON, S.G.F., *Creation Legends of the Ancient Near East*, Hodder and Stoughton, London 1963.

BROCKELMANN, Carl, *History of the Islamic Peoples*, Capricorn Books, New York 1947.

BROWNE, Edward G., *A Literary History of Persia*, Vols I-IV. Cambridge University Press, Cambridge 1964.

BUDGE, E.A. Wallis, *The Seven Tablets of Creation*, 2 vols, 1902.

CAMPBELL, C.G., *Tales from the Arab Tribes*, Drummond, London 1949.

CAVENDISH, Richard, *Mythology, An Illustrated Encyclopaedia*, Orbis, London 1980.

CERAM, C.W., *Gods, Graves and Scholars*, Gollancz, London 1971.

CERNY, J., *Ancient Egyptian Religion*, Hutchinson, London.

CHARLES, R.H., *The Book of Enoch*, John Murray, Oxford 1912.

CHELEBI, Suleyman, *The Mevlidi Sherif*, translated by F. Lyman MacCallum, London 1943.

CHELKOWSKI, Peter J., *Ta'ziyeh, Ritual and Drama in Iran*, New York University Press, New York 1979.

CHEYNE, T.K., *Traditions & Beliefs of Ancient Israel*, A & C Black, London 1907.

COLIN, G.S., *Recueil des Textes en Arabe Marocain. I. Contes et Anecdotes*, Paris 1937.

COMTE, Fernand, *Mythology*, Chambers, Edinburgh 1991.

CROSS, Fernand, *Canaanite Myth and Hebrew Epic*, Harvard University, Cambridge, Mass. 1973.

CROSS, Frank Moore, *The Ancient Library of Qumran*, G. Duckworth, London 1958.

CUMONT, Franz, *Oriental Religions in Roman Paganism*, Kegan Paul, London 1911.

DALLEY, Stephanie, *Myths from Mesopotamia*, Oxford University Press, Oxford 1989.

DERMENGHEM, Emile (ed.) *Contes Fasis, recueillis par Moh. el Fasi*, Paris 1926.

DESROCHES-NOBLECOURT, Christiane, *Life and Death of a Pharaoh: Tutankhamen*, Penguin, Harmondsworth 1972.

DOWNING, Charles (trans.), *Armenian Folktales and Fables*, Oxford University Press, Oxford 1972.

DRIEL, G. Van, *The Cult of Assur*, Assen, Holland 1969.

DRIVER, Godfrey R., *Canaanite Myths and Legends*, T & T Clark, Edinburgh 1956.

DRIVER, Godfrey R., *The Judaean Scrolls*, Oxford 1965.

EISENMAN, Robert and WISE, Michael, *The Dead Sea Scrolls Uncovered*, Element Books, Shaftesbury 1992.

FERDOWSI, Abo 'l-Qasim, *The Epic of the Kings*, translated by Reuben Levy, Routledge & Kegan Paul, London 1967.

FISCHER, August, *Das Liederbuch eines Marokkanischen Sangers*, Leipzig 1918.

FRAZER, James George, *Folklore in the Old Testament*, MacMillan, London 1923.

GHIRSCHMAN, R., *Iran*, Pelican, Harmondsworth 1954.

GIBB, E.J.W., *A History of Ottoman Poetry*, Vol. I, Luzac, London 1958.

GIBB, H.A.R., KRAMERS, J.H., SCHACHT, J., BOSWORTH, C. Edmund and DONZEL, E. Van, *Encyclopaedia of Islam*, E.J. Brill, Leiden 1960.

GRAY, John, *The Canaanites*, Thames & Hudson, London 1964.

GRAY, John, *Near Eastern Mythology*, Hamlyn, London 1969.

GRIMAL, Pierre, *Stories from Babylon and Persia*, Burke, London 1964.

GRIMWOOD-JONES, Diana, and HOPWOOD, Derek (eds.), *Middle East and Islam: A Bibliographical Introduction*, Inter-documentation Company, Zug-Leiden 1972.

GUILLAUME, A., *The Life of Muhammad*, Oxford University Press, Oxford 1955.

GURNEY, O.R., *The Hittites*, Penguin, Harmondsworth 1952.

HART, George, *A Dictionary of Egyptian Gods and Goddesses*, Routledge, London 1987.

HERKLOTS, G.A. and JA'FAR Sharif, *Islam in India or the Qanun-i-Islam*, Curzon Press, London 1972.

HERODOTUS, *The Histories*, translated by Aubrey de Selincourt, Penguin, Harmondsworth 1954.

HINNELLS, John R., *Persian Mythology*, Hamlyn, London 1975.

HINNELLS, John R. (ed.), *Dictionary of Religions*, Penguin, Harmondsworth 1984.

HOLLISTER, John Norman, *The Shi'a of India*, Luzac, London 1953.

HOOKE, S.H., *Babylonian and Assyrian Religion*, Hutchinson, London 1953.

HOOKE, S.H. (ed.), *Myth, Ritual and Kingship . . . in the Ancient Near East and in Israel*, Clarendon, Oxford 1958.

HOOKE, S.H., *Middle Eastern Mythology*, Pelican, Harmondsworth 1978.

HUGHES, Thomas Patrick, *A Dictionary of Islam*, Premier Book House, Lahore 1964.

IONS, Veronica, *Egyptian Mythology*, Hamlyn, London 1965.

IQBAL, Afzal, *Life & Work of Rumi*, Institute of Islamic Culture, Lahore 1956.

IRVING, T.B. (trans. and comm.), *The Qur'an, The First American Version*, Amana Books, Brattleboro, Vermont 1985.

IZZARD, Molly, *The Gulf: Arabia's Western Approaches*, John Murray, London 1979.

JACOBSEN, Thorkild, *The Treasures of Darkness, A History of Mesopotamian Religion*, Yale University Press, New Haven 1976.

JAMES, E.O., *The Ancient Gods*, Weidenfeld & Nicolson, London 1960.

JASTROW, Morris, *The Religion of Babylonia and Assyria*, Ginn & Co., Boston 1898.

JASTROW, Morris, *Hebrew and Babylonian Traditions*, T.F. Unwin, London 1914.

KEITH-FALCONER, Ion G.N., *Kalilah and Dimnah or the Fables of Bidpai*, Philo Press, Amsterdam 1970.

KHAN, M. Ebrahim, *Anecdotes from Islam*, Sh. Muhammad Ashraf, Lahore 1966.

KNAPPERT, Jan, *Moroccan Tales of Mystery and Miracle*, Outrigger Publishers, Hamilton, New Zealand 1976.

KNAPPERT, Jan, *Islamic Legends*, 2 vols., E.J. Brill, Leiden 1985.

KRAMER, Samuel Noah, *Sumerian Mythology*, American Philosophical Society, Philadelphia 1944.

KRAMER, Samuel Noah, *The Sumerians, their History, Culture and Character*, University of Chicago Press, Chicago 1963.

KRAMER, Samuel Noah, *In the World of Sumer*, Wayne State University Press, Detroit 1986.

KRAMER, Samuel Noah and MAIER, John, *Myths of Enki, the Crafty God*, Oxford University Press, Oxford 1989.

LANE, Edward W., *An Account of the Manners and Customs of the Modern Egyptians*, London 1842.

LANE, Edward W. (trans.), *The Thousand and One Nights*, 3 vols., East-west Publications, London 1973.

LANE, Edward W., *Arabian Society in the Middle Ages*, Curzon Press, London 1971.

LANGDON, Stephen Herbert, *The Babylonian Epic of Creation*, Oxford University Press, Oxford 1923.

LANGDON, Stephen Herbert, *Sumerian and Babylonian Psalms*, Geuthner, Paris 1909.

LANGDON, Stephen Herbert, *Sumerian Liturgical Texts*, University Museum, Philadelphia 1917.

LEWIS, Bernard, *The Assassins*, Weidenfeld & Nicolson, London 1967.

LEWIS, Geoffrey, *The Book of Dede Korkut*, Penguin, Harmondsworth 1982.

LITTMANN, Enno, *Mohammed im Volksepos*, Kommission hos Ejnar Munksgaard, Copenhagen 1950.

LITTMANN, Enno, *Ahmed il-Bedawi*, Akademie der Wissenschaften, Wiesbaden 1950.

LITTMANN, Enno, *Islamisch – Arabische Heiligenlieder*, Akademie der Wissenschaften, Wiesbaden 1951.

LORIMER, D.L.R., and Lorimer E.O., *Persian Tales*, Macmillan, London 1919.

MACDONALD, Duncan B., *The Religious Attitude and Life in Islam*, Khayats, Beyrouth 1965.

MACKENZIE, Donald A., *Myths of Babylonia and Assyria*, Gresham, London n. d.

McCALL, Henrietta, *Mesopotamian Myths*, British Museum, London 1990.

McNEIL, John R. *et al.*, *The Age of God-Kings 3000–1500* BC, Time-Life Books, Amsterdam 1987.

MITCHELL, T.C., and COLLON, D., *Sumerian Art*, British Museum, London 1969.

MONTGOMERY, James A., and HARRIS, Zellig S., *The Ras Shamra Mythological Texts*, American Philosophical Society, Philadelphia 1935.

MONTGOMERY WATT, William, *Muhammad at Mecca*, Clarendon, Oxford 1953.

MONTGOMERY WATT, William, *Companion to the Qur'an*, Allen & Unwin, London 1967.

MONTGOMERY WATT, William, *Bell's Introduction to the Qur'an*, University Press, Edinburgh 1970.

MONTGOMERY WATT, William, *Muhammad at Medina*, Clarendon, Oxford 1966.

MOOR, Johannes C. De, *An Anthology of Religious Texts from Ugarit*, E.J. Brill, Leiden 1987.

MOSCATI, Sabatino, *The World of the Phoenicians*, Cardinal, London 1973.

MUHAJIR, Ali Musa Raza, *Lessons from the Stories in the Quran*, Sh. Muhammad Ashraf, Lahore 1965.

NASR, Seyyed Hossein, *Islamic Spirituality*, 2 vols., Crossroad, New York 1987, 1991.

NICHOLSON, R.A., *A Literary History of the Arabs*, London 1923.

NICHOLSON, Reynold A., *The Mystics of Islam*, Routledge & Kegan Paul, London 1963, 1966.

NICHOLSON, Reynold A., *Rumi, Poet and Mystic*, Routledge, London 1956.

NORRIS, H.T., *Saharan Myth and Saga*, Clarendon, Oxford 1972.

NOY, Dov, *Folktales of Israel*, Routledge & Kegan Paul, London 1963.

Oxford, *The Cyclopaedic Concordance . . . to the Study of the Bible*, SPCK, London n.d.

PADWICK, Constance E., *Muslim Devotions*, SPCK, London 1961.

PATAI, Raphael, and GRAVES, Robert, *Hebrew Myths: the Book of Genesis*, Arrow Books, London 1989.

PEERMAHOMED EBRAHIM TRUST (ed.), *The Necessity of Imamat*, Peermahomed Ebrahim Trust, Urdu Bazar, Karachi 1971.

POSENER, Georges, *A Dictionary of Egyptian Civilisation*, Methuen, London 1962.

PROOSDIJ, B.A.V., *Babylonian Magic and Sorcery*, E.J. Brill, Leiden 1952.

RAUF, M.A., *The Life and Teaching of the Prophet Muhammad*, Longman, London 1964.

RINGGREN, Helmer, *Religions of the Ancient Near East*, Westminster Press, Philadelphia 1973.

ROBERTS, J.J.M., *The Earliest Semitic Pantheon*, Johns Hopkins University Press, Baltimore 1972.

ROGERS, Alexander, *The Shahnamah of Fardusi*, Heritage, Delhi 1973.

SADHU, S.L., *Folk Tales from Kashmir*, Asia Publishing House, London 1962.

SA'DI, Shaykh Muslihu'd-Din, *The Rose Garden*, translated by Edward B. Eastwick (1852), Octagon, London 1974.

SAGGS, H.W.F., *The Greatness that was Babylon*, Sidgwick & Jackson, London 1962.

SALEH, Khairat Al, *Fabled Cities, Princes and Jinn from Arab Myths and Legends*, Eurobooks Peter Lowe, Wallingford 1984.

SANDARS, N.K., *Poems of Heaven and Hell from Ancient Mesopotamia*, Penguin, Harmondsworth 1971.

SANDARS, N.K., *The Epic of Gilgamesh*, Penguin, Harmondsworth 1973.

SCHIMMEL, Annemarie, *Mystical Dimensions of Islam*, University of North Carolina Press, Chapel Hill 1975.

SCHIMMEL, Annemarie, *And Muhammad is His Messenger*, University of North Carolina Press, Chapel Hill 1985.

SCHWARZBAUM, Haim, *The Mishle Shu'alim (Fox Fables) of Rabbi Berechiah Ha-Nakdan*, Institute for Jewish and Arab Folklore Research, Kiron, Israel 1979.

SIMSAR, Muhammad A., *Tales of a Parrot by Ziya'u'd-Din Nakhshabi*, Akademische Verlagsanstalt, Graz, Austria 1978.

SMALLWOOD, E.M., *The Jews Under Roman Rule*, E.J. Brill, Leiden 1981.

SMITH, Margaret, *Readings from the Mystics of Islam*, Luzac, London 1972.

SMITH, Sydney, *Early History of Assyria to 1000 BC*, Chatto & Windus, London 1928.

SMITH, W. Robertson, *Lectures on the Religion of the Semites*, A & C Black, London 1894.

SOLLBERGER, Edmond, *The Babylonian Legend of the Flood*, British Museum, London 1971.

SPARKS, H.F.D. (ed.), *The Apocryphal Old Testament*, Clarendon, Oxford 1984.

SPENCE, Lewis, *Myths and Legends of Babylonia and Assyria*, G. Harrap, London 1916.

SPENCER, Sidney, *Mysticism in World Religion*, Pelican, Harmondsworth 1963.

STEVENS, E.S., *Folk-tales of Iraq*, Oxford University Press, London 1931.

STUMME, H., *Tunesische Marchen und Gedichte*, Leipzig 1893.

SURMELIAN, Leon, *Daredevils of Sassoon*, Allen & Unwin, London 1964.

THOMAS, (attributed) *The Gospel According to Thomas*, E.J. Brill, Leiden 1959.

THOMPSON, Henry O., *Biblical Archaeology*, Paragon House, New York 1987.

VERMES, G., *The Dead Sea Scrolls in English*, Pelican, Harmondsworth 1968, revised edition 1992.

WILHELM, Gernot, *The Hurrians*, Aris & Phillips, Warminster 1989.

WISEMAN, D.J. (ed.), *Peoples of Old Testament Times*, Clarendon, Oxford 1973.

WOHLSTEIN, Herman, *The Sky-God An-Anu*, Paul Stroock, New York 1976.

YADIN, Yigal, *The Scroll of the War of the Sons of Light Against the Sons of Darkness*, Oxford 1962.

ZWEMER, Samuel M., *Studies in Popular Islam*, Sheldon, London 1939.

TITLE	QUANT	PRICE
The Elements Of... Series		
Islam Shaykh Fadhlalla Haeri 160pp		£5.99
Judaism Brian Lancaster 144pp		£5.99
Meditation David Fontana 144pp		£5.99
Myticism R A Gilbert 144pp		£5.99
Native American Tradition Arthur Versluis 144pp		£5.99
Natural Magic Marian Green 144pp		£5.99
Pendulum Dowsing Tom Graves 144pp		£5.99
Prophecy R J Stewart 144pp		£5.99
Psychosythesis Will Parfitt 144pp		£5.99
The Qabalah Will Parfitt 144pp		£5.99
The Runes Bernard King 144pp		£5.99
Shamanism Nevill Drury 144pp		£5.99
Sufism Shaykh Fadhlalla Haeri 144pp		£5.99
Tai Chi Paul Crompton 144pp		£5.99
Taoism Martin Palmer 144pp		£5.99
The Tarot A T Mann 160pp		£5.99
Visualisation Ursula Markham 144p		£5.99
Zen David Scott & Tony Doubleday 144pp		£5.99
SUBTOTAL		£
Plus postage and packing of £1 per book in the UK or £1.50 per book overseas.		£
TOTAL		£

To: **Element Books Ltd, Longmead, Shaftesbury, Dorset, SP7 8PL**
I enclose a cheque for £............. made payable to Element Books Ltd; or please debit my *ACCESS/VISA/AMEX/Diners Club
card No: ....
*Delete as applicable   Expiry Date: ....../......
Name:..
Address:...
....
Signature: ....

ELEMENT • LONGMEAD • SHAFTESBURY •DORSET SP7 8PL
TELEPHONE: 0747 51339 FAX: 0747 51394

TITLE	QUANT	PRICE
The Elements Of... Series		
The Aborigine Tradition James Cowan 144pp		£5.99
Alchemy Cherry Gilchrist 144pp		£5.99
The Arthurian Tradition John Matthews 144pp		£5.99
Astrology Janis Huntley 144pp		£5.99
The Baha'i Faith Joseph Shepperd 144pp		£5.99
Buddhism John Snelling 144pp		£5.99
Celtic Christianity Anthony Duncan 144pp		£5.99
The Celtic Tradition Caitlin Matthews 144pp		£5.99
The Chakras Naomi Ozaniec 144p		£5.99
Christian Symbolism John Baldock 144pp		£5.99
Creation Myth R J Stewart 144pp		£5.99
Dreamwork Strephon Kaplan-Williams 144pp		£5.99
The Druid Tradition Philip Carr-Gomm 144pp		£5.99
Earth Mysteries Philip Heselton 144pp		£5.99
Feng Shui Man Ho Kwok & Joanne O'Brian 144pp		£5.99
The Goddess Caitlin Matthews 144pp		£5.99
The Grail Tradition John Matthews 144pp		£5.99
The Greek Tradition Murry Hope 144pp		£5.99
Herbalism David Hoffmann 144pp		£5.99
Human Potential Nevill Drury 144pp		£5.99
SUBTOTAL		£
Plus postage and packing of £1 per book in the UK or £1.50 per book overseas.		£
TOTAL		£

To: Element Books Ltd, Longmead, Shaftesbury, Dorset, SP7 8PL
I enclose a cheque for £............. made payable to Element Books Ltd;
or please debit my *ACCESS/VISA/AMEX/Diners Club
card No: ....
*Delete as applicable   Expiry Date: ....../......
Name:..
Address:..
....
Signature: ....

ELEMENT • LONGMEAD • SHAFTESBURY • DORSET SP7 8PL
TELEPHONE: 0747 51339 FAX: 0747 51394